D1207273

The McGraw-Hill Series
Economics

Public Finance

Laurence S. Seidman
University of Delaware

McGraw-Hill
Irwin

Boston   Burr Ridge, IL   Dubuque, IA   New York   San Francisco   St. Louis
Bangkok   Bogotá   Caracas   Kuala Lumpur   Lisbon   London   Madrid   Mexico City
Milan   Montreal   New Delhi   Santiago   Seoul   Singapore   Sydney   Taipei   Toronto

McGraw-Hill
Irwin

PUBLIC FINANCE

Published by McGraw-Hill/Irwin, a business unit of The McGraw-Hill Companies, Inc., 1221 Avenue of the Americas, New York, NY, 10020. Copyright © 2009 by The McGraw-Hill Companies, Inc. All rights reserved. No part of this publication may be reproduced or distributed in any form or by any means, or stored in a database or retrieval system, without the prior written consent of The McGraw-Hill Companies, Inc., including, but not limited to, in any network or other electronic storage or transmission, or broadcast for distance learning.

Some ancillaries, including electronic and print components, may not be available to customers outside the United States.

This book is printed on acid-free paper.

1 2 3 4 5 6 7 8 9 0 QPD/QPD 0 9 8

ISBN   978-0-07-337574-8
MHID   0-07-337574-8

Publisher: *Douglas Reiner*
Developmental editor: *Karen Fisher*
Editorial coordinator: *Noelle Fox*
Marketing manager: *Dean Karampelas*
Project manager: *Kathryn D. Mikulic*
Lead production supervisor: *Michael R. McCormick*
Design coordinator: *Joanne Mennemeier*
Lead media project manager: *Cathy L. Tepper*
Cover design: *JoAnne Schopler*
Typeface: *10.5/12 Times Roman*
Compositor: *Hurix*
Printer: *Quebecor World Dubuque Inc.*

Library of Congress Cataloging-in-Publication Data

Seidman, Laurence S.
    Public finance / Laurence S. Seidman.—1st ed.
        p. cm.
    Includes index.
    ISBN-13: 978-0-07-337574-8 (alk. paper)
    ISBN-10: 0-07-337574-8 (alk. paper)
    1. Finance, Public. I. Title.
HJ141.S374 2009
352.4—dc22
                                2008025383

www.mhhe.com

For my wife Ann, my son Jesse, and my daughter Suzanna

About the Author

Laurence S. Seidman

Laurence S. Seidman is Chaplin Tyler Professor of Economics at the University of Delaware. He received his B.A. in Social Studies from Harvard University and his Ph.D. in economics from the University of California, Berkeley. He taught at the University of Pennsylvania and Swarthmore College before coming to the University of Delaware. He has taught lower- and upper-level undergraduate public finance classes for over two decades using six different public finance textbooks.

Larry is the author of many books on public finance topics including: *The USA Tax: A Progressive Consumption Tax* (MIT Press, 1997), *Funding Social Security: A Strategic Alternative* (Cambridge University Press, 1999), *Helping Working Families: The Earned Income Tax Credit* (with co-author Saul Hoffman, Upjohn Institute, 2003), and *Pouring Liberal Wine into Conservative Bottles: Strategy and Policies* (University Press of America, 2006).

Larry has written numerous public finance articles in economics journals including the *American Economic Review* ("Taxes in a Life Cycle Growth Model With Bequests and Inheritances," June 1983), the *Journal of Political Economy* ("Conversion to a Consumption Tax: The Transition in a Life Cycle Growth Model," April 1984), the *Journal of Public Economics* ("Taxes and Capital Intensity in a Two-Class Disposable Income Growth Model," November 1982), the *National Tax Journal, International Tax and Public Finance*, and the *Public Finance Review*. He has published many public finance articles in policy journals including *Tax Notes, Health Affairs,* and *Challenge.* Larry is an invited member of the National Academy of Social Insurance.

A Note to Professors

This textbook can *actually* be covered in one semester. A semester has about 13 weeks and my book has 13 chapters averaging about 25 pages per chapter. My aim in writing this book was to present the most important public finance materials in a straightforward way to help both students and professors.

Why not write a longer textbook and let each professor pick and choose? The problem with a longer book is that there are always some essential materials in every chapter. If a textbook has seven tax chapters but there's only time to cover three, it becomes difficult for a professor to assign the crucial material. To make sure students get all of the essentials, a professor must assign sections of all of the chapters. Splicing a long book chapter by chapter and page by page isn't easy for either the professor or the students.

I fully realize that many professors will want to teach some material that I've omitted. That's great. By all means, supplement my book with any of your favorite classroom material (also, please send it to me so I can consider including it in my next edition). Some supplementary materials were also developed to help you out, including a test bank and PowerPoint presentations. My concise book gives you the time to add your favorite materials.

My book can easily be adapted for use in both lower- and upper-level classes. This text is written so it can be used by a professor (like me) who teaches one class with principles of economics students and another class with intermediate economics students. Assign the entire text to both classes. Assign the indifference-curve appendixes to the intermediate economics class. Take your choice with your principles of economics class: If you want to use indifference-curve diagrams, assign some or all of the appendixes; if you don't, skip the appendixes.

I've written my text based on firsthand experience teaching and grading a wide variety of students. I've had the opportunity to learn what materials different students can and cannot handle. My classroom experience has guided my judgment on what level of difficulty to use, what is too hard and what is too easy, what is challenging yet teachable and how to teach it, and what to include and what not to include. The way I've written each section reflects the feedback I've received from undergraduates in my lower-level course and in my upper-level course.

I sincerely hope that you'll decide that this is the best one-semester Public Finance textbook available for you and your students.

Larry Seidman
University of Delaware

Complete

Research

Laurence Seidman's *Public Finance* incorporates research from across the discipline, extending beyond the classroom to provide empirical tie-ins with real world examples.

Appendixes

Several chapters contain appendixes for further exploration, allowing a professor to customize the course to fit time constraints and the varying competencies of students.

Core and Special Interest Chapters

A concise course does not mean that professors cannot teach the interesting topics. *Public Finance* contains all of the necessary core materials and tools that are integral to any public finance course. Seidman also includes interesting topics like environmental pollution, Social Security, health insurance, and education.

Chapter **Two**

Externalities and the Environment

Chapter **Nine**

Consumption Taxes

Concise

Brief Contents

Can Be Covered in One Semester

Why assign a book where the class will skip nearly half of the pages? Seidman's *Public Finance* concisely covers all of the essentials of public finance, allowing courses the time flexibility to delve more deeply into specific material.

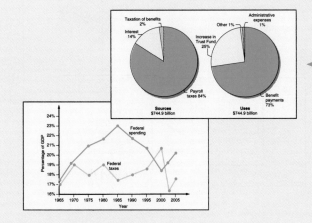

Exhibits

Seidman's *Public Finance* offers a complete look at the material by employing easy-to-read graphs, tables, and charts that supply an intuitive, at-a-glance understanding of the material without dense prose and lengthy passages.

Clear

Examples

Each chapter of Seidman's *Public Finance* features hypothetical and real-world examples. These clear applications apply directly to the material and enable students to relate the concepts of public finance to their everyday lives, heightening the understanding of the subjects presented.

Writing Style

Written with students in mind, *Public Finance* is an approachable text. The concise sections and understandable examples are engaging and informative for students.

Graphs

The graphs in the text provide thorough illustration of the major concepts in public finance. Accompanied by explanation in the text, the graphs clarify and highlight the examples and core topics in the book. Additional appendixes for more advanced students also feature indifference-curve graphs and explanations.

Starting a Health Insurance Company

Now imagine that you've just graduated from college in this society, and you decide to start a health insurance company. But can you make money selling health insurance? There are many factors to consider as you crunch the numbers.

Initially you assume that insurance won't change anyone's medical bill—5% will still have a $61,000 bill and 95% will still have a $1,000 bill—and that no one has inside information about her own health prospects, so everyone assumes her chances are 5% and 95%, respectively. For every 100 people who buy your insurance, 5 people are likely to incur a $61,000 bill, and 95 people, a $1,000 bill. Hence, your expected total bill from hospitals and doctors for your enrollees will be

$$5(\$61,000) + 95(\$1,000) = \$305,000 + \$95,000 = \$400,000$$

To obtain premium revenue of $400,000 from your 100 enrollees, you must charge a premium of $4,000 per enrollee. As long as you charge a premium of at least $4,000 and enrollees are willing to pay your premium, for every 100 persons you will take in at least $400,000 in revenue, thereby covering your expected cost of $400,000.

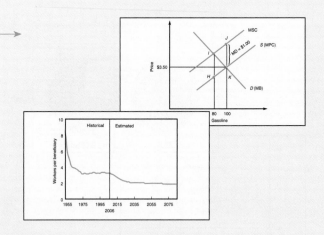

Current

Up-to-Date Features

The first edition includes today's research and real-world examples, highlighted throughout the text.

- In the News: Examples of public finance in the headlines and in the surrounding world.
- Case Study: Current work and findings on topics in public finance and public policy.
- Current Research: Empirical studies presenting new results using actual data.

Real-World Issues

With chapters devoted to the environment, Social Security, health insurance, and taxation, the text explores the current and controversial topics on everyone's mind. Taking a public finance approach, students will investigate how to resolve upcoming problems like global warming and the Social Security shortfall.

Acknowledgments

I am very grateful to the professors who reviewed draft chapters for this book and contributed so many constructive comments and suggestions for the final draft; I read their reviews carefully and worked hard to respond to their feedback and incorporate their suggestions.

Raymond Batina
Washington State University

Jeffrey Carlson
Illinois State University

Catherine Chambers
University of Central Missouri

R. Edward Chatterton
Lock Haven University

Howard Chernick
Hunter College, CUNY

Dennis Coates
University of Maryland, Baltimore City

Steven Craig
University of Houston

F. Trenery Dolbear, Jr.
Brandeis University

Patrick Dolenc
Keene State College

William Dougan
Clemson University

David Gay
University of Arkansas

Karen Gebhardt
Colorado State University

Soma Ghosh
Bridgewater State College

Julia Hansen
Western Washington University

David Harris
Benedictine College

Yu Hsing
Southeastern Louisiana University

Larry Huckins
Baruch College, CUNY

Samia Islam
Boise State University

Leroy Allan Jenkins
University of Nebraska, Kearney

Catherine Krause
University of New Mexico

Sara LaLumia
College of William and Mary

Elroy Leach
Chicago State University

Amlan Mitra
Purdue University, Calumet

Lawrence Martin
Michigan State University

William O'Brien
Worcester State College

James O'Toole
Chico State University

Robert Seeley
Wilkes University

Daniel Nathan Shaviro
New York University

Anthony Sindone
Indiana University, South Bend

John A. Sondey
South Dakota State University

Abdol Soofi
University of Wisconsin, Platteville

Edward R. Stuart
Northeastern Illinois University

Mark Tsien-Yung Law
University of Vermont

Tracy Turner
Kansas State University

Mary Lois White
Albright College

James Wilde
University of North Carolina, Chapel Hill

Michael Wolkoff
University of Rochester

I give thanks to my superb editors at McGraw-Hill, Noelle Fox and Karen Fisher, for their detailed recommendations on the substance and style of every chapter, paragraph, and sentence. I also thank McGraw-Hill project manager Kathryn Mikulic for coordinating the production process. I owe a debt to my exceptional economics graduate student assistant at the University of Delaware, Drew Sawyer, for his meticulous checking of all substantive details in the entire book. I am grateful to my public finance students at the University of Delaware who gave me detailed feedback on draft chapters of my book over the past few semesters. I thank my two colleagues at the University of Delaware, Ken Lewis and Saul Hoffman, for our joint research over the years that prepared me to write this book. I am grateful to Karen Gebhardt at the University of Colorado for her work on the PowerPoint presentations. I owe thanks to the many public finance economists whose writings have educated me. Finally, I am grateful to my wife Ann, my son Jesse, and my daughter Suzanna.

Brief Contents

Table of Contents

Public Finance

Chapter **One**

Introduction to Public Finance

Royalty-Free/CORBIS

The purpose of this introductory chapter is to give you the flavor of the material that will follow in the rest of this book. Its aim is to whet your appetite, not satisfy it. Don't be concerned when questions are raised but answers aren't given or when terms are used that are not fully explained. That's the purpose of the rest of the book.

Let's begin our tour of public finance economics with a basic question: Why do we have a government? Why are there taxes and government spending? Why public finance? Most courses in economics correctly teach that the free market usually does a good job in producing goods and services. Economists therefore find it useful to begin by asking the following questions:

Why not leave everything to "the market"?

Why have any taxes and government spending?

THE ROLE OF GOVERNMENT IN MAKING A FREE MARKET POSSIBLE

In a state of nature with no government, there would be no free market. A free market consists of the voluntary interaction of producers and consumers of goods and services. Without a government, criminals would prey on productive people, stealing the goods they produce and the income they earn. Anticipating theft, potentially productive people would stop producing. Almost everyone agrees that a government is necessary to protect producers and their property and thereby to make a free market possible. True, it is possible to imagine private vigilante groups trying to protect themselves from criminals. But most agree that it would be much more effective to establish a government to provide protection for everyone against criminals. Thus, there is little dispute that a government should be established to operate a police force and a court system to protect private property and make a free market possible.

Of course, only a small limited government with low taxes would be needed to protect property and make possible a free market. So the question becomes: Is it necessary or desirable for government to do more than protect people and their property from criminals? To answer this question, we must first appreciate why the free market usually works well for consumers and also appreciate why it nevertheless has certain particular problems that may provide a reason for further government intervention.

WHY THE FREE MARKET USUALLY WORKS WELL FOR CONSUMERS

It is not hard to see why the free market usually works well for consumers. Producers can profit only if they produce what consumers want and avoid producing what consumers don't want. Producers can profit by offering consumers higher quality at the same price as the competition or the same quality at a lower price than the competition. Producers of the same quality product can retain customers and profit only if they charge a price no higher than their competitors. The lower their cost, the lower the price they can afford to charge, so producers have an incentive to try to hold costs down by more efficient management and use of resources. If any producer is temporarily able to set a price well above cost and to make a large profit because there is currently no competition, new firms will enter and compete, forcing the producer to lower the price. Firms find it profitable to compensate workers more when they work hard and efficiently, so individuals have an incentive to work hard and efficiently. Producers can profit by developing new products or better-quality products. Consumers benefit from these competitive pressures on producers and workers.

Economists go further and show that the free market will usually generate just the right quantity—the *socially optimal* quantity—for consumers of each good or service. When economists say that the free market usually results in efficiency, they mean that the market not only pressures producers to minimize the cost of producing any product of a given quality—this is called productive efficiency—but also that it usually allocates the optimal quantity of resources to the production of good X versus good Y, which is called allocative efficiency.

But what is the "right" quantity of good X for consumers? The production of each unit of good X uses resources (labor, materials, etc.) that could have been used to produce other goods like good Y. If consumers value the next unit of good X more than its cost, then it is best for consumers if the next unit of X is produced. But if consumers value the next unit of good X less than its cost, then it is best for consumers if the next unit of X is not produced and the resources are allocated to make a different good, Y or Z.

FIGURE 1.1

Supply and Demand
The market goes to
the intersection.

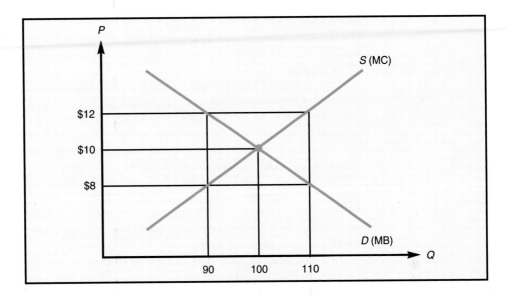

Figure 1.1 shows the market supply-demand diagram for good X. The market price is $10, and the quantity bought and sold is 100. The price is set in the competitive market, and given the price, each buyer decides the quantity he wants to demand, and each seller decides the quantity he wants to supply; hence, buyers and sellers are price takers. At a price of $10, the buyers want to buy 100 (demand D is 100) and the suppliers want to supply 100 (supply S is 100). If the price is initially $8, demand would exceed supply so that the price would get bid up to $10. If the price is initially $12, supply would exceed demand and competition would drive the price down to $10.

Note that in the supply-demand diagrams in this book, supply and demand curves are drawn as straight lines, but the term *curve* will generally be used because the actual relationship between price and quantity may be curved rather than straight.

Thus far our discussion of Figure 1.1 illustrates positive economics—an explanation of what happens without saying whether it is good or bad. Now comes a key question in normative economics, which does try to say whether it is good or bad: In Figure 1.1 is 100—the quantity at the intersection of curves S and D—the right quantity of good X for consumers? The answer is usually yes. To see why, we must first establish that the height of the supply curve is the marginal cost (MC) of producing that unit and the height of the demand curve is the marginal benefit (MB) to a consumer of that unit.

Why is the height of the S curve the marginal cost (MC)—the cost of producing the next unit? Producers find it profitable to increase production of X another unit as long as the MC is less than the price P, and they find that it is profitable to stop when MC is about to rise above P. If the price is $8, the S curve says that producers would supply 90—this means they would find it profitable to produce the 90th unit but not the 91st. So it must be the case that the MC of the 90th unit is slightly less than $8, and the MC of the 91st unit is slightly greater than $8. We say that the MC of the 90th unit is (approximately) $8—the height of the S curve.

Why is the height of the D curve the MB? Consumers buy another unit of X as long as its marginal benefit (MB)—the maximum dollar amount they would be willing to pay for it—exceeds its price P. If the price is $12, consumers would demand 90—this means they would buy the 90th unit but not the 91st. So it must be the case that the MB of the 90th unit is slightly greater than $12, and the MB of the 91st unit is slightly less than $12. We say that the MB of the 90th unit is (approximately) $12—the height of the *D* curve.

Now we can see why it would be best for consumers if more than 90 units of X were produced. Consider the 91st unit. The height of the supply curve is the marginal cost (MC), so the MC of the 91st unit is about $8. The height of the demand curve is the marginal benefit (MB) to the consumer of that unit, so the MB of the 91st unit is about $12. Since the consumer values the 91st unit more than it costs, it should be produced. The same is true of each additional unit until the 100th.

Symmetrically, it would be best for consumers if fewer than 110 units of X were produced. Consider the 110th unit. Its MC is about $12, and its MB is about $8. Since the consumer values the 110th unit less than it costs, it should not be produced—it would be better if the resources were used elsewhere to make other goods. The same is true of each unit until the 100th.

Thus, 100 units of good X is just the right quantity for consumers. This is exactly the quantity produced in a free market by competitive firms seeking profit. The market produces the quantity at the intersection of the *D* and *S* curves. The quantity that is best for consumers is the quantity at the intersection of the MB and MC curves. Since the height of the *D* curve equals MB and the height of the *S* curve equals MC, the free market produces the optimal quantity of good X.

Of course, not every market is perfectly competitive, but many markets are competitive enough so that Figure 1.1 conveys the basic reason why the free market usually works well for consumers and tends to produce roughly the right quantity of most goods and services.

It should be emphasized that this analysis assumes that the marginal cost paid by each producer equals the entire marginal cost to society—the marginal social cost (MSC)—and the marginal benefit to each consumer equals the entire marginal benefit to society—the marginal social benefit (MSB).

TAXES, SUBSIDIES, REGULATIONS, AND INEFFICIENCY

Whenever the free market generates just the right quantity for consumers, any government intervention that changes the quantity causes an inefficiency ("deadweight loss")—a reduction in society's welfare. Note that by "inefficiency" in this context economists mean an *allocative* inefficiency: the government intervention causes too many or too few resources to be allocated to the production of good X relative to other goods and services; if the free market produces the quantity of good X that is best for consumers, then a government intervention that changes the quantity is *not* best for consumers.

A tax imposed by the government causes a *decrease* in the quantity below the optimal quantity. Figure 1.2 shows the effect of a $4 per unit tax *levied on producers*. Figure 1.3 shows the effect of a $4 per unit tax *levied on consumers*. Let's explain each.

In Figure 1.2, a tax of $4 per unit levied on *producers* increases their MC by $4 because the producer has to send $4 to the government for each unit sold. This shifts up their supply curve $4 to *S′*, so the market moves to the intersection of *S′* and *D*, decreasing the quantity from 100 to 90. Note that the consumer pays a price of $12 to the producer who sends $4 to the government and keeps $8.

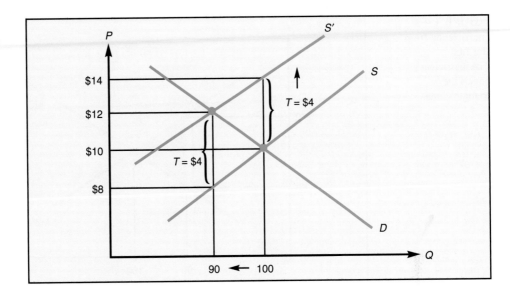

FIGURE 1.2

A Tax on Producers
The supply curve
shifts up.

In Figure 1.3, a tax of $4 per unit levied on *consumers* decreases the price that consumers are willing to pay producers by $4 because the consumer has to send $4 to the government for each unit bought. This shifts down their demand curve $4 to D', so the market moves to the intersection of D' and S, decreasing the quantity from 100 to 90. Note that the consumer pays a price of $8 to the producer and a tax of $4 to the government.

Whether the $4 tax is levied on producers or consumers, it causes the same decrease in quantity from 100 to 90 and therefore the same amount of inefficiency. The magnitude of the inefficiency from the $4 per unit tax (whether levied on producers or consumers) equals the area of the triangle *BAD* in Figure 1.4. Why? Starting at 90 units (the quantity under the tax), for each additional unit there would be a net gain to society equal to the vertical distance MB-MC; no further net gains would be possible once MB equals MC. Adding the vertical distances MB-MC, unit by unit, yields the

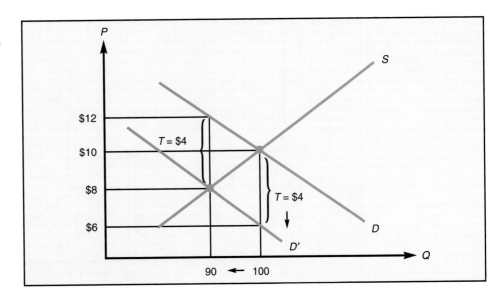

FIGURE 1.3

A Tax on Consumers
The demand curve
shifts down.

FIGURE 1.4
Inefficiency from the Tax
The inefficiency equals the triangle's area.

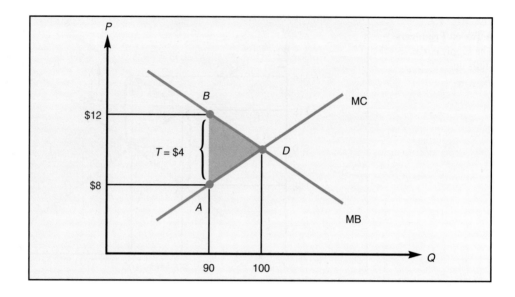

area of the triangle *BAD*. The tax prevents this net gain, *BAD*, from taking place, so the area of the *BAD* triangle equals the inefficiency (deadweight loss) from the tax. In this example, the inefficiency is $20 because the area of a triangle equals ½ (base × height) = ½ ($4 × 10).

Note that if MB and MC were curves rather than straight lines, then *BAD* would be a "triangle" with two sides curved rather than straight so that the formula for the area, ½ (base × height), would be an approximation. Throughout this book, we simplify by assuming that *BAD* is a triangle with three straight sides so that the formula gives its exact area.

Symmetrically, a subsidy given by the government causes an *increase* in the quantity above the optimal quantity. Figure 1.5 shows the effect of a $4 per unit subsidy given to *producers*. Figure 1.6 shows the effect of a $4 per unit subsidy given to *consumers*. Let's explain each in turn.

FIGURE 1.5
A Subsidy to Producers
The supply curve shifts down.

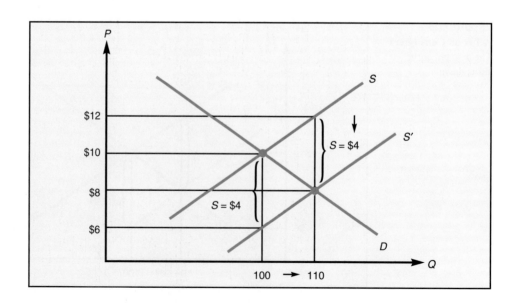

FIGURE 1.6

A Subsidy to Consumers
The demand curve shifts up.

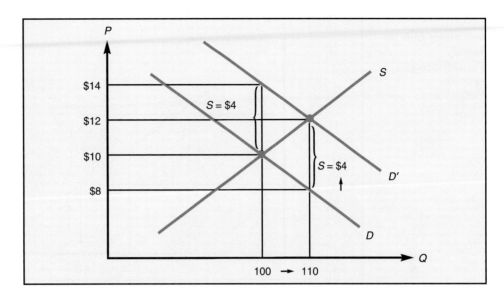

In Figure 1.5, a subsidy of $4 per unit given to producers decreases their MC by $4 because the producer receives $4 from the government for each unit sold. This shifts down their supply curve $4 to S', so the market moves to the intersection of S' and D, increasing the quantity from 100 to 110. Note that the consumer pays a price of $8 to the producer who also receives $4 from the government.

In Figure 1.6, a subsidy of $4 per unit given to consumers increases the price they are willing to pay producers by $4 because the consumer receives $4 from the government for each unit bought. This shifts up their demand curve $4 to D', so the market moves to the intersection of D' and S, increasing the quantity from 100 to 110. Note that the consumer pays a price of $12 to the producer and receives a subsidy of $4 from the government.

Whether the $4 subsidy is given to producers or consumers, it causes the same increase in quantity from 100 to 110 and therefore the same amount of inefficiency. The magnitude of the inefficiency from the $4 per unit subsidy (whether given to producers or consumers) equals the area of the triangle *BAD* in Figure 1.7. Why? Starting at 110 units (the quantity under the subsidy), for each unit less there would be a net gain to society equal to the vertical distance MC-MB; no further net gains would be possible once MC equals MB. Adding the vertical distances MC-MB, unit by unit, yields the area of the triangle *BAD*. The subsidy prevents this net gain, *BAD*, from taking place, so the area of the *BAD* triangle equals the inefficiency from the subsidy. In this example, the inefficiency is $20 because ½ (base × height) = ½ ($4 × 10).

Instead of the $4 tax, suppose the government imposed a regulation limiting the quantity to 90. Then the inefficiency would be the same as under the $4 tax and would be equal to the area of the triangle *BAD* in Figure 1.4.

Instead of the $4 subsidy, suppose the government imposed a regulation requiring a quantity of 110. Then the inefficiency would be the same as under the $4 subsidy and would be equal to the area of the triangle *BAD* in Figure 1.7.

It is important to emphasize that a tax, subsidy, or regulation causes an inefficiency *whenever* the free market would generate just the right quantity for consumers. The free market does this for most goods and services. However, it does not do it for *all* goods and services. When it doesn't, the *proper* tax, or subsidy, or regulation, would increase,

FIGURE 1.7
Inefficiency from the Subsidy
The inefficiency equals the triangle's area.

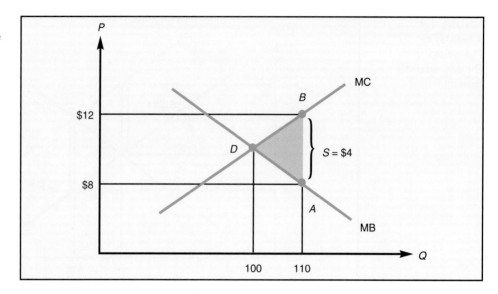

not decrease, consumer welfare. So whether a tax, subsidy, or regulation is a villain or hero depends on whether the free market would generate the optimal quantity of the particular good or service.

It is also important to emphasize that even when the free market would generate the optimal quantity, a tax on good X to raise revenue to finance a beneficial government program might raise welfare. A tax on X would raise welfare as long as the benefit from the government program financed by the tax is greater than the burden from the tax *including* the inefficiency caused by the tax.

PROBLEMS FOR THE FREE MARKET

Although the free market usually works well for consumers, it has several specific problems. We consider them in turn.

Externalities: Chapters 2 and 6

Suppose there is a significant cost generated by the production of good X that is *not* charged to the producers of X. For example, suppose that the production of each unit of X causes $4 of damage to the environment. The *marginal social cost* (*MSC*) is defined as the regular MC plus the marginal environmental damage. As shown in Figure 1.8, the MSC curve is $4 higher than the *S* curve. The *S* curve has a height equal to MC—the marginal cost actually charged to the firm which determines how much the firm wants to supply.

The socially optimal quantity occurs at the intersection of the MSC curve and the MB curve—90 units of good X. Consider the 100th unit. The consumer is willing to pay $10 for the 100th unit, but the cost of the 100th unit is $14—$10 in resources and $4 in environmental damage. It would best if the 100th unit were not produced—and the same for the units from the 99th to the 91st—but the market goes to where *D* and *S* intersect (at 100 units), so the market generates too much of a good when its production involves a cost that is not charged to the producers—a **negative externality**. The free market generates too much of any good that has a negative externality.

FIGURE 1.8
Market Inefficiency When There Is a Negative Externality
The inefficiency equals the triangle's area.

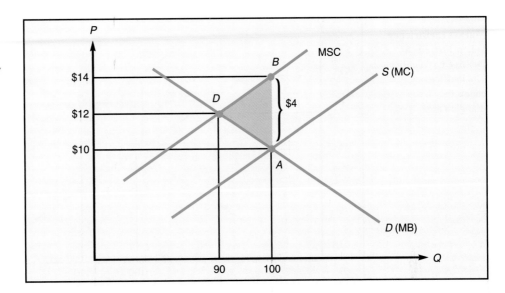

Starting at 100, the quantity under the free market, for each unit less there would be a net gain to society equal to the vertical distance MSC-MB; no further net gains would be possible once MSC equals MB. Adding the vertical distances MSC-MB, unit by unit, yields the area of the triangle *BAD*. The area of the *BAD* triangle equals the inefficiency generated by the free market when there is a negative externality. In this example, the inefficiency is $20 because ½ (base × height) = ½ ($4 × 10).

Now suppose that the consumption of a good—for example, medical care (M)—benefits not only the people who consume it but also people who don't consume it. This could happen for a number of reasons. When a person receives medical treatment for a contagious disease or is vaccinated to prevent it in the first place, other people benefit because they are less likely to catch it. Also, some healthy people feel better whenever sick people have the medical care they need, either because they care about sick people or because they think that they will get similar treatment if they become sick. For example, suppose the consumption of each unit of M causes $4 of benefit to other people. The *marginal social benefit (MSB)* is defined as the regular MB to the consumer plus the marginal benefit to other people. As shown in Figure 1.9, the MSB curve is $4 higher than the *D* curve.

The socially optimal quantity occurs at the intersection of the MSB curve and the MC curve—110 units of good M. Consider the 100th unit. The consumer is willing to pay $10 for the 100th unit, and other people are willing to pay $4 for the same unit, so the MSB is $14; however, the cost of the 100th unit is only $10. So it would be best if the 100th unit were produced—and the same for the units from the 101st to the 110th. The market goes to where *D* and *S* intersect, 100 units, so the market generates too little of a good when the consumption of the good involves a benefit to other people—a positive externality. The free market generates too little of any good that has a positive externality.

Starting at 100, the quantity under the free market, for each unit more there would be a net gain to society equal to the vertical distance MSB-MC; no further net gains would be possible once MSB equals MC. Adding the vertical distances MSB-MC, unit by unit, yields the area of the triangle *BAD*. The area of the *BAD* triangle equals the inefficiency generated by the free market when there is a positive externality. In this example, the inefficiency is $20 because ½ (base × height) = ½ ($4 × 10).

FIGURE 1.9
Market Inefficiency When There Is a Positive Externality
The inefficiency equals the triangle's area.

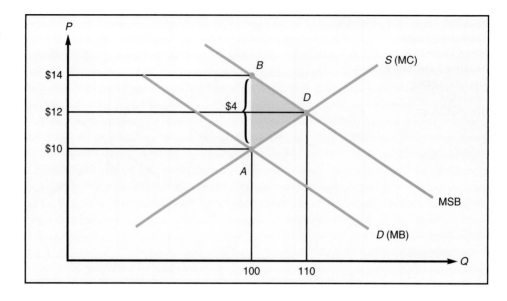

What kind of government intervention is appropriate when there is an externality? We will see in Chapter 2, "Externalities and the Environment," that when there is a negative externality, the government should levy a tax of proper magnitude to eliminate the inefficiency; such a tax is called a corrective tax. We will see in Chapter 6, "Health Insurance," that when there is a positive externality, the government should provide a corrective subsidy of proper magnitude to eliminate the inefficiency. Note that when there is a negative externality, a *tax* of proper magnitude is a hero, not a villain, and when there is a positive externality, a *subsidy* of proper magnitude is a hero, not a villain. In Chapter 2 we examine policy to treat a particular negative externality—damage to the environment. In Chapter 6 we consider the possibility that medical care generates a positive externality—a benefit to other people when sick patients receive medical care—and we try to determine which policy would be appropriate to treat it.

Public Goods: Chapter 3

Suppose it is either difficult or undesirable to exclude somebody from benefiting from a service even if the person refuses to pay for it voluntarily. Consider military protection against an attack by a foreign country. If government played no role in national defense, would private business firms operating through a free market supply adequate protection against a foreign attack directly to any consumer willing to pay for it? Imagine a large private corporation that trains employees to be soldiers, purchases military equipment and weapons, and tries to sell protection against a foreign attack to individual consumers. Consumers would know that if the corporation provides protection to others against foreign attack, they will automatically be protected even if they refuse to pay. Each selfish consumer would therefore wait for others to buy protection from the corporation. This is called the free-rider problem. If most consumers are selfish and wait, a free market will produce too little military protection.

If a company sells fire protection, it would be possible to exclude people who refuse to pay from being protected. However, when a fire breaks out in a home, many would regard it as undesirable to have a fire company let it burn because the homeowner has not bought protection. Moreover, the best way to protect adjacent homeowners who have paid for fire protection would be to extinguish the fire. Knowing this, some selfish consumers would take their chance of not buying protection, counting on receiving protection should their home catch fire. If there are too many selfish consumers, then too many won't pay and the fire company will not be able to afford the personnel and equipment to provide adequate protection.

Economists call a good or service a public good if it is hard to exclude someone who refuses to pay from benefiting and if one person's consumption doesn't diminish consumption by others. Military protection against foreign attack, police protection against criminals, and firefighter protection against home fires are all public goods. As we will see in Chapter 3, most analysts agree that the government should intervene by levying taxes to acquire the funds to buy the public good from a private firm or to produce the service itself.

Social Insurance: Chapters 5 and 6

Whereas virtually all economists agree that government intervention is warranted for externalities and public goods, economists disagree about social insurance. By social insurance we mean old age insurance, health insurance, unemployment insurance, disability insurance, and workplace-injury insurance (workers' compensation). Some economists think social insurance should be left to the private market with little or no government intervention, while other economists think government should play a major role in the provision of social insurance. Economists who support government intervention disagree about the kind of intervention. Here we will comment on old age insurance in Chapter 5 and health insurance in Chapter 6.

Old Age Insurance

Some economists believe that preparing for old age should be left to the market; they contend that individuals should be free to choose how much of their income to consume and how much to save. Each person in middle age should take responsibility for preparing for retirement by saving enough each year to build an adequate retirement fund. Once retired, the person should use the retirement fund to buy old age insurance (an annuity) from a private insurance company which would then make monthly payments to the person for as long as he lives. Individuals who choose to consume more while they are young should have to accept the consequences of consuming less when they are old. If someone arrives at old age without enough funds to subsist, perhaps government should provide a minimum welfare payment to enable subsistence just as it might for younger poor people, but government should not operate a special old age insurance program.

Economists who favor government intervention for old age insurance believe it is unrealistic to expect everyone to prepare adequately for retirement. True, some people could have prepared for retirement but chose instead to live and spend lavishly while young; these lavish spenders do not deserve help. However, many would be inadequately prepared for retirement through no fault of their own. Some may have lost their career job in middle age because of a decline in demand for their company's product and had to take another job with a much lower wage during their last decade of work. Some may have suffered a serious health problem that prevented them from working and caused them to withdraw their savings. Some may have worked hard full time throughout their career, but their low economic aptitude kept them from earning enough to save adequately for retirement. Some may have saved adequately but suffered bad luck on their investments.

Economists who favor government intervention for old age insurance differ over which kind of intervention would be best. One option is for the government to operate a **Social Security** program in which workers and employers pay enough payroll taxes each year to finance benefits promised to current retirees based on their wage histories. A second option would be for the government to require workers to save and invest a specific percentage of their earnings in a private retirement fund of their choice. Under this option, government might require workers to have a large percentage of their retirement fund invested in safe assets like U.S. Treasury bonds and to buy old age insurance—an annuity—either from a private company or perhaps from the government upon retirement. Government might supplement the saving of low-income workers to make sure they accumulate enough to buy an adequate annuity when they retire. Several other options for government intervention are also available. All this is discussed in Chapter 5.

Health Insurance

Economists who believe that health insurance should be left to the market contend that individuals should be free to choose a job that offers health insurance, or buy health insurance from a private insurance company, or decide to go without health insurance. Hospitals should be required to provide life-saving emergency medical care to uninsured people, but the uninsured should then be required to pay as much of their hospital bill as possible. The prospect of such payments would provide an incentive for individuals to obtain health insurance.

Economists who favor government intervention for health insurance believe it is unrealistic to expect everyone to obtain adequate health insurance. True, some people who don't obtain adequate insurance chose to spend lavishly on other things rather than buying insurance; these lavish spenders do not deserve financial help (although most citizens believe the children of lavish spenders should get necessary medical care). Some people may have been much too confident about not needing medical care; perhaps they deserve to be taught a lesson. However, many would be inadequately insured through no fault of their own. Some may have been unable to obtain a job that provided adequate health insurance and when they tried to buy insurance, found that they could not obtain it or could do so only at a very high premium. Why couldn't they buy insurance at a reasonable premium? Their family might have a member suffering from a chronic costly medical problem, and private insurers often either reject an application for insurance from a high-cost family or set the premium very high to cover the high expected cost. Even a family without a chronic costly medical problem might have difficulty affording health insurance if its income is low—after all, premiums are high because medical costs are high—and the family's income may be low due to low economic aptitude, not laziness. True, even a low-income family (provided it's healthy) may be able to find insurance with an affordable premium if it is willing to pay the first several thousand dollars (the deductible) of medical care before the insurance kicks in; but then this low-income family may have trouble affording the first several thousand dollars of medical care.

Some economists who favor government intervention for health insurance believe that medical care generates a positive externality that warrants a subsidy to sick patients. They contend that when sick people get medical care, other people benefit for two different reasons: first, they may be less likely to catch a contagious disease; second, they may feel better knowing that sick people are getting the medical care they need but cannot afford on their own. If this positive externality is significant, then a significant subsidy to sick patients to help them pay for medical care is socially optimal. Insurance provides the subsidy—the patient pays part of the medical bill but the insurer pays the rest. Helping people obtain private insurance or providing government insurance may therefore be socially optimal due to a positive externality.

Economists who favor government intervention for health insurance differ over which kind of intervention would be best. One option is for the government to operate a health insurance program in which workers and employers pay enough payroll taxes each year so that government has the funds to pay a large percentage of all medical bills. The U.S. government operates such a program—**Medicare**—for the elderly, but not for working families. A second option would be for the government to help families obtain private health insurance by providing tax credits to individuals who obtain insurance through an employer or on their own. A third option would be for the government to provide last-resort insurance at an affordable premium for anyone unable to obtain private insurance at an affordable premium. Several other options for government intervention are also available. All this is discussed in Chapter 6.

A final important point about social insurance should always be kept in mind: Social insurance is redistributive—it reduces inequality between low- and high-income households. Social insurance programs are financed by taxes that collect many more dollars from the typical high-income household than from the typical low-income household. But the dollars are spent more evenly. For example, Medicare spends roughly the same amount for hospital care for the average low-income patient as for the average high-income patient.

Income Distribution, Taxation, and Efficiency: Chapters 7, 8, and 9

Although economists agree that the free market usually works well for consumers, they disagree about whether the distribution of income generated by the free market is fair. Economists agree that the tax system can be used to modify the after-tax distribution of income. Economists also agree that such modification would cause some efficiency loss to the economy. They disagree about how much efficiency would be lost, whether the resulting distribution of after-tax income would be fairer than the market distribution, and if so, whether the gain in fairness outweighs the loss in efficiency.

Income Distribution

Most economists agree that the free market distribution of income tends to promote economic efficiency. The free market usually (though not always) distributes higher income to people who have higher economic productivity. Firms find it profitable to pay more to attract high-productivity workers, and the higher their actual productivity, the higher their pay. Consequently, individuals have an incentive to obtain the education and training needed to raise their productivity and to work hard on the job to increase their productivity. Firms find it profitable to give low pay or even zero pay (a dismissal) to workers whose low or poor effort makes their productivity low. Consequently, individuals have an incentive to work hard and efficiently in order to avoid low or zero pay. Investors have an incentive to channel funds into productive ventures that pay high returns. Inventors have an incentive to develop new products and processes that yield high profits and hence high remuneration. Entrepreneurs and investors have an incentive to take risks that may generate high earnings.

Economists disagree, however, over whether pay that varies according to economic productivity is always fair. Most think it is fair to the degree that a person's economic productivity reflects his own effort to acquire education and training and to work hard. An individual's economic productivity may reflect economic aptitude as well as effort; many individuals may be unable to become a surgeon, corporate lawyer, investment banker, CEO of a large firm, or star athlete or entertainer, no matter how hard they try to acquire education and training. Some people may exert extraordinary effort but still generate low productivity.

Moreover, income received in a free market may reflect good or bad luck rather than simply high or low productivity. One person buys corporate stocks and the timing turns out to be right—just after the purchase the stock market rises sharply and the person sells the stocks making a huge capital gain. A year later another person buys stocks and the timing turns out to be wrong—the market plunges and stays down for several years; needing cash, that individual is forced to sell at a huge capital loss. Two small oil and gas companies face the same probability of striking oil: One strikes oil, makes a big profit, and pays its managers big bonuses; the other strikes nothing, makes a big loss, and cuts the pay of its managers. One aspiring actor has a connection that gets him a part in a movie that turns out to be huge success, and soon after he is offered huge compensation for his next movie; another equally talented aspiring actor lacks the connection, fails to get a breakthrough part, and ends up leaving acting for an ordinary job with ordinary pay.

Taxation

A progressive income tax can be used to make the distribution of after-tax income less unequal than the market distribution of before-tax income. A **progressive tax** applies a higher tax rate to high-income households, a **proportional tax** applies the same tax rate to all households, and a **regressive tax** applies a higher tax rate to low-income households. Consider an example of a progressive tax. Suppose high-income person H has $100,000 of income, and low-income person L, $10,000, so H has 10 times the income of L. If both face the same 20% tax rate, H's after-tax income would be $80,000 and L's, $8,000, so H would have 10 times the after-tax income as L ($80,000 ÷ $8,000 = 10); with a proportional tax, the after-tax income ratio is the same as the before-tax income ratio. However, suppose H is taxed 20.8% and L, 12%, so that H pays $20,800 in tax and L pays $1,200. Then H would have 9 times the after-tax income of L ($79,200 ÷ $8,800 = 9). Hence, a progressive tax makes the ratio of after-tax incomes less than the ratio of before-tax incomes.

Is a progressive tax fairer than a proportional tax? If H and L have the same economic aptitude but H works hard and L is lazy, then many citizens would object to trying to narrow their inequality with a progressive tax. But if L works just as hard as H but has much lower economic aptitude, many would conclude that some narrowing of inequality through a progressive tax might be fair. If the main reason that high-income people earn more than low-income people is that they try harder, then a progressive tax might seem unfair, but if the main reason is economic aptitude or luck, then a progressive tax might seem fair.

Efficiency

It should be recognized that there is an efficiency loss to the economy from a progressive tax because it discourages efforts to earn more, and the greater the progressivity, the greater the efficiency loss. In the above example where H is taxed 20.8% and L 12%, H has 9 times as much after-tax income as L; the reduction from 10 to 9 would still leave most individuals with plenty of incentive to try to get the education and training needed to have H's rather than L's skill. The higher the tax rate set on H and the lower the tax rate on L, the less would be the incentive. In the extreme, suppose H were taxed 100% of any income above $10,000. Then it wouldn't pay for a person to get the education or training to have high skills instead of low skills. Clearly, such an extremely progressive tax would cause a large efficiency loss, as individuals who could potentially have very high productivity forgo the education and training and settle for mediocre productivity.

Thus, there is a trade-off: The more progressive the tax system, the greater its reduction in inequality, but the greater its efficiency loss to the economy. Each citizen will therefore prefer a different degree of progressivity depending on how that citizen personally weighs reducing inequality versus reducing efficiency.

All these issues are discussed in depth in Chapters 7, 8, and 9.

Education: Chapter 11

Whereas many citizens take it for granted that government should operate most elementary and secondary schools, most economists do not. Economists begin by asking why we can't rely on the free market to provide elementary and secondary schools. If the government did not operate public schools, private schools would spring up in every community, charge tuition, and engage in a competition to attract parents to enroll their children. This competition would compel schools to try to achieve high quality at an affordable price in order to attract and retain consumers—parents and their children—just as it does for countless other goods and services. Each private school would recognize that if it provides lower quality for the same tuition as its competitors, or the same quality at a higher tuition, it will gradually lose enrollees and revenues and be forced to contract. This competitive pressure would benefit consumers.

Economists recognize, however, that another feature of a free market would pose a problem. A free market generates a wide variety of levels of quality and price for most goods and services. High-income people generally buy high-quality products at high prices, while low-income people buy low-quality products at low prices. Most citizens find this inequality acceptable for most goods and services, but many citizens would be troubled by wide variations in the quality of each child's education according to parental income. Most citizens therefore conclude that government should operate most schools and charge no tuition.

Economists point out, however, that it would be possible to reduce variation in quality without having government operate the schools. Government could levy taxes, whereby high-income households contribute more dollars than low-income households, and then distribute the same amount of dollars per child to each family earmarked for spending on school tuition. Such a program would raise the quality that low-income parents could afford. The government could further narrow differences in quality by giving a larger amount of dollars per child to low-income households than to high-income households. Thus, economists point out it would be possible to reduce quality differences without having government operate most schools.

Nevertheless, a special problem arises with a private school market because many parents care about the family backgrounds of the other children who attend their child's school—economists call this a **consumption externality**. As a consequence, private schools don't sell their product to any buyer the way stores do. Private schools use selective admissions and screen applicants. As explained in Chapter 11, this consumption externality—a central feature of a private school market—may cause difficulties that provide a justification for a public school system.

Low-Income Assistance: Chapter 12

In a free market economy, individuals with low productivity are paid low wages. As a consequence, without government assistance their family's consumption of goods and services would be low—in particular, they would be unable to afford adequate health insurance and medical care. What, if anything, should the government do about this?

One answer is that the government should not intervene, so that most youngsters will then learn that unless they work hard at school and pursue higher education or vocational training, they risk a life of low productivity, low wages, and low consumption. An absence of government assistance would create a strong incentive for youngsters to acquire the skills and productivity needed to escape poverty. Many citizens, however, believe that people who work hard and responsibly should receive enough income to escape poverty and obtain necessary medical care even if their productivity is low. To achieve this, some kind of government intervention is necessary. But what kind?

The options are discussed in Chapter 12. First, the government can provide health insurance to low-income people. In fact, **Medicaid**—government health insurance for low-income people—is by far the largest expenditure for low-income families in the United States. Second, the **Earned Income Tax Credit (EITC)**—a refundable tax credit that benefits even people who owe no income tax—increases the income of low-income workers without reducing job offers by employers, in contrast to an increase in the minimum wage. Third, other refundable tax credits can be used for education, health insurance, and saving. Fourth, most people who are laid off from their jobs receive **unemployment compensation**—cash benefits—from the government; persons physically or mentally unable to work often receive **disability insurance**, and persons injured on the job usually receive **workers' compensation**.

PROBLEMS FOR THE GOVERNMENT

When the free market works poorly, it is often the case that government intervention will work better, but not always. Government sometimes performs poorly when it attempts to remedy poor market performance.

Political Economy: Chapter 3

In Chapter 3 we ask how the government should make decisions concerning public goods. Once we examine what government should do, we then turn to how government actually behaves and makes decisions. The analysis of how government should and actually does make decisions concerning goods and services is sometimes called **political economy**.

To examine this, in Chapter 3 we consider an imaginary island where the free market works well for most goods and services but does not provide adequately for the defense of the island against pirates. A wall surrounding the island can be built to protect against a pirate raid. But how thick should the wall be? The thicker the wall, the costlier it is to build, but the better it will protect against a pirate raid. How should the thickness of the wall be decided? Should there be voting? Should a unanimous vote be required or simply a majority vote? Taxes must be levied to pay for the cost of building a wall of a specified thickness. But how much tax should be assigned to each family? And how should this tax assignment be decided?

While the island can teach many lessons about public goods and political economy, it is of course necessary to examine more realistic government problems and behavior. Chapter 3 next turns to the study of elections, logrolling among legislators, lobbying, special interests, government bureaucracies, political corruption, and the rationale for a constitution to restrain the legislature and the executive.

Cost-Benefit Analysis: Chapter 4

Consider these decisions facing the government: Should it build a new highway? How much should it spend to improve the safety of a highway? How much of a reduction in carbon emissions should it try to get the private sector to achieve? Should it pay for new costly medical treatment X? Should it intervene militarily? Each of these decisions involves weighing cost against benefit. Chapter 4 explains how cost-benefit analysis should be done in these examples and more generally in order to guide government decisions. It also explains mistakes to be avoided when doing cost-benefit analysis.

Which Level of Government? Chapter 10

When the free market works poorly and government intervention seems warranted, a question arises: Which level of government—federal, state, or local—should intervene? Chapter 10 examines the roles of local government and state government.

The strategy of Chapter 10 is to first consider a society in which all households have similar incomes and then to turn more realistically to a society in which households differ significantly in income. If all households in society had similar incomes, local government would often (though not always) be preferable to a higher level of government (state or federal). The reason is that numerous local governments would compete to attract households by offering an attractive mix of public services and taxes. Local governments would compete for residents the way firms compete for consumers, and this competition would be beneficial, just as it is for other goods and services. Of course, even in a society with similar incomes, state or federal government should build highways and the federal government should provide national defense.

But when incomes differ significantly among households, the presumption in favor of local government may need partial reconsideration. Why? Local governments often prefer to attract high-income households that are more able to finance local schools and other public services and less likely to inject street crime. As a consequence, a separation process develops whereby high-income people locate in high-income communities and use zoning to exclude middle- and low-income households. In turn, middle-income households locate in middle-income communities and use zoning to exclude low-income households. With communities differing significantly by income, local financing of public schools would result in a wide variation of school quality across communities. To reduce this inequality, at least some of the financing must come from a higher level of government—state or federal—which can collect more tax dollars from high-income than low-income households and then distribute more dollars to low-income than high-income schools.

What kind of tax should a local government use? The federal government relies on income tax and payroll tax, state governments rely on sales tax and income tax, but local governments rely on property tax. Chapter 10 discusses why and examines the pros and cons of a property tax.

Borrowing Instead of Taxing: Chapter 13

When should the government borrow instead of tax? Borrowing is tempting for a government just as it is for a household. By borrowing, a household can consume more than it earns. By borrowing, a government can provide more programs that voters want without levying the taxes they don't want. But a household that borrows must eventually repay the loan plus interest, so a household should generally limit its borrowing to long-term productive investments and emergencies. Is the same true of a government? Chapter 13 explains how the commonsense concern about excessive borrowing applies to a government just as it does to households and business firms. But it also explains why government borrowing may sometimes be warranted. Chapter 13 then looks at the borrowing record of the U.S. government and the projected outlook for its borrowing in the future.

TAXES AND GOVERNMENT SPENDING IN THE UNITED STATES

Facts and numbers come alive when they are analyzed and explained. Analyzing and explaining are what we will be doing from Chapter 2 to 13 of this public finance textbook. Nevertheless, there are several public finance facts and numbers that you should see, learn, and even memorize before the analysis and explanation begins. Some of these facts and numbers will surprise you when you see them and will surprise your friends or parents when you tell them. Keep them in front of your mind when you're with friends or parents, and in back of your mind as you study the rest of this textbook. Here are a few questions for you and your friends and parents. *Don't* read the answer *until* you've tried to answer the question; you'll have more fun, and you'll remember the answer better when you read it.

1. Select one of the following percentages of gross domestic product (the total output of the economy) to complete the facts below: 10%, 20%, 30%, 40%, 50%, 60%, 70%.
   a. U.S. taxes (federal plus state plus local) as a percentage of GDP: ___%
   b. U.S. federal taxes as a percentage of GDP: ___%
   c. U.S. state and local taxes as a percentage of GDP: ___%
   d. OECD[1] taxes as a percentage of GDP: ___%
   e. Scandinavian[2] taxes as a percentage of GDP: ___%

   Table 1.1 gives the answers, and Figure 1.10 illustrates them.
   Question: Does Table 1.1 mean that the United States should raise its taxes as a percentage of GDP ?
   Answer: Not necessarily. Even though U.S. taxes are a lower percentage of GDP than most other economically advanced countries, it is possible that taxes are much too high in other countries and still too high in the United States. Until we study the effects of taxation and the government programs financed by taxes, we can't know whether U.S. taxes should be left at 30%, raised above 30%, or cut below 30%. Table 1.1 can't tell us what's best, only what is. It shows that the U.S. is a low-tax country compared to other economically advanced countries.

2. Select one of the three phrases to complete this sentence:[3] Federal tax revenue as a percentage of GDP today is (*much higher than, about the same as*, or *much lower than*) 40 years ago.

   As can be seen in Figure 1.11, federal tax revenue as a percentage of GDP today is *about the same as* forty years ago—roughly 18%; over the past 40 years tax revenue

---

[1] OECD is the acronym for the Organization for Economic Cooperation and Development, which includes mainly economically advanced countries.

[2] Denmark, Finland, Norway, and Sweden.

[3] The source for the questions that follow is the U.S. Congressional Budget Office (CBO), *The Budget and Economic Outlook: Fiscal Years 2008 to 2017* (January 2007 edition).

TABLE 1.1

Taxes as a Percentage of GDP

Source: Organization for Economic Cooperation and Development (OECD), *Revenue Statistics* (2007 edition); U.S. Congressional Budget Office (CBO), *The Budget and Economic Outlook: Fiscal Years 2008 to 2017* (January 2007 edition).

U.S. taxes	30%
U.S. federal taxes	20
U.S. state and local taxes	10
OECD taxes	40
Scandinavian taxes	50

FIGURE 1.10

Taxes as a Percentage of GDP

The U.S.'s percentage is 30%, OECD's is 40%.

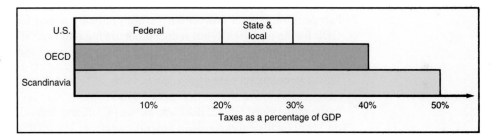

has ranged between 16% and 21% of GDP. Similarly, federal *spending* as a percentage of GDP today is *about the same as* 40 years ago—roughly 20%; over the past 40 years spending has ranged between 18% and 23% of GDP. The difference between federal spending and tax revenue in a given year—the federal deficit—averaged about 2% of GDP over the past 40 years but reached a peak of 6% in the mid-1980s. The federal government borrows whenever it runs a deficit. The federal government borrows, not by going to a bank, but by selling U.S. government securities (bonds) to the public—to domestic and foreign households and businesses, to state and local governments, and to foreign governments.

FIGURE 1.11

Federal Spending and Taxes as a Percentage of GDP

The gap was greatest in the 1980s.

Source: U.S. Congressional Budget Office.

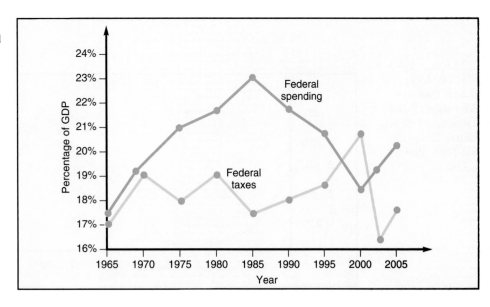

If the federal deficit (and hence federal borrowing) is large, then federal debt—how much the federal government owes lenders (bond holders)—grows faster than GDP, and debt as a percentage of GDP increases; if the deficit (and hence borrowing) is small, then debt grows slower than GDP, and debt as a percentage of GDP falls.

3. Select from the following percentages to complete the paragraph below: 25%, 35%, 50%, 100%.

   During World War II, the increase in military spending was financed mainly by borrowing so by the end of the war federal debt was over ____% of GDP. Over the next three decades, GDP grew faster than federal debt (borrowing was relatively small) so by the mid-1970s federal debt was down to ____% of GDP. Over the next two decades, greater federal borrowing gradually raised federal debt to ____% of GDP by the mid-1990s, but reduced borrowing and fast GDP growth brought debt down to about ____% of GDP by 2000 where it remains today.

   The correct answers are 100%, 25%, 50%, 35% respectively; debt as a percentage of GDP since 1965 is shown in Figure 1.12.

   In the mid-1990s, federal debt was 50% of GDP, and federal interest payments were about 3% of GDP or about 15% of federal spending (3% ÷ 20% = 15%). Today federal debt is 35% of GDP, and federal interest payments are 2% of GDP or 10% of federal spending (2% ÷ 20% = 10%). Thus, the reduction in debt has reduced the share of federal spending that must be devoted to paying interest.

4. Choose the correct terms from the following list to complete the paragraph below: *personal income, payroll, corporate income, sales,* and *property.*

   The ____ tax raises about 45% of federal revenue, the ____ tax raises about 35%, and the ____ tax raises about 10%. State revenue comes mainly from the ____ tax and the ____ tax, while local revenue comes mainly from the ____ tax.

   The correct answers are *personal income, payroll, corporate income, sales, personal income,* and *property,* respectively. As shown in Figure 1.13, the personal income tax is the most important source of federal revenue with the payroll tax (FICA on most pay stubs) for Social Security and Medicare a strong second. Although other economically

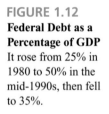

FIGURE 1.12
Federal Debt as a Percentage of GDP
It rose from 25% in 1980 to 50% in the mid-1990s, then fell to 35%.

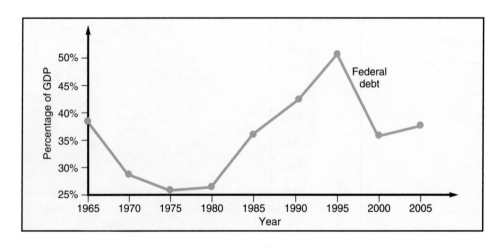

FIGURE 1.13

Components of Federal Revenue and Spending

Source: Bureau of Economic Analysis NIPA tables: (*a*) Federal Revenue, Table 3.2; (*b*) Federal Spending, Table 3.16.

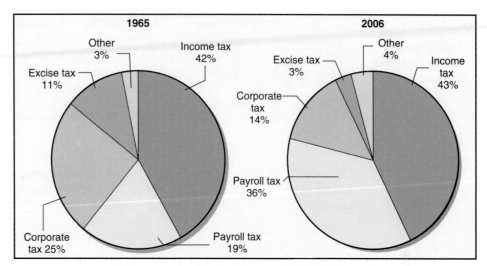

(*a*) Components of Federal Revenue (% of Total Revenue)

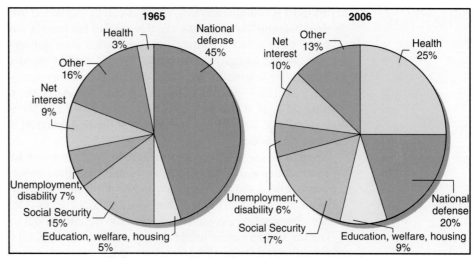

(*b*) Components of Federal Spending (% of Total Spending)

advanced countries levy a tax similar to a sales tax as an important revenue source (the value-added tax, or VAT), the U.S. federal government does not. In the United States, state governments rely on a sales tax and/or a personal income tax. Local governments levy a property tax to fund public schools and other services.

A serious problem looms on the horizon. The Congressional Budget Office projects that "The Big Three" social insurance programs—Social Security, Medicare, and Medicaid—will, due to population and medical cost trends, rise as shown in Table 1.2.

Currently the deficit is about 2% of GDP (spending 21% of GDP, taxes 19%). If the CBO projections for the Big Three prove accurate and if other components of federal spending stay constant as a percentage of GDP, then federal spending will rise from

TABLE 1.2
Medicare, Medicaid,
and Social Security
("The Big Three") as
a Percentage of GDP

	"The Big Three"	Fed Spending	Fed Taxes	Fed Deficit
2000	8%	20%	20%	0%
2010	10	22	20	2
2020	12	24	20	4
2030	14	26	20	6
2040	16	28	20	8

22% of GDP in 2010 to 28% in 2040. If federal tax revenue stays 20% of GDP, the federal deficit will rise to 8% of GDP in 2040. Recall that the annual federal deficit has averaged 2% of GDP over the past 40 years.

Summary

Perhaps the most basic role of government is to protect people and private property from criminals—protection that is essential for making the free market possible. The free market usually works well for consumers and produces roughly the right quantity of most goods and services, and this can be explained using the basic supply and demand diagram. Nevertheless, the free market has certain problems.

When there are externalities, the free market does not produce the right quantity. For a good with a negative externality, the free market produces too much; for a good with a positive externality, too little. When a good or service—like national defense or police protection—benefits everyone because they can't be excluded from benefiting whether they pay or not, the good or service is called a *public good*, and there is a free-rider problem. Most economists agree that the best practical solution to the free-rider problem is taxation.

Whereas virtually all economists agree that government intervention is warranted for externalities and public goods, economists disagree about social insurance. Some economists think old age insurance and health insurance should be left to the market, while other economists think such insurance should be provided by government. Economists who support government intervention disagree about the kind of intervention.

The tax system can be used to modify the after-tax distribution of income. A progressive income tax would reduce inequality because it applies higher tax rates to high-income households than to low-income households. Economists agree that this would cause some weakening of incentives and an efficiency loss to the economy, but they disagree about how much.

Whereas most citizens take it for granted that government should operate most elementary and secondary schools, most economists do not take it for granted and ask whether a private school market could work better. A special problem arises with a private school market because many parents care about the family backgrounds of the other children who attend their child's school. As a consequence of this *consumption externality*, private schools don't sell their product to any buyer the way stores do. Private schools use selective admissions and screen applicants. This feature of a private school market may cause difficulties that provide a rationale for a public school system.

In a free market economy, individuals with low productivity get paid low wages. As a consequence, without government assistance, their family's consumption of goods and services would be low—in particular, they would be unable to afford adequate health insurance and medical care. If citizens want low-productivity people to obtain necessary medical care and live above poverty, government intervention would be necessary.

Although the free market has certain problems, so does government. The analysis of how government should and actually does make decisions concerning goods and services is called *political economy*. A choice must be made about which level of government—federal, state, or local—should intervene. Cost-benefit analysis should be used to guide government decisions. Although government borrowing sometimes is warranted, the commonsense concern about excessive borrowing applies to a government just as it does to households and business firms.

Several interesting facts and numbers concerning taxation and government spending should be kept in mind. Tax revenue as a percent of GDP is 30% in the United States, 40% on average in economically advanced countries (OECD), and 50% in Scandinavia. In the United States, federal tax revenue as a percent of GDP is 20%, while state and local tax revenue is 10%. The Big Three social insurance programs—Medicare, Medicaid, and Social Security—together are projected to increase from 10% of GDP in 2010 to 16% of GDP in 2040.

Roughly 45% of federal revenue comes from personal income tax, while roughly 35% comes from payroll (FICA) tax and 10% from corporate income tax. State revenue comes mainly from sales tax and income tax; local revenue, from property tax. Borrowing during World War II drove federal debt above 100% of GDP; in the three decades after the war from the mid-1940s to the mid-1970s, federal debt as a percentage of GDP gradually declined to 25%; over the next two decades it rose gradually to 50% and then declined to about 35% by 2000 where it remains today.

Key Terms

free market, *2*
efficiency, *2*
productive efficiency, *2*
allocative efficiency, *2*
positive economics, *3*
normative economics, *3*
marginal cost (MC), *3*
marginal benefit
 (MB), *3*
marginal social
 cost (MSC), *4*
marginal social benefit
 (MSB), *4*
inefficiency, *4*

negative externality, *8*
positive externality, *9*
corrective tax, *10*
corrective subsidy, *10*
free-rider problem, *10*
public good, *11*
social insurance, *11*
Social Security, *12*
Medicare, *13*
progressive tax, *14*
proportional tax, *14*
regressive tax, *14*
consumption
 externality, *15*

Medicaid, *16*
Earned Income
 Tax Credit (EITC), *16*
unemployment
 compensation, *16*
disability insurance, *16*
workers'
 compensation, *16*
political economy, *16*
cost-benefit
 analysis, *17*
federal deficit, *19*
federal debt, *20*

Questions

For questions 1 to 4, assume there is no externality.

1. Using a diagram, explain why a tax on producers of good X causes inefficiency. Show the dollar amount of the inefficiency.

2. Using a diagram, explain why a tax on consumers of good X causes inefficiency. Show the dollar amount of the inefficiency.

3. Using a diagram, explain why a subsidy to producers of good X causes inefficiency. Show the dollar amount of the inefficiency.

4. Using a diagram, explain why a subsidy to consumers of good X causes inefficiency. Show the dollar amount of the inefficiency.

5. Suppose the production of a good X damages the environment (there is a negative externality). Using a diagram, show the dollar amount of inefficiency generated by the free market. What policy can correct the market to eliminate the inefficiency?

6. Suppose the consumption of a good M benefits not only the people who consume it but also the people who don't consume it (there is a positive externality). Using a diagram, show the dollar amount of inefficiency generated by the free market. What policy can correct the market to eliminate the inefficiency?

7. Explain the free-rider problem for military protection against foreign attack.

8. Give arguments against and for some government role concerning old age insurance.

9. Give arguments against and for some government role concerning health insurance.

10. Explain how a progressive income tax reduces inequality but causes some inefficiency.

11. Assign the percentages 10%, 20%, 30%, 40%, and 50% to the following: U.S. taxes, U.S. federal taxes, U.S. state and local taxes, OECD taxes, and Scandinavian taxes.

12. What does the CBO project will happen to "The Big Three" from 2010 to 2040?

13. Go online and find several interesting numerical *percentages* (not dollar amounts)—percentages of GDP or percentages of total spending—about components of U.S federal, state, and local spending. Begin by checking out national defense, Medicaid (federal versus state), and education (federal versus state versus local). Why do you think these percentages are interesting or surprising?

Appendix

The Indifference-Curve/Budget-Line Diagram

In this appendix we introduce the indifference-curve/budget-line diagram. This diagram will be used in the appendices of Chapters 6, 7, 10, 11, and 12. Read this appendix before reading the appendix to any of those chapters.

Figure 1A.1 is an indifference-curve/budget-line diagram. Each point indicates a particular quantity of good X, and a particular expenditure Y on other goods. We explain the individual's budget line, then the individual's indifference curves, and finally why the individual chooses the point on the budget line that is on a higher indifference curve than any other point on the budget line.

If the individual spent no income on good X, point A would be chosen. If the individual spent all income on good X, point B would be chosen. In Figure 1A.1 income is $100, and the price P of good X is $5; then at point A, Y = $100, and at point B, X = 20 units. The individual's *budget line* is the line AB. Given the income, the individual can afford any point on the budget line—any combination (X, Y) on the line AB.

Consider point J which is on the individual's budget line when P = $5; at point J, X = 10 and Y = $50, so J is (10, $50). The person can afford to buy 10 units of X, thereby spending $50 on X, and would have $50 left over to spend on other goods. If P were higher, then the budget line would be AC, which is steeper than AB. In Figure 1A.1 if P were $10, then at point C, X would be 10. If the price is $5, then the slope of the budget line is −$5, because the individual must spend $5 *less* on other goods to get *one more unit* of X. More generally, *the slope of the budget line equals* −P. Suppose the individual's income increases above $100 (not shown); then the vertical axis intercept would shift up above A. Since the price is still P = $5, the slope of the budget line would remain the same; hence, the increase in income would shift the budget line out *parallel* to AB.

Which of the points on the budget line AB should the individual choose? The answer is the point that gives the individual a higher *utility* (subjective satisfaction)

FIGURE 1A.1

The Indifference Curve Diagram

The person chooses the point on the budget line that is tangent to an indifference curve.

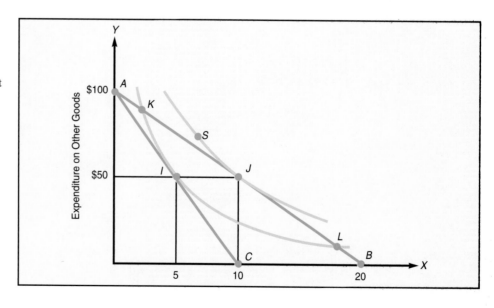

than any other point on the budget line. As will be explained in a moment, it turns out that at this point, and only at this point, the budget line *AB* is tangent to an indifference curve—for example, point *J*—while at any other point on the budget line—for example, point *K* or *L*—the indifference curve cuts through the budget line instead of being tangent to it.

But what is an indifference curve? Through any point (*X, Y*) in the diagram, it is useful to draw a curve connecting all other points that would give the person the same utility. For example, consider point *I*; suppose that point *K* would give the person the same utility as point *I*. Then through *I*, draw a curve that goes through *K*; each point on this curve would give the person the same utility. Similarly, consider point *J* and suppose that point *S* would give the individual the same utility. Then through *J*, draw a curve that goes through *S*; each point on this curve would give the person the same utility. It would be natural to call these curves "utility curves," but they are called **indifference curves.** Why? Because the person would be indifferent to having point *I* or point *K* or point *L*. Just remember that any point on an indifference curve would give the person the same utility as any other point on that indifference curve.

Consider two indifference curves, one through point *S*, the other through point *I*. Point *S* would give the person a higher utility than point *I* because *S* has more units of good X and also a larger expenditure *Y* on other goods. Since point *J* would give the person the same utility as point *S*, point *J* would give the person more utility than point *I*. Thus, the more "northeast" or higher is an indifference curve, the higher is its utility. Now consider three points the person can afford if the budget line is *AB*: *J, K*, and *L*. The person would prefer *J* to either *K* or *L* because *J* is on a higher indifference curve. The person would prefer point *J*, where the indifference curve is tangent to *AB*, to any other point on *AB* because any other point on *AB* is on a lower indifference curve than *J*. Thus, out of all the points on *AB*, the person would choose *J*.

Chapter **Two**

Externalities and the Environment

Royalty-Free/CORBIS

This chapter concentrates on an extremely important *negative* externality—environmental pollution. Economic analysis has led virtually all economists to make a controversial recommendation: charge polluters a price (either by levying a pollution tax or by requiring polluters to buy a permit for each unit of pollutant they emit) in order to discourage pollution. By contrast, many noneconomists recommend other approaches to reducing pollution. Some would require (mandate) each polluter to cut back a particular amount or switch to a particular low-polluting technology or manufacture a low-polluting product. Others would subsidize low-polluting technologies or products. This chapter explains why economists prefer charging polluters a price.

Recall from Chapter 1 that an externality exists whenever producers or consumers do *not* have to pay for a cost they generate or do *not* receive a payment for a benefit they generate. It should be emphasized that an externality can be *negative or positive*.

A **negative externality** exists whenever producers or consumers do *not* have to pay for a cost they generate. Suppose there is a significant cost generated by the production of good X—for example, damage to the environment—that is *not* charged to the producers of X. With a negative externality, output of good X is too high because producers or consumers of the good ignore a cost of the good that is external to them—a cost they do not have to pay. For example, firms produce too much of a polluting good (a good that generates pollution when it is produced or consumed) because the cost of pollution to society is *external* to the polluting firms—they are not charged for using air and water quality the way they are charged for using labor or materials.

A **positive externality** exists whenever producers or consumers do *not* receive payment for a benefit they generate. With a positive externality, output of good M (for example, medical care) is too low because producers or consumers of the good ignore a benefit of the good that is external to them—a benefit to others. For example, too few people get flu immunizations because they ignore the benefit to others who would not catch the flu from them. Positive externalities are important in medical care and education, and we analyze these positive externalities in Chapters 6 and 11.

THE ECONOMIST'S APPROACH TO POLLUTION

Environmental Pollution

Economists generally recommend a particular kind of intervention by government to reduce (abate) environmental pollution. They recommend that the government charge polluters a price in order to discourage pollution. The greater the environmental harm from a pollutant, the higher should be the price for emitting it. The price can take two forms: a pollution tax or a permit price. Whichever form the pollution price takes, it would confront producers with the environmental cost of their production. Before polluting, they would consider the cost and therefore consider shifting to a production process entailing less pollution. If they continue polluting, they would try to pass on the cost to consumers through a higher product price, and the higher price would give consumers an incentive to shift away from a product that entailed pollution. The result would be a reduction in pollution.

If the government levies a pollution tax or sells permits, it raises revenue. But the aim is to reduce pollution, not raise government revenue. Therefore, the government should return the revenue to the population by cutting other taxes or sending out cash rebates to households. If the pollution revenue is recycled in this way, then the tax burden on the population would *not* increase; the pollution taxes would be revenue replacers, not revenue raisers. Although revenue recycling would remove part of the burden on people from pollution taxes, people would still bear some burden because they would consume less of certain goods—namely goods that entail pollution. However, they would benefit from the improved environmental quality.

Most economists regard pollution as an example of a **market failure**—an allocation of resources by the market that is *not* socially optimal. Why does the market fail? The problem is that no one owns the air and water—in other words, there is a failure of **property rights**. When something is free, it is used wastefully. By contrast, anything that is owned is seldom free because, naturally, the owner insists on charging a price for its use. Any potential user is deterred from frivolous use. But who owns the air above city C or the water in river R? No one owns it, so no one charges a price for using it—that is, polluting it. In a free market, consequently, pollution is excessive.

The solution to excessive pollution is straightforward to most economists. Whenever pollution harms many citizens, usually the most practical solution is for the government to assume ownership on behalf of the public and then do what a typical private owner of a resource does: charge a price for its use. The market fails because a key element—ownership of a valuable resource—is absent. The solution is to restore the market by restoring the missing ingredient: ownership of the resource and a price for its use.

A Price for Pollution

The government can charge a price in two ways: by a tax and by a permit price. Under the tax method, the government sets a tax per unit of pollutant X. Polluters are then free to respond; for each unit they pollute, they must pay the tax. Under the permit method, the government decides the aggregate quantity of pollutant X it is willing to tolerate. It then sells that quantity of permits to polluters, whereby each permit allows the owner to emit one unit of pollutant X. Emission of a unit of the pollutant without a corresponding permit would be illegal, triggering a steep fine or other penalties. The government would set the permit price in an auction to clear the market—the price at which the demand for permits by bidding firms equals the quantity the government has decided to supply. The permit method is also called **cap and trade** because a *cap* is set on the total quantity of pollution—the quantity of permits—and firms that initially obtain permits are allowed to *trade* them so there is an active secondary market in permits (just as there is in corporate stocks and bonds).

Under the tax method, the government fixes the price per unit of pollutant X, but the response of polluters determines the aggregate quantity of pollution. Under the permit (*cap and trade*) method, the government fixes the aggregate quantity of pollutant X (sets the *cap*), but the bidding of polluters for permits determines the price of a permit—hence, the price per unit of pollutant X. Which method is better? It depends. We return to this question shortly. But note this: Both pricing methods raise comparable revenue for the government.

Charging polluters a price forces them to **internalize the externality**. Previously, the harm they were causing the environment was *external* to them because they did not have to pay for it. By charging a price, the government makes the cost *internal* to the polluters—they must now pay for using up a valuable resource—the environment—just as they must pay for using up other valuable resources like labor and materials. Like any other internal (private) cost, they try to pass it on to buyers by raising the price of the product. This causes consumers to cut down on the purchase of the product and hence reduces pollution.

Coase's Prescription When Victims Are Few: Assign a Property Right

Before analyzing what to do when many citizens are harmed—the case that is relevant to major pollutants such as sulfur dioxide (acid rain) and gaseous carbon products (global warming)—it is interesting to consider what to do when only a few victims are involved. Several decades ago, the economist Ronald Coase pointed out that the government need not charge a price. Instead, the government can simply establish a standard private property right which makes the owner legally entitled to receive payment for any use of her property. With that property right in place, the potential polluter would end up confronting a price equal to the damage caused to the environment, and she would be optimally deterred from polluting.

Coase gave an example where a rancher's cattle eat the crop of a neighboring farmer. The government can simply establish that the victim—the farmer—has a property right that enables her to obtain full compensation under the law from the rancher for damages to the crop—by bringing the case to court if necessary. If the cost in legal fees and time spent going to court is small relative to the crop damage, the farmer will sue. Knowing this, the rancher would have an incentive to avoid damaging the farmer's crop.

Coase also noted that if, instead, the rancher were given a property right permitting her cattle to eat the farmer's grass, the farmer would offer to pay the rancher to restrain her cattle; so once again, the rancher would have an incentive to restrain her cattle. Thus, whether the property right is assigned to the farmer or the rancher, the rancher would have an incentive to restrain her cattle. Thus, the government need not impose a price; assigning a property right would generate the proper financial incentive to restrain the cattle.

Suppose the rancher were surrounded by numerous independent farmers and her cattle ate a small quantity of each farmer's crop. Even if each farmer were given a property right, the damage to each farmer might be less than the cost in legal fees and time spent going to court to sue for damages. If so, each farmer would not sue. Knowing this, the rancher would have no incentive to restrain her cattle. It might be possible for a law firm to try to organize a *class action suit* of all damaged farmers, but financing such a suit—the **transactions costs**, or the costs involved in organizing the suit and contacting the numerous parties to the suit—may be prohibitive for achieving voluntary collective action.

Thus, if many farmers were each harmed a small amount by a particular rancher, it would be more practical for the government to charge the rancher a price per unit of crop damaged. Usually only a few farmers are damaged by a particular rancher, so establishing a property right is all that is needed to solve that problem. However, in the case of major environmental pollutants, many citizens are harmed. Most economists agree that for these pollutants, the best practical solution is to have the government charge polluters a price per emission.

The Trade-Off between Environmental Quality and Output

Consider a highly lethal pollutant: The slightest emission would cause enormous damage. What do economists recommend? The same thing as any other sensible citizen: Ban it. But economists view a ban as an extreme case of our two pricing methods. Under the tax method, the more harmful the pollutant, the higher should be the tax per unit of pollutant; in the extreme, the tax should be so high that no polluter could afford to emit even a single unit. Under the permit method, the more harmful the pollutant, the smaller should be the aggregate number of permits that the government sells; in the extreme, the number sold should be zero.

Economists contend that citizens should recognize the basic trade-off shown in Figure 2.1. Getting more environmental quality involves giving up some output. For example, suppose that under a free market with no governmental environmental policy, a low environmental quality would result (level F). How can environmental quality be raised? One way is for firms to switch to cleaner but more costly production techniques. Another way is for firms to cut back on output involving pollution. Still another is for firms to produce and pollute exactly as before, but for the government to use up resources to treat the pollution. Whichever method is used to improve environmental quality, there will be less output for consumers to enjoy. To raise environmental quality (from level F toward level A), the economy must move along the trade-off curve and accept less output.

What point on the trade-off curve is best for people's welfare? Imagine that the economy is initially at point F. Then imagine reducing output just enough to raise

FIGURE 2.1

The Trade-Off between Output and Environmental Quality
Raising environmental quality requires a reduction in output.

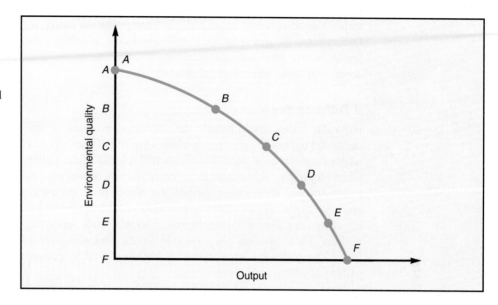

environmental quality to level *E*, so the economy would move "northwest" on the trade-off curve from point *F* to point *E*. Suppose people subjectively value the improvement from level *F* to level *E* more than the required loss in output. Then it should be done. Starting from *E*, consider reducing output just enough to reach quality level *D*. Once again, if people value the improvement from *E* to *D* more than their loss in output, it should be done. Suppose the environmental improvement outweighs the output loss until level *B* is reached. Starting at level *B*, suppose people subjectively value an improvement from *B* to *A less* than the required loss in output. Then an improvement to *A* should *not* be done, and point *B* would be the point on the trade-off curve that is best for people's welfare.

The Virtues of Pollution Prices

Once the target for pollutant X has been determined, why not just assign a quota (ceiling) to each polluter of X to ensure that the aggregate quantity of X equals the target? Once the aggregate target has been set, how do we decide which firms should do the polluting—that is, how do we *allocate* pollution among the polluters? For example, suppose current aggregate pollution of chemical X is 5,000 units, there are 100 polluters of X, and it is decided that the aggregate target for pollutant X should be 1,000 units (a cutback of 80%). One simple approach would be to *command* each polluter to emit no more than 10 units of X. But this doesn't take into account the varying production levels of the 100 polluters. A simple approach that does take this into account would be to command each polluter to cut back 80% from its current emissions (emit only 20% of its current level). Another approach would be to *control* the production technology that firms can use in order to reduce the emissions of X; this *technology-forcing* approach is generally taken by the U.S. government and most other governments around the world.

Unfortunately, this **command and control** method is a poor way to handle the allocation problem. First, the 100 polluters of X produce a variety of products. Consumers value some products more than others. Surely we want the allocation to take account of consumer preference for the products. Second, the polluters differ in technological options. Some can cut back pollution easily with little additional cost. Others must incur a substantial additional cost to achieve the same reduction. Since polluters will pass on cost increases to consumers, we want the allocation to take account of these technological options.

A Pollution Tax

Pollution prices would handle the allocation problem nicely. First, consider the tax method. Suppose the government sets a tax of $40 per unit of pollutant X. The polluter whose products have good substitutes will reason: "I can't afford to pay this tax because when I try to pass the cost on to my customers by raising my price, they will simply shift to substitutes." By contrast, the polluter whose products are highly valued by consumers will reason: "I can afford to pay the tax because when I try to pass the cost on to my customers, they will keep buying." So who ends up cutting pollution sharply? The polluter whose product has good substitutes. And who ends up cutting back relatively little? The polluter whose product is highly valued by consumers. This is exactly the pattern of cutback we want.

Next, consider the polluter with technological options that enable a reduction in pollution at little additional cost: "Rather than pay the tax, it is cheaper for me to switch technologies and reduce pollution." By contrast, consider the polluter with few technological options. Only at high cost can pollution be reduced: "I'm still better off paying the tax, because it would be even more expensive for me to switch technologies." So who cuts back pollution sharply? The polluter with good technological options. And who cuts back pollution relatively little? The polluter with few technological options. This is exactly the pattern of reduction we want.

Of course, when each polluter of X decides how much to pollute if the tax is $40, it may turn out that aggregate pollution of X will be 1,200 or 800 instead of the target, 1,000 units. If pollution is 1,200 units, then the government should raise the tax above $40; if pollution is 800, then the government should lower the tax below $40. Eventually, the government will find the tax that approximately achieves the aggregate target of 1,000.

Pollution Permits

Now consider the permit method. The government would sell 1,000 permits, so the supply of permits would be fixed at 1,000. The practical aspects of how the government would actually sell or auction the permits requires careful thought and should be based on the practical methods that have been used, for example, when the government sells U.S. Treasury bonds. Here we sketch a simple hypothetical method which may not be the most practical. Under this method, the government would get polluters to reveal their demand for permits by asking them to place orders for permits at each of the following prices: $30, $40, and $50. The polluters would submit their orders at each price. For example, at a price of $30, polluters might order (demand) 1,200, while at a price of $50, polluters might order 800 permits. Suppose that at a price of $40, polluters would want to order 1,000 permits. The government would then announce that the permit price is $40 and would sell each polluter the number of permits each polluter ordered at that price.

If the price of a permit is $40, then a $40 per unit pollution tax should produce exactly the same pattern of pollution reduction across polluters and yield aggregate pollution equal to 1,000. After all, a polluter doesn't care whether the $40 price per unit is called a permit price or a tax. She will figure her profit and do the same thing.

Therefore, whether the price is charged through the tax or permit method, the desirable pattern of cutback across polluters is induced.

A price system results in the socially optimal allocation of pollutant X across polluters. There is a more general principle at work here. A price system results in the socially optimal allocation of any resource across users—whether the resource is labor, capital, materials, or pollutants. This is why economists want to use prices to allocate pollution among polluters.

We can disagree over what the target for pollutant X should be. Should it be 800 units or 1,200 units instead of 1,000? But once the target has been set, we can surely agree on this: Let's achieve the pollution target with the minimum sacrifice in output. That is exactly what pollution prices can do. Pollution prices induce a socially desirable pattern of pollution reduction across polluters. This means that the target is achieved with the minimum loss in the value of output.

Objections to Pollution Prices and Economists' Responses

When discussing pollution prices, one major question arises: Isn't a pollution price a "license to pollute" and therefore ethically questionable? This objection confuses two distinct questions: First, what should be the aggregate target? Second, given the target, how should we allocate the pollution among polluters? Prices apply only to the second issue, while the objection is really concerned with the first issue—the setting of the target. Let the case be made for a zero target. If it is persuasive, then we should simply ban the pollutant. However, if it is not persuasive and we decide to tolerate a certain quantity of pollutant X, then we should achieve the target with the minimum sacrifice in output. That is where prices come in.

Won't the polluters just pass on these pollution prices to "innocent" consumers by raising product prices to cover these charges? Yes, they certainly will. The purpose of pollution prices is to confront consumers with the environmental cost of the products they buy. *The price system is an information system.* The price of each good is supposed to convey information to the consumer—namely, the cost of producing it. If the price is less than cost, then the consumer is misled and demands too much of the good; if the price is greater than cost, then the consumer demands too little of the good. The free market fails because the price of "polluting output" (output that generates pollution in its production or use) is too low relative to the price of "pollution-free output" (output that generates no pollution in its production or use). Why is the price of polluting output too low? Because it doesn't include the environmental cost. Why doesn't it include the environmental costs? For the simple reason that polluters are not charged for polluting. Why aren't they charged? Because there is no owner of air or water to impose the charge. Consumers are induced by the false price signals to consume too much polluting output and too little pollution-free output. The whole point of pollution prices is to raise the price of polluting output relative to the price of pollution-free output so that consumers receive accurate information and, as a result, shift consumption from polluting goods to pollution-free goods and services.

But won't pollution taxes raise the tax burden on the population? No, because the government should return the pollution revenue to the population by cutting other taxes or sending people cash transfers. Pollution taxes are revenue replacers, not revenue raisers.

Practical Problems to Pollution Pricing

Let's consider a few practical problems with the two pricing methods. Perhaps the most important practical problem is this: Pricing requires measuring each polluter's emissions, while mandating low-pollution technologies does not. In some cases, measuring may be too costly or unfeasible. Naturally, economists recommend using pricing only if the cost of measuring is less than the benefit of pricing.

The tax method has another problem: It can never guarantee that the pollution target will be met precisely. In response to a given tax per unit, polluters may emit too much or too little. If too much, the government can raise the tax; if too little, the government can lower it. However, the government may never hit it exactly right. On the other hand, the tax method ensures that abatement will not occur if it is very costly, because if the tax is $40, polluters will only abate if the cost of abatement is less than $40.

While the permit method guarantees that the target will be achieved, it has other problems. With the permit method, very costly abatement may occur, because the permit price that results from supply and demand may turn out to be very high, and if the permit price turns out to be $200, then polluters will abate as long as the *cost* is less than $200. Moreover, there are also practical problems. Will the sale (auction) occur on a single day for the year? Permits must surely be tradable so that firms can buy and sell them as their production plans evolve. But how well will the permit market work? Will firms buy permits simply because they expect to sell the permits at a higher price or because they want to keep competitors from getting the permits they need to produce? Will there be any restriction on who can buy or sell permits? Will the permit price fluctuate erratically in response to speculation and psychology? The tax method has none of these problems.

Thus far, neither the United States nor any other nation has relied heavily on pollution prices to implement environmental policy. However, the cause of pollution prices has slowly begun to make progress. Some recent experiments with pollution prices in the form of tradable permits (which we discuss later in this chapter) give grounds for hope. Nevertheless, we must confess that governments still generally mandate specific production techniques for polluters, and we continue to achieve a given level of environmental quality with an unnecessarily large sacrifice in output.

Charging a Price versus Mandating or Subsidizing Clean Technologies

Instead of charging polluters a price (through a tax or tradable permits), why not require (mandate) producers to use particular clean, low-polluting technologies or make particular clean products? Or why not give a subsidy (through tax breaks or direct payments) to firms or consumers for adopting clean production technologies or clean products? For example, instead of taxing oil or gasoline according to the pollution generated, why not require auto manufacturers to produce cars with a particular gas mileage or require homes to have a particular insulation? A mandate for producers seems very direct, and its cost consequences are hidden; therefore, this approach is often popular with the public. Giving tax breaks or direct payments is surely more popular politically than charging a price. However, economists almost unanimously recommend charging polluters a price *and* generally *oppose* either mandates or subsidies to producers or consumers of clean technologies and products. Why?

First, economists emphasize that charging polluters a price automatically stimulates the production and consumption of clean technologies and products. When the price of a polluting good rises, consumers not only have an incentive to buy less of the polluting good but also have an incentive to switch to clean alternative products; therefore, producers automatically have an incentive to produce clean products. Note that charging polluters a price leaves *a completely level playing field among potential alternatives*. There is no favoring of one clean process or product over another by the government. The market is left to develop the alternatives and present them to potential consumers.

Second, any list of mandates for particular clean technologies and products is likely to reduce pollution at an unnecessarily high cost to consumers. Consider two examples: (1) requiring electric utilities to use "scrubbers" to remove sulfur dioxide when coal containing sulfur is burned and (2) requiring auto manufacturers to produce cars with a specified gas mileage—corporate average fuel efficiency (CAFE) standards. For some electric utilities, it may be cheaper to switch from high-sulfur coal to low-sulfur coal rather than install scrubbers. Electric utilities, like other firms, pass on costs to consumers through higher prices. By contrast, if electric utilities are charged a price for emitting sulfur dioxide, they will have an incentive to choose the least-cost method of reducing emissions, and this will minimize the price increase to consumers.

CAFE standards raise the cost of producing cars, but once cars are purchased, drivers have *no* incentive to reduce their driving. By contrast, taxing oil or gasoline gives drivers an incentive both to buy cars that get better gas mileage *and* to drive less; with a tax, each driver would have an incentive to choose the least-cost way of reducing the use of gasoline—either buying a car with better gas mileage, reducing driving, or both. With a tax, if it is not very costly to raise the gas mileage of cars, then most drivers will switch to high-gas-mileage cars; if it is very costly to raise gas mileage, many drivers will stick with low-gas-mileage cars but will strive to reduce their driving. By contrast, if it is very costly to raise gas mileage, a high CAFE standard will impose a very high cost on all car buyers. In 2007, Congress passed and the president signed into law a new energy bill that raised the CAFE standard from 25 miles per gallon (set three decades ago) to 35 miles per gallon by 2020. Congress did not consider the alternative, recommended by many economists, of raising the federal tax on gasoline which is currently 18.4 cents a gallon—much lower than it is in most economically advanced countries. One reason Congress chose CAFE over a gas tax is that the cost to consumers of raising the CAFE standard is hidden, while the cost of raising the tax on gasoline would be very visible.

Third, any list of subsidies for particular clean technologies and products must inevitably result in *a distorted playing field among potential alternatives*. Any process or subsidy that is included in the list will have an improper advantage over any that is omitted. Technologies or products that are yet to be invented would initially have to be omitted; potential inventors would have no guarantee that embarking on a costly effort would ultimately result in an adequate subsidy. Even if a well-intentioned board of technicians tried to be neutral among products included in the list, it would be extremely difficult for the technicians to figure out how to subsidize all products on the list equally.

Fourth, political lobbying for subsidies would distort the playing field among potential alternatives. The list and magnitude of subsidies in practice would not be determined by a board of technicians. It would be determined by politicians who would be subjected to lobbying by producers and consumers seeking subsidies for their particular alternative. Producers differ in lobbying strength, and lobbying strength would shape the magnitude of the subsidies that result from the political process.

Fifth, switching to clean alternatives is not always the socially optimal response. Suppose all the clean alternatives are very costly—they use up a lot of resources. Then it might be socially optimal for consumers to drive less or wear sweaters indoors rather than switch to costly high-gas-mileage cars or clean driving fuels or clean heating technologies. A subsidy makes a clean alternative appear cheaper than its real use of resources. Producers and consumers are induced to produce and consume more than they would if they recognized that the real cost is higher. The price system is an information system—each price is supposed to signal the marginal social cost of the product so that producers and consumers can make decisions based on accurate information. A polluting good is underpriced unless the government charges polluters a price equal to the environmental cost. If clean alternatives to the polluting good are subsidized, the clean alternatives will also be underpriced. The economically correct solution is accurate pricing for both the polluting good and its clean alternatives: Producers of the polluting good should be charged a price equal to the environmental cost, and clean alternatives should not be given a subsidy.

Sixth, subsidies require raising taxes, cutting other government programs, or borrowing to pay for them. Whoever pays the taxes that are raised, or benefits from the programs that are cut, or pays the interest in the future on the new borrowing, will bear the burden of the subsidies. Moreover, as we will see in Chapter 7, most taxes impose some inefficiency on the economy. The burden due to subsidies is the same whether the subsidies are delivered by explicit direct payments to firms or consumers by the government, or by tax breaks to producers or consumers. The tax breaks mean that the producers or consumers are allowed to pay less tax if they produce or consume the subsidized alternative. However, the government collects less tax revenue from them. To make up for this cut in revenue, the government must raise other taxes or cut programs or borrow.

Thus, virtually all economists recommend resisting the temptation to impose mandates or give subsidies to producers and consumers of alternative clean products. The economically best solution is to charge the polluters a price equal to the environmental cost and avoid either mandates or subsidies to producers or consumers.

ECONOMIC ANALYSIS OF A POLLUTION TAX AND TRADABLE PERMITS

A Pollution Tax

We will now show, using a supply and demand diagram, that a competitive market generates too much of a *polluting good—a good whose production or use generates pollution*—however, if a tax is imposed, the competitive market will produce less of the good, and if just the right tax is imposed, the competitive market will produce just the right quantity of the polluting good.

The Right Tax Generates the Right Quantity of a Polluting Good

A competitive market is governed by demand and supply, as shown for gasoline in Figure 2.2. The lower the price, the greater the quantity demanded by the buyers of gasoline. The higher the price, the greater the quantity supplied by the sellers of gasoline. The market will go to the intersection point: The price of gasoline will turn out to be $3.50, and the quantity actually bought and sold will be 100.

The height of the supply curve equals the **marginal private cost (MPC)**. Sellers compare the cost they will actually have to pay to produce another gallon—their marginal private cost—to the price they will get for it. As long as their MPC is less than the price, they make more *profit* by producing another gallon. For example, when the price is $3.50, sellers keep producing as long as the MPC is less than $3.50—according to the diagram, 100 gallons. So the cost of producing the 100th gallon must be just under $3.50 because it would be produced if the price were $3.50. The cost of producing the 101st gallon must be just above $3.50 because it would not be produced if the price were $3.50.

FIGURE 2.2

The Socially Optimal Quantity of a Polluting Good
The quantity where MB equals the MSC is socially optimal.

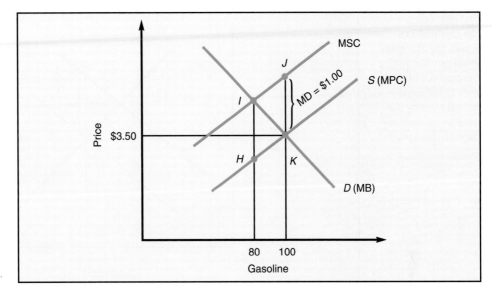

When deciding how much to supply, producers (sellers) care only about the costs they actually pay—the wages they pay for labor, and the prices they pay for materials and machines. They ignore any cost they don't pay for—damage to the environment. The **marginal social cost (MSC)** of a polluting good equals the regular marginal cost due to using up inputs (labor, materials, and machines) plus the **marginal damage (MD)** to the environment. In the absence of a tax, the MPC is less than the marginal social cost (MSC). The MSC curve is above the MPC curve (when there is no tax) by an amount equal to the MD.

In Figure 2.2, the MD that occurs from the car's exhaust when a gallon of gasoline is burned in an auto engine is $1.00 at any quantity of gasoline. What does it mean to say the MD is $1.00? Here is one answer many economists give. Suppose that if people were informed by health experts of the health consequences, they would together be willing to pay a total of $1.00 to avoid the damage that occurs per gallon burned; then economists would conclude that well-informed people judge the MD per gallon to be $1.00.

The height of the demand curve equals the **marginal benefit (MB)**. The MB is the maximum amount that consumers would be willing to pay for that unit. Why? Consider the 100th gallon in Figure 2.2. If the price were $3.50, drivers would be willing to buy 100 gallons, but not a gallon more, so the 100th gallon was a very close decision—to buy or not to buy. That means that the maximum amount drivers are willing to pay for the 100th gallon is very slightly above $3.50, or approximately $3.50. As the number of gallons drivers have already bought increases, the MB declines.

The **socially optimal quantity** of a polluting good is where the MB equals the MSC. In Figure 2.2, the socially optimal quantity is 80 gallons. For each gallon up until the 80th, the MB exceeds the MSC, so society enjoys a net gain (even taking into account the environmental damage) when each gallon is produced. But for each gallon after the 80th, society would suffer a net loss when each gallon is produced (the benefit is not worth the cost of using up regular inputs plus damaging the environment).

The competitive market goes to the intersection of *D* and *S*, so the competitive market (in the absence of a tax) generates 20 gallons more than the socially optimal

FIGURE 2.3
The Optimal Tax Equals the Marginal Damage
The market will move to the socially optimal quantity if a tax is levied equal to marginal damage.

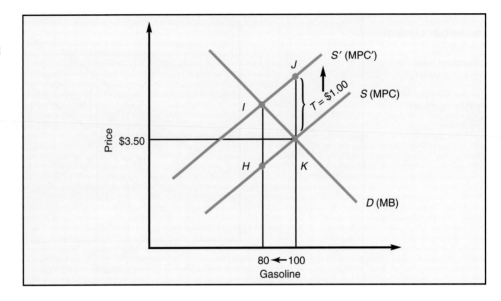

quantity—100 instead of 80. The competitive market gets the quantity of the polluting good wrong because one key component of the marginal social cost—the marginal damage to the environment—is *external* to the participants in the polluting-good market. No market participant has to pay for the environmental damage being generated, so no participant takes it into account. Hence, there is an *externality* problem. When a good has a *negative externality*, the market generates too much of the good.

What can be done to reduce the quantity of gasoline from 100 gallons to the socially optimal quantity of 80? Levy the right tax—a tax T equal to the damage per gallon $1.00—as shown in Figure 2.3. The effect of a $1.00 tax per gallon would be to shift up the supply curve by $1.00 because the tax would increase the marginal private cost sellers have to pay by $1.00. With a tax equal to the marginal damage, the new MPC′ equals the MSC, and the new supply curve S'(MPC′) coincides with the marginal social cost (MSC) curve. The market would therefore move to the intersection of the D curve with the new S' curve, so the quantity of gasoline generated by the market would fall from 100 to 80 gallons.

Levying a tax equal to the environmental damage—$1.00 per gallon—internalizes the externality. Previously, the damage gasoline use was inflicting on the environment was external to market participants because they did not have to pay for it. By levying a tax equal to the marginal damage, the government makes the environmental cost internal to the market participants. For this reason, a tax levied to internalize an externality is called a **corrective tax**. Its purpose is not to raise revenue but to correct the market. It is sometimes called a **Pigouvian tax**, after the British economist Arthur Pigou who proposed it for this purpose nearly a century ago.

If the tax T is set equal to the marginal damage MD, the reduction in the polluting good—gasoline—from 100 to 80 gallons—confers a *net* benefit on society. It is useful to divide this net benefit into two parts, which can be seen in Figure 2.4. The first part is the *gross* benefit from the reduction in environmental damage; each unit that is cut avoids a marginal damage of $1.00, the vertical distance MD between the MSC curve and the MPC curve. Adding up the gross benefit over all units cut gives the area *HIJK*; the area of *HIJK* equals $1.00 × 20 = $20.

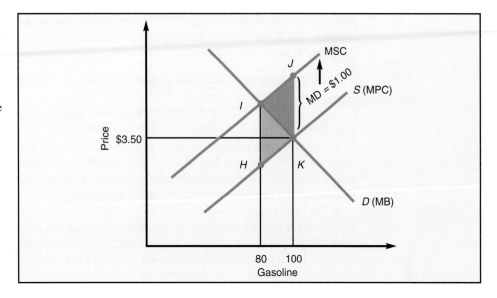

If the environmental benefit were *not* counted, the cutback would impose a loss on the economy; that loss would equal the area *HIK*. Why? Consider the cutback of the 99th unit. From Figure 2.4, the MB that consumers would have been willing to pay for this unit is a bit greater than $3.50—call it $3.53—so the loss to consumers from not having this unit is $3.53. On the other hand, by not producing the 99th unit, there is a resource saving equal to the MPC which is a bit less than $3.50—call it $3.48—and these resources can be redeployed to make other goods. So the loss to society from not producing the 99th unit is $3.53 − $3.48 = $0.05. Similarly, the loss from not producing the 98th unit is $3.56 − $3.46 = $0.10. Finally, the loss from not producing the 80th unit is $4.10 − $3.10 = $1.00. Adding the losses over all units cut gives the area *HIK*; the area of the triangle *HIK* equals ½($1.00 × 20) = $10.

Thus, cutting back pollution to the social optimum confers an environmental benefit equal to the area *HIJK* ($20) and imposes a loss on the economy due to the reduction in the polluting good that is equal to the area *HIK* ($10). Hence the net benefit to society of the cutback equals the area *IJK* = *HIJK* − *HIK* = $20 − $10 = $10. Even though this cutback confers a net benefit, it is often said that cutting back pollution imposes a cost or loss on the economy by reducing the quantity of the polluting good that consumers enjoy; this cost (loss) is area *HIK* ($10). While it is useful to measure this loss *HIK* ($10), it should always be remembered that the cutback confers an environmental benefit *HIJK* ($20), and hence a net benefit to society equal to *IJK* = *HIJK* − *HIK* = $20 − $10 = $10.

In this example the MD is $1.00 regardless of the quantity of gasoline, so the proper tax is $1.00. Suppose the MD increases with the quantity of gasoline. What tax should be levied? The answer is easily obtained by modifying Figure 2.2. If MD increases, then the vertical gap between MSC and MPC widens as gasoline increases. Imagine redrawing the MSC curve in Figure 2.2 so it is steeper than the MPC curve to make the vertical gap widen as quantity increases, and locating the intersection of the new steeper MSC curve and the *D* (MB) curve. This is the socially optimal quantity of gasoline. *At this optimal quantity*, note the MD, the vertical gap between MSC and MPC; the proper tax equals that MD. If that tax is levied, the S curve will shift up parallel by the amount of the tax and the new S' curve will intersect the D curve at the socially optimal quantity so the market will move to that quantity. Thus:

If MD varies with quantity, the proper tax equals the MD at the quantity where the MSC and MB curves intersect.

Use Pollution Tax Revenue to Cut Other Taxes

The purpose of pollution taxes is not to raise revenue—it's to discourage pollution. So when pollution taxes are levied, other taxes can be cut or direct cash transfers can be sent to households or firms (in Chapter 8 on the U.S. income tax, we will see that a cash transfer can be implemented by a refundable tax credit).

If the federal government levies the pollution tax and collects the revenue, other federal taxes can be cut, such as the federal income tax. If a state government collects the pollution tax revenue, other state taxes can be cut, such as the state sales tax. If a local government collects the pollution tax revenue, other local taxes can be cut, such as the local property tax. Alternatively, whichever government collects the pollution tax revenue can return the revenue by sending cash transfers to households.

Different ways of returning the pollution tax revenue to the private sector will have different effects. If household income tax rates are cut, then revenue will be returned to households according to how much income tax they pay. If sales (or value-added) taxes are cut, prices of consumer goods will be lower so even low-income people who pay no income tax will benefit; thus, cutting sales (or value-added) taxes is an equitable way to offset the burden of pollution taxes. If an equal-dollar cash transfer (refundable tax credit) is given to all households, then all households will receive the same dollar boost in income.

The crucial point is that pollution taxes should be viewed as *revenue replacers*, not revenue raisers. They are levied to reduce pollution, not to raise government revenue. However, if all the revenue is returned to the population, does this mean that pollution taxes impose no burden? No. Pollution taxes cause less of certain goods—namely goods that involve pollution. The reduction in these goods imposes a burden on society (in Figure 2.4, *HIK*). On the other hand, the improved environmental quality is a benefit (in Figure 2.4, *HIJK*). As long as the benefit is larger than the burden, the pollution taxes are socially desirable.

Tax Emissions, Not the Polluting Good

Let's return to the gasoline example and consider another important point. Different kinds of gasoline generate different quantities of pollution per gallon. Given this fact, should the government vary the tax per gallon according to the quantity of pollution? The answer is yes. By varying the tax according to the pollution per gallon, producers of gasoline are given an incentive to produce (and consumers of gasoline, an incentive to use) the kind of gasoline that involves less pollution. In other words, there should be the same tax per unit of pollution, not per gallon of gasoline. The government should tax emissions (pollution), not the polluting good.

Consider another example where it is very important to levy the tax on emissions, not on the polluting good: Sulfur dioxide generated in the production of electricity. When the generation of electricity involves burning coal containing sulfur, sulfur dioxide is produced. If sulfur dioxide is emitted into the air, acid rain is produced with harmful effects, according to scientists. However, it would be a mistake to levy a tax per unit of electricity (the polluting good). Why? Because the producers of electricity—electric utilities—can vary the quantity of sulfur dioxide that is emitted per unit of electricity produced. The utilities can use low-sulfur coal instead of high-sulfur coal, or they can install a scrubber, as we discussed earlier. They can switch to another fuel that contains no sulfur. It is important to give electric utilities an incentive to make choices that reduce the quantity of sulfur dioxide emitted into the air per unit of electricity produced. A tax per unit of electricity won't provide such an incentive, but a tax per unit of sulfur dioxide emitted will. Thus, the government should levy a tax per unit of sulfur dioxide emitted into the air, not a tax per unit of electricity produced, just as it should vary the gasoline tax according to the pollution from that particular kind of gasoline.

We can state our general conclusion: Whenever feasible, levy the tax per unit of pollution—per emission—not per unit of polluting good. In the remainder of this chapter, we will assume that the tax is per unit of pollution, not per unit of good.

To Minimize Cost, Levy the Same Tax on All Firms Emitting Pollutant X

This section demonstrates a point that is of the utmost importance for public policy:

> *To minimize the cost of achieving a given reduction in pollutant X, the same tax per emission should be levied on all firms emitting pollutant X.*

To show this important point, we work with a diagram, Figure 2.5, that has emissions (pollution), instead of the quantity of the polluting good (such as gasoline), on the horizontal axis. In this diagram, the marginal damage (MD) is the amount of damage per emission (per unit of pollution). We simplify our example and diagram by assuming that the marginal damage stays constant as the quantity of emissions increases so that the MD curve is a horizontal line; the marginal damage is $40 per unit of pollutant X at all levels of emissions. The main conclusions of this section would still remain valid if MD varied with the quantity of pollution.

There are two firms emitting this pollutant. Suppose in the absence of any government policy that each firm, coincidentally, emits 50 units. Although the two firms emit the same chemical pollutant, assume that the two firms produce different goods and therefore would incur different costs for abating pollution. Each firm can abate pollution—reduce its emissions starting from 50 units by moving leftward—but at a cost. For example, emissions can be reduced by installing equipment that reduces the pollution that accompanies a given quantity of its output or by switching to a more costly but less polluting production process.

For each firm, starting from an emissions level of 50, each unit abated entails a higher marginal abatement cost (MAC). For example, as shown in Figure 2.5, as firm H (the high abatement cost firm) moves left from 50 emissions, its MAC_H rises sharply; and as firm L (the low abatement cost firm) moves left from 50 emissions, its MAC_L rises slowly.

It is socially optimal for each firm to abate another unit of pollution as long as its MAC is less than the MD ($40). Thus, starting from 50 emissions, firm H should abate 10 and continue to emit 40, while firm L should abate 40 and continue to emit 10.

A tax T of $40 per emission—a tax T equal to the marginal damage (MD) per emission—would induce each firm to abate the socially optimal quantity. The manager of each firm would recognize that it is profitable to abate a unit as long as its MAC is less than the tax it would otherwise have to pay to emit the unit. So starting at 50 emissions, each firm would find it profitable to reduce emissions as long as its MAC is less than the tax of $40. Thus, firm H would keep abating pollution until its emissions have

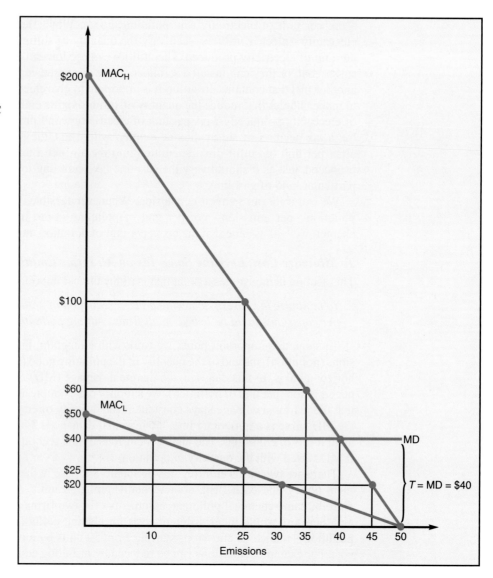

FIGURE 2.5
**The Optimal
Cutback of Pollution**
A tax equal to
marginal damage will
induce each firm to
cut back until its MAC
equals MD.

been cut to 40, while firm L would keep abating until its emissions have been cut to 10. Here's the key point:

If the government sets the tax T *equal to the marginal damage MD, what the firms then do for profit will unintentionally be what is best for society.*

To appreciate this achievement of the tax, suppose instead that the government required each firm to abate 25 units; equivalently, the government permitted each to emit 25 units. At first glance, the government requirement might appear reasonable—each firm would be required to abate the same quantity, 25, and each firm would be permitted to emit the same quantity, 25.

However, the result of this government requirement would not be socially optimal. From Figure 2.5 you can see that abating the 25th unit costs firm H $100 (its MAC is

$100), while the MD is only $40—so the requirement forces firm H to abate more than is socially optimal. Conversely, abating the 25th unit costs firm L $25; since the MD is $40, it would be socially optimal for L to abate still further.

When each firm complies with the government requirement to abate 25 and emit 25, their MACs differ: MAC_H is $100, while MAC_L is only $25. Whenever MACs differ, it is possible to reduce the total cost of abatement while achieving the same total abatement: Just let the high MAC firm H abate less and the low MAC firm L abate more. In the diagram, starting from 25, letting firm H abate 1 unit less (emit 1 unit more) avoids a cost of $100, while having firm L abate 1 unit more (emit 1 unit less) incurs a cost of only $25—for a net cost saving of $75 ($100 − $25), while keeping total abatement the same and total emissions at 50. Starting from 25, when H abates 15 units less (and emits 15 units more, or 40) and L abates 15 units more (and emits 15 units less, or 10), the two MACs become equal ($40), and no further total cost reduction is possible. This is sometimes called the **equimarginal principle**:

> *The total cost incurred to achieve a pollution target has been minimized only if each polluter reduces pollution until its marginal abatement cost is the same as every other polluter.*

The reason is simple. If two polluters have unequal MACs, then total cost can be reduced while keeping total pollution the same by having the low MAC firm abate more (and emit less) while having the high MAC firm abate less (and emit more). A policy conclusion follows immediately:

> *To induce polluters to equalize their MACs, charge all polluters the same tax per emission of pollutant X.*

As long as the same tax per emission is levied on all firms, their MACs will end up equal, because each firm will find it profitable to abate until its MAC equals the tax it faces. Thus, the emissions tax—provided it is the same for all firms emitting the pollutant—will result in equal MACs across firms and will therefore achieve a given total abatement at minimum possible total cost.

The message of economists to policy-makers is this: Resist arguments for varying the tax per emission among polluters of chemical X. An extreme variation is a zero tax—in other words, exempting certain polluters from the tax. Firms emitting the same pollutant differ along many dimensions, and firm managers, owners, and workers will present arguments to the government about why their firm's tax should be low or even zero (an exemption). But if the tax is varied across firms, then MACs will end up unequal, and the reduction in pollution will not be achieved at minimum possible cost.

Tradable Permits

Instead of levying a tax, suppose the government requires firms to have a permit for each unit of pollution that it emits; it would be illegal for a firm's emissions to exceed its permits (punishment would be imposed on the firm or its managers for violating the law). The government decides how much pollution will be tolerated and then supplies exactly that number of permits to firms. This method is called cap and trade because the government puts a *cap* (ceiling) on the amount of pollution by supplying that amount of permits, and then firms are allowed to *trade* (buy and sell) permits at whatever price emerges among them in a permit market.

How do firms get the permits? We consider two alternatives. Under the first, the government *sells* permits to firms. Under the second, the government *gives* permits to firms. Under both plans, after obtaining permits from the government on January 1, firms can buy or sell permits—the permits are tradable (marketable) throughout the year; on the following December 31, firms must hold a number of permits equal to its emissions during that calendar year or else face punishment.

Government Sells Permits

First, consider the plan in which the government sells or auctions permits to firms, illustrated in Figure 2.6; as shown, the government has decided to supply 50 permits. But how would the government set the price of a permit? Suppose the government announces a *tentative* price and asks firms to place orders for permits at this price. If the total quantity of permits "demanded" at this tentative price by the firms is greater than the quantity of permits the government is supplying (50), then the government would raise the tentative price and ask firms to place orders at the new price. Raising the price would decrease the demand for permits.

Symmetrically, if the total quantity of permits demanded at this tentative price by the firms is less than the quantity of permits the government is supplying (50), then the government would lower the tentative price and ask firms to place orders at the new

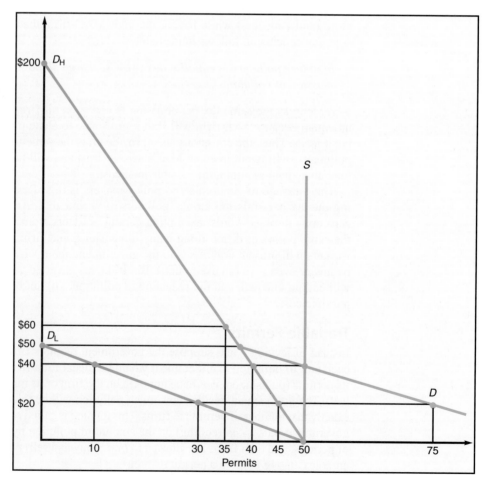

FIGURE 2.6
The Permit Market
The permit price is determined by the intersection of the supply and demand for permits.

price; lowering the price would increase the demand for permits. When the government finds the tentative price where the demand for permits equals its supply—$40 in Figure 2.6—it makes that tentative price the final price and sells the permits. Whatever the initial tentative price in Figure 2.6—whether lower or higher than $40— the government's final price will end up where demand equals supply (50).

What determines the position and slope of the permit demand curve D in Figure 2.6? The permit demand curve is simply the horizontal sum of the permit demand curves of each firm. So what determines the position and slope of the permit demand curve of firm L and of firm H?

Each firm's permit demand curve is simply its MAC curve drawn in Figure 2.5.

Suppose the tentative price of a permit is $40. Then each firm would find it profitable to do the same thing it would do if it faced a tax of $40. It would reduce its emissions as long as its MAC is less than $40. Hence, firm L would want to emit 10, and firm H, 40. So at a price of $40, L would demand 10 permits, and H, 40 permits, so total demand would be 50 permits. Thus, to obtain the permit demand curve D in Figure 2.6, we simply draw firm L's MAC and label it D_L, draw firm H's MAC curve and label it D_H, and at each price, horizontally add D_L plus D_H to get D; the D curve is simply the horizontal sum of D_L and D_H. Note that if the price were $20, D_L would be 30 and D_H, 45, so D would be 75. For any price less than $40, D would be greater than S (50). Note that if the price were greater than $50, D_L would be 0, so D would equal D_H. For any price greater than $40, D would be less than S (50). Thus, the government would adjust its tentative price until it arrives at a final price of $40.

Selling Permits versus Levying a Tax

So how does this plan differ from levying a tax of $40? At first glance, there appears to be no difference. Each firm's emissions should be the same whether it must pay a permit price of $40 or pay a tax of $40; hence, in both cases, total emissions should be 50. Moreover, the government should collect the same total revenue—$40 times the number of emissions (50 units), or $2,000.

However, there is an important difference. If the tax had been set at $20, then firms would have emitted more than 50 units (in fact 75); and if the tax had been set at $60, then firms would have emitted less than 50 (in fact 35). So under the permit plan, if the government decides to supply 50 permits, then emissions will definitely end up at 50 units, but with the tax, the government can't be sure that emissions will end up at 50. On the other hand, with the tax, the government can be sure of the MAC each firm will incur for the last unit the firm abates; for example, if the tax is $40, each firm will abate until its MAC rises to $40 and will not abate units with an MAC above $40. Thus, a tax of $40 ensures that abatement will not be undertaken if its cost exceeds $40. By contrast, when the government decides to supply 50 permits, it can't be sure which permit price will end up making the demand for permits equal to 50, so it is possible that very costly abatement will be undertaken.

Therefore, the difference is this: With the tax, the government makes sure that abatement that is too costly will not be undertaken—the tax puts a definite limit on the cost to the economy of abatement, but not a definite limit on emissions. With the permits, the government makes sure that emissions will not exceed the target—the permits put a definite limit on emissions, but not a definite limit on the cost of abatement to the economy.

Of course, the tax method need not allow emissions to be permanently excessive; if pollution is excessive in the short run, the tax can be raised. Similarly, the permit plan need not allow abatement costs and the price of polluting goods to be excessive permanently; if they are excessive, the supply of permits can be raised, reducing permit prices, abatement costs, and the price of polluting goods. This increase in the supply of permits could be triggered automatically whenever the permit price rises above some designated value.

So which policy is better? It depends on which goal the citizenry gives a higher priority for a particular pollutant. If the citizenry wants to be sure of never exceeding the pollution target, then the permit plan is better. However, if the citizenry wants to be sure of never causing firms to incur high abatement costs (resulting in large price increases to consumers of polluting goods), then the tax is better.

A Hybrid Policy: A Permit System with a Safety Valve

It is possible to compromise and partially address both concerns with a hybrid policy. The hybrid policy is *a permit system with a safety valve*. The government would choose an initial pollution target and try to sell the corresponding amount of permits to firms. If the price needed to reduce permit demand to the initial supply turns out to be too high, the government would promptly raise the supply of permits to keep the permit price below a target ceiling. The safety valve is the prompt expansion of permit supply by the government to keep the permit price (and therefore the MAC that firms incur) from rising too high. The hybrid policy is a compromise: The initial pollution target is no longer rigid, but it is subject to prompt relaxation in the event that meeting it would cause firms to incur an excessive abatement cost.

Government Gives Permits

In the second alternative, the government gives, rather than sells, the 50 permits to the firms; however, if a firm wants to emit more than its permit "gift," it can buy *extra permits* from a firm that is willing to emit less than its gift and sell its *excess permits*. Some firms will demand extra permits, and some firms will supply excess permits. The price of permits will adjust until the demand for extra permits equals the supply of excess permits. So which permit price will equate demand and supply?

If the price were $40, each firm will realize that no matter how many permits it was given, the cost *to the firm* of another emission is $40. That's clearly true for a firm that wants to emit more than it was given—it has to buy additional permits at a price of $40. But even if the firm is content to emit less than it was given, the last unit it emits costs $40 because it prevents the firm from selling that permit at a price of $40. No matter how many permits the firm was given, emitting another unit costs $40. But then under this plan, if the permit price is $40, each firm will emit exactly the quantity it would have emitted if it had been taxed $40. From Figure 2.5, with a tax of $40, firm L would want to emit 10 and firm H would want to emit 40:

> *Even if the permits are given to firms, each firm's emissions will still be determined by its MAC curve in Figure 2.5.*

According to Figure 2.5, if the price were $20, L would want to emit 30 and H, 45; if the price were $40, L would want to emit 10 and H, 40; and if the price were $60, L would want to emit 0 and H, 35.

Table 2.1 shows that the permit price will end up $40 no matter how the government gives out 50 permits to L and H. Here's why: According to the MAC lines in Figure 2.5, if the price were $40, L would want to emit 10 and H, 40.

In the top block of the table, the government gives L 25 and H 25 permits. If the price were $40, L would want to emit 10, so it would supply 15 excess permits, and

TABLE 2.1   **Demand for *Extra* Permits and Supply of *Excess* Permits**

Gifts from the Government: L 25, H 25								
P	**L emits**	**L's gift**	**L demands**	**L supplies**	**H emits**	**H's gift**	**H demands**	**H supplies**
$20	30	25	5	0	45	25	20	0
$40	10	25	0	**15**	40	25	**15**	0
$60	0	25	0	25	35	25	10	0
Gifts from the Government: L 45, H 5								
P	**L emits**	**L's gift**	**L demands**	**L supplies**	**H emits**	**H's gift**	**H demands**	**H supplies**
$20	30	45	0	15	45	5	40	0
$40	10	45	0	**35**	40	5	**35**	0
$60	0	45	0	45	35	5	30	0
Gifts from the Government: L 5, H 45								
P	**L emits**	**L's gift**	**L demands**	**L supplies**	**H emits**	**H's gift**	**H demands**	**H supplies**
$20	30	5	25	0	45	45	0	0
$40	10	5	**5**	0	40	45	0	**5**
$60	0	5	0	5	35	45	0	10

H would want to emit 40, so it would demand 15 extra permits; hence with the total supply of excess permits (15) equal to the total demand for extra permits (15), the price would stay $40. By contrast, if the price were $20, L would want to emit 30, so it would demand 5 extra permits, and H would want to emit 45, so it would demand 20 extra permits; hence with the total demand for extra permits (25) greater than the total supply of excess permits (0), the price would rise. And if the price were $60, L would want to emit 0, so it would supply 25 excess permits, and H would want to emit 35, so it would demand 10 extra permits; hence with the total supply of excess permits (25) greater than the total demand for extra permits (10), the price would fall. Thus, the price would end up $40.

In the middle block of the table, the government gives L 45 and H 5 permits. If the price were $40, L would want to emit 10, so it would supply 35 excess permits, and H would want to emit 40, so it would demand 35 extra permits; hence with the total supply of excess permits (35) equal to the total demand for extra permits (35), the price would stay $40. By contrast, if the price were $20, L would want to emit 30, so it would supply 15 excess permits, and H would want to emit 45, so it would demand 40 extra permits; hence with the total demand for extra permits (40) greater than the total supply of excess permits (15), the price would rise. If the price were $60, L would want to emit 0, so it would supply 45 excess permits, and H would want to emit 35, so it would demand 30 extra permits; hence with the total supply of excess permits (45) greater than the total demand for extra permits (30), the price would fall. Thus, the price would end up $40.

In the bottom block of the table, the government gives L 5 and H 45 permits. If the price were $40, L would want to emit 10, so it would demand 5 extra permits, and H would want to emit 40, so it would supply 5 excess permits; hence with the total supply of excess permits (5) equal to the total demand for extra permits (5), the price would stay $40. By contrast, if the price were $20, L would want to emit 30, so it would demand 25 extra permits, and H would want to emit 45, so it would demand

0 extra permits; hence with the total demand for extra permits (25) greater than total supply of excess permits (0), the price would rise. And if the price were $60, L would want to emit 0, so it would supply 5 excess permits, and H would want to emit 35, so it would supply 10 excess permits; hence with the total supply of excess permits (15) greater than the total demand for extra permits (0), the price would fall. Thus, the price would end up $40.

When H and L buy permits from the government or pay a tax, their cost of production increases, shifting up their supply curve for their product and raising its price. It is sometimes thought that these product price increases can be avoided if the government gives permits to polluters instead of selling them, but this is not so. If polluters are given tradable permits, we have just seen that the permit price will end up the same as if they had been sold permits ($40 in our example). With a permit price of $40 they will face the same increase in the *marginal* cost of producing the good as they would if the government sold permits at a price of $40 or levied a $40 tax. Because the height of the supply curve of a good equals its *marginal* cost, the shift up of the supply curve of polluting goods is the same, and therefore the increase in the price of polluting goods is the same in the short run. Thus, this analysis leads to an important conclusion:

> *Giving permits to polluting firms will also shift up the supply curve of each polluting good and thereby raise the price of polluting goods, just like selling permits or levying a tax.*

Selling versus Giving

Of course, firms want the government to give rather than sell permits. However, taxpayers should want the government to sell rather than give permits. If the government gives the permits, then it collects no revenue, so it will be unable to cut other taxes. By contrast, with either a pollution tax or the sale of permits, the government raises revenue and can therefore cut other taxes.

Moreover, giving rather than selling permits may result in more pollution in the long run if "new" polluters as well as "old" are given free permits. This gift will induce more firms to enter the polluting industry. Even if each firm curtails its pollution, the larger number of firms may end up generating more total pollution in the long run than if the permits were sold. To get an industry to generate the optimal quantity of any good over the long run, all firms must pay all costs generated by their production, and firms should not receive gifts or subsidies that induce additional entry into the industry. When firms use up air and water quality, they should have to pay for it without receiving a gift; otherwise, too many will enter the polluting industry.

To prevent this harmful long-run effect, free permits could be given only to old polluters (grandfathering) and not be given to new polluters who would have to buy all their permits. But this favoring of old firms over new firms would create another problem: It would reduce competitiveness in the industry and would constitute a harmful barrier to entry. Even if a new firm could offer a better product at lower cost, it might be unable to compete because it would have to buy all its permits.

Thus, giving permits is definitely inferior to selling permits. Unfortunately, it has thus far been easier to gain political support for giving permits rather than either selling permits or levying a tax, because polluting firms prefer it and taxpayers don't realize that giving away permits prevents tax cuts that could occur if permits were sold or emissions taxed.

APPLICATIONS: ACID RAIN AND GLOBAL WARMING

Tradable Permits for Sulfur Dioxide to Reduce Acid Rain

When coal containing sulfur is burned to generate electricity, sulfur dioxide is produced. If sulfur dioxide is emitted into the air, acid rain forms and falls to earth with harmful effects. Sulfur dioxide pollution can be cut by reducing the production of electricity or by reducing the quantity of sulfur dioxide that gets emitted per unit of electricity produced. The utilities can use low-sulfur coal instead of high-sulfur coal or install a scrubber to capture most of the sulfur dioxide so that it is not emitted into the air. They can also switch to another fuel that contains no sulfur. The aim of environmental policy should be to achieve a given reduction in sulfur dioxide pollution at minimum cost. To minimize cost, firms potentially emitting sulfur dioxide should be confronted with the same price per emission. The price can be implemented by levying a tax or selling tradable permits.

Before 1990, the price strategy was not used in the United States for sulfur dioxide. Using the traditional command and control approach, the U.S. Environmental Protection Agency (EPA) in the early 1970s established a maximum sulfur dioxide emissions rate for every *new* coal-burning generator of electricity. That meant that every new plant could not emit more than a specific number of pounds of sulfur dioxide per million BTUs of fuel burned; but the more fuel it burned, the more it could emit. No incentive was given for reducing emissions per se. Applying the regulations only to new plants gave polluters a perverse incentive to keep using old "dirty" plants as long as possible.

The path-breaking Clean Air Act Amendments of 1990, however, authorized the gradual phasing in of a national program of tradable permits for sulfur dioxide by electric utilities to begin after a five-year delay for preparation. Tradable permits (allowances) are *given* (according to a formula), *not sold*, to electric power plants. Each plant is given a number of permits roughly proportional to its past use of fuel. Plants can then buy or sell permits. Each permit allows a plant to emit one ton of sulfur dioxide. Any plant emitting more tons (whether from old or new plants) than its permits allow is punished with a stiff fine ($2,000 per ton in the initial year, currently larger because it is indexed to inflation). Each year, permits are given to plants to cover emissions that year or in a future year (so permits can be "banked" for future use). The number of permits given out has declined gradually each year in order to gradually reduce total pollution. Each electric power plant is required to continuously measure and record its emissions. The EPA monitors permit trading and emissions and levies fines for excess emissions.

Under the program, total emissions have fallen, permit prices have turned out to be lower than expected, trading costs have been low, there has been little delay from litigation, and it is estimated that there has been a substantial reduction in the total cost of achieving pollution reduction as permits have been traded from plants with low abatement costs to plants with high abatement costs. At times, however, there have been erratic fluctuations in permit prices.

A market mechanism does not prevent mistakes, but it does generate quick adaptation to new information. Initially, many electric utility firms evidently expected a higher permit price and, as a consequence, placed orders for scrubbers that cost a bit less than the expected high price. But when the permit price turned out to be low because of the unexpected availability at moderate cost of low-sulfur coal from the Powder River Basin in Wyoming, some utility firms regretted their purchase of scrubbers, but others were able to cancel their order for scrubbers and switch from high-sulfur to low-sulfur coal—a more cost-effective response.

Costs of the Permit System

It should be acknowledged that a tradable permit system entails costs that are avoided by technology mandates such as requiring every utility to install a scrubber. With permits, emissions must be accurately measured, monitored, and audited; and transactions costs are incurred by buyers and sellers in the permit market. There is a risk that the permit price will be subject to speculation that generates erratic price fluctuations based on psychology rather than cost. But it appears that these costs have been substantially less than the cost saving that results from letting each plant decide how to respond to the permit price.

To ensure political support from the electricity industry for the Clean Air Act Amendments in 1990, the legislation prescribed that the government give, not sell, the permits to electric utility firms. As noted earlier, this has two shortcomings. First, this gift or subsidy to the industry will in the long run lead to higher output and emissions than socially optimal. Second, because no revenue is raised, the government cannot cut other taxes. It remains to be seen whether it is politically possible to charge polluters a price—either by selling permits or levying an emissions tax—without giving the polluting industry a gift or subsidy.

A Carbon Tax or Tradable Permits to Reduce Global Warming

According to most scientists, gaseous carbon emissions (such as carbon dioxide) from the burning of carbon fuels are contributing to global warming. If so, it would be worth reducing carbon emissions if the cost of reduction is less than the future harm from global warming. Economists agree that rather than use command and control technology regulations, a price should be put on carbon emissions to give potential emitters an incentive to cut back. The price can be implemented either through a carbon tax or carbon permits. Because carbon emissions anywhere in the world contribute to global warming, ideally potential emitters in all countries should be faced with the same carbon emissions price so that a given reduction in global warming can be achieved at minimum cost to the world economy.

There are two policy decisions that must be made. First, which should be used: a carbon tax or carbon permits (cap and trade)? Second, how can low-income countries like China and India be induced to participate in cutting carbon emissions? Earlier in this chapter we discussed the pros and cons of a tax versus permits; the application to carbon is examined in the box titled "A Carbon Tax versus a Carbon Cap and Trade Program." The second decision—the participation of low-income countries—is discussed in the remainder of this section where we consider how to induce the participation of low-income countries under either a carbon tax treaty or a carbon permits (cap and trade) treaty.

A Carbon Tax Treaty

Consider how a carbon tax treaty would address this problem.

For administrative feasibility, carbon would be taxed *upstream* at the point it enters the economy through a few thousand fuel producers rather than *downstream* when it is actually emitted (in gaseous form) by millions of drivers and homeowners and by thousands of factories and electric utility plants. Thus coal would be taxed when mined, and oil and natural gas when pumped or refined or imported. Each would be taxed according to its carbon content. The fuel producers and importers subject to the carbon tax would then pass the tax on in higher prices so that all fuel users in the economy would face these higher prices. According to a Congressional Budget Office (CBO) study, a carbon tax of $100 per ton, which would raise the price of gasoline about $0.30

Case Study   A Carbon Tax versus a Carbon Cap and Trade Program

At a conference in Washington, D.C., in October 2007 hosted by the Hamilton Project of the Brookings Institution, two economists presented papers advocating two different carbon price policies for reducing carbon emissions in the United States. Professor Robert Stavins of Harvard's Kennedy School of Government advocated a carbon cap and trade program, and Professor Gilbert Metcalf of Tufts University, a carbon tax.*

Before discussing their differences, it is important to emphasize that they both agree about the following points: (1) either carbon price policy would be much better than command and control technology regulations; (2) a carbon price policy should raise revenue so that other taxes can be reduced (Stavins therefore proposes that initially half, and eventually all, the permits be auctioned by the government rather than given free to firms); (3) to simplify practical administration, the carbon price should be imposed *upstream* when carbon enters the U.S. economy from a few thousand coal mines, oil refineries, natural gas pipelines, and importers, rather than *downstream* when it is emitted by millions of firms, drivers, and dwellers; and (4) the government should pay the going carbon price to any downstream carbon emitter who captures and sequesters carbon gas instead of releasing it to the atmosphere.

Stavins makes these arguments for preferring cap and trade to a tax. First, any new tax meets stiff political resistance. Second, if some permits are given out free, recipients may politically support rather than oppose the program. Third, some upstream carbon firms may successfully lobby for partial or full exemption from a tax. Fourth, cap and trade is more certain to hit the pollution reduction target than a tax—this fact appeals to environmentalists. Fifth, the European Union countries are adopting cap and trade so harmonization will be easier if the United States does too.

Metcalf makes these arguments for preferring a tax to cap-and-trade. First, historically cap and trade programs have given permits out for free and not collected revenue that can be used to reduce other taxes. Second, there will be wasteful political lobbying by firms for free permits. Third, the administration of a tax is time-tested, whereas administering cap and trade is a new challenge. Fourth, in the short run it is more important to avoid excessive abatement cost than excessive emissions because there is plenty of time to adjust emissions before global temperature is affected. Fifth, cap and trade has the volatility of stock market prices which can disrupt planning.

*The papers are available at the Hamilton Project Web site, http://www.brookings.edu/projects/hamiltonproject.aspx.

a gallon, would reduce carbon emissions in the United States about 15%. The prices of all goods that use a lot of carbon fuel in their production would rise relative to the price of goods and services produced with little carbon fuel, providing an incentive to reduce the use of carbon fuels. Carbon tax revenue would be recycled by cutting other taxes and sending households cash transfers.

To minimize the cost of reducing global warming, all countries should implement the same carbon tax. This important point can be seen by reinterpreting Figure 2.5 as applying to two firms L and H in two countries. With no tax, L and H each emit 50. If each country imposes a $40 carbon tax, then L would cut back 40 and emit 10, while H would cut back 10 and emit 40, so total emissions would be cut from 100 to 50. The MAC of the last unit cut back by L would equal the MAC of the last unit cut back by H (each MAC would equal $40, the tax) so the total cost of cutback is minimized.

How much more would it cost if H alone cut back 50 instead of H cutting back 10 and L cutting back 40? If H cuts back 50, the last unit cut back has an MAC of $200, so the *average* MAC would be ½ × $200 = $100. Thus, the total cost of H cutting back 50 would equal 50 × $100 = $5,000. By contrast, if H cuts back 10 and L cuts back 40, the last unit each cuts back would have an MAC of $40, so the *average* MAC for both H and L would be $20. Thus, the total cost of cutting back 50 would equal 50 × $20 = $1,000. In this example, the total cost if H alone cuts back 50 would be 5 times ($5,000 vs. $1,000) the total cost if the cutback of 50 is shared optimally between H and L.

Thus, to minimize total cost, all countries should levy the same carbon tax and share in the cutback until each country's MAC equals the tax. Any treaty that exempts any countries from levying the tax raises the cost of achieving a given reduction in global warming.

However, low-income countries make two points. First, they note that high-income countries have emitted most of the carbon over the past two centuries and are responsible for most of the buildup thus far. Second, they say they have a right to grow their economies to improve the standard of living of their people.

Is there any way to address these objections of low-income countries while heeding economists' point that all firms in all countries must face the same price to minimize the total cost of reducing world emissions? The answer is yes. It can be done if high-income countries are willing to compensate low-income countries, through revenue transfers, for agreeing to implement the carbon tax.

Consider one way this can be done. Each country would decide whether to participate in an international carbon tax treaty. Under the treaty, the country would agree to levy the specified carbon tax—for example, $40 per ton—on all domestic emitters (the magnitude of the tax would be set by treaty participants). Each country would keep its own tax revenue and either return the revenue to its own population by cutting other taxes or use it to finance its own government programs. Then under a formula based on country per capita income (also set by treaty participants), participating countries with high per capita incomes would contribute revenue that would then be distributed to participating countries with low per capita incomes. For example, the United States would be one of the countries contributing revenue, and China would be one of the countries receiving revenue.

In our H and L example, consider a treaty where each government H and L would agree to levy a tax of $40 on its own polluters. Even if country L has no benefit from the reduction in global warming, L should agree to levy this tax on its own polluters *if* country H pays country L at least $800. Why? Because the cost to country L of cutting back 40 is $800 (the MAC of the 40th unit cut back is $40, so the average MAC is $20, so $20 × 40 = $800).

Should country H be willing to pay country L $800? It depends on how much benefit country H expects to receive from the reduction in global warming. In response to the $40 tax, H would cut back 10 (from 50 to 40), so the cost of cutback to H's economy is $200 (because the MAC of the 10th unit cut back is $40, so the average MAC is $20, so $20 × 10 = $200). Thus, the cost of cutback plus the payment to country L equals $1,000 ($200 + $800). As long as country H believes its benefit from reducing global warming exceeds $1,000, it should be willing to pay L $800 to participate in the treaty.

If country L believes it would get some benefit from a reduction in global warming, then L should be willing to join the treaty for a payment from H that is less than $800. For example, if L believes its benefit would be $200, it should be willing to join the treaty if H pays it $600 because its total benefit ($200 + $600) would cover its cost of cutback ($800).

One thing is for certain:

It is better for H to cost-reimburse L in order to get L to help with the cutback rather than for H to do all the cutting back by itself.

Why? Because the first unit that L cuts back has a near-zero MAC. It would therefore be better for H to get L to start cutting back at L's initially low MAC, and to reimburse L an amount equal to L's low MAC, than for H to keep cutting back by itself at an ever-rising MAC.

It would be better for country H to pay country L $800 to join the treaty (so that L cuts back 40 and H cuts back 10) rather than for H to cut back 50 by itself. The cost to H of cutting back 50 would be $5,000 (from Figure 2.5, the MAC of the 50th unit H cuts back would be $200, so the average MAC is $100, so $100 × 50 = $5,000), whereas if L joins the treaty, the cost to H is only $1,000 ($200 for its own cutback of 10 plus its payment of $800 to L).

Of course, country H wants to pay country L the minimum amount needed to get L to join the treaty, while L wants to get as much as it can from H. So there will be tough negotiations over the redistribution formula.

A Carbon Tradable Permits Treaty

An alternative way to achieve the minimum cost of cutback for the world would be a tradable permits treaty that would establish an international permit market. The treaty would set a world target for total carbon emissions and would then distribute without charge this total amount of permits among participant country governments according to an agreed upon formula. Each country government would sell (or give) a certain quantity of permits to its own firms that emit carbon and sell the rest of its permits in the international permit market. Each firm in any country that signs the treaty would be required to possess as many permits as it emits; it would meet this requirement by buying or selling permits in the international permit market. Each country government would agree to monitor its own carbon polluters to make sure each polluter emits an amount of carbon no greater than the amount of permits it possesses. If the international permit market runs smoothly, carbon polluters in all countries would face the same permit price and adjust their pollution until their own MAC was equal to that price. Hence, the MACs of all polluters would be equal.

How would a tradable permits treaty accomplish the redistribution necessary to induce low-income countries to participate? By using a formula that gives a relatively large number of permits to low-income countries and a relatively small number of permits to high-income countries. Through the international permit market there would then be a transfer of income from high-income countries to low-income countries.

In our example, suppose under the treaty formula the government of country L is given 30 permits and the government of country H is given 20 permits. We showed earlier that no matter how the 50 permits are initially distributed between H and L, the price will end up $40, and firms in L will want to emit 10, while firms in H will want to emit 40. So the government of L will sell (or give) 10 permits to its firms and sell 20 permits to the government of H which will then sell (or give) 40 permits to its firms. Thus, the government of L will sell 20 permits at $40 per permit to the government of H, thereby resulting in a redistribution of $800 from country H to country L.

A Hybrid Carbon Treaty: A Permit System with a Safety Valve

As noted earlier, it would be possible to implement a hybrid: a permit system with a safety valve. The treaty would set an initial pollution target and distribute the corresponding amount of permits to the governments of all participating countries. But if the market price of a permit rises above the ceiling price adopted under the treaty by participant country governments, the treaty would authorize and implement a prompt expansion of the supply of permits that would continue until the market price is brought back down to the ceiling price.

The Political Challenge

Developing, maintaining, and implementing such a treaty—whether it uses a tax or tradable permits—would be politically challenging. Obviously low-income countries would want to maximize revenue transfers while high-income countries would want to minimize transfers. An agreement would have to be reached concerning the voting mechanism among treaty participants that would be used to decide the tax and the formula for transferring income or the total number of permits and the formula for distributing permits to countries. In order to try to win a favorable modification of the formula, some countries might claim they were considering withdrawing from the treaty, so there would always be the risk of country withdrawals. However, it should be recognized that similar problems occur under most international treaties.

Instead of a carbon tax or tradable permits, an international treaty was negotiated in Kyoto, Japan, in 1997 under which each high-income country was assigned a specific numerical emissions target, and low-income countries were exempt. The method of achieving its target was left to each high-income country.

Note the differences between the carbon tax or tradable permits described above and the Kyoto treaty. With the tax or tradable permits, there are no emission targets for individual countries; instead the tax is set with the aim of inducing a target total world emissions, or there is an emissions target for the world that sets the total number of permits to be distributed. With the tax or permits, each carbon emitter in each country has an incentive to reduce its own emissions until its marginal abatement cost (MAC) equals the tax or permit price; because the tax or permit price is the same for all firms in all countries, MACs would end up equal among all emitters, thereby achieving the reduction in world carbon emissions at minimum cost. With Kyoto, MACs will not be equalized, so emission reduction will not be achieved at minimum cost.

Although many high-income countries have ratified the Kyoto treaty, the United States has not, and low-income countries such as China are exempt from the treaty. Thus, the two largest carbon emitters, the United States and China, are not restrained by the treaty.

Summary

Economic analysis has reached several important conclusions. The right tax—a tax equal to the marginal damage to the environment—gets the market to generate the right quantity of a polluting good. Pollution tax revenue should be used to cut other taxes or send households cash transfers. Whenever feasible, the tax should be levied per emission, not per unit of the polluting good. A tax per emission that is the same for all emitters of pollutant X minimizes the cost of abating the pollution. Tradable permits are an alternative way to charge polluters a price in order to discourage pollution. There are pros and cons to tradable permits versus pollution taxes: With tradable permits, the quantity of emissions is certain, but the cost to the economy of abatement is not limited; with a tax, the quantity of emissions is uncertain, but the cost to the economy of abatement is limited. It is better for the government to sell, rather than give, permits to polluters, because then the revenue can be used to cut other taxes; even when permits are given, the price that evolves as permits are traded among polluters tends to minimize the cost of reducing pollution in the short run though not the long run.

Key Terms

externality, *27*
negative externality, *28*
positive externality, *28*
market failure, *28*
property rights, *28*
cap and trade, *29*
internalize the
  externality, *29*

transaction costs, *30*
command and control, *31*
marginal private cost
  (MPC), *36*
marginal social cost
  (MSC), *37*
marginal damage
  (MD), *37*

marginal benefit
  (MB), *37*
socially optimal
  quantity, *37*
corrective tax, *38*
Pigouvian tax, *38*
equimarginal
  principle, *43*

Questions

Questions 1 to 4 refer to the production of good X.

1. Production of good X generates pollution. Draw a supply-demand diagram for good X (assume the market is competitive). Assume that initially the government has *no* environmental policy. Your diagram should have three straight lines: label them S, D, and MSC (marginal social cost). S and D intersect at point K. Assume the environmental damage per unit of good X is $30. With no policy, 100 units of X are produced and the price of a unit of X is $120, but the socially optimal (best) amount of X, taking account of the environmental damage, is 60 units, shown at point I. Show all these numbers and points K and I on your diagram.

2. For the 100th unit of good X:
   a. What is the marginal benefit (MB) to consumers? $_____
   b. What is the marginal private cost of production (MPC)? $_____
   c. What is the marginal damage (MD) to the environment? $_____
   d. What is the marginal social cost (MSC)? $_____
   e. What is the marginal net loss to society? $_____

3. Using your diagram from question 1, label the triangle *IJK* that shows the net loss to society from the production of units 61 through 100; the net loss is $_____.

4. What tax per unit of good X would achieve the social optimum? $_____
   a. This tax will shift the S curve (*up, down*), so the price of X will (*increase, decrease*) and the quantity of X will (*increase, decrease*).
   b. Give the letters of the area that shows the environmental benefit: _____ (*Hint:* You'll need a new letter H); the environmental benefit is $_____.
   c. Give the letters of the area that shows the loss to society (ignoring the environmental gain) from the (*increase, decrease*) in the quantity of X: _____; the loss is $_____.
   d. Give the letters of the area that shows the net gain to society (the environmental benefit minus the loss to society from less X): _____; the net gain is $_____.

5. Draw Figure 2.5 with firms H and L except that each firm emits 60 (not 50) with no policy, the marginal damage (MD) of each emission is $48 (not $40), the vertical intercept of MAC$_H$ is $240 (not $200), and the vertical intercept of MAC$_L$ is $60 (not $50).

6. It is best for society to reduce an emission whenever MAC is less than (MD, tax).

7. It is best for a firm to reduce an emission when MAC is less than (MD, tax).

8. A tax of $____ would induce the firms to achieve what is best for society.

9. Suppose instead of a tax the government sells 60 permits.
   a. If the price were $24, L would demand _____ and H would demand _____.
   b. If the price were $48, L would demand _____ and H would demand _____.
   c. Thus, the price would turn out to be $ _____.

10. Assume H is a carbon polluter in a high-income country and L in a low-income country, and the goal is to cut total carbon emissions by 60. This can be done at minimum total cost if H cuts back _____ and L cuts back _____; then the total cost would be $ _____.

11. Instead, suppose H cuts back 60 and L cuts back 0; the total cost would be $_____.

12. Instead, suppose L cuts back 60 and H cuts back 0; the total cost would be $_____.

13. Suppose country H proposes a treaty where each government H and L would agree to levy a tax of $48 on its own polluters. If country L is unaffected by global warming, L should still agree to levy this tax on its own polluters if H pays L at least $_____. Why?

14. Under a tradable permits treaty where the total number of permits is 60, if country L is unaffected by global warming, country L should still agree to the treaty if it is given at least _____ permits. Why?

15. Go online and find out whether there are any bills that have been introduced in Congress to levy a carbon tax or to establish a carbon cap and trade program. Describe the main features of these bills.

Chapter Three

Public Goods and Political Economy

Royalty-Free/CORBIS

Economists rightly emphasize that competitive markets generally work well for most goods and services and that it is best for government to avoid interference in these markets. But there is a kind of good that markets cannot be expected to handle well: a *public good*. It is usually best for a public good to be *financed* by taxation and paid for by government.

The actual *production* of the public good may be done either by government or private firms, but two problems arise. First, what is the socially optimal quantity of a particular public good? Second, how should decisions be made concerning public goods? The analysis of how government should and actually does make decisions concerning goods and services is sometimes called political economy. Once we have examined what government should do, we will then turn to how government actually behaves and makes decisions.

THE CONCEPT OF A PUBLIC GOOD

A public good has two properties: (1) nonexcludability and (2) nonrivalry. Nonexcludability means that it is hard to exclude any person from benefiting from the good or service even if the person won't pay for it. Nonrivalry means that consumption of the good or service by one person does not prevent consumption of the good by other people; in fact, all individuals simultaneously consume the same quantity of the good. By contrast, a private good has excludability—it is easy to exclude a person from benefiting from the good or service if the person refuses to pay for it, and it has rivalry—consumption of the good by one person prevents consumption by other people. A private good is consumed by only one person.

Let's give some examples. National defense is a public good: If a military force is established, equipped, and stands ready to defend the nation, it is hard to exclude any person from being defended; moreover, the quantity of defense is the same for all people.

Police protection from criminals is a public good: If police deter potential criminals and apprehend actual criminals, it is hard to exclude any person from being protected. Air quality is a public good: It is hard to exclude any person from the air quality; moreover, the air quality is the same for all people in a given locality.

What about fire protection? Is this service excludable to someone who won't pay for it? It would be possible for a fire department to refrain from putting out a fire in the house of a homeowner who didn't pay for fire protection. But in many cases this would jeopardize adjacent houses of homeowners who did pay for protection. Moreover, many citizens consider it wrong to let a fire burn down a house just because the owner hasn't paid. So in practice local fire protection is a nonexcludable service.

Some goods or services have one of the two properties but not the other. A cable TV program is excludable but not rival: It is easy to exclude someone who refuses to pay from receiving the program; but one person's watching (consuming) the program does not prevent another from watching it. A crowded city street is rival but not excludable: When one car is driven on the street, it increases congestion and slows down other cars—reducing the consumption of the street by other drivers, but it is hard to exclude any particular car from entering the street (technology could change this—while toll booths on city streets are not feasible, electronic scanners might be, so cars could be billed for the use of city streets).

Note that economists do not call anything provided by the government a "public good." Although a public good usually ends up being financed by government, some public goods are provided by the private sector. Government also provides goods and services that are not public goods—that is, goods or services that are excludable and/or rival. For example, schooling is not a public good because it would be easy to exclude a child from school if his parents refused to pay.

Nonexcludability, the Free-Rider Problem, and Taxation

Nonexcludability implies that it may be hard to get some individuals to voluntarily pay an adequate share of the cost of a public good because they know that they can't be excluded from benefiting if the good is produced.

True, some individuals will voluntarily pay because they believe it is morally right to contribute—they get a warm glow from doing the right thing. If national defense were funded by voluntary contributions rather than taxes, some individuals would donate large sums and many individuals would contribute something. Another reason some individuals contribute voluntarily is because they are altruistic—they are willing to contribute to help others in need. Large sums are voluntarily donated to charities by some individuals, and many individuals donate something. Thus, it is certainly true that there would be substantial voluntary donations to finance many public goods.

However, without taxes, some individuals would choose to be **free riders**—people who reason, "I'll let others pay and then enjoy the benefits." True, if everyone tries to free ride, there would be no public goods supplied because no one would be willing to pay for them. Yet each free rider reasons this way: "If others pay and I don't, the public good will be supplied and I'll benefit. But if I pay and others don't, very little of the public good will be supplied and I'll hardly benefit. So either way, I won't pay."

Hence, even if many individuals would contribute something voluntarily, many would not contribute an adequate share of the cost and some would not contribute at all. Therefore, reliance on voluntary contributions would result in an underprovision of the public good.

The standard approach to the free-rider problem is taxation. Since everyone benefits, everyone should be compelled to contribute. The compelling must be done by the government, and the compulsory payment is called a **tax**.

Taxation has shortcomings. First, it is certainly true that some people would voluntarily contribute substantially to a national defense fund, and taxation will crowd out voluntary contributions; once government assumes responsibility for providing national defense and levies a tax, voluntary contributions to a national defense fund will surely dry up. Second, compulsion diminishes individual freedom; with compulsion, each household must pay its tax instead of having the freedom to decide how much to contribute to national defense. Third, an income tax reduces the reward to working more or saving more, because each person keeps less of what he earns for working or saving. Fourth, the legislative process by no means ensures that the socially optimal quantity of the public good will be provided. Fifth, taxation gives government power which might be used harmfully.

On the other hand, there are three shortcomings to relying on voluntary contributions. First, while some would contribute substantially, some would not, so there would be underfinancing and underprovision of the public good. Second, it would be unfair: Contributors with a conscience would be taken advantage of by free riders; even among contributors, some would give a much larger percentage of their income than others. Third, it would be inefficient: There would be no satisfactory mechanism for achieving the socially optimal level of defense—the level that best balances its benefit against its cost.

Who Should Produce a Public Good?

Notice that we have *not* said who should actually *produce* the public good—government or private firms. Once government raises the revenue through taxes, it then has the option of producing the public good with its own employees or purchasing the public good from private firms. Consider national defense: The government employs soldiers but purchases planes from private firms. It would be possible instead for the government to own and operate factories that use government employees to build planes. Thus, a public good, because of nonexcludability, must be *financed* by taxation and *paid for* by government. However, it may actually be produced by either government with its own employees or by private firms.

Why does the government buy planes produced by private firms instead of producing its own planes? One reason is that there is a large market for planes in the private sector. Private airlines buy a large number of planes to serve a huge number of private airline passengers. Air travel is a private good—if you refuse to pay, you won't be allowed on the plane—so there is a large private sector that provides air travel. Consequently, private firms are already producing a large number of planes for the private sector. Competition among these firms has improved their efficiency. It therefore makes sense for the government to take advantage of this efficiency by purchasing planes from these firms rather than producing its own planes.

By contrast, why does the federal government employ its own soldiers, and why does a city government employ its own police officers? Private firms produce the planes for the federal military and the cars for the city police department because these firms are already producing planes and cars for a huge private sector. It is true that private firms employ armed security guards that provide protection to private firms, but these private firms do not employ a huge number of heavily armed soldiers or police officers. Many citizens would probably be alarmed at the prospect of private firms possessing heavy firepower and manpower. Most citizens seem to take it for granted that sizable armed forces and police forces should be under the control of elected public officials.

An interesting illustration of private versus public production has occurred during reconstruction efforts in Iraq. The U.S. military has been in charge of the reconstruction, but many reconstruction projects have been contracted out to private firms such as Kellogg, Brown, and Root, a subsidiary of the large firm Halliburton (before becoming U.S. vice president, Dick Cheney was the CEO of Halliburton). Such contracting may make sense. There is a large private sector involved in construction projects throughout the world, so several large private firms have developed expertise in implementing such projects. Provided that the contracting process involves competitive bidding among a sufficient number of independent private firms and that contracts are awarded on objective merits, it seems sensible to generally use private firms rather than have the U.S. military perform the construction projects.

Such projects require armed security to proceed safely in Iraq. Although the U.S. military attempts to provide general security in Iraq, security at particular reconstruction projects is usually provided by private firms. From time to time, armed private security forces, such as the firm Blackwater, have engaged insurgents trying to disrupt a project. There have been several incidents in which innocent Iraqis have been harmed by these private security forces. The behavior of these private armed security forces has been criticized by Iraqi citizens and by the government of Iraq. This has put the U.S. government in a difficult situation. The U.S. government has direct control over and responsibility for the behavior of U.S. soldiers in Iraq, but it does not have direct control over the behavior of armed private security forces of U.S. reconstruction firms. The private security firms and their employees operate outside the U.S. military's chain of command, yet the U.S. military, and the U.S. government, is often blamed for the actions of employees of these firms. Critics have charged that private armed security forces should be prohibited and that all armed security should be provided by the U.S. military. Others reply that, except for a few incidents, private security forces have generally operated satisfactorily and reduced the burden on the U.S. military.

Thus, it is not always clear who should produce a public good. The best practical approach should be decided case by case.

The Island Wall

To appreciate the problems posed by a public good, imagine an island with three families. Suppose ships visit the island to sell private goods like food or clothing. The seller can easily exclude any family that refuses to pay, so there is no free-rider problem. As long as there is competition among visiting ships, the price of each item will be kept close to its cost, and the free market for private goods will work efficiently on the island without any cooperation by the families with each other.

However, suppose another ship with a construction crew visits the island offering to produce a public good: a defensive wall around the island. Without a wall, the island is vulnerable to a raid by pirates. The wall is a public good because an islander who refuses to pay can't be excluded from benefiting from the wall. The thicker the wall, the better the protection. To simplify, assume that any wall that is built has the same height, uses the same material, and surrounds the entire island; the only issue is how thick to make the wall.

The Socially Optimal Quantity of the Public Good

Before we examine what the three families *will* do, let's figure out what they *should* do by using Figure 3.1. The height of each family's MB curve shows the maximum dollar amount that family would pay for an additional foot of thickness. We assume that each family would pay most for the first foot and then less for each additional foot.

> *We label the families H (high), M (medium), and L (low) according to the height of the family's MB curve.*

Family H (high MB) would pay a higher dollar amount for each foot than family M (medium MB), who in turn would pay a higher amount than family L (low MB). Note that the letter H, M, or L refers to the MB, not the income, of the family.

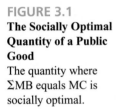

FIGURE 3.1
The Socially Optimal Quantity of a Public Good
The quantity where ΣMB equals MC is socially optimal.

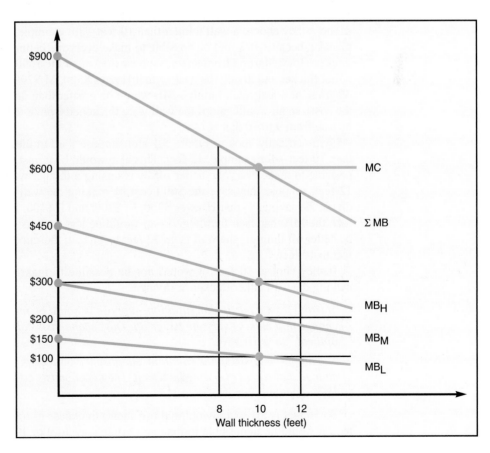

Assume that the marginal cost (MC) of each additional foot of thickness stays constant as the wall gets thicker and that the construction crew charges a price per foot P equal to this MC because there is competition from other construction ships that might visit the island.

Now consider the numbers in Figure 3.1. A 1-foot-thick wall costs $600 to build, and each additional foot of thickness costs $600, so the MC line is horizontal at a height of $600. It just so happens that the heights of the MB curves (which happen to be straight lines for these families) are in the ratio of 3:2:1; at any level of thickness, the ratio MB_H:MB_M:MB_L is 3:2:1. For example, at a thickness of 10 feet, MB_H = $300, MB_M = $200, and MB_L = $100.

It will prove useful to draw a *sum of the MBs curve* (ΣMB, where the symbol Σ means "sum") above the three family MB curves to indicate the vertical sum of the MB curves of the three families. For example, at a thickness of 10 feet, ΣMB = $600 ($300 + $200 + $100); while at a thickness of 0 feet, ΣMB = $900 ($450 + $300 + $150).

The reason for summing the MBs of all three families is that protection from the wall is nonrival—each family's protection does not diminish the others—so when the wall is made a foot thicker, the total marginal benefit for the three families is the sum of the MBs of each family. By contrast, with a private good for which consumption is rival, only the MB of the person who consumes the good matters (everyone else has no benefit). Hence, for a public good, we care about the ΣMB of all who simultaneously consume it, while for a private good we care only about the MB of the one person who consumes it.

Then it would be best if the three families choose the 10-foot-thick wall, the thickness at which the ΣMB curve intersects the MC curve. Why? Look at Figure 3.1 and suppose they choose a wall thinner than 10 feet—for example, 8 feet. This would be a mistake, because it would be possible to make everyone better off by making the wall thicker. How? Starting from 8 feet, suppose they incur the $600 cost of making the wall a foot thicker and divide the cost so that H pays $300, M $200, and L $100. From the diagram, at 8 feet, each family's MB would be greater than its cost-share (its share of the cost), so all would gain if the wall were thickened from 8 to 9 feet; the same would be true from 9 to 10 feet.

Symmetrically, look at Figure 3.1 and suppose the families choose a wall thicker than 10 feet—for example, 12 feet. This also would be a mistake because it would be possible to make everyone better off by choosing a thinner wall. How? Starting from 12 feet, suppose they save the $600 cost by making the wall a foot thinner and then divide the saving, so that H saves $300, M $200, and L $100. From the diagram, at 12 feet, the MB that each family gives up would be less than its cost saving, so it would be better off thinning the wall from 12 feet to 11 feet; the same would be true from 11 feet to 10 feet.

If they choose 10 feet, it would *not* be possible to make everyone better off by making the wall either thicker or thinner.

> *Starting from a particular situation, suppose it would be impossible to make a change that makes everyone better off. Then economists call the situation "Pareto optimal," or* efficient.

> *Starting from a particular situation, suppose it would be possible to make a change that makes everyone better off. Then economists call the situation "not Pareto optimal," or* inefficient.

So 10 feet is the socially optimal (efficient) thickness of the wall. Starting from 10 feet, it would be impossible to make a change (say, to 9 or 11 feet) that would make

Current Research   Optimal Protection against Crime

Protection against crime is a public good: If the quantity of protection is increased—for example, through additional police officers—every law-abiding citizen benefits, and none can be excluded from benefiting. Figure 3.1 applies to protection against crime: The socially optimal protection against crime is the quantity at which the ΣMB curve intersects the MC curve. But in practice, how can ΣMB be estimated so that it can be compared to MC?

An empirical application is given by economists Philip Cook and Jens Ludwig in their book on gun violence.* Protection against gun violence is a public good, so optimal protection is the quantity at which the ΣMB curve intersects the MC curve. Cook and Ludwig estimate ΣMB by employing a method widely used by economists to determine the optimal quantity: a survey of willingness to pay (this method is called *contingent valuation*). They use data from a nationally representative phone survey of about 1,200 adults in fall 1998 conducted by the National Opinion Research Center of the University of Chicago; their dollar estimates are for 1998. The respondents were asked whether they would vote for or against a program that would reduce criminal gun violence by 30% but raise their taxes by $X ($X was $50, $100, or $200); the respondents were told that the program "would reduce gun thefts and illegal gun dealers and make it more difficult for criminals and delinquents to obtain guns." From the survey answers, Cook and Ludwig estimate that in 1998, the average American household would have been willing to pay about $200 to reduce criminal gun violence, implying that the American public of roughly 100 million households would have been willing to pay about $20 billion in total. Extrapolating, Cook and Ludwig estimate that the American public would have been willing to pay about $80 billion in 1998 to virtually eliminate criminal gun violence.

Their estimates would enable the plotting of a ΣMB curve in Figure 3.1 where the horizontal axis would be the percentage reduction in criminal gun violence and the vertical axis would show ΣMB—the dollar amount the public would be willing to pay to reduce criminal gun violence by an additional 1%. Based on estimates of the program's cost and effectiveness by experts in law enforcement and criminology, an MC curve could be plotted in Figure 3.1 showing the dollar cost of reducing criminal gun violence an additional 1%. Then the socially optimal reduction in criminal gun violence through this program would be the quantity at which the ΣMB curve intersects the MC curve, and the socially optimal expenditure on this program is the amount that would bring about the reduction in gun violence.

Of course, how much a household is willing to pay to reduce gun violence might depend on the method used to reduce it. The wording of the question suggested that the method would involve increasing the supervision and monitoring of the sale and possession of guns. An alternative method for reducing gun violence would be to increase the number of police officers patrolling the streets. Thus, the Cook and Ludwig study provides evidence and estimates concerning the public's willingness to pay for only one particular method of reducing gun violence.

*Philip Cook and Jens Ludwig, *Gun Violence: The Real Costs* (Oxford University Press, 2000).

everyone better off. By contrast, either 9 or 11 feet is inefficient: Starting from either 9 or 11 feet, it would be possible to make a change—specifically, a move to 10 feet—that could make everyone better off if the cost-shares are properly assigned. We arrive at this important conclusion:

> *The efficient quantity of a public good is the quantity at which the sum of the MBs of all who consume the good equals the MC. By contrast, the efficient quantity of a private good is the quantity at which the MB of the person who consumes the good equals the MC.*

Hence, using the symbol Σ to indicate the sum:

> *At the efficient, socially optimal quantity of a public good, ΣMB = MC.*
> *At the efficient, socially optimal quantity of a private good, MB = MC.*

POLITICAL ECONOMY

How should the three island families decide whether to purchase a defense wall? We now turn to political economy—how the families might collectively make decisions concerning the public good.

Political Economy on the Island

If the construction ship crew foolishly approaches each family alone with a price of $600 per foot, it will be disappointed. Each family alone (even H) would be unwilling to buy even a 1-foot wall if it must pay the entire $600 per foot itself, because as can be seen in Figure 3.1, no family's MB curve is as high as $600 even for the first foot. At zero feet, even H's MB curve is below the MC of $600.

It is important to recognize that H's MB curve might have been higher, so that at zero feet, H's MB curve might have been above the MC of $600. If this had been the case, then H alone would have been willing to pay for at least a 1-foot wall, even if H were charged the entire MC of $600. Thus, it is possible that a single buyer would be willing to pay more than the MC for a certain quantity of a public good. A good example of this is discussed in the box on a particular global public good: the military protection of a valuable world resource.

If the construction crew is sensible, it will ask the three families to get together and decide what they would collectively be willing to do. Assume that the families get along well and are glad to cooperate. Also assume each family is honest (you certainly are) and tells the others the truth about its own MB curve. Then the families sit down and together draw Figure 3.1.

Suppose the families agree that, since their MBs are in the ratio of 3:2:1, they will share the cost in the ratio of 3:2:1. In other words, costs will be shared in the same ratio as benefits. Since the price per foot is $600, they agree that H will pay $300 per foot; M, $200; and L, $100; each family's horizontal cost-share line is shown in Figure 3.1.

The cost-share is the price that the family must pay per unit of the public good.

With cost-shares decided, each family looks at its own MB curve, compares the height of its MB at each foot of thickness to its cost-share (price), and decides how thick a wall it would want. Note that each family's MB curve is its demand curve, because at each price that the family faces (its cost-share), the curve tells how many feet of thickness the family would want to buy (demand).

Every family would decide that it wants a wall 10 feet thick; up until 10 feet, each family's MB exceeds its cost-share, but beyond 10 feet, each family's MB is less than its cost-share. Pleased and relieved that they unanimously prefer a 10-foot-thick wall, they inform the construction crew. The 10-foot-thick wall is constructed and purchased collectively by the families, and each family enjoys a net benefit from the wall because, for each foot of thickness built, each family's MB exceeds its cost-share; moreover, had another foot (the 11th) been built, each family's MB would have been less than its cost-share, so 10 feet was the best wall for all three families given their cost-shares.

This happy outcome—the unanimous choice of the socially optimal (efficient) quantity of the public good—depended on several things. First, the families had to cooperate. Second, they had to be honest about their own MBs. Third, they had to agree to share the cost in the same ratio as their MBs.

Suppose instead that the families had agreed to equal-dollar cost-shares so each would pay $200 per foot. Then from Figure 3.1, H would have wanted more than 10 feet, while L would have wanted less. So there would have been no unanimity. Or

Case Study   A Global Public Good: Military Protection of a Valuable World Resource

Oil is a valuable resource on which many economies around the world currently depend. If a hostile dictator were to gain control of enough of the world's oil to significantly manipulate its price or disrupt its supply, that dictator could harm the standard of living for ordinary people in many countries. Military protection to prevent a valuable world resource like oil from the control, manipulation, and disruption by a hostile dictator is a global public good: Each nation would benefit from such protection whether or not it had paid for the protection. Thus, there is a potential free-rider problem: Each nation may wait for others to provide and pay for such military protection; but if all nations wait, such military protection will not be forthcoming. However, it is possible that the benefit of military protection to a single large nation dependent on oil would be great enough to cover the entire cost of protection; if so, that nation would be willing to provide the military protection by itself if necessary.

Such was apparently the case for the United States in August 1990 when Iraq's dictator Saddam Hussein suddenly moved his Iraqi army into Kuwait, taking control of its oil fields. Kuwait is a small, oil-rich country that borders Saudi Arabia. Whether Saddam Hussein wanted to move the Iraqi army into Saudi Arabia can of course be debated. President George H. W. Bush made it clear that the United States would be willing, if necessary, to pay the entire cost of defending the oil fields of Saudi Arabia from Saddam Hussein's army and forcing his withdrawal from Kuwait. The Bush administration judged that the United States' MB from defending the Saudi and Kuwaiti oil fields—from which the United States gets an important fraction of its oil—would exceed the entire cost. The United States immediately poured troops into Saudi Arabia, making it clear the United States was ready to fight, alone if necessary, to protect Saudi Arabia and Kuwait.

Of course, other nations—Saudi Arabia, Kuwait, Western European countries, Japan, and so forth— also had substantial MBs for the defense of Saudi Arabia and Kuwait. During the fall of 1990, the Bush administration worked diplomatically to gain support from other nations—either to contribute troops or commit to help pay for a military intervention to drive the Iraqi army out of Kuwait.

A majority of Congress voted to support such a military intervention if Saddam Hussein did not withdraw voluntarily.

In January 1991, after months of warning Saddam Hussein to withdraw, the United States (with military support from several other nations and political support from the majority of countries) attacked the Iraqi army in Kuwait, defeated it in less than a month, and forced it to withdraw from Kuwait. President Bush made the decision not to pursue the Iraqi army once it had withdrawn from Kuwait— specifically, not to attempt a military assault on Baghdad or try to remove Saddam Hussein from power. Following the success of the military operation, the United States was able to secure substantial financial reimbursement from Saudi Arabia, Kuwait, Japan, Germany, and other nations—these nations chose *not* to be free riders—so that the United States ended up bearing only a fraction of the cost.

By contrast, in 2003 President George W. Bush was unable to secure either troop or financial contributions from this set of countries (the United States did obtain support from Britain and several other countries) to invade Iraq, secure its capital Baghdad, and remove Saddam Hussein from power. As a consequence, the United States has ended up bearing most of the cost of the military invasion and pacification of Iraq from spring 2003 to the present.

Why the difference? It is possible that these other nations wanted a U.S. military invasion to remove Saddam Hussein from power, but they chose to be free riders. However, it is also possible that these nations felt the benefit from an invasion and pacification of Iraq was not worth its cost. In 1990, Saddam Hussein had moved his army into Kuwait, and the announced purpose of the Bush administration was to lead a coalition to drive the Iraqi army out of Kuwait but not to invade Baghdad and remove Saddam Hussein from power. In 2003, the announced purpose of the Bush administration was to dismantle the weapons-of-mass-destruction program that it believed Saddam Hussein was pursuing and to remove him from power. The nations that were unwilling to contribute may have judged the benefit to be less than its cost, and their unwillingness to contribute financially may have been due to this judgment rather than free riding.

suppose that the cost-shares had been set in the same ratio as family incomes. *If* the ratio of family incomes just happened to be the same as the ratio of MBs, 3:2:1, then the cost-shares would have been the same as before ($300, $200, and $100), and once again there would have been a unanimous choice of 10 feet. This is possible; perhaps the reason for their 3:2:1 ratio of MBs was their 3:2:1 ratio of incomes. However, it is not certain. Suppose their incomes in fact were equal, and their 3:2:1 ratio of MBs was due solely to their differing attitude about the likelihood of a pirate raid; then if cost-shares were set according to income, each would pay $200 per foot, and there would be no unanimity.

A Unanimity Rule

Suppose the families agree in advance that they will only order a defensive wall with a particular thickness from the construction crew if their support is unanimous—all three families support it. To achieve unanimity, they must agree to cost-shares that are in the same ratio as their MBs. Thus, if equal-dollar cost-shares are initially proposed, they will discover that they are unable to find a wall thickness that achieves unanimous support. They will therefore be compelled to alter the cost-shares and try again. Eventually they will arrive at the 3:2:1 ratio for cost-shares that achieves unanimity—all three will then support a 10-foot wall and enjoy a net benefit when it is constructed.

Thus, an advantage of a unanimity rule is that it prevents an action—the building of a wall with particular thickness and with a particular cost-share ratio—in which some families do not enjoy a net benefit. The rule forces the families to keep renegotiating the cost-share ratio until they find one that enables every family to enjoy a net benefit from constructing the wall.

We have implicitly assumed that the three families are honest about their MB curves and do not behave strategically. But a family might be tempted to be dishonest by understating its own MB in order to be assigned a lower cost-share. Knowing that unanimity is required, a family may hold out, refusing to support any wall proposal until the others agree to assign it a very low cost-share. If all families hold out, no wall will be built.

Majority-Rule Voting and the Median Voter

Suppose the three families, in light of the deadlock that might occur with a unanimity rule, agree to decide the thickness of the wall by majority-rule voting; if two of the three families vote for a particular wall, the purchase will be made. What will happen?

> *Each family must know its cost-share in order to know how to vote; each will decide how to vote by comparing its MB to its cost-share.*

Suppose initially that the cost-shares are H $300 per foot, M $200 per foot, and L $100 per foot. They agree to vote on the following question: "Should we thicken the wall by at least one more foot?" Starting from zero feet, all three vote for the first foot (because each family's MB in Figure 3.1 exceeds its cost-share), all three vote for the second, and they continue until all three vote for the tenth. Then all three vote against the eleventh. So with these cost-shares, voters unanimously prefer a 10-foot wall.

But if a family's cost-share is raised from its dollar number given above, it will prefer less than 10 feet; if cost-share is lowered, it will prefer more. Which family will want the thickest wall? It depends on how cost-shares are assigned. Once cost-shares are assigned, the MB curves in Figure 3.1 tell how much thickness each family would prefer. Given the cost-shares, rank the three families according to their preference from thickest to thinnest.

The family in the middle of the ranking is called the median voter. As we have just seen, the median voter may be family H, M, or L depending on how cost-shares are assigned.

With majority voting, the outcome will be what the median voter prefers.

For example, given cost-shares, suppose one family prefers 8 feet, another family prefers 12 feet, and the median voter something between 8 and 12 feet—call it *N* feet. Then starting from zero feet, all three will vote to increase thickness until 8 feet; two will vote to go to *N* feet; but then two will vote against going above *N* feet, so *N* feet will be the outcome.

Note that the outcome may not be the socially optimal quantity (10 feet). If *N* is 10, then 10 feet will be chosen—the social optimum. But if *N* is 9 or 11, the social optimum will not be chosen.

The socially optimal quantity will be chosen under majority-rule voting if the median voter prefers it; otherwise, not. To get the median voter to prefer the social optimum, it is necessary to assign the median voter the cost-share that will cause that voter to prefer the socially optimal quantity.

Majority-Rule Voting: Single- and Double-Peaked Preferences

Thus far, decisions have been made foot by foot: Should the thickness of the wall be raised from 8 to 9 feet, from 9 to 10 feet? We now consider a different way of arriving at a decision. Suppose that, given a particular assignment of cost-shares, family H prefers a thick wall, M prefers an intermediate wall, and L prefers a thin wall, so there is a deadlock. Suppose the families agree to conduct pair-wise votes between two options to try to break the deadlock: Whichever option (thick, intermediate, or thin) wins the first pair-wise vote is then matched against the remaining option.

Given cost-shares, the preferences are shown in Table 3.1. For example, H's first choice is thick, second choice is intermediate, and third choice is thin. For the moment, ignore family D, and assume the three families voting are H, M, and L.

If H, M, and L vote between intermediate and thick, then intermediate beats thick because M and L vote for intermediate. If H, M, and L vote between intermediate and thin, then intermediate beats thin because M and H vote for intermediate. With these preferences, pair-wise voting yields a clear winner: intermediate.

But if family L were replaced by family D, the result would be different. We will see shortly that D stands for *double-peaked preferences*. Like L, D's first choice is thin. But unlike L, D's third choice is intermediate. Why? D believes that an intermediate wall gives no more protection than a thin wall and so is definitely not worth its additional cost; D believes that to get more real protection the wall must be thick. Hence, D ranks thin first, thick second, and intermediate third. With H, M, and D voting, thick beats intermediate because H and D vote for thick; then thin beats thick because M and D vote for thin; but then intermediate beats thin because M and H vote for intermediate. Thus, none (thick, intermediate, or thin) can defeat the other two. If a pair-wise vote is held,

TABLE 3.1
Majority-Rule Voting

Choice	H	M	L	D
First	Thick	Intermediate	Thin	Thin
Second	Intermediate	Thin	Intermediate	Thick
Third	Thin	Thick	Thick	Intermediate

FIGURE 3.2
Voter Preferences
Only voter D has two
peaks.

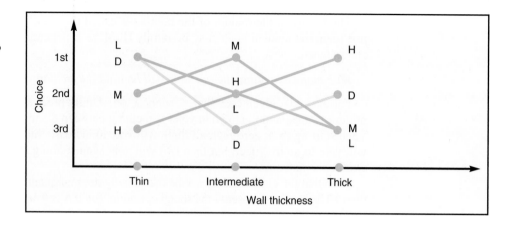

FIGURE 3.2
Voter Preferences
Only voter D has two
peaks.

and then the first winner is run against the remaining option, the remaining option always wins—so there is "cycling": The prize for winning moves round and round from option to option; there is no clear, stable winner. This is sometimes called the *voting paradox*.

Figure 3.2 shows the preferences of the four families: H, M, L, and D. All but D have single-peaked preferences; that is, when each family's preferences are plotted, there is one peak. By contrast, D has double-peaked preferences—when its preferences are plotted, there are two peaks. If some families have double-peaked preferences, pair-wise voting may result in cycling with no clear, stable winner.

An Island Government When There Are Many Families

Suppose that the island has many families. There is no practical way for all the families to sit down together voluntarily, decide on each family's cost-share, and choose the thickness of the wall. Suppose a government is established to tackle this problem. Assume that a government with a legislature and an executive (a president, prime minister, or governor) has been established, and the construction ship crew approaches the government with its offer to build a defensive wall.

The legislature will need to have the power of taxation. If the legislature simply appealed to families to make voluntary contributions, what would happen? Some families would contribute substantially because they believe it is morally right to help finance a defensive wall. But many families would contribute little or nothing because a defensive wall is a public good, so if the wall is built, no family can be excluded from benefiting.

What should the government do? Look back at Figure 3.1, but instead of three MB curves, imagine many. The socially optimal wall thickness is where the ΣMB curve (the vertical sum of the MB curves of all the families) intersects the MC curve. If the government knew each family's MB curve, it should assign each family a *tax price* (cost-share) that makes the family prefer the social optimum—a tax price that equals the height of the family's MB curve at the social optimum. The government should then purchase the socially optimal (efficient) wall thickness from the construction firm and levy the taxes needed to finance it. Families would unanimously support the government's choice of the socially optimal wall thickness.

Optimal Taxation

Suppose that the height of every family's MB curve happened to be exactly proportional to its income—if one family has four times the income of another, its MB curve is four times higher than the other's. Then the government should make each family's tax price (cost-share) proportional to its income—it should levy a **proportional tax**. With a proportional income tax, when the government provides a public good, it taxes a $120,000 income family four times the dollar amount that it taxes a $30,000 income family.

Of course, the relationship between MB and income may not be proportional. If one family has four times the income of another, its MB curve may be eight times as high, or only twice as high, not four times a high. If eight times as high, then the government should make each family's tax price rise faster than its income—when income is multiplied by 4, the tax should be multiplied by 8. This is called a **progressive tax**. If only twice as high, then the government should make each family's tax price rise slower than its income—when income is multiplied by 4, the tax should be multiplied by 2. This is called a **regressive tax**.

Thus, if the height of every family's MB curve varies with its income, then exactly how it varies with income determines whether the optimal income tax is proportional, progressive, or regressive. It must be emphasized that by *optimal*, we mean solely with respect to the objective of achieving unanimous citizen support for the socially optimal quantity of the public good. In Chapter 8, "Income Taxes," we will see that other objectives, such as fairness and incentives to work and save, should be taken into account when choosing whether to make an income tax progressive, proportional, or regressive.

Practical Obstacles

Unfortunately, it is not obvious whether MB curves for a particular public good rise faster or slower than income, so we can't be sure whether the government should choose a progressive, proportional, or regressive income tax just for the objective of achieving the socially optimal quantity of the particular public good with unanimous citizen support.

Moreover, there may well be wide variation in the height of MB curves among families with the same income. Consider two families with the same income. One may be very concerned about a pirate raid and therefore have a high MB curve, while the other may be unconcerned about a pirate raid and therefore have a low MB curve. The government can't vary a family's tax according to its suspected concern. Even if the government were inclined to ask citizens about the intensity of their concern, citizens would have an incentive to understate it in order to be assigned a low tax. Dishonest citizens would understate their concern, so assigning taxes based on survey results would be unfair.

The fact is that the government cannot know each family's MB curve for a particular public good. Recall that this was a problem even with just three families, because each family had an incentive to understate its MB to the other two families in order to obtain a smaller cost-share. It would surely be a serious problem with many families. The best the government can do is use a very rough proxy for MB-like income.

But more fundamentally, it is naive to simply assume that the government will want to achieve the social optimum or that it will want to assign cost-shares that win unanimous support among citizens for the social optimum. Who makes the government's decisions? Is it a legislature (perhaps with the approval of the executive)? How are legislators elected? What is the impact of primary elections by political parties? Why is there logrolling and pork-barrel legislation? Is there sometimes government failure, just as there is sometimes market failure? Is there sometimes government corruption? What is the impact of lobbying—by private interests or by government bureaucracies?

It's time to leave our island and return to a realistic examination of governmental institutions and behavior.

THE BEHAVIOR OF GOVERNMENT

Voting, Legislators, Policies, and Elections

Decisions about public goods are made by a legislature (perhaps with the approval of an executive)—not by citizens directly. The legislators are elected by the citizens to represent them. Of course, this does not automatically mean that the legislature will do what the citizens want. Whatever other motives they may have, legislators generally want to be reelected. Let's consider how this may affect the legislators' voting on a public good.

Candidates Dove and Hawk

Consider an election campaign between two candidates, Dove and Hawk, and assume the election will be decided by one issue: spending on national defense. The voters want to know the percentage of the budget each candidate favors spending on national defense. As shown in Figure 3.3, the preference of the voters ranges from 0% spending (extreme Dove) to 40% spending (extreme Hawk), and voter opinion is spread out smoothly between 0% and 40%, so that the median voter prefers 20%: half the voters—Dovish voters—prefer spending between 0% and 20% on national defense, and half the voters—Hawkish voters—prefer spending between 20% and 40% on national defense. Dove's personal preference is to spend 10%, while Hawk's personal preference is 30%. Each realizes that whoever takes a public position further from the middle of the electorate (20%) will lose the election. If both candidates want to avoid losing the election, both will announce public support for spending 20%.

There are two reasons why the two candidates might not move to the middle (20%). First, each would like to be elected while keeping as close to his personal preference as possible. Each may have gone into politics partly due to genuine concern about defense spending. Second, each candidate had to have his party's nomination—in Dove's party, voter preference ranged from 0% to 20%, while in Hawk's party, voter preference ranged from 20% to 40%. In the primary election that determined the party's nominee, each candidate took a public position right in the middle of his party's voters (Dove 10%, Hawk 30%). This is one reason that each candidate won his primary election and is now his party's candidate in the general election. Changing positions now might have two negative effects. First, voters might question his honesty. Second, his own base—the supporters in his own party who are helping raise money for campaign ads—might lose enthusiasm. This would reduce the ad campaign, making it harder to win over undecided voters.

FIGURE 3.3

Primary and General Election Voting
To win the primary, Dove favors 10% and Hawk favors 30%; but to win the general, 20% would be best.

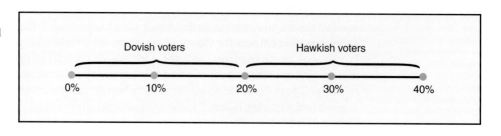

Why Does an Individual Citizen Vote?

Let's raise a basic question: Why does an individual citizen bother to vote? After all, a citizen might reason: "My vote has virtually no chance of deciding the election, and I have other things to do with my time." Many citizens do reason this way and don't bother to vote. But many citizens do vote despite recognizing that their own vote won't decide the election. Why do they do it? Among the reasons are the following:

- Many citizens believe that if most citizens decided not to vote, democracy would fail and society would be worse off. Consequently, these citizens believe it is their duty to set an example and do what they want other citizens to do; they vote to keep democracy from failing. They believe that not voting is not doing their civic duty—it's free riding.

- Many citizens like to officially express their preferences about who should hold political office and what policies they favor or oppose. In economist's language, these citizens receive utility (satisfaction) from voting that outweighs its time cost, even when they know it won't affect the outcome of the election.

- Many citizens fear that others will think badly of them if they don't vote.

Because of these and other influences, we observe a variety of patterns in elections. In some, candidates of both parties take positions close to the middle of the entire electorate. In other elections, candidates of both parties stick to positions close to the middle of their own party and stay quite a distance away from the middle of the entire electorate.

Logrolling

Instead of legislators voting on one issue at a time, issues can be packaged, and this can make a difference to the outcome when legislators differ with respect to intensity of preference. Suppose representative Hawk is strongly in favor of high defense spending but weakly opposed to spending for national parks, while representative Nature is strongly in favor of spending for national parks but only weakly opposed to high defense spending. If the issues are voted on separately, Hawk and Nature cancel each other's votes: Hawk votes for high defense spending and Nature votes against it, while Nature votes for high national park spending and Hawk votes against it. If more than half the votes are required for passage, then neither passes.

To break the deadlock, Hawk and Nature make a deal: Each agrees to vote for the other's priority. Then both pass. Hawk is willing to accept a small loss from high national park spending to get a large gain from high defense spending, and Nature is willing to accept a small loss from high defense spending to get a large gain from high national park spending. To break a deadlock (where nothing passes), they have agreed to trade votes and engage in logrolling: "I'll vote for your highest priority if you'll vote for mine."

The logrolling can be accomplished through one bill and one vote or two bills and two votes. Under the one-bill approach, a bill containing high defense spending and high national park spending is put to a vote, and both Hawk and Nature vote for it. Under the two-bill approach, both vote for the first bill authorizing high defense spending, and then both vote for the second bill authorizing high national park spending.

It might seem that logrolling benefits both legislators and their constituents (if their constituents have the same priorities) and should, therefore, be viewed positively. Yet logrolling is often viewed negatively. Why?

Suppose the legislature has voted $10 million to fund a list of local projects. Now a bill is being drafted with a list of local projects that will receive the funding. Legislators are logrolling with each other—each says, "I promise to vote for the project in your district if you vote for the project in my district." Suppose that most of the projects have only a small positive value to local residents—specifically, local residents would not have been willing to pay taxes to fund the projects. Then the logrolling certainly seems wasteful, with each legislator striving to get a pork-barrel project funded in his district by vote trading with other legislators who have the same objective—a project that the district's voters would not have been willing to fund with their own taxes.

The real problem here is not the logrolling over particular projects, but the voting of $10 million by the legislature in the first place. Once the pot of $10 million has been made available, then each legislator views it as "free" money—why not try to get some of it for his own district? If local projects have primarily local benefits, then they should be funded locally, not nationally, so that local taxpayers have to weigh the cost of paying local taxes against the benefit of the project.

It should be noted that local pork-barrel projects funded by a pot of federal money are only a small fraction of government spending. Stopping pork-barrel spending would not get most government spending "under control" because most government spending is social insurance (federal), defense (federal), and education (state and local). However, pork-barrel spending is nevertheless worth curtailing.

Lobbying, Special Interests, Campaigns, Bureaucracies, and Corruption

Imagine a complete ban on **lobbying**—communication from citizens or groups to legislators about their reasons for supporting or opposing a proposed bill. How would legislators become informed about problems that need to be addressed or about the pros and cons of past or proposed legislation? Surely any attempt to completely prevent such communication would be undesirable and impractical. Nevertheless, there is a concern about certain kinds of lobbying.

Consider an example: Domestic business firms producing clothing seek a tariff on imports of clothing that would compete with their own domestic sale of clothing. A tariff would raise the price of clothing and give a large boost to the domestic firms' revenues and, therefore, to the incomes of their workers, managers, and stockholders. Private special interests engage in rent seeking—to use government to obtain higher returns than they could otherwise achieve.

Why don't consumers lobby against the tariff on imports of clothing? Because the tariff would have only a small impact on the typical consumer who devotes only a small percentage of his budget to clothing. Each consumer is hurt only slightly, so it is not worth it for any consumer to spend money lobbying against the tariff—in fact, it is not worth it for any consumer to even pay attention. Besides, consumers face a free-rider problem. Lobbying against the tariff is a public good. If it succeeds, all consumers of the product benefit whether they contributed to the lobbying effort or not. Therefore, lobbying against the tariff receives little funding. By contrast, it is worth it for domestic firms in the clothing industry to spend a lot of money lobbying for the tariff because the tariff will cause a significant boost in their revenues. Thus, narrow special interests raise a lot of money to lobby for legislation that benefits them, but broad general interests raise little money to counter it.

Legislators need funds to run for reelection. Special interests are able and willing to offer funds to legislators who vote for their special interest legislation, while the general public offers little funding to legislators who resist. Thus, there is an imbalance.

Case Study The Politics of Subsidies and Tariffs

In Chapter 2, "Externalities and the Environment," we explained why economists support charging a price to polluters (either through a tax or tradable permits) and oppose giving clean alternatives a subsidy (either through direct payments or tax breaks). Here we elaborate on the role of lobbying and politics by looking at the case of ethanol. It should be emphasized that the same account could be written about many other subsidies and tariffs.

Economists recommend charging producers of oil or gasoline a price that reflects its environmental cost and then letting ethanol compete with other clean alternatives in the marketplace without having the government subsidize any potential alternative or place a tax or tariff on any alternative. Ethanol is a clean alternative to gasoline that can be obtained from corn or sugarcane. The United States grows a lot of corn, and Brazil grows a lot of sugarcane. The political result has been that Congress has enacted a subsidy of about $1.00 a gallon for ethanol obtained from U.S. corn and placed a tariff of about $0.50 a gallon on ethanol obtained from Brazilian sugarcane. Producers, people, and politicians from U.S. corn-growing regions have worked hard politically to get Congress to enact both the subsidy and the tariff. They have argued that the ethanol subsidy helps the U.S. environment and energy independence and that the tariff is justified to offset the subsidy that Brazilian sugarcane producers receive from their government. Some environmental groups have lobbied for the subsidy but generally not for the tariff.

Many individual Americans, whether they realize it or not, have a small loss imposed on them from the ethanol subsidy and tariff. The tariff raises the price of sugarcane ethanol from Brazil by about $0.50 a gallon and reduces the competitive effect of Brazilian ethanol on the price of U.S. ethanol and gasoline. The ethanol subsidy causes some reduction in the price of U.S. ethanol and gasoline to drivers, but taxpayers must make up for the revenue loss that results from ethanol tax breaks and direct payments which are estimated to be approaching $10 billion a year. With 300 million Americans, that comes to about $30 per person ($10 × 10^9 divided by 300 × 10^6 = $33). With such a small effect per person, it is rational for most Americans to ignore it politically.

By contrast, producers and people in corn-growing regions have received a much larger per person benefit from the ethanol subsidy and tariff. It is therefore much more important for members of Congress from corn-growing regions to get the ethanol subsidy and tariff enacted than it is for members of Congress from other regions to prevent enactment. Even senators in states where most people don't grow corn know that their corn farmers care much more about this issue than other voters; how they vote on ethanol will be carefully watched by corn farmers but rationally ignored by most constituents.

There is a final factor politically favoring the ethanol subsidy and tariff. It just happens that the Iowa caucus is the first vote in the presidential primaries. As a consequence, presidential candidates seeking both the Democratic and Republican nominations spend many months campaigning in Iowa. These candidates usually quickly see the virtues of a U.S. corn ethanol subsidy and a tariff on imported ethanol. In fact, any representative or senator who anticipates possibly running for president recognizes the political cost of voting against an ethanol subsidy and tariff. Even after the candidate is elected president, it is not too easy to suddenly abandon the pledges made in Iowa.

Once again, it should be emphasized that there is nothing unusual about ethanol or the producers, people, and politicians in corn-growing regions. The same political story occurs for many products in many regions. The benefit per person from achieving a subsidy and tariff is large for the producers and people in the affected regions, while the loss per person for the vast majority is small.

Legislators are under pressure to raise funds to finance their campaigns, and special interests, not general interests, have an incentive and an ability to raise and offer campaign funds to legislators.

It might seem desirable to reduce politicians' dependence on raising funds for election campaigns. Various proposals for campaign finance reform have been proposed. For example, it has been proposed that campaigns be publicly financed through taxes.

But this raises difficult questions. How would public funds be allocated? Would funds go only to the two major parties? Does it violate freedom of expression if individuals are prohibited from spending their own money to express their views on political issues and support particular candidates?

The influence of special interests works through another channel. Elected government officials—legislators and executives—and their staffs may plan to leave government eventually and return to the private sector. They may want to obtain jobs with private firms that are currently lobbying them because of their position in government. If they respond favorably to the lobbying today, they may have a greater chance of being offered a job tomorrow. This is known as the *revolving door* problem.

Thus far we have described possible abuse initiated by the private sector. Abuse may also be initiated by the public sector. Government bureaucrats who administer bureaus—government departments in charge of particular programs—have an incentive to expand their programs and operations because expansion brings more pay, power, and prestige. They therefore have an interest in enlisting the support of private sector organizations to lobby legislators to expand their programs. They may be tempted to promise special treatment for private sector groups that help them win expansion. Rather than being dispassionate neutral players, bureaucrats may well be a dedicated and effective force for expanding government.[1]

The interaction of special interests in the private sector and in government bureaucracies creates prospects for corruption—that is, illegal and unethical behavior that sacrifices the public interest for personal gain. Private special interests may pay (bribe) government officials—directly (with cash) or indirectly (with gifts or a job upon leaving government)—to favor them in legislation or in regulation. Government bureaucrats may reward private organizations that help them expand their bureaus and programs, or they may make life difficult for private firms under their regulation unless these firms support their expansion or make payoffs to them.

Public Choice, Government Failure, and Constitutions

The *public choice* school of economists has argued that legislators, executives, and government bureaucrats are generally biased toward expanding government beyond what is best for the public.[2] According to this perspective, it is naive to assume that "government" is a neutral and benevolent servant of the public. On the contrary, legislators, executives, and bureaucrats have an incentive and, unless restrained by a constitution, the power to enact and implement laws and regulations that inflate government and do more harm than good—that is, a tendency to government failure is the rule, not the exception.

Public choice economists argue that legislators, executives, and bureaucrats need to be restrained by a constitution that limits their power to expand government and do harm. For example, the constitution should contain provisions such as a limit on the percentage of GDP that a government can spend, a requirement that the budget be balanced, and a limit on how many terms an elected official can serve.

Although most economists accept the basic point that government, like markets, may fail, many question the specific points of the public choice school. They note that pervasive advertising in our society promotes private sector goods, not government programs, so that there may be a bias toward private sector goods. Legislators and

[1] William Niskanen, *Bureaucracy and Representative Government*. Aldine, 1971.

[2] Geoffrey Brennan and James Buchanan, *The Power to Tax: The Analytical Foundations of a Fiscal Constitution*. Cambridge University Press, 1980.

executives surely have an incentive to be reelected, but it is not obvious that expanding government is always the best way to be reelected. For example, Presidents Reagan and George W. Bush were successful in getting elected by promising tax and spending cuts. Similarly, many legislators have been successful in elections by giving a high priority to cutting taxes and spending.

Bureaucrats no doubt want to expand their departments and programs, but it is legislators (with the approval of the executive), not bureaucrats, who decide the size of departments and programs. Some constitutional limits may be useful, but others may impose a straitjacket that prevents desired flexibility by government. For example, in a recession, government budgets automatically go into deficit because tax revenues drop, and a requirement to promptly balance the budget (which can only be achieved by either raising taxes or cutting government spending) is likely to reduce demand, thereby making the recession worse, so any balanced budget requirement must be carefully drawn to avoid this problem (this issue is discussed in Chapter 13 on government borrowing).

Summary

A public good is a good or service that has two properties: (1) nonexcludability and (2) nonrivalry. Nonexcludability means that it is hard to exclude any person—even if the person won't pay for it—from benefiting from the good or service. Nonrivalry means that consumption by one person of the good or service does not prevent consumption by other people; in fact, all individuals simultaneously consume the same quantity of the good. Nonexcludability means that it is hard to get many individuals to voluntarily pay for a public good because each person knows that he can't be excluded from benefiting if the good is produced, so each is tempted to be a free rider who benefits without paying. The standard approach to the free-rider problem is taxation. Because everyone benefits, everyone should be compelled to contribute.

The problems posed by a public good were illustrated through the example of an island wall. The three families on the island must decide whether to have a defensive wall built, and if so, how thick it should be. Given the preferences of the three families and the cost of the wall, there is a socially optimal wall thickness. If the families agree to share the cost of the wall in proportion to their benefit, they will unanimously agree on how thick to make the wall. But if the cost-shares are assigned differently, they will disagree on how thick to make the wall. If they are unwilling to alter the cost-shares to achieve unanimity, they will need a mechanism to break the deadlock. Majority-rule voting is one mechanism. Sometimes majority-rule voting works well and yields the social optimum as a stable, clear winner. However, other times majority-rule voting does not yield the social optimum, and sometimes it does not even yield a stable, clear winner.

Political economy is the study of how government should behave with respect to goods and services and how it actually behaves. We considered legislators, policies, elections, logrolling, lobbying, special interests, campaign financing, bureaucracies, corruption, public choice, government failure, and constitutions.

Key Terms

political economy, *57*
public good, *58*
nonexcludability, *58*
nonrivalry, *58*
private good, *58*
altruistic, *58*
free riders, *59*

tax, *59*
efficient, *62*
inefficient, *62*
cost-share, *64*
global public
  good, *65*
median voter, *67*

proportional tax, *69*
progressive tax, *69*
regressive tax, *69*
logrolling, *71*
lobbying, *72*
bureaucrats, *74*
corruption, *74*

Questions

Questions 1 to 7 concern a different wall on a different island with families A, B, and C.

1. The ratio $MB_A:MB_B:MB_C$ is 5:2:1 at any thickness. For example, at a thickness of 0 feet, $MB_A = \$1,000$, $MB_B = \$400$, $MB_C = \$200$, and at a thickness of 5 feet, $MB_A = \$500$, $MB_B = \$200$, $MB_C = \$100$. The marginal cost (MC) of building an additional foot of thickness is $800. Draw the diagram, label the curves (lines), and show numbers.

2. Would it be socially optimal to increase wall thickness above 0 feet? Would it be socially optimal to decrease wall thickness below 10 feet? Explain why or why not.

3. Suppose A, B, and C are taxed the same dollar amount ($_____ per foot). Then A would prefer (*more, less*) than 5 feet, while C would prefer (*more, less*) than 5 feet.

4. A, B, and C would all prefer 5 feet if their taxes are $_____, $_____, and $_____ per foot.

In questions 5 to 7, "optimal tax" means the tax that induces all families to prefer the socially optimal thickness.

5. Suppose A's income is 5 times C's income. Then the optimal tax to finance the wall is (*progressive, proportional, regressive*), because A has 5 times as much income as C and pays _____ times as much tax.

6. Suppose A's income is 3 times C's. Then the optimal tax to finance the wall is (*progressive, proportional, regressive*), because A has 3 times as much income as C and pays _____ times as much tax.

7. Suppose A's income is 7 times C's. Then the optimal tax to finance the wall is (*progressive, proportional, regressive*), because A has 7 times as much income as C and pays _____ times as much tax.

Questions 8 and 9 concern voting. The preferences are shown in the table. Each family (H, M, L, and D) votes between two choices (such as thick and thin) and then between two other choices.

Choice	H	M	L	D
First	Thick	Intermediate	Thin	Thin
Second	Intermediate	Thin	Intermediate	Thick
Third	Thin	Thick	Thick	Intermediate

8. With H, M, and L voting, but not D, what happens? Why?

9. With H, M, and D voting, but not L, what happens? Why?

10. Using a diagram, discuss primary and general elections involving Dove and Hawk.

11. Discuss subsidies and tariffs for ethanol. Explain the effects of either a subsidy or a tariff.

12. Go online and read about the controversy in the 1990s to enact an amendment to the U.S. Constitution that would require Congress and the president to adhere to a balanced budget. Briefly summarize the position of advocates and opponents.

13. Go online and read about pork-barrel projects. What do you think should be done about them?

Chapter **Four**

Cost-Benefit Analysis

Charles Smith/Corbis

Cost-benefit analysis is the measuring of the costs of a project and the benefits of a project to help decide whether to undertake the project and what the scale of the project should be. Consider these decisions facing government: Should a particular highway be built? Should improvements be made in a highway to make it safer? How much should carbon fuel use be cut (through a carbon tax or permits) to reduce global warming? Should Medicare pay for costly treatment X? Should a military intervention be undertaken? In these and many other decisions, economists recommend weighing cost against benefit to help guide the decision. In this chapter, using these examples, we examine how cost-benefit analysis can help us arrive at better decisions in the public sector.

The basic principle of cost-benefit analysis is simple:

A project should be undertaken if its benefit to society exceeds its cost to society. The scale of such a project should be increased as long as the marginal social benefit (MSB) exceeds the marginal social cost (MSC) so that the optimal scale occurs where MSB equals MSC.

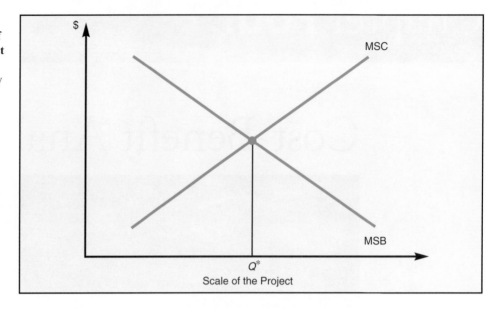

Scale of the Project

The optimal scale of an investment project is shown in Figure 4.1. At any scale of the project less than Q^*, the MSB exceeds the MSC so it is socially optimal to increase the scale another unit. At any scale of the project greater than Q^*, the MSB is less than the MSC so it is socially optimal to decrease the scale another unit. Hence, the optimal scale is Q^*. The challenge comes in measuring and comparing the marginal social benefit, which comes in the future, to the marginal social cost, which occurs in the present.

In discussing cost-benefit analysis, economists and others often drop the word *marginal* and simply say that an investment should be undertaken as long as the benefit exceeds the cost. We follow this convention by usually omitting the word *marginal*. Remember, however, that the question is not simply whether a project should be undertaken but also whether the scale (quantity or quality) of the project is optimal. Finding the optimal scale involves comparing the marginal benefit from raising the quantity or quality an *additional* (*marginal*) unit with the marginal cost of that additional unit.

Some noneconomists have criticized cost-benefit analysis because they believe it is unethical to weigh a benefit such as a life saved or a reduction in global warming against money—its cost. But cost, though measured in money, means **opportunity cost**—the benefit that could have been enjoyed by using the resources to produce other goods and services. Thus, cost-benefit analysis is a means of comparing the benefit from one project to the benefit people could have enjoyed by using the resources to make other goods or services.

COST-BENEFIT ANALYSIS

Private firms and individuals use cost-benefit analysis all the time. Firm managers compare the cost of a new factory or machine to its benefit: the increase in future profits. Individuals compare the cost of higher education or training to its benefit: the increase in future earnings. The principles of cost-benefit analysis therefore apply to firms, individuals, and government. Whoever is weighing cost against benefit faces essentially the same problem: measuring costs, measuring benefits, and recognizing the role of the interest rate in converting a future value to a "present value." When government uses cost-benefit analysis, measuring benefits is often difficult because the analyst must rely on imperfect methods, such as revealed preference and contingent valuation. We begin with an example in which a private firm weighs cost against benefit. We then consider several examples in which the government weighs cost against benefit.

A PRIVATE FIRM

Building a Factory

Consider a firm with expanding demand for its product. With its current factory the firm is already producing at capacity, so to take advantage of the expanding demand, the firm would have to build another factory. To decide whether it is worth building another factory, the firm must compare the cost of building the factory with the benefit—the additional profit that can be made by producing and selling more. In order to keep things as simple as possible, we assume there is no taxation.

Suppose that the factory would be built in one year (year 0) and that it will last only one year (year 1) before wearing out. The construction cost in year 0 would be $100,000, and the profit (*excluding any interest cost due to borrowing*) in year 1 would be $110,000. Should the firm build it? The answer depends on whether the interest rate at that time is greater or less than 10%.

Building with Borrowing

Suppose the firm must borrow $100,000 in year 0 to pay for the construction cost, and will repay the loan in year 1. If the interest rate is 5%, the firm must repay $105,000; the profit of $110,000 would more than cover the loan repayment, and the correct decision is to build. However, if the interest rate is 15%, the firm must repay $115,000; the profit of $110,000 would not cover the loan repayment, and the correct decision is not to build.

Present Value

It is useful to consider an equivalent way of arriving at the decision. The $100,000 cost occurs this year—in the present—but the $110,000 profit occurs next year—in the future. Is the $110,000 next year enough? We take the present value (PV) of the $110,000 which equals $110,000/(1 + r)$ where r is the interest rate:

$$\text{PV of \$110,000 in year 1} = \frac{\$110,000}{(1 + r)}$$

If $r = 10\%$, the PV of $110,000 in year 1 equals $100,000 today in year 0.

The **present value (PV)** of a future amount at a future date is the amount you would need to put in the bank today to have that future amount by that future date.

In this example, you would have to put $100,000 in the bank today (year 0) to have $110,000 by next year (year 1). Clearly, present value depends on the interest rate.

Present value is sometimes called the *present discounted value* to emphasize the fact that it is obtained by dividing the future value by a number greater than 1—that is, discounting the future value. In particular, the future value is divided by (1 + the discount rate); in our example, the discount rate is the interest rate. We omit the word *discounted* and use the term *present value* and the abbreviation *PV*.

	r = 5%	r = 15%
PV of profit	$104,762	$ 95,652
Cost of project	100,000	100,000
Correct decision	Build	Don't build

Taking the present value is the opposite of compounding. If you put $100,000 in the bank in year 0 and the interest rate r is 10%, it would compound to $110,000 in year 1. So having $110,000 in year 1 is equivalent to having $100,000 in year 0. Hence, with $r = 10\%$, the PV of $110,000 in year 1 is $100,000.

If $r = 5\%$, the PV of $110,000 equals $104,762; and if $r = 15\%$, the PV of $110,000 equals $95,652. This leads us to the correct decision rule shown in Table 4.1: Build the factory if the PV of the future profit, $110,000, is greater than the cost, $100,000; don't build the factory if the PV of the profit is less than the cost.

Building without Borrowing

Suppose the firm has the cash from past profits to build another factory without borrowing. The decision to build *still* depends on whether the interest rate is greater or less than 10%—equivalently, on whether the PV of the profit exceeds the cost ($100,000). At first glance, it might seem that without borrowing, the interest rate is irrelevant, but this is not so. If the firm doesn't build the factory, it can keep its $100,000 in the bank so that it earns interest. If $r = 5\%$, the bank account would grow to $105,000 next year, so it would be better to build the factory and earn a profit of $110,000 next year. However, if $r = 15\%$, the bank account would grow to $115,000 next year, so it would be better not to build the factory.

Thus, whether or not the firm must borrow, it remains true that the correct decision is to build the factory if and only if the PV of the profit (computed using the actual interest rate) exceeds the cost. The numbers in Table 4.1 remain relevant. If $r = 5\%$, the PV of the profit will be $104,762 so the factory should be built. If $r = 15\%$, the PV of the profit will be $95,652 so the factory shouldn't be built.

Multiyear Profits

Now suppose that the factory lasts two years instead of one. Profit is $55,000 in year 1 and $60,500 in year 2. Then the present value of profits over the two years is

$$\text{PV of profits} = \left[\frac{\$55,000}{(1 + r)}\right] + \left[\frac{\$60,500}{(1 + r)^2}\right]$$

where r is the interest rate. Note that the year 1 profit is divided by $(1 + r)$ but the year 2 profit is divided by $(1 + r)^2$. Note also that if there were a year 3 profit, it would be divided by $(1 + r)^3$. If r is 10%, then:

$$\text{PV of profits} = \left(\frac{\$55,000}{1.10}\right) + \left(\frac{\$60,500}{1.10^2}\right) = \$50,000 + \$50,000 = \$100,000$$

If r is less than 10%, the PV of the profits will be greater than the cost ($100,000), and the factory should be built. If r is greater than 10%, the PV of the profits will be less than the cost ($100,000), and the factory should not be built. Thus, the correct decision rule remains the same: Build the factory if the PV of future profits is greater than the cost; don't build the factory if the PV of profits is less than the cost.

GOVERNMENT

Building a Highway

The same logic and analysis applies when the investment project is undertaken by government. While private firms invest in factories, government invests in *infrastructure,* such as roads and bridges. Let's consider the use of cost-benefit analysis to evaluate the construction of a highway.

The cost of the highway has two components: construction costs (e.g., labor, equipment, and asphalt) and future maintenance (repair) costs. Computing the present value by "discounting" future maintenance costs, and adding construction costs, gives the present value of the cost of the highway.

The benefit is how much drivers would be willing to pay to use the highway in all future years. Discounting each year's benefit and summing over all future years gives the present value of the benefits of the highway. But how can the benefits be estimated in practice?

Highways save drivers time, so it would be possible to estimate how many hours are saved. If we can then put a dollar value on the time that is saved, we would have an estimate of the benefits of the highway because this is what drivers should be willing to pay to use the highway. But how can we put a dollar value on time saved?

In order to put a dollar value on time saved, drivers can be placed along a spectrum, and different drivers' willingness to pay must be estimated and then aggregated. At one end of the spectrum are truck drivers carrying cargo. At the other end are people seeking noncommercial objectives, such as recreation, visiting friends, or vacation. In between are people commuting to work. For truck drivers with cargo, the issue is dollars and cents. The managers in business firms transporting cargo can figure out how much money they would save by reducing the time required to ship their goods; these managers should be willing to pay an amount equal to this saving from the time reduction. The first task of the cost-benefit analyst would be to estimate this cost saving of firms shipping cargo; this constitutes one important component of the total benefit of the highway. In the rest of this section, we concentrate on commuters and then provide a brief comment on noncommercial drivers.

There are at least three ways for the cost-benefit analyst to estimate the benefit to commuters: increased output, actual market behavior (revealed preference), and hypothetical questions and answers (contingent valuation). Let's consider each in turn.

Increased Output

One approach to measuring the benefits of time saved is to estimate how much more output commuters could produce at work. Economists generally assume that the wage a worker is paid provides a rough measure of the output the worker produces. Suppose a commuter would save an hour a day by using the highway. If the commuter works the hour instead of driving and is paid a wage of $20 an hour, economists estimate that the highway has enabled $20 more output to be produced. If the commuter works 250 days per year (5 days a week for 50 weeks), her additional annual wage income enabled by the highway is $5,000. Summing actual wage income enabled by the highway over all commuters yields an estimate of the annual aggregate increase in output made possible by the highway. The PV of benefits is obtained by discounting future annual benefits and summing over the life of the highway.

Actual Market Behavior (Revealed Preference)

Another approach to measuring the benefits of time saved is to look at commuter location preferences. Prior to the building of the highway, suppose we observe two homes in two different suburbs of the city, and each home is inhabited by a commuter who works in the city. The two homes are identical, and the suburban towns are identical; the only difference between the homes is the difference in commuting time to work (an hour a day for a roundtrip). The commuter in the home closer to the city actually paid $20,000 more for her home than the other commuter. It might then be argued that the actual payment of two different prices for the two homes "reveals" the value of time saved. Dividing $20,000 by the number of hours saved over a career of commuting yields an estimate of the value of an hour.

Of course, the conditions described above—identical homes, identical towns—seldom hold. Home prices differ because of differences in many factors, only one of which is commuter time. Given this reality, what can be done? Economists recommend using actual data to try to quantify the relationship between all these factors and home prices. Looking at actual data on the price of homes that differ in rooms, square feet, neighborhood safety, schools, and so on, as well as commuter time, economists can fit a regression equation to the actual data to provide a quantitative estimate of how much each factor affects the price of a home. By controlling for the impact of other factors in this way, it is possible to estimate the effect of commuter time on the price of a home and therefore assign a value to the benefit of saved time.

Hypothetical Questions and Answers (Contingent Valuation)

Another way to put a dollar value on time saved is to ask drivers hypothetical questions. A survey can be administered that asks commuters how much they would be willing to pay to reduce their daily commute one hour. This method is called *contingent valuation* because the question is hypothetical—the respondent knows she will not actually have to make the payment. Supporters of this method contend that it directly elicits the information needed and that survey results can be a reasonably reliable guide to how much individuals would pay if the choice were actual rather than hypothetical.

Critics contend that the surveys produce unreliable results. They note that the answers may be sensitive to the exact wording, presentation, and context of the questions. For example, consider the following four ways of asking about the dollar value of saving an hour commuting:

1. How much would you pay to reduce your daily commute one hour?
2. Considering traffic, how much would you pay to reduce your daily commute one hour?
3. Considering what you could earn at work, how much would you pay to reduce your daily commute one hour?
4. Considering the time you could spend with your children, how much would you pay to reduce your daily commute one hour?

It is possible that despite the different wording most respondents would give roughly the same answer. It is also possible that the different wording would elicit substantially different answers. If so, which answer should be regarded as the best measure of benefit?

Supporters of contingent valuation reply that actual market behavior is also subject to similar problems. Consider the price that a commuter is willing to pay for a home closer to the city where she works. When the commuter decides the price to offer the seller for the home, she may think about commuting in traffic or calculate what she could earn at work or think about spending time with her children; what she chooses to think about may affect the price she offers and the actual price at which the home is purchased.

The order in which a consumer confronts goods at a department store or in a catalog may also affect willingness to pay and what the consumer purchases. If a consumer enters the store at one end or reads the catalog from the beginning, she may buy one set of goods; if she enters the store at the other end or reads a catalog from the end, she may buy another set of goods. A consumer's purchasing behavior may also be very different depending on whether she can use a credit card or must pay cash. A consumer may buy certain goods or services not because she gets direct utility from it but because she thinks others will approve of her behavior.

Supporters of contingent valuation contend that techniques are improving based on experience conducting surveys. Survey research is a field that must be taken seriously and treated rigorously: The design of the sample, the conducting of interviews, and the framing of questions all affect responses. Respondents must be asked about specific and realistic situations, not abstractions. Instead of asking, "What would you pay to prevent pollution in bays and harbors?" ask, "What would you pay for a new program that would limit damage from any future oil spill in the bay or harbor nearest to where you live?" To get respondents to take the questions seriously, they might be informed that the government is likely to use the results of the survey to decide whether to undertake the program in question. Polls like these are often used by news outlets to evaluate the benefit or popularity of proposed legislation.

Hypothetical Questions and Answers to Noncommercial Drivers

Similar questions can be asked to noncommercial drivers whose purpose is recreation, visiting friends, or vacation. For example, "How much would you pay to reduce by an hour your travel time for recreation, visiting friends, or vacation?" To evaluate a particular highway project, it would be useful to ask drivers about specific trips that could actually be made more quickly by the proposed highway.

Benefits of Improving the Safety of a Highway

Back to the new highway: Not all benefits can be measured by time saved. Compare the *safety* of three highways. Highway C has a single narrow lane in each direction with no guardrail or shoulder. Highway B has two narrow lanes in each direction with a guardrail and narrow shoulders. Highway A has several wide lanes in each direction, the two directions are separated by guardrails and substantial distance, and there are wide shoulders. The safer the highway, the greater the cost of building it. So which should be built?

The benefit of building the highway safer is the reduction in deaths and injuries. We must determine how this benefit can be valued so it can be compared to the cost. How can a value be put on lives saved and injuries avoided? Some people object to putting a specific dollar value on lives saved, but a decision about which highway to build must still be made. For many economists, the sensible thing to do is to try to put an approximate value on lives saved, which can then be compared to the cost in order to help make a sensible decision.

The methods for putting some sort of value on lives saved are the same as discussed above for putting a value on time saved commuting: increased output, actual market behavior (*revealed preference*), and hypothetical questions and answers (*contingent valuation*).

Increased Output

If someone dies on a busy highway, we can determine the output that person would have produced if she had survived without injury. An estimate of this output is the wage income the person would have earned over the rest of her life. This can be estimated by extrapolating from the person's actual past wage income.

Most economists find this method of estimating the value of a life saved unsatisfactory. Consider the implications. It may be true that person H would have produced 10 times more output than person L, but do we really want to value H's life as 10 times as valuable as L's? What about a person who doesn't work in the marketplace for a wage? The value of saving that person's life is surely not zero. Some economists suggest assigning a dollar value to the leisure time that people enjoy—at least this ensures that every life gets some dollar value. Finally, the benefit from a safer highway is greater than simply the work and leisure that the person can enjoy. The benefit includes the avoidance of suffering by the rest of the family—in coping with the shock of the accident and life thereafter. People might pay a lot to avoid such suffering, but this is ignored by focusing solely on the output that the deceased person would have produced.

Actual Market Behavior (Revealed Preference)

We can observe how much people actually pay in the marketplace to reduce their chance of dying. There are two ways to pay. The first is by buying a good or service that reduces the chance of dying. The second is by choosing a lower-paying job because it is less dangerous. Let's consider each.

Cars have various features that reduce the chance of dying in an accident—airbags, structural strength, and so forth. When people have a choice of whether to buy the safety feature or not, their decision reveals how much they value reducing the odds of dying. If a person chooses to pay $5,000 more for an auto structure that has a 1 in 100 chance of saving the life of a family member, then that person is revealing that she values a 1 in 100 chance of saving a family member's life by at least $5,000.

Suppose a coal miner has a 1 in 100 chance of death on the job, while a clerk who works in the mining town has no chance of death on the job, but a coal miner is paid $5,000 more than the clerk. The pay difference is called a **compensating differential**. It might be inferred that a person who chooses to be a clerk instead of a miner values a 1 in 100 chance of saving her own life by at least $5,000. Of course, this inference is based on the assumption that the only reason the person prefers to be a clerk rather than a miner is to minimize the chance of death on the job.

Hypothetical Questions and Answers (Contingent Valuation)

Another way to put a value on a life is to ask a hypothetical question. A survey can be administered that asks people the following question: "How much would you pay to reduce your chance of death on the highway from 2 in 1,000 to 1 in 1,000?"

Critics contend that the answer may depend on the exact wording of the question. Imagine another way of asking the question: "Considering the shock to your family if a relative died on a highway, how much would you pay to reduce the chance of death on the highway from 2 in 1,000 to 1 in 1,000?"

It is possible that most respondents would give roughly the same answer to both questions, but it is also possible that the different wording would elicit substantially different answers.

Supporters of contingent valuation reply that actual market behavior has a similar problem. When a consumer in a car showroom is about to choose safety features for

On August 1, 2007, the interstate highway bridge over the Mississippi River at Minneapolis, Minnesota, collapsed, killing 13, injuring 80, and stranding many cars precariously over the river. The shock of the collapse reverberated around the country. Many claimed that the collapse shows that U.S. bridges and highways (infrastructure) are inadequately maintained and inadequately inspected. The American Society of Civil Engineers estimates that roughly a quarter of U.S. bridges are "structurally deficient or functionally obsolete" and calls for a very large federal expenditure to remedy the deficiency.

Economists, however, recommend that cost-benefit analysis be applied to decisions concerning infrastructure maintenance and inspection. Clearly, additional maintenance and inspection have a benefit, but they also have a cost. Additional maintenance or inspection should be undertaken as long as the marginal benefit exceeds the marginal cost, but additional maintenance or inspection should not be undertaken once the

marginal benefit drops below the marginal cost. Hence, there is a socially optimal amount of maintenance and inspection—the amount at which the marginal benefit equals the marginal cost.

Thus, a bridge collapse is tragic for its victims but in itself does not tell us whether maintenance and inspection have been socially optimal. To decide this question, there is no substitute for estimating the dollar cost of additional maintenance and inspection and comparing it to an estimate of the dollar benefit from reducing the probability that a collapse will occur. One way of estimating the dollar benefit would be to survey a representative sample of the population and ask them how much they would be willing to pay to reduce the probability of collapse by another percentage point (say from 2% to 1%). The aggregate amount that people would be willing to pay should then be compared to the cost incurred in reducing the probability another percentage point as estimated by bridge engineers.

her new car, she may or may not think about the shock to her family and the hardships they would face if she were killed in a highway accident. What the consumer happens to think about at the moment of decision may determine her decision.

The Value of a Statistical Life

Whenever a project would save lives, it is handy for practitioners of cost-benefit analysis to have a rough dollar estimate of the **value of a statistical life (VSL)**—the value of the life of someone we don't know personally. If a highway safety project is estimated to save 10 lives per year and the VSL is estimated to be about $8 million, then the project's benefit from lives saved can be estimated as about $80 million per year, which can then be compared to the project's cost to decide whether the project should be undertaken. Harvard economists Kip Viscusi and Joseph Aldy, after a comprehensive review of empirical research, report a median estimate of the VSL that in 2008 dollars would be about $8 million (they reported an average VSL of about $7 million in 2003 which translates into about $8 million today due to inflation).[1]

It is important to emphasize that the estimate of $8 million per life should be used with great caution. Many controversial assumptions and techniques are used in studies to arrive at a dollar estimate of a statistical life. Varying these assumptions and techniques might well cause a large change in the VSL estimate. Moreover, the appropriate value of the VSL might vary according to the project being considered. The figure of $8 million per life doesn't distinguish between a young life and an old life—while some citizens would value any life the same, others would not. The $8 million figure also doesn't distinguish between the kind of death that is avoided, but people may feel

[1] Kip Viscusi and Joseph Aldy, "The Value of a Statistical Life: A Critical Review of Market Estimates throughout the World," *Journal of Risk and Uncertainty* 27, no. 1, pp. 5–76.

differently about whether the death that is avoided by the project would have been from a highway accident, drowning, burning, bombing, shooting, and so forth, and they might be willing to pay different dollar amounts to reduce the chance of particular kinds of death.

Mistakes to Avoid

Supporters of proposed projects are naturally tempted to overestimate benefits. Objective analysts should be on guard to avoid several mistakes. We consider each in turn.

Counting Job Creation as a Benefit

How often have you heard a politician defend a government spending project by saying it will "create jobs"? This assertion implies that a cost-benefit evaluation of a project should count as a benefit the jobs created. But it shouldn't. Why not? Because the issue is whether to create jobs in the project being evaluated or let jobs be created elsewhere in the local economy. Hence, labor used in the project should be counted as a cost, not a benefit.

Double Counting the Same Benefit

Building a highway reduces commuter time which causes the value of suburban homes to rise. The value of time saved should be counted as a benefit, but it would be double counting to add the rise in value of the suburban homes.

Counting Secondary Benefits

Benefits should be measured as the amount that direct users of the project would be willing to pay for its use. For example, the benefit of a highway is the amount drivers would be willing to pay in tolls to use it. The demands of all drivers—individuals and employees of companies—should be counted. What shouldn't be counted are indirect secondary benefits to individuals and business firms that do not use the highway.

REDUCING GLOBAL WARMING

Cost-benefit analysis can also be applied to a broader issue like global warming. How much should each country cut back on its emission of greenhouse gases such as carbon dioxide in an effort to combat global warming? Cutting back is costly—carbon fuel combustion must be reduced, thereby reducing driving and goods that are produced using fuel. Assume such a cutback is likely to reduce global warming in the future. Such a reduction in warming would benefit many (though not all) countries. Cutting back should occur as long as the marginal cost of further cutback is less than the marginal benefit of further reduction in future warming.

Suppose a carbon tax is the method used to induce the cutback. If the tax is $50 per ton, then it will be profitable for fuel producers to cut back as long as the marginal cost of cutback is less than $50 and to stop when the marginal cost reaches $50. This must be compared to the marginal benefit resulting from that last unit of cutback. If the marginal benefit is greater than $50, then the tax should be raised to induce more cutback. The tax should be adjusted until the marginal cost equals the marginal benefit.

The benefit occurs in the future when there would be less warming as a consequence of less emission today. Suppose it is estimated that the additional future warming from another ton emitted today would reduce crops by X, raise air-conditioning by Y, and flood coastal property worth Z. If these total $50, current cutback is optimal; if they total more than $50, further cutback is optimal; and if they total less than $50, less cutback is optimal.

Uncertainty and the Risk of Catastrophe

Suppose there is a small chance that failure to reduce global warming will lead to catastrophe—enormous values for $X, $Y, and $Z. Then it is unsatisfactory simply to use the most likely values of $X, $Y, and $Z and compare them to the cost of reducing global warming. The analysis should incorporate the possibility that the future benefit of reducing global warming will be huge—avoiding a catastrophe.

One way to incorporate the possibility of catastrophe is to use a weighted average of the most likely values and the catastrophic values of $X, $Y, and $Z, where the weights for the catastrophic values equal the estimated probability of occurrence. Of course, the probability can only be estimated, not known with certainty, but some adjustment is surely better than simply ignoring the possibility of catastrophe in weighing cost against benefit to arrive at a decision.

The Social Discount Rate

To compare today's cost to tomorrow's benefit, analysts must discount the future benefit to obtain the present value. They must determine what should be the **social discount rate**—the rate analysts use to compute the present value of future benefits. The higher the social discount rate, the lower the PV of future benefits, and the less likely that the marginal benefit will exceed the marginal cost for the proposed government policy.

For a business firm seeking profit, the market interest rate at which the firm can actually borrow is utilized as the discount rate. For a government that is building or improving a highway, the market interest rate at which the government can actually borrow is also generally utilized as the proper discount rate. In both cases, the market interest rate indicates what could have been generated by the funds through alternative investments if the funds were not used by the firm or the government.

For a very long-term problem that spans generations, like global warming, there is less of a consensus about whether the market interest rate is the appropriate discount rate. Some economists contend that because the central issue is the trade-off between the well-being of different generations (rather than the same generation at different ages in its life cycle), the social discount rate—the rate the government should use for a cost-benefit evaluation of a long-term policy—should be lower than the actual market interest rate at which the government can borrow.

Other economists favor using the market interest rate. They argue that if a particular policy fails the cost-benefit test using a market interest rate, this means that the policy is not the best way for the current generation to help a future generation. Instead, the current generation should use the funds to save and invest productively for the future, earning a return equal to the market interest rate. Rather than cut back today's output to cut back carbon, the current generation should save and invest more, leaving future generations with a higher capital stock to compensate for the warming. For an example of the importance of the discount rate, see the box "The Debate over the 2006 Stern Review on Global Warming."

Cost-Effectiveness Analysis

Needless to say, estimating the future benefits of reducing global warming is extremely difficult. A more modest goal is to make sure that any reduction in global warming is done at minimum cost to the economy. This requires **cost-effectiveness** analysis

Current Research   The Debate over the 2006 Stern Review on Global Warming

In November 2006, a comprehensive report on global warming was released in Britain with the endorsement of then Prime Minister Tony Blair. The report's primary author was the economist Nicholas Stern, and the report was called *The Stern Review on the Economics of Climate Change*. The *Stern Review* estimated that a failure to sharply and promptly reduce greenhouse gas emissions to a particular target would cause damage equal to 5% of GDP per year. Hence, the benefit of reducing emissions from the projected level under business as usual to the Stern target would be 5% of global GDP per year. The *Stern Review* estimated that the cost of this sharp and prompt emissions reduction would be only 1% of global GDP per year.

In his 2007 review of the *Stern Review*, economist William Nordhaus of Yale University,* who has constructed empirical economic models of global warming, reports that his most recent model, also based on cost-benefit analysis, prescribes a much more moderate gradual "ramping up" of emissions reduction than the *Stern Review*. Nordhaus's model prescribes a carbon tax today of $17 per ton, while the *Stern Review* prescribes a carbon tax today of $311 per ton.

According to Nordhaus, the main reason for the huge difference in their policy recommendations is the choice of the value for the social discount rate. In his review, Nordhaus says that the *Stern Review* uses a near-zero social discount rate, so that benefits that occur in the far future from reducing global warming are given the same weight as costs that occur in the present. Nordhaus says that if the *Stern Review* had used the standard positive social discount rate used in most cost-benefit studies (roughly 3%), which gives much less weight to benefits in the far future than costs in the present, its prescription would have been similar to his model's prescription. Nordhaus runs his economic model first with his standard social discount rate of 3% and then with the *Stern Review*'s 0.1% discount rate. He finds that with his discount rate a carbon tax of $17 per ton should be imposed today rising gradually to $84 in 2050 and $270 in 2100, so that the optimal rate of emissions reduction is 6% today, 14% in 2050, and 25% in 2100. But when he runs his model with the *Stern Review*'s near-zero discount rate (0.1%), he finds that his model would then prescribe the optimal carbon tax today to be $159 (instead of $17), and optimal emissions reduction in 2015 would be 50%. The *Stern Review* itself prescribes a carbon tax today of $311, so the discount rate is not the sole reason for the huge difference, but it is clearly a key reason for the difference.

Another reason for the difference is the way the two models compare persons with different levels of consumption. If productivity continues to advance with technological progress, then people in the future will enjoy much higher per capita consumption than people today. Emissions reduction today to reduce global warming tomorrow means sacrificing consumption by people today in order to prevent a sacrifice in consumption by people in the future. However, people in the future will be able to "afford" a sacrifice in consumption more than people today, because they will be starting from a much higher level of consumption due to technological progress. Nordhaus says that the *Stern Review* does not sufficiently recognize this difference.

How can we decide which social discount rate and which comparison of persons with different levels of consumption are the proper ones to use in a cost-benefit analysis of global warming? Nordhaus offers one way. He says to look at the actual saving rate of most economies. Saving is the main way that people sacrifice today in order to benefit in the future. Nordhaus argues that the actual saving rate reveals how much people value future consumption relative to present consumption and how they compare a sacrifice starting from different levels of consumption. He says that the values he uses in his model generate a saving rate for the economy that corresponds to the actual saving rate observed, while the *Stern Review*'s values imply a saving rate much higher than we observe.

* William D. Nordhaus, "A Review of the *Stern Review on the Economics of Climate Change*," *Journal of Economic Literature* 45, no. 3 (September 2007), pp. 686–702.

rather than cost-benefit analysis. With cost-effectiveness analysis, no attempt is made to compare the benefit with the cost. Cost-effectiveness analysis focuses on achieving a given objective at minimum cost. The case for imposing the same carbon tax on all emitters in all countries is that whatever the reduction in global warming, that reduction will be achieved at minimum cost to the economy (as explained in Chapter 2). Cost-effectiveness analysis, unlike cost-benefit analysis, does not try to determine the optimal level of reducing global warming.

PAYING FOR A COSTLY MEDICAL TREATMENT

One of the most difficult and important applications of cost-benefit analysis concerns medical care. Advances in technology, medication, and medical procedures have made it possible to cure medical conditions that previously could not be treated, but often the new technology, medication, or procedure is expensive. Naturally, patients and their families usually want access to the best treatments, which also tend to be costly. The key issue becomes: Will the insurer—government or private—pay for costly treatment X? Any economist would reply that there should be a weighing of the benefit of X against its cost to arrive at a decision.

Nevertheless, many people say they are ethically opposed to having cost considered. As long as the technology, medication, or procedure is judged "safe and effective," they believe the insurer should pay for it. They contend that insurers should be obligated to pay unless they can prove that X is either unsafe or ineffective. Conversely, insurers contend that until X has been proved safe and effective, they should not be required to pay for it. What insurers and patients have in common is that neither will admit that cost should be considered.

But imagine that treatment X, judged safe and effective, can extend the life of a patient from 100 to 101 years but at a cost of *$1 million* per patient. Should Medicare, the health insurance program for retirees that is operated by the federal government, pay for treatment X for patients who are 100 years old? Suppose that if Medicare pays, 1,000 patients who are 100 years old would request treatment X so the cost to Medicare would be *$1 billion*. Is it really sensible to ignore cost, or should the criterion instead be that X must not only be safe and effective but also have an acceptable cost-benefit ratio?

One way to measure the benefit in this situation would be to ask hypothetical questions and answers—the method of *contingent valuation*—as we discussed under highway safety. But to whom should the questions be directed? One option would be to ask old sick persons and their families how much they would be willing to pay to obtain treatment X. Another option would be to ask middle-age persons how much they would be willing to pay today to have treatment X available should they need it when they become old and sick. It seems likely that old sick persons and their families would pay more than middle-age persons and their families who have the same income. If so, the measure of benefit might be an average of how much they would be willing to pay.

The question can be refined further. One question might ask people how much they would pay to extend life from 100 to 101; another question, from 90 to 91; another, from 80 to 81. It seems likely that people would be willing to pay less for an extension from 100 to 101 than from 80 to 81. Suppose people are willing to pay more than the cost of treatment X for the extension from 80 to 81 but less than the cost for extension from 100 to 101. Should public policy consider "age rationing"—making treatment X available to 80-year-olds but not 100-year-olds? These are surely difficult issues—so difficult that some are inclined to say they oppose any kind of cost-benefit analysis for these questions.

But what is the alternative? If someone says that "life is priceless" and weighing cost is "immoral," then any treatment X that might save any lives would always be approved. But the resources absorbed by treatment X then cannot be used to save lives through treatment Y; nor can the resources be used in other ways to make life better for people. So the issue is not life versus money. Resources used here cannot be used elsewhere—resources have an opportunity cost. The issue is how best to use resources to promote the well-being of people. Economists contend that some kind of cost-benefit analysis, despite its difficulties, is a useful tool to help allocate resources to promote such well-being.

INTERVENING MILITARILY

Should a particular military intervention be undertaken? The answer should be based on weighing the cost of the intervention against its benefit—in other words, on a cost-benefit analysis. Of course, the answer cannot be given solely by economic analysis. Evaluating the benefit of the particular military intervention must rely heavily on the disciplines of history, international relations, political science, and military science. However, economics can contribute to an evaluation of the cost of a particular military intervention. When a military intervention is being contemplated, it should matter to the citizenry whether the cost is estimated to be $150 per person or $6,000 per person. A citizen may support the intervention if its estimated cost per person is $150, but she might oppose the intervention if its estimated cost per person is $6,000. Yet quite often there is little serious analysis or discussion of the estimated cost per person prior to a military intervention. Moreover, even when an aggregate analysis is done, it is seldom translated into a cost per person so that each citizen can ask herself, "Am I personally willing to bear this $X burden—that is, to give up $X of consumption of goods and services?"

The economic cost of a military intervention is much larger than the military budgetary cost that is incurred during the war. There are the costs of the lives lost and the suffering of veterans who must live with serious injuries. There are the medical costs and disability payments to veterans that will occur for many years. If the war is financed by borrowing instead of taxes, there are interest costs. There is the cost of replacing military hardware destroyed during the war. The war may raise the price of a valuable resource such as oil.

The best way to appreciate the complexity of applying cost-benefit analysis to a military intervention is to examine an actual example. The box titled "The 2003 U.S. Military Intervention in Iraq" shows cost-benefit analysis in practice.

Case Study   The 2003 U.S. Military Intervention in Iraq

In summer 2002, the Bush administration challenged Iraq's dictator Saddam Hussein to dismantle his program for developing weapons of mass destruction (chemical, biological, and nuclear) or face military consequences. Preparations for a U.S. military intervention in Iraq took place in fall and winter 2002; in spring 2003, the United States and several allies invaded Iraq and ousted Saddam Hussein from power. In May 2003, with U.S. combat deaths at about 150 people, President Bush declared major combat operations to be over. U.S. military forces, however, remained in Iraq to try to maintain stability. In December 2003, Saddam Hussein was captured by U.S. forces. Continuing resistance from insurgents took a steady toll of U.S. soldiers. By July 2004, cumulative U.S. combat deaths approached 1,000. The U.S. military pacification of Iraq has continued to the present with cumulative U.S. combat deaths passing 4,000.

In September 2002, as the Bush administration prepared for a military intervention in Iraq, economist Lawrence Lindsey, the head of President Bush's National Economic Council, publicly estimated that the cost of such an intervention might be roughly $150 billion (Lindsey said between $100 and $200 billion).[1] The Bush administration (the White House and Defense Department) quickly disagreed with Lindsey and estimated the cost of an intervention as only about 30% of Lindsey's estimate (the administration said less than $50 billion—we'll infer $45 billion) based on the experience of the Unites States' 1991 removal of Saddam Hussein's Iraqi military from Kuwait and the United States' post-9/11 attack on the ruling terrorist-supporting Taliban (who had been hosting Osama bin Laden's Al-Qaeda training camps) in Afghanistan. These aggregate numbers were not translated to cost per person at the time, but it is worth noting here that Lindsey's cost of $150 billion (1 billion is 10^9) translates to $500 per person (because with 300 million Americans, 150×10^9 divided by 300×10^6 equals 0.5×10^3 or $500). The estimate of the Bush administration was therefore that the cost per person would be 30% of $500, or *$150 per person* (45×10^9 divided by 300×10^6 equals 0.15×10^3 or $150).

NORDHAUS

In late 2002, Yale economist William Nordhaus published a much higher estimate—40 times as great.[2] The main reason for the huge difference is that Nordhaus rejected a "quick victory" scenario. Nordhaus conceded that a quick victory would involve a cost of about $100 billion (halfway between Lindsey's estimate and the administration's estimate)—roughly twice the administration's estimate of $45 billion; on a per person basis, roughly $300 per person instead of the administration's $150 per person. He contended that it was likely that the intervention would be followed by "a prolonged conflict and nasty outcomes" due to a long-lasting resistance against the U.S. military occupation. He presented a table with numerical cost estimates showing "the array of costs that might be incurred if the war drags on, occupation is lengthy, nation-building is costly, the war destroys a large part of Iraq's oil infrastructure, there is lingering military and political resistance in the Islamic world to U.S. occupation, and there are major adverse psychological reactions to the conflict." He estimated a cost of $1.9 trillion—$1,900 billion, or 19 times greater than the $100 billion cost of a quick victory and about 40 times the administration's estimate of $45 billion. Translated to a cost per person, Nordhaus's estimate is roughly $6,000 per person, because with 300 million Americans, $1,900 \times 10^9$ divided by 300×10^6 equals 6.3×10^3 or roughly *$6,000 per person—40 times the administration's estimate of $150 per person.*

WALLSTEN AND KOSEC

In mid-2006, Scott Wallsten and Katrina Kosec, two analysts at the American Enterprise Institute, noted that while the U.S. federal budgetary cost of the Iraq war and pacification over the three years since the invasion had cost about $300 billion, they estimated that the full economic cost of the war as of mid-2006 was about $500 billion—half a trillion.[3] An important cost omitted from the budget is the cost of death and injuries. Based on studies by Harvard economist Kip Viscusi on the value of a statistical life (VSL), they assigned a cost of $7.5 million to each

(continued)

Case Study   The 2003 U.S. Military Intervention in Iraq   *(continued)*

American life lost. At the time of their study, 2,400 U.S. soldiers had died in Iraq, implying a cost of $18 billion. Similarly, based on studies of the cost of injuries of varying severity, they estimated a cost of $23 billion for the 18,000 U.S. soldiers who had been wounded. Because of Iraq's lower per capita income, they used lower values for each Iraqi dead or wounded, but they still arrive at an Iraqi casualty cost of $150 billion. About 40% of U.S. troops in Iraq were from National Guard and Reserves who left their civilian jobs; they estimated this redeployment reduced U.S. output over the period by about $12 billion. They estimated that the war saved about $100 billion by stopping Saddam Hussein from killing his usual 10,000 Iraqis per year and by making economic sanctions of Iraq unnecessary. Subtracting this $100 billion from the $500 billion yielded a net cost of the war of $400 billion *as of mid-2006*. Dividing by 300 million yields a cost per person of about $1,300 *as of mid-2006*.

STIGLITZ AND BILMES

Also in 2006, economists Joseph Stiglitz and Linda Bilmes estimated that the full cost of the Iraq War would end up exceeding $2.3 trillion, or roughly *$7,500 per person* ($2,300 × 10^9 divided by 300 × 10^6 equals 7.7 × 10^3); note that $7,500 per person is *50 times* the Bush administration's prewar estimate of $150 per person (and 25% higher than Nordhaus's prewar estimate of $6,000 per person).[4] They too argued that the economic cost of the war is much larger than the federal budgetary cost during the war. They contended that a major component of long-term cost is medical care and disability benefits to veterans. Another cost is replacing the military hardware destroyed in the war. Another is the interest cost due to the financing of the war by borrowing rather than taxes. They use $6.5 million as the value of each life lost and add in an estimated cost of living with serious injuries. They included the lost output to the economy of redeploying civilians to the military. Finally they estimated that the war raised the world oil price by $10 per barrel, imposing a corresponding cost on oil users.

All these analyses focused on the cost, but a cost estimate alone would not have been enough to determine a citizen's decision. Suppose that in fall 2002 the American public had been given an estimated cost per person of military intervention in Iraq. Each citizen would then have to weigh this estimated cost against the *perceived* benefit of an intervention. *Ideally*, each citizen would be given accurate information about the state of Saddam Hussein's program to develop weapons of mass destruction and what he planned to do if he succeeded in developing such weapons—for example, move his army into Kuwait and Saudi Arabia to take control of their oil fields, or sell some of his new weapons to Al-Qaeda, or move his army through Jordan into the West Bank to confront the Israeli army. *Ideally*, each citizen would also have accurate information about what the U.S. government planned to do after the invasion: Would the United States withdraw its military as soon as Saddam Hussein was removed from power and was no longer a threat to do any of the above; or instead would it keep its military in Iraq fighting against insurgents for as long as necessary to bring stability and democracy to the country?

The cost of removing Saddam Hussein from power and then leaving would be much less than the cost of removing him and then staying and fighting insurgents for as long as it takes to achieve stability and democracy. *In practice*, in fall 2002 citizens did *not* have reliable information about the state of Saddam Hussein's weapons programs or his military intentions, nor did the U.S. government. Citizens were also uncertain about their own government's postinvasion plans (perhaps the U.S. government was also uncertain).

Thus, a cost estimate alone would not have decided the issue for a citizen. However, an accurate cost estimate would still have been helpful.

---

[1] Quoted in "Bush Economic Aide Says Cost of Iraq War May Top $100 Billion," *The Wall Street Journal*, September 16, 2002.

[2] William Nordhaus. "The Economic Consequences of a War with Iraq," chap. 3 in *War with Iraq: Costs, Consequences, and Alternatives* (American Academy of Arts & Sciences, 2002), pp. 51–85.

[3] Scott Wallsten and Katrina Kosec, "The Iraq War: The Economic Costs," *The Milken Institute Review*, Third Quarter 2006, pp. 16–23.

[4] Joseph Stiglitz and Linda Bilmes, "Encore," *The Milken Institute Review*, Fourth Quarter 2006, pp. 76–83.

Summary

In this chapter we saw how cost-benefit analysis can be helpful in arriving at better decisions in the public sector. A project should be undertaken if its benefit to society exceeds its cost to society; moreover, the scale of such a project should be increased as long as the marginal social benefit (MSB) exceeds the marginal social cost (MSC) so that the optimal scale occurs where the marginal social benefit equals the marginal social cost.

Private firms and individuals often use cost-benefit analysis. Firm managers compare the cost of a new factory or machine to its benefit (the increase in future profits), and individuals compare the cost of higher education or training to its benefit (the increase in future earnings). The principles of cost-benefit analysis therefore apply to firms, individuals, and government.

When a firm considers building another factory, the firm must compare the cost of building the factory with the benefit—the additional profit that can be made by producing and selling more. Specifically, the firm should compare the present value (PV) of the increase in future profits to the cost.

The benefit of building a highway is what drivers would be willing to pay to use the highway in all future years. Highways save drivers time. It would be possible to estimate how many hours are saved; putting a dollar value on the time saved yields an estimate of the benefits of the highway because this is what drivers should be willing to pay to use the highway.

The benefit of building the highway safer is the reduction in deaths and injuries. People reveal their preference by how much they actually pay in the marketplace to reduce their chance of dying. They pay by buying a good or service that reduces the chance of dying or by choosing a lower-paying job because it is less dangerous. Alternatively, a survey can be administered that asks people how much they would pay.

Mistakes to avoid when doing cost-benefit analysis include counting jobs created as a benefit, double counting the same benefit, and counting secondary benefits.

The benefit of reducing carbon emissions is how much people would be willing to pay to reduce future global warming. Emissions should be cut back as long as the marginal cost of cutback is less than the marginal benefit. To compare future benefits to current costs, the benefits must be converted to present value by discounting using the social discount rate.

One difficult and important application of cost-benefit analysis concerns whether the government should pay for a costly medical treatment. Advances in technology, medication, and medical procedures have made it possible to cure medical conditions that previously could not be treated, but often the new technology, medication, or procedure is expensive. Economists prescribe a weighing of the benefit of the treatment against its cost. The issue is not "life versus money" but rather how best to use resources to promote the well-being of people.

A military intervention should be subjected to cost-benefit analysis. Although an estimate of the benefit must rely on the disciplines of history, international relations, political science, and military science, economists can provide an estimate of the cost. In particular, economists can make sure that costs outside the military budget are counted and that an aggregate cost estimate is translated into a cost per person, so that each citizen can grasp cost against perceived benefit. An interesting application of cost-benefit analysis is the 2003 U.S. military intervention in Iraq.

Key Terms

cost-benefit analysis, *79*
opportunity cost, *80*
present value (PV), *81*
revealed preference, *83*

contingent
valuation, *83*
compensating
differential, *86*

value of a statistical
life (VSL), *87*
social discount rate, *89*
cost-effectiveness, *89*

Questions

1. Suppose a factory would be built in one year (year 0) and last only a year (year 1). The construction cost in year 0 would be $100,000 financed by borrowing and the profit in year 1 would be $120,000. Should the firm build the factory? Explain why or why not.

2. Suppose the factory lasts two years instead of one, and the profit is $60,000 in year 1 and $72,000 in year 2. Should it be built? Explain.

3. For a new highway, how would you calculate the benefit to firms that transport their cargo by truck?

4. One way to estimate the benefit of a new highway is increased output. Explain.

5. Another way to estimate the benefit of a new highway is to measure how suburban home prices vary by commuting time from the city. Explain.

6. Still another way to estimate the benefit of a new highway is to ask hypothetical questions to drivers. Explain.

7. If a highway is made safer, the benefit is fewer deaths and injuries. Explain the following two ways that economists put a dollar value on fewer deaths and injuries: (*a*) revealed preference and (*b*) contingent valuation.

8. Give three mistakes that the cost-benefit analyst should avoid.

9. How does the social discount rate affect cost-benefit analysis for global warming?

10. How can contingent valuation help answer: "Should Medicare pay for treatment X?"

11. Discuss the costs of the Iraq War since 2003.

12. Go online to read about the controversy over putting a dollar value on a life saved in cost-benefit analysis. Write about your opinions on VSL.

13. Go online to find an example of cost-benefit analysis not discussed in this chapter. Explain how this analysis was used to reach a final decision.

Chapter **Five**

Social Security

PhotoLink / Photodisc / Getty Images

Under the U.S. Social Security system, a payroll tax is levied on workers and employers (employers mail the workers' share as well as their own to the government), and the revenue is used to pay benefits to retirees (who previously paid into the system when they were workers). We describe the U.S. Social Security system in detail later in this chapter.

Although you are a long way from retirement, Social Security is already relevant to you. First, if you've worked for a paycheck, you've probably noticed that a FICA tax was taken out of your paycheck—that's the payroll tax for Social Security. Second, you may have heard it said that when you reach retirement in a few decades, you will get little or no Social Security benefits because of the financial difficulties of the program. Is this true? Might you be better off if you could direct your payroll taxes to your own individual investment account that might earn a higher return than Social Security will give you when you retire? Third, most policy makers are saying that Social Security needs to be reformed soon to protect your generation, and various conflicting proposals have been offered. For example, President Bush offered a proposal in 2005 and spent a great deal of effort trying to persuade the public to support it and Congress to pass it. Most Democrats in Congress opposed the president's plan, and some offered their own ideas for reform. A political deadlock occurred, and no reform plan was enacted. Social Security reform is an issue that will continue to be debated in election campaigns, so you should think about it now.

This chapter has three sections. The first section presents an analysis of four different ways to prepare for retirement; the second describes the U.S. Social Security program in detail; the third considers options for Social Security reform.

FOUR WAYS TO PREPARE FOR RETIREMENT

Before examining the U.S. Social Security system and proposals for reform, it is important to pause to carefully consider the possible ways to prepare for retirement and the advantages and disadvantages of each way. Table 5.1 shows four ways to prepare for retirement.

Workers Support Retirees

In the first row of Table 5.1 "Workers support retirees," under the first column, "Individually," the entry is "Historical." Throughout the long sweep of history until recently, this was probably the most important and widely used way, and it is therefore labeled "Historical." When parents became too old to work in the fields or hunt, their own children took care of them by providing food. The support from workers to "retirees" was handled within individual families. When you got too old to work, you depended on your own children; they would take care of you just as you had taken care of your parents when they became too old to work. Thus, there was a *compact between the generations* within individual families. One advantage of this way is that the care is between people with personal bonds—workers are helping their own parents.

One disadvantage to this method is that not everyone has children who are able and willing to care for them. Some people either never had children or had children who died before middle age; some children are selfish; some children are unable to help their parents because they don't earn enough—for example, because they have a chronic illness or disability or because they have special burdens such as chronically sick children.

Move to the right in the first row to the second column, "Collectively"; the entry is "U.S. Social Security." Under this method, utilized by the U.S. Social Security system, the government taxes all workers and then sends benefit checks to all retirees. Hence, workers collectively support all retirees. The advantage of this method, compared with the historical method, is that old people are not dependent on their own children; the existence, attitude, or ability of their own children is no longer crucial to their well-being in old age. Each old person is supported collectively by all children in society.

TABLE 5.1
Preparing for Retirement

	Individually	Collectively
Workers support retirees	Historical	U.S. Social Security
Each generation self-sufficient	Recent	Possible

The move to the right in the first row can be viewed as providing *insurance* against the possibility that a person's own children will be unable or unwilling to support that person in old age. A person who regards it as risky to depend on his own children might find the move to the right in the table appealing.

There is another feature of collective rather than individual support that may be an advantage or disadvantage, depending on your philosophy. Under the collective Social Security system, the legislature (with executive approval) decides the formula for how much tax each worker pays and how much benefit each retiree receives. For example, if worker H earns three times as much as worker L, will H pay three times as much, more than three times as much, or less than three times as much tax as L? And when they retire, will H receive three times, more than three times, or less than three times the benefit that L receives? The legislature could, for example, choose formulas that achieve a partial redistribution from high- to low-wage workers, so that H pays three times the tax that L pays but receives twice (not three times) the benefit that L receives. Such partial redistribution characterizes the formula chosen by Congress for the U.S. Social Security system.

There are some disadvantages to workers collectively supporting retirees. First, it must be a compulsory system to work effectively and fairly—compulsory taxes must be levied—and any compulsion is always somewhat regrettable. Compulsion is necessary because if the collective system instead relied on voluntary contributions from workers, many workers would naturally prefer to give to their own parents rather than the collective fund. Also, it would be impossible to promise a particular benefit to retirees because the benefit would depend on what workers felt like giving each year.

Second, the collective system is impersonal. Instead of support from children to their own parents, there are tax payments and benefit checks among strangers. Under the U.S. Social Security system, workers are of course free to ask employers to attach personal notes to their parents with their payroll taxes, but even if employers agree, Congress has not authorized the inclusion of workers' personal notes in benefit checks to their parents. Of course, workers are free to try to convince their own parents that their benefit checks are coming from their own children's payroll taxes.

Each Generation Self-Sufficient

Now let's turn to the second row of Table 5.1, "Each generation self-sufficient"; in the first column, "Individually," the entry is "Recent." In more recent times (the past few decades), there has been an attempt by more workers to save for their own retirement so that they would not be dependent on the next generation when they get old—either individually (their own children) or collectively (the U.S. Social Security system). Under this way, workers can put their saving in the bank or buy government bonds, corporate bonds, or corporate stocks. The saving will earn interest, dividends, or *capital gains* (e.g., if they buy corporate stock and its price goes up over time). When they retire, they will gradually draw down their bank account or sell their bonds or stocks and use the cash to finance their consumption.

It is important to mention another way individuals can save. They can buy a home, financed mostly by borrowing from a bank (a mortgage), but then gradually pay off the loan; these gradual payments are saving—uses of income not for consumption, but to gradually get out of debt. By retirement, they may succeed in owning the home and no longer having any debt. They can then sell the home, move into a more modest rental apartment, and finance their consumption (including rent) by gradually drawing down the proceeds from the home sale. So instead of building up wealth for retirement in the form of a bank account, bonds, or stocks, individuals can build up wealth in a home by gradually paying off the debt initially needed to buy the home.

Move to the right in the second row to the second column of Table 5.1. Could each generation save for its own retirement collectively? It's possible, although it has seldom been attempted. Under this method, the government would tax all workers and save the revenue by putting it in a savings account or by buying bonds or stocks, earning interest, dividends, or capital gains, respectively. When workers retire, the government would gradually draw down the bank account or sell the bonds or stocks and use the cash to pay benefits to retirees to finance their consumption. Collectively, each generation would be saving for and financing its own retirement.

The Rate of Return

In each of the four ways of preparing for retirement, there is a **rate of return** for the typical worker. What is the rate of return? In any retirement system, a worker makes a sacrifice during the work stage of life and receives a benefit in the retirement stage. In a government system, the worker's sacrifice is a tax; in a private system, the worker's sacrifice is a contribution to a retirement fund. Think of each stage as having a length of 30 years. The rate of return compares the person's benefit in retirement to the sacrifice that person made as a worker. For example, suppose a worker sacrifices $100 while working and then receives a benefit of $150 in retirement. The benefit exceeds the sacrifice by $50, so the ratio of the gain ($50) to the sacrifice ($100) is 50%—hence, the rate of return (on the sacrifice) is 50%. So the rate of return r^* is defined as:

$$r^* = \frac{(B_2 - T_1)}{T_1} = \left(\frac{B_2}{T_1}\right) - 1$$

where B_2 is the person's benefit as a retiree (in the second stage of life) and T_1 is the sacrifice that person made as a worker (in the first stage of life). As indicated above, there are two equivalent formulas for the rate of return. From the first, $r^* = (\$150 - \$100)/\$100 = 50\%$; from the second, $r^* = (\$150/\$100) - 1 = (1.5) - 1 = .5 = 50\%$. As long as B_2 is greater than T_1, the rate of return r^* is positive. This simple example and definition assume that the worker makes one sacrifice T_1 and receives one benefit B_2. Note that r^* is the rate of return *per period* where a period is 30 years; the rate of return over 30 years is a much larger percentage than an annual rate of return—the rate of return per year.

To simplify our analysis in this section:

We assume that there are two stages of life of equal length: work and retirement; T$_1$ is the sacrifice made in the work stage and B$_2$ is the benefit received in the retirement stage.

What determines the rate of return? The answer is different for the two rows in Table 5.1.

Rate of Return When Workers Support Retirees

In the first row of the table, workers support retirees. Imagine that you're a worker, and you make a contribution T_1. Now you retire. What determines the benefit you receive? The more workers there are to support you and the higher the wage of those workers, the higher will be your benefit. That's true whether worker support is individual (within each family) or collective, but we focus specifically on the collective case. There are two things that will raise your benefit B_2 relative to your sacrifice T_1. First, faster growth in the labor force, so that as workers retire, a greater number of workers replace

TABLE 5.2   A Rate of Return Example

Period	Workers	Wage	Tax	Revenue	Retirees	Benefit	Rate of Return
1	100	$10,000	**$2,000**	$200,000	—	—	
2	125	10,000	2,000	250,000	100	**$2,500**	25%
1	100	10,000	**2,000**	200,000	—	—	
2	100	12,000	2,400	240,000	100	**2,400**	20
1	100	10,000	**2,000**	200,000	—	—	
2	125	12,000	2,400	300,000	100	**3,000**	50

them. Second, faster growth in the wage per worker. Thus, in the first row of the table where workers support retirees, the faster the labor force and wage growth, the higher the rate of return.

Let's examine this with a numerical example shown in Table 5.2. Assume that there are two equal-length life stages: work and retirement. Each person works in stage 1 and retires in stage 2. Think of the length of each stage and of each period in the table as 30 years. Assume that there are 100 workers in period 1 (so there will be 100 retirees in period 2), and each worker earns a wage of $10,000 and pays a 20% payroll tax of $2,000. What will each worker receive as a benefit upon retirement in period 2? In the workers-support-retirees system, each period the tax revenue raised from workers is paid out as benefits to retirees so:

$$BR = tWL$$

where t = the payroll tax rate

W = the wage per worker (so $T = tW$ is the tax per worker)

L = the number of workers

B = the benefit per retiree

R = the number of retirees

Here we simplify by assuming that all wage income is subject to payroll tax.

We consider three cases shown in the three blocks of Table 5.2. In the first block of the table, the number of workers grows from 100 in period 1 to 125 in period 2 (25%), while the wage stays constant at $10,000, and tax per worker stays constant at $2,000. Revenue in period 2 will be $250,000, and the benefit per retiree in period 2 will be $2,500, so the rate of return is ($2,500/$2,000) − 1 = 25%.

In the second block, the number of workers stays constant at 100, while the wage grows from $10,000 in period 1 to $12,000 in period 2 (20%), so tax per worker grows from $2,000 to $2,400 (20%). Revenue in period 2 will be $240,000, and the benefit in period 2 will be $2,400, so the rate of return is ($2,400/$2,000) − 1 = 20%.

Finally, in the third block, the number of workers grows from 100 to 125 (25%), and the wage grows from $10,000 to $12,000 (20%). The benefit in period 2 will be $3,000, so the rate of return is ($3,000/$2,000) − 1 = 50%.

In the box, we show how to derive a formula that links the rate of return $r*$ to the growth rate of labor g_L and the growth rate of the wage g_W.

The formula is only valid when the payroll tax rate, the growth rate of labor, and the growth rate of the wage remain constant over time.

The Derivation of $r^* = g_L + g_W + g_L g_W$ When Workers Support Retirees

Each year, benefits equal payroll tax revenue, so

$$BR = tWL,$$

where B = the benefit per retiree

R = the number of retirees

t = the tax rate

W = the wage per worker (so $T = tW$ is the tax per worker)

L = the number of workers

In period 1, $B_1 R_1 = tW_1 L_1$, and in period 2, $B_2 R_2 = tW_2 L_2$. The rate of return r^* is defined as

$$r^* = \left(\frac{B_2}{T_1}\right) - 1$$

In this formula we now substitute for B_2 and T_1. Since $B_2 R_2 = tW_2 L_2$, then $B_2 = tW_2 L_2 / R_2$; and $T_1 = tW_1$; so

$$\frac{B_2}{T_1} = \frac{\left(\dfrac{tW_2 L_2}{R_2}\right)}{tW_1} = \left(\frac{W_2}{W_1}\right)\left(\frac{L_2}{R_2}\right)$$

because t cancels out. Then

$$\left(\frac{W_2}{W_1}\right)\left(\frac{L_2}{R_2}\right) = \left(\frac{W_2}{W_1}\right)\left(\frac{L_2}{L_1}\right)$$

because $R_2 = L_1$ (the number of retirees in period 2 is equal to the number of workers in period 1). Since $W_2/W_1 = 1 + g_W$ and $L_2/L_1 = 1 + g_L$, then

$$\frac{B_2}{T_1} = (1 + g_W)(1 + g_L) = 1 + g_L + g_W + g_W g_L$$

so

$$r^* = \left(\frac{B_2}{T_1}\right) - 1 = g_L + g_W + g_L g_W$$

The formula is

$$r^* = g_L + g_W + g_L g_W$$

Note that each g is the growth rate per *period* where a period is 30 years (a 30-year growth rate is a much larger percentage than an *annual* growth rate—the growth rate per *year*). Let us check to see that the formula gives the correct answer for the three blocks in Table 5.2:

$$r^* = \quad g_L \quad + \quad g_W \quad + g_L g_W$$

First Block: $\quad\quad r^* = 25\% + \quad 0\% + (25\%)(\ 0\%) = 25\%$

Second Block: $\quad r^* = \quad 0\% + 20\% + (\ 0\%)(20\%) = 20\%$

Third Block: $\quad\quad r^* = 25\% + 20\% + (25\%)(20\%) = 50\%$

Our formula does indeed give the correct answer. Note that the last term in the formula, $g_L g_W$, is the smallest of the three terms, so by ignoring the last term, r^* approximately equals $g_L + g_W$:

The rate of return approximately equals the growth rate of the labor force plus the growth rate of wages: $r^* \approx g_L + g_W$.

Note that the payroll tax rate t is *not* in the formula for r^*. As long as the payroll tax rate t is constant over time, its magnitude has no effect on r^*. The reason is that a higher t means bad news and good news for your rate of return: The bad news is that you pay a higher tax in your work stage; the good news is that you receive a higher benefit in your retirement stage. The bad and good exactly cancel so that raising t has no effect on your r^*. If you look at the derivation in the box, you can see where t cancels out.

Of course, if the government increases t just as you retire so that the t during your retirement is greater than the t you paid as a worker, this increase in t will increase your r^*; symmetrically, if the government decreases t just as you retire so that the t during your retirement is less than the t you paid as a worker, then this decrease in t will decrease your r^*.

In our example in Table 5.2, everything is in terms of a time period of 30 years, where each person works for one period and retires for one period. But suppose each person works for X years and retires for Y years, where X and Y differ? And suppose we use annual rates for g_L and g_W—for example, suppose g_L is 1% per year and g_W is 2% per year. And finally suppose we use an annual rate for r^*—after all, when we put money in our bank account, we want to know the interest rate per year. For example, an r of 3% means that if we put \$100 in our account, it will earn \$3 of interest in one year, and we then say that we've earned an annual rate of return of 3%. Does the formula, $r^* = g_L + g_W + g_L g_W$, remain valid?[1]

The answer is *yes*.[2] The growth rate of labor g_L is roughly 1% per year, and the growth rate of the real (inflation-adjusted) wage g_W is roughly 2% per year (because g_W usually equals the growth rate of labor productivity—output per worker—which is roughly 2% per year), so the annual rate of return when workers support retirees is approximately equal to 3% ($r^* \approx 3\%$) because with *annual rates*:

$$r^* = g_L + g_W + g_L g_W$$

$$r^* = 1\% + 2\% + (1\%)(2\%)$$

$$r^* \approx 3\%$$

Rate of Return When Each Generation Is Self-Sufficient

Now let's return to the second row of Table 5.1, where each generation is self-sufficient. Workers save in bank accounts or by buying bonds or stocks, and when they retire, they obtain the principal (what they saved) plus earnings. When banks lend the saving to firms or when workers buy bonds or stocks, the saving is then invested in real capital—equipment, plant, and technology. Assume that every \$100 that is invested raises the revenue that firms generate by \$6 per year—in other words, assume that the **marginal product of capital (mpk)** is 6%.

Next comes a key assumption: If there is competition among firms for workers' saving, firms will end up having to offer workers roughly \$6 of interest, dividends, or *capital gains* (the rise in the price of stock) on every \$100 of their saving—a rate of return of 6% (firms can't afford to offer more than the mpk). *If* this assumption is correct and *if* there is no tax, then workers would receive a rate of return on their saving equal to the marginal product of capital, so r^* would equal the mpk.

So which is likely to be larger, $(g_L + g_W + g_L g_W)$ or mpk? The growth rate of labor g_L is roughly 1% per year, and the growth rate of the real (inflation-adjusted) wage g_W on average roughly equals the growth rate of labor productivity which is roughly 2% per year, so the rate of return when workers support retirees is roughly 3% per year. Estimating the marginal product of capital is difficult; the mpk varies across firms and

---

[1] The appendix to this chapter shows how to define and calculate your annual rate of return r* under Social Security if you work for 40 years and retire for 20 years.

[2] Laurence Seidman, "Social Security and Demographics in a Life Cycle Growth Model," *National Tax Journal* 36, no. 2 (June 1983), p. 219.

over time. A plausible rough estimate for the average value (across firms and over time) of the mpk is perhaps about 6% per year. Thus:

It seems likely that the rate of return when each generation is self-sufficient would be several percentage points higher than the rate of return when workers support retirees.

With each generation self-sufficient, however, it is very important to distinguish between the two cases: individual and collective. With collective saving and investment, each worker receives the same rate of return—the return earned on the huge portfolio of bonds and stocks. With individual saving and investment, each worker receives the rate of return that his own small portfolio earns. His own portfolio will consist of a particular set of bonds and stocks of a particular set of companies. Even if the average mpk in the economy is 6%, the mpk of his set of firms may differ significantly from 6%. Moreover, there may be a significant divergence between the rate of return he receives on his saving from interest, dividends, or capital gains and the mpk of his companies.

For example, suppose he buys stock in a corporation that he expects to have an mpk of 6%. Suppose, further, that the corporation does not pay any dividends, so the return will be received entirely in the form of a capital gain—a rise in the price of the stock. If the mpk turns out to be 6%, the stock price *should* rise 6%, thereby providing a 6% return. However, stock prices depend on psychology as well as the mpk. Sometimes the rise in stock prices is larger than the mpk, but sometimes it's smaller—sometimes stocks even fall despite a positive mpk. Thus, with individual saving and investment, the rate of return on an individual's portfolio can diverge sharply from the average mpk in the economy. Even if that average mpk (across firms and over time) is 6%, an individual saver who retires when the stock market is booming might receive a rate of return of 16% (10 points higher), but an individual saver who retires when the stock market has plunged might receive a rate of return of –4% (10 points lower).

The Impact on the Economy

Imagine two economies being born. One will provide for retirement by having workers supporting retirees. The second will provide for retirement by having each generation be self-sufficient. Let's consider each in turn.

When the workers-support-retirees economy is born, the first workers don't save because they know that they will be supported in retirement by the next generation of workers. Therefore, there is no real investment and no accumulation of real capital (i.e., machinery). When the first workers retire, the next generation of workers makes transfers to the retirees; the retirees consume their transfers, so once again, no real investment occurs. Thus, no real capital accumulates in the workers-support-retirees economy.

By contrast, when the self-sufficient economy is born, the first workers know that they must save for their own retirement, so they save. Their saving finances real investment by firms so that real capital (i.e., machinery) is produced and accumulates. When the first workers retire, they sell their bonds and stocks—their claims to ownership of the machinery—to the next generation of workers. Thus, the self-sufficient economy operates with a permanent capital stock.

Because the self-sufficient economy accumulates more real capital than the workers-support-retirees economy, it generates more output each year.

Now consider this question: Does a collective workers-support-retirees system (the northeast entry in Table 5.1) like the U.S. Social Security system reduce saving, investment, and the capital stock of the economy?

The answer depends on the type of system it replaces. If the collective workers-support-retirees system replaces an individual workers-support-retirees system (the northwest entry in Table 5.1), then the answer is no; instead of workers giving transfers to their own parents to consume, the workers give transfers (through payroll taxes) to other parents to consume.

However, if a collective workers-support-retirees system replaces a system where each generation is self-sufficient, then the answer is yes. With self-sufficiency, workers save for their own retirement by providing funds to firms to invest in real capital. With a workers-support-retirees system, instead of providing funds to firms to invest in real capital, workers pay taxes that provide funds for retirees to consume. So the capital stock would be lower.

Thus, a workers-support-retirees system has two disadvantages relative to a self-sufficient system: First, the rate of return is lower and second, the capital stock and output of the economy are lower. If the current system is workers-support-retirees (like the U.S. Social Security program), it might seem desirable to switch to a system where each generation is self-sufficient. Unfortunately, breaking out of a workers-support-retirees system is hard to do.

Breaking Out Is Hard to Do

Suppose a new generation of workers in a workers-support economy wants to become self-sufficient and save for its own retirement. Instead of sending transfers to retirees, these workers decide that they would rather buy bonds and stocks, which upon retirement they would sell to finance their consumption. The obvious problem is this: What happens to current retirees if these workers buy bonds and stocks instead of sending retirees transfers? Clearly, the retirees would be in trouble, and they would feel they had been treated very unfairly; when these retirees were working, they didn't buy bonds and stocks—instead, they sent transfers to retirees in the expectation that the same would be done for them when they retired. Changing the system on them when they are retired would no doubt make them quite angry. How would you feel if it happened to you?

So if a new generation of workers wants to become self-sufficient without ditching retirees, the workers must *double-save*: They must save (i.e., consume less than their wage income) in order to send transfers to retirees, and then they must save again to buy bonds and stocks for themselves. When they retire, they will sell their bonds and stocks to finance their consumption and will not receive any transfers. If one generation of workers is willing to double-save and receive no transfer from workers when they retire, thenceforth each generation of workers will only have to save once—for itself—by buying bonds and stocks. If the transition from one system to another occurs in a single generation, that generation must double-save while receiving a single benefit. That's quite a sacrifice for one generation of workers to make.

It would be fairer to spread out the sacrifice over several generations. Instead of double saving—saving 100% more—the first generation of workers might save only 50% more. For example, instead of double saving—saving $200 instead of $100—the first generation of workers might save $150, sending $90 to retirees (instead of the $100 retirees were expecting) and saving $60 for itself; and then the second generation of workers might save $150, sending $80 to retirees (instead of the $90 retirees were expecting) and saving $70 for itself. Eventually, a future generation of workers would send nothing to retirees and save only for itself. From then on, each generation would be completely self-sufficient. But during the transition, several generations of workers would be doing extra saving and bearing an extra burden, and several generations of retirees would be receiving somewhat less than they had been expecting.

The key point is this: To convert from a workers-support-retirees system to a self-sufficient system, there must be sacrifice. Either the current retirees can be ditched, forcing them to bear the entire sacrifice even though they supported the previous generation of retirees when they worked, or one generation of workers must double-save but get only a single benefit, or the sacrifice must be spread out over several generations of workers and retirees. There is no painless way to convert from a workers-support-retirees system to an each-generation-self-sufficient system. Conversion may be worth it in the long run. But in the short run, breaking out is hard to do.

Defined Benefit versus Defined Contribution

Even if breaking out weren't hard to do, there is another important difference to consider in deciding whether to switch Social Security from a collective workers-support-retirees system to an individual self-sufficient system. The collective workers-support-retirees system is a *defined-benefit* plan, whereas the individual self-sufficient system is a *defined-contribution* plan.

Under a **defined-benefit plan**, a worker is promised a retirement benefit that is linked by a formula to that worker's preretirement wage history (a traditional pension would be one example of a defined-benefit plan). The formula can be set to give low-wage workers a **replacement rate** (the ratio of the monthly benefit to the preretirement monthly wage) that is greater than, equal to, or less than high-wage retirees. The defined benefit is an **annuity**: It is paid monthly for as long as the retiree lives, so that the total benefit the person receives during retirement depends on how long the person lives. The annuity can have an automatic inflation adjustment by which the monthly benefit is raised whenever the price of goods in the economy rises (the U.S. Social Security annuity has an automatic inflation adjustment, but many private defined-benefit pension plans do not).

Under a **defined-contribution plan**, a worker's retirement benefit is the sum that has actually accumulated for the worker from designated contributions made by the worker and employer over the worker's career plus the investment income (interest, dividends, and capital gains) that has been earned in the worker's account; a 401(k) would be an example of a defined-contribution plan. The worker owns the assets in the account and controls how the account is invested. Upon retirement the retiree may choose when and how much to draw down the accumulated sum during retirement (the retiree may use the sum to purchase an annuity from a private firm that sells annuities).

U.S. Social Security has always been a defined-benefit plan. Several decades ago, most private pensions were also defined-benefit plans: The typical firm promised each worker a benefit that depended on that worker's preretirement wage history at that firm. A serious shortcoming of a private sector defined-benefit plan is that often a worker must stay with the same firm until retirement to receive benefits. As more workers began to switch firms during their careers, many workers began to prefer that their pension plan be defined contribution, so they could take accumulated funds with them when they switched firms.

Many employers also found defined-contribution plans appealing. With a defined-contribution plan, the employer's obligation is to regularly contribute a specified amount to a worker's pension fund. By contrast, with a defined-benefit plan the employer promises to pay a specified benefit many years in the future when each worker retires. The employer must therefore estimate, under great uncertainty, how much to put away each year in order to meet this future obligation. The employer therefore risks not accumulating enough to pay promised benefits. Thus, increasingly, the private sector has moved toward defined-contribution plans. However, this means that the typical worker is now bearing an investment risk—his retirement benefits depend on his fund's investment history, not his wage history.

The Implication for Social Security

What is the implication for Social Security of this private sector shift away from defined-benefit and toward defined-contribution plans? Two opposite responses are possible.

Under the first, it can be argued that the private sector shift reflects the preference of workers for defined-contribution plans, and Social Security should follow this trend by also switching from defined benefit to defined contribution. Each worker's Social Security benefit would be whatever has actually accumulated for the worker; the benefit would no longer be linked to the worker's wage history by a formula. At any time, each worker would be able to check the amount that has accumulated in his fund and plan accordingly. With each worker keeping track of his fund and receiving periodic statements (like bank statements) from the Social Security Administration, it is extremely doubtful that Congress would ever dare to interfere with a worker's fund. By contrast, Congress has periodically changed Social Security's defined-benefit formula. So defined-contribution Social Security would be less subject to political risk than defined-benefit Social Security.

Under the second, it can be argued that it seems prudent to keep Social Security as primarily a defined-benefit plan. The main objection workers have to defined-benefit plans at private firms—that switching firms results in a forfeiting of benefits—is not relevant to Social Security because workers who switch firms remain under Social Security coverage. An arrangement that may appeal to workers would be coverage by a defined-contribution plan through their employer (or on their own) and coverage by a defined-benefit Social Security program. In this way, a typical worker's retirement benefit would depend partly on the contributions to and investment history of his own defined-contribution fund and partly on his own wage history through Social Security's defined-benefit program.

Social Security's defined-benefit plan has important advantages. A retiree's benefit is based on his own wage history, not investment history—so while there is political risk of a change in the benefit formula, there is no investment (stock market) risk. The benefit is an annuity which pays a monthly benefit until the person dies. The benefit has an automatic full cost-of-living adjustment—if inflation rises during retirement, automatically so does the monthly Social Security benefit. It is not always possible for an individual to purchase a private annuity at a reasonable price that has a full cost-of-living adjustment because of adverse selection in the private annuity market. It can be argued that Social Security's defined-benefit inflation-protected annuity is becoming more, not less, important as the private sector shifts from defined-benefit to defined-contribution pensions.

Under Social Security's progressive defined-benefit formula, moreover, there is some redistribution from high- to low-wage workers when they retire: If person H earned three times the wage and paid three times the payroll tax each year as person L, person H would receive a monthly benefit perhaps twice but not three times as great as person L because of the progressive benefit formula. For anyone who favors such partial redistribution, this is an important virtue of defined-benefit Social Security.

TABLE 5.3
Collective
Workers-Support-
Retirees System
versus Individual
Self-Sufficient
System for Social
Security

	Collective Workers Support Retirees	Each Individual Self-Sufficient
Average rate of return $r*$	$g_L + g_w + g_L g_w = 3\%$	$mpk = 6\%$
Capital and output of economy	Lower	Higher
Individual ownership and control	No	Yes
Benefit depends on	Wage history Defined-benefit	Investment income Defined-contribution
Risk of variation of $r*$	Low	High
Benefit automatically an annuity paid monthly as long as retiree lives	Yes	No
Benefit automatically inflation protected	Yes	No
Partial redistribution from high-wage to low-wage workers	Yes	No

In considering possible reforms of Social Security, it is important to take account of the fact that many individuals will be preparing for retirement privately as well as through Social Security, while some individuals—either by choice or because they can't afford it—will be preparing only through Social Security. Individuals who are also preparing privately will be accumulating funds in individual investment accounts—funds they own and control but that are subject to investment (stock market) risk. Individuals who are not preparing privately will not accumulate any funds in an individual investment account unless such accounts are established as part of Social Security.

Table 5.3 summarizes the points we have made in this chapter, comparing a collective workers-support-retirees system and an individual self-sufficient system for Social Security.

THE U.S. SOCIAL SECURITY SYSTEM

Background

Social Security was enacted in the United States in 1935 as the crowning jewel of President Franklin D. Roosevelt's New Deal. The original plan was for workers (and their employers) to pay payroll taxes (a percentage of wage income up to a ceiling), have one large Social Security fund build up, and upon retirement receive benefits from the single large fund that they had helped to build. In Table 5.1, the original plan was the southeast entry: Each generation collectively would be self-sufficient in providing for its own retirement. In the late 1930s, payroll taxes were paid, the single fund began to build up, and few benefits were paid out because few retirees had paid into the fund while they were working—according to the original plan, they were therefore not eligible for benefits.

However, there was a lot of sympathy for the retirees of the late 1930s. The Great Depression had forced many of them to use up their savings when they became unemployed. Many, through no fault of their own, faced old age without savings. Couldn't anything be done to help them? The answer was yes. Instead of sticking to the original plan, Social Security could take the payroll tax revenue coming in and use it to send benefits to these unfortunate retirees. In Table 5.1, the system could be moved from the southeast entry up to the northeast entry: Collectively workers would support retirees.

Immediately the question arose: What will become of today's workers when they retire because there won't be any buildup of a large fund? And immediately came an answer: When they retire, the payroll taxes of the next generation of workers (and their employers) will be used to pay their benefits. So around 1940 Social Security adopted the new plan and began paying out benefits instead of building up a large fund. The new plan came to be called **pay-as-you-go (PAYGO)** because when people worried, "How will benefits be paid if no fund builds up," they were told, "Don't worry, we'll pay as we go—we'll use tomorrow's payroll taxes to pay tomorrow's benefits." PAYGO is another name for the northeast entry in Table 5.1: Collectively workers support retirees.

Needless to say, the new plan was a great deal for people retiring in the 1940s. Take Ida Fuller of Vermont. Legend has it that she was about to retire when Social Security was enacted, so prior to retirement she (and her employer) paid only about $20 of payroll tax. But once she retired she had the fortitude to live to a very old age, collecting about $20,000 in Social Security benefits! Before getting too angry at Ida and other retirees of that era, remember that most of them suffered economic hardship through no fault of their own due to the Great Depression. At any rate, there's no way to get the money back from these retirees—they've been dead for half a century.

For the next 40 years until 1980, Social Security followed the PAYGO plan. Each year, payroll tax revenue would be sent out to pay benefits. For people retiring in the 1950s, Social Security was not quite as spectacular a deal as it had been for people retiring in the 1940s, but it was still a very good deal: the 1950s retirees had only paid payroll tax during the last decade or two of their work careers, but they were now receiving benefits financed by payroll taxes on the entire workforce. Each decade, Social Security became less of a great deal. By 1980, virtually every retiree had paid payroll taxes over his entire work career, so for each retiree, the taxes he had paid were no longer much less than the benefits he received during retirement.

The Ratio of Workers to Retirees

In the early 1980s not only was Social Security no longer a spectacular deal, but a demographic threat loomed on the horizon. It was recognized by experts that in three decades (around 2010) the numerous baby boomers—born in the decade and a half following World War II—would stop being workers who paid payroll taxes and become retirees entitled to Social Security benefits. Also, medical advances would enable many of these boomers to live to a very old age; they would spend many years in retirement receiving benefits.

This prediction made by experts in the early 1980s proved accurate. Figure 5.1 shows how the ratio of workers to retirees (the number of workers per retiree) has declined in the United States and the projected path for the future. In 1955, the ratio was over 8 workers per retiree. In 2006 the ratio was 3.3 and is projected to decline to 2.1 by 2032. Thus:

Over the next two and half decades, the ratio of workers to retirees in the United States is projected to fall from 3 to 2.

FIGURE 5.1

Social Security's Demographic Challenge

The ratio of workers paying Social Security taxes to people collecting benefits will fall from 3.3 in 2006 to 2.1 by 2032.

Source: 2007 Annual Report of the Board of Trustees of the Federal Old Age and Survivors Insurance and Disability Insurance Trust Funds, table IV.B2.

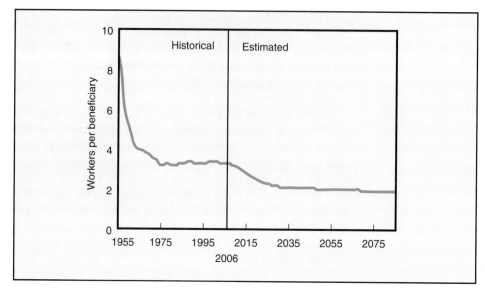

When a demographic shift reduces the ratio of workers to retirees, then unpleasant consequences must follow: Either the replacement rate must fall, or the tax rate must be raised, or both. To see this, let's consider a hypothetical numerical example. In a workers-support-retirees system, benefits paid out each year equal tax revenues paid in, so

$$BR = tWL$$

$$(\$45)(100) = (.15)(\$100)(300)$$

where B = the benefit per retiree ($45)

R = the number of retirees (100)

t = the payroll tax rate (15%)

W = the wage per worker ($100)

L = the number of workers (300)

This year, total benefits paid out equal total taxes paid in ($4,500). Here we simplify by assuming all wage income is subject to payroll tax. Note that the ratio of the benefit ($45) to the wage per worker ($100), the replacement rate B/W, equals 45%. Dividing by W, and then by R, yields:

$$\frac{B}{W} = t\left(\frac{L}{R}\right)$$

$$\frac{\$45}{\$100} = (.15)\left(\frac{300}{100}\right)$$

$$.45 = (.15)(3)$$

Suppose that as time passes, the number of retirees gradually rises from 100 to 150 while the number of workers remains at 300; the ratio of workers to retirees, L/R, gradually falls from 3 (300/100) to 2 (300/150). Then either the replacement rate B/W must fall or the tax rate t must be raised. If the tax rate is kept at 15%, then the replacement rate will fall gradually from 45% to 30% (a 33% decline in the replacement rate):

$$\frac{B}{W} = t\left(\frac{L}{R}\right)$$

$$\frac{\$30}{\$100} = (.15)\left(\frac{300}{150}\right)$$

$$.30 = (.15)(2)$$

Instead, if the replacement rate is to be kept at 45%, then the tax rate must be gradually raised from 15% to 22.5% (a 50% increase in the tax rate):

$$\frac{B}{W} = t\left(\frac{L}{R}\right)$$

$$\$45/\$100 = (.225)300/150$$

$$.45 = (.225)(2)$$

The Buildup of the Trust Fund

In the early 1980s, policy makers tried to figure out what could be done in advance to reduce the severity of the coming financial crunch for Social Security due to the projected decline in the ratio of workers to retirees. A bipartisan commission, headed by Alan Greenspan (prior to his becoming Federal Reserve chairman in 1987) recommended raising payroll taxes to build up the Social Security Trust Fund. Payroll taxes are deposited into the Trust Fund, and benefits are paid from the Trust Fund, so each year if taxes collected exceed benefits paid, the Trust Fund will build up. Rather than build up cash, the fund would use the cash to buy safe U.S. Treasury bonds that pay interest, and the interest income would help pay benefits when the baby boomers retired. With bipartisan support—so that neither political party could blame the other—Congress passed the payroll tax increase—and over the next two decades, the fund grew steadily; there is now about $2.3 trillion worth of U.S. Treasury bonds held by the Social Security Trust Fund earning substantial interest income every year. Currently the combined employer plus employee payroll tax rate is 12.4% (much higher than before the 1980s) applied to an employee's wage income up to an annual ceiling that is much larger than before the 1980s—and this number is automatically raised each year to keep pace with increases in wage income: $97,500 in 2007 and $102,000 in 2008.

The current buildup postpones, but is not large enough to eliminate, Social Security's financial problem. The chief actuary of the Social Security Administration reports that if the current tax and benefit rules are unchanged, then in about two decades the Trust Fund will have to start gradually cashing in its Treasury bonds to get enough cash to pay scheduled benefits—tax revenues and interest won't be enough to pay scheduled benefits—and by 2040 there will be no bonds left in the Trust Fund.

So what will happen after 2040? Will Social Security stop paying benefits? No. At current tax rates, every year Social Security will continue to collect payroll tax revenue that it will immediately send out to retirees to pay benefits. Payroll taxes collected each year, not bonds or cash piled up in the Trust Fund, have always been the main source of revenue to pay Social Security benefits.

However, there will be a serious problem after 2040. Social Security's chief actuary estimates that, with current tax rates, the payroll tax revenue collected after 2040 will be only about 70% of scheduled benefits under current benefit rules. That's why, prior to 2040, the Trust Fund will have to cash in some of its Treasury bonds every year to be able to pay scheduled benefits. So when the bonds are gone, there will be a 30% gap. What will happen? At one extreme, Congress could raise $100 instead of $70 in payroll taxes and keep benefits unchanged; at the other extreme, Congress could cut benefits from $100 to $70, keeping payroll taxes unchanged. Most likely, Congress will split the difference: It will probably raise payroll taxes from $70 to $85 (roughly a 20% increase, from the current combined employer plus employee rate of 12.4% to roughly 15%), and cut benefits from $100 to $85 (a 15% cut, from a current replacement rate of about 40% to 34%).

Description of the Current U.S. Social Security Program

Social Security is financed by a payroll tax authorized by the **Federal Insurance Contribution Act (FICA)**. Legally, half the tax is levied on the worker and half on the employer. Administratively, the employer sends both halves to the government (the employer withholds the worker's half from the worker's paycheck), so workers do not write any checks to the government to pay for Social Security.

The worker and the employer each owe a tax equal to 6.2% of wage income up to a **payroll tax ceiling** of $102,000 in 2008; each year the ceiling is automatically increased with the wage growth in the economy. For a worker who earns $102,000 in 2008, the employer sends 12.4%, or $12,648, to the government. If a worker examines his pay stubs, he will see that $6,324 (6.2%) has been taken out of his paychecks over the year; he will not see the other $6,324 that the employer legally owes and also sends to the government. If a worker earns more than $102,000 in 2008, no further payment is made to the government for the rest of the year. For example, for a worker who makes $136,000 in 2008, tax payments will be made for three-quarters of the year from January through September, before earnings reach $102,000; from October through December, no payments will be made, and the worker will note a jump in his take-home pay during the last three months of the year.

Table 5.4 shows the payroll tax rate, the taxable ceiling, and the maximum tax in selected years from 1983 to 2008; the taxable ceiling is adjusted automatically each year according to wage growth in the economy (Congress can make an additional adjustment to the ceiling by voting to do so). The employee tax rate increased from 5.4% in 1983 to 6.2% in 1990 where it has remained. In 2008, the maximum employee tax was $6,324, and the maximum combined (employee plus employer) payroll tax was $12,648. As we will see in Chapter 7, most economists believe the employee bears most of the burden of the employer's payroll tax because employers set wages lower in order to pay that tax; hence, the maximum employee payroll tax burden approached $12,648 in 2008.

TABLE 5.4 **Payroll Tax Rate, Taxable Ceiling, and Maximum Tax, from 1983 to 2008**

Year	Employee Tax Rate	Taxable Ceiling	Maximum Employee Tax	Combined Tax Rate	Maximum Combined Tax
1983	5.4%	$ 35,700	$1,928	10.8%	$ 3,856
1984	5.7	37,800	2,155	11.4	4,309
1990	6.2	51,300	3,181	12.4	6,361
2007	6.2	97,500	6,045	12.4	12,090
2008	6.2	102,000	6,324	12.4	12,648

The official name for the Social Security program is **Old Age, Survivors, and Disability Insurance (OASDI)**—the combined 12.4% pays for OASDI. Each employee pays 5.3% for the OAS program and 0.9% for the DI program for a total of 6.2%, so of the combined 12.4%, 10.6% is for OAS and 1.8% is for DI. Thus, Social Security provides benefits to workers who become disabled as well as to retirees. It should be noted that there is an additional combined 2.9% (legally 1.45% on the employer, 1.45% on the worker) on *all* wage income (no ceiling) that pays for Medicare's hospital insurance (HI). So in 2008, if a worker making $102,000 examines his pay stubs, he will see that an additional $1,479 (1.45%) has been taken out of his paychecks over the year for Medicare HI; he will not see the other $1,479 that the employer legally owes for Medicare and sends to the government. Note that if the worker made twice as much ($204,000), then twice as much would have been taken out for Medicare but nothing more for Social Security (because of the $102,000 ceiling).

Social Security Eligibility

A person must work and pay payroll tax for 40 quarters (10 years) to be eligible to collect Social Security benefits. The earliest age at which a person can begin collecting monthly benefits—the **earliest eligibility age (EEA)**—is 62, but if the person chooses to wait until an older age to start, the monthly benefit will be larger. Once a person starts, he will receive a monthly annuity payment—a payment that continues until death no matter how long he lives. An annuity provides insurance against outliving one's savings. Once a person has started receiving a monthly benefit, each year the person's monthly payment is increased automatically with price inflation in the economy—for example, if inflation was 3% last year, then this year the person's monthly payment will be automatically set 3% higher than last year.

The amount of the monthly benefit depends on the person's wage history—specifically, on the worker's **average indexed monthly earnings (AIME)**. To compute a worker's AIME, the government doesn't simply average the person's annual wage incomes because wage incomes were much lower years ago. Instead, the government takes a person's wage income in each past year and "multiplies it up" to adjust for the average rise in wage incomes in the economy since that year. Then it takes the average of these adjusted annual wage incomes and divides by 12 to put it on a monthly basis. The result is called the person's AIME.

It is important to emphasize that there is a feature of AIME that limits the Social Security benefit of a worker with high wage income and thereby contributes to the progressivity of the Social Security benefit formula. In computing a high-income person's AIME over his career, only monthly wage income up to a ceiling—the same ceiling that limits how much he was taxed for Social Security—is used; hence, wage income above this ceiling is not counted either for Social Security taxes or benefits. Thus, the AIME of a person with high wage income is less than the person's actual average monthly wage income—for a very high-income person, it is much less. Just as the wage of a high-income person is taxed only up to a ceiling, so the benefit of a high-income person is computed by counting in AIME only his monthly wage income up to that same ceiling.

Progressive Benefit Formula

The retiree's monthly benefit, also called the retiree's **primary insurance amount (PIA)**, is based on his AIME. Instead of making a person's PIA a flat percentage of his AIME, Congress long ago enacted a **progressive benefit formula**

FIGURE 5.2
**Social Security's
Benefit Formula**
Congress has set a
progressive benefit
formula: 90%, 32%,
15%.

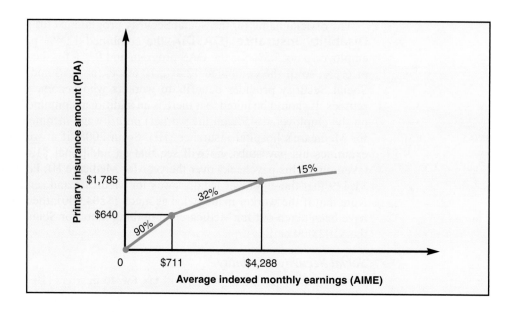

that favors low earners more than high earners. The benefit bracket percentages are shown in Figure 5.2. The *bend points* where the percentages change are $711 and $4,288 in 2008.

The benefit bracket percentages set by Congress are 90%, 32%, and 15%.

In 2008 for the first $711 of AIME, the PIA increased 90 cents for each dollar of AIME, so an AIME of $711 yielded a PIA of $640. For the next $3,577 of AIME, the PIA increased 32 cents for each additional dollar of AIME, so a person with an AIME of $4,288 ($711 + $3,577) had a PIA of $1,785 (because [.90 × $711] + [.32 × $3,577] = $640 + $1,145 = $1,785). Above this AIME of $4,288, the PIA increased 15 cents for each additional dollar of AIME. Recall that, as explained above, the AIME of high earners is limited by counting wage income only up to the taxable ceiling, so the PIA is similarly limited (even without cutting the bracket rate from 15% to 0%). In 2008, a person who retired at 62 and who had worked steadily since age 22 with earnings always above the taxable ceiling had an AIME of $7,260 and a PIA of $2,230; because the person is retiring at 62 instead of waiting until his **full benefits age (FBA)** of 67, his monthly benefit would be 75% of his PIA, or $1,673, or about $20,076 for the year.

Hence, due to the progressive benefit formula, the replacement rate falls as wage income rises. Applying the rates 90%, 32%, and 15% to AIME in order to get PIA, it turns out that:

The replacement rate is roughly 60% for a low-income worker, 40% for an average worker, and 20% for a high-income worker.

It should be noted, however, that on average low-income workers do not live as long as high-income workers; hence, even though low-income workers receive a higher replacement rate in retirement, they receive it for fewer years on average.

Social Security Benefits

Social Security will provide benefits for a spouse who did not work in the marketplace or pay any payroll tax; he will receive a benefit equal to half of his spouse's, and if his spouse dies, he receives her full benefit. If a spouse works in the marketplace, he receives whichever is larger: a benefit based on his own wage history or half of his spouse's benefit.

Social Security also provides benefits to workers who become seriously disabled and unable to work. Disability benefits are roughly 15% of total Social Security benefits. A worker must be screened, evaluated, and wait nearly a half year before receiving benefits. The benefit is comparable to what the person would have received if he had worked until 65.

If a person waits until the full benefits age to start Social Security, then he receives the full PIA, but if the person starts at an earlier age, he receives less than the PIA. The monthly benefit is reduced if one retires earlier—for example, a person with an age of full benefits of 65 who starts retirement at 62 (the earliest age permitted) receives a monthly benefit equal to 80% of his PIA. If he waits until after 65 to start retirement, he receives a monthly benefit greater than his PIA. For many years, the FBA was 65, but Congress has enacted a schedule that gradually raises the FBA to 67. For people born before 1938, the FBA is 65; for people born between 1943 and 1954, it is 66; and for people born after 1959, it is 67. *A person with a full benefits age of 67 who starts collecting benefits at 62 receives a monthly benefit equal to 75% of his PIA.*

Between ages 62 and 64, Social Security has an earnings test: For each dollar earned above a threshold (roughly $12,000), the monthly benefit is reduced by 50 cents. This is really not a tax, just a postponement, because once the person's wage income falls below the threshold or once the person reaches 65, he will get it back with interest. The earnings test used to apply to people 65 and over, but Congress has recently exempted them.

Figure 5.3 shows the sources and uses of Social Security revenue. In 2007, 84% of its revenue came from payroll taxes, 14% from interest on its bonds, and 2% from income tax levied on benefits; 73% of its revenue went to pay benefits, 25% to increase its holdings of U.S. Treasury bonds, 1% to administer Social Security, and 1% for an exchange with another government fund.

FIGURE 5.3
Sources and Uses of Social Security Revenue
Sources: 84% payroll taxes, 14% U.S. bond interest.
Uses: 73% benefits, 25% increase in U.S. bonds, 1% administration.

Source: 2007 Annual Report of the Board of Trustees of the Federal Old Age and Survivors Insurance and Disability Insurance Trust Funds, table II.B1.

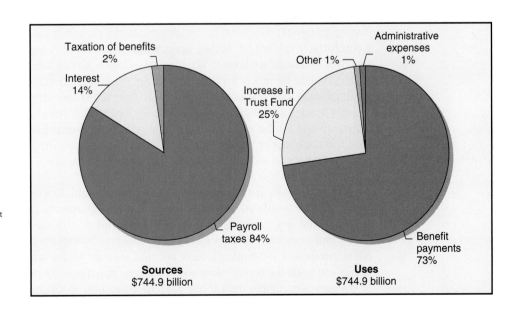

Taxation of benefits 2%
Interest 14%
Payroll taxes 84%

Sources
$744.9 billion

Other 1%
Administrative expenses 1%
Increase in Trust Fund 25%
Benefit payments 73%

Uses
$744.9 billion

The Impact on Work

For a worker with annual wage income less than $102,000 in 2008, the combined employer-employee payroll tax for Social Security is 12.4% of wage income. Does the tax reduce the number of hours worked? Most workers probably treat the FICA tax like any other tax and view take-home pay as their reward for work. If so, it is possible that the Social Security payroll tax causes some discouragement to work. Most economists believe, however, that the effect on heads of households is small because their labor supply is inelastic—it does not vary much in response to taxes. The effect on spouses who would be second earners may be somewhat larger because their labor supply is sometimes more optional and hence more elastic.

There is a feature of the benefit structure of Social Security that may somewhat discourage second-earner spouses from working *if they are aware of it*: the 50% spousal benefit. Even if a second-earner spouse doesn't work, he will be entitled to a benefit equal to 50% of the primary earner's benefit. Therefore, unless he earns enough to qualify for a larger benefit, working would not bring him any additional future Social Security benefit. What can be done to reduce the discouragement to work faced by potential second-earner spouses due to the 50% spousal benefit? One option would be to gradually phase down the spousal benefit from 50% to perhaps 33%. It would be interesting to conduct a survey to see how many working-age spouses are aware of the 50% spousal benefit and whether they say it has affected their decision about working.

The Impact on Saving, Investment, and Capital Accumulation

Suppose the choice for workers is between saving for their own retirement and paying taxes that finance benefits to current retirees (with the expectation that the same will be done for them when they retire). Aggregate saving, investment, and capital accumulation would be higher in the economy if workers save for their own retirement than it would be if they paid taxes that financed retiree consumption.

One way to see this is to recognize that as workers work and pay Social Security taxes, thereby increasing the Social Security benefits to which they will be entitled when they retire, they are accumulating wealth—**social security wealth**. If workers made deposits in their bank account or bought bonds or stocks, they would be accumulating private wealth. In either case, they would be able to receive a flow of benefits during retirement. Workers have to accumulate a certain amount of wealth to finance a comfortable retirement. If they accumulate social security wealth by paying taxes as they work, they do not have to accumulate as much private wealth; nor can they afford to accumulate as much private wealth. So workers who accumulate social security wealth should save less and consume more than they otherwise would have.

How much social security wealth does a given worker have? Although it might seem natural to add all the taxes the worker has paid into Social Security, a better measure is to add the benefits that the worker will receive upon retiring. A worker should care about future social security benefits when deciding how much less to save (how much less private wealth to accumulate).

In order to compare a worker's social security wealth to the private wealth that the worker has accumulated in a bank account, it is important to realize that the worker's bank account will continue to earn compound interest in the years until the worker retires and starts receiving social security benefits. To make a fair comparison, we can either compound the worker's bank account forward to see what it would grow to by retirement or do the reverse with social security benefits—we can discount (the reverse of compounding) them back to the present to see how much the worker would need to have today in a bank account to be able to provide the same benefit in retirement. So we can either take the future value of the bank account or take the *present value* of the social security benefits. Economists generally prefer to take the present value of the benefits as the measure of a worker's social security wealth, which can be compared to the private wealth currently in the worker's bank account plus the value of the worker's bonds, stocks, and home.

For most low-income workers, their social security wealth is almost their entire wealth—they have accumulated little private wealth (in a bank account, bonds, or stocks or in a home). By contrast, for most high-income workers, their social security wealth is less than half their entire wealth because they have accumulated substantial private wealth.

In a series of empirical studies, one economist, Martin Feldstein of Harvard, has estimated that Social Security has cut U.S. private saving roughly in half, causing a large reduction in the capital stock of the economy. As with most empirical studies, there are various assumptions, techniques, and data that can be questioned, and a few other researchers have instead found that the effect of social security wealth on reducing private wealth and the capital stock is substantially smaller. Although the magnitude of the effect is in dispute, it seems highly likely that most middle-aged workers would save more if there were no Social Security program.

The Impact on Retirement

In the United States, more workers start retirement at age 62 than at any other age. The percentage of working people who retire at age 62 is roughly 25%, while the percentage of people who retire at either age 61 or 63 is roughly 10%. It seems likely that this spike in retirement at age 62 is due to the fact that Social Security's earliest eligibility age (EEA) is 62. The second most popular age to start retirement is the full benefits age (FBA). In the United States, there is another spike in the number of people who retire at the FBA, 65; many people consider this to be Social Security's "normal" retirement age. In the United States, for each year a person delays starting Social Security benefits, the starting benefit is increased enough to compensate a worker with an average lifetime for the late start; of course, a person with a shorter-than-average lifetime will be less than fully compensated, while a person with a longer lifetime will be more than fully compensated.

It seems likely that the numerical values that Congress chooses for Social Security's EEA and FBA have an important impact on the age workers choose to retire. International evidence strongly supports the link between Social Security and retirement; similar spikes are generally observed in other countries. In France and the Netherlands, social security's EEA is 60, and there is no increase in the starting benefit if a worker delays retiring beyond age 60; not surprisingly, the percentage of workers retiring in each country has a huge spike at age 60. In the early 1970s Germany reduced its social security EEA by five years, and during the next decade the average age at which German workers retired also fell by about five years.

REFORMING SOCIAL SECURITY

The debate over reforming Social Security has been intense during the past decade. Both President Clinton, a Democrat, and President George W. Bush, a Republican, warned the nation that substantial legislative action must be taken by Congress to protect Social Security for the next generation. The two presidents disagreed about what

Case Study   The Clash of Two Distinguished Economists over Social Security

Two of the most distinguished and influential public finance economists of the past few decades are Martin Feldstein of Harvard and Peter Diamond of the Massachusetts Institute of Technology. Each has been elected president of the American Economic Association. Each has written numerous important and influential journal articles on all aspects of public finance economics. Feldstein has been an adviser to Republican Presidents Reagan, Bush, and Bush, while Diamond has been an adviser to Democratic President Clinton. Both agree about the basic framework and principles of public finance economics. Both agree that Social Security should be reformed. However, they differ on their recommendations for Social Security reform, and their disparity is due primarily to differences in personal philosophy rather than differences in economic analysis.

To understand why they give different recommendations, recall Table 5.3. Feldstein favors "each individual self-sufficient" and recommends that individual private accounts be introduced into Social Security. Diamond favors "collective workers support retirees" and recommends a combination of tax increases and benefit cuts. Each emphasizes different rows of Table 5.3. Feldstein emphasizes the first three rows: His approach yields the higher average rate of return, higher capital and output for the economy, and provides individual ownership and control. Diamond emphasizes the remaining rows:

His approach links a worker's benefit to wage history rather than investment income, has a low risk of variation in r^*, provides an annuity that is paid as long as the person lives and is automatically adjusted for inflation, and achieves a partial redistribution from high- to low-wage workers.

For a deeper understanding of where Feldstein and Diamond agree and disagree, read four articles—two by Feldstein and two by Diamond. In January 2004, Diamond took the podium at the annual meeting of the American Economic Association and gave his presidential address entitled "Social Security"—his address was published in the March 2004 issue of the *American Economic Review*. One year later in January 2005, Feldstein took the podium at the annual meeting of the American Economic Association and gave his presidential address entitled "Rethinking Social Insurance"—his address was published in the March 2005 issue of the *American Economic Review*. Then the spring 2005 issue of the American Economic Association's *Journal of Economic Perspectives* published two articles: one article by Diamond—coauthored by Peter Orszag, then an economist at the Brookings Institution, now the director of the Congressional Budget Office—entitled "Saving Social Security" (which gave a concise exposition of their 2004 book, *Saving Social Security: A Balanced Approach*) and one article by Feldstein entitled "Structural Reform of Social Security."

that action should be, and after a decade of debate, Congress has deadlocked and taken no action. Almost all experts agree with the two presidents that it would be a serious mistake to do nothing about Social Security. Looming on the horizon is the very serious "2040 problem." Yet even knowledgeable experts disagree about what should be done; for two specific examples, see the box "The Clash of Two Distinguished Economists over Social Security." This section describes the problems facing Social Security and presents the alternative options for treating these problems.

Treating the 2040 Problem

According to the analysis of the Office of the Chief Actuary of the Social Security Administration, if payroll tax rates remain constant, benefits due under the current Social Security benefit formula will be fully paid until 2040 by supplementing payroll taxes with revenue from interest earned on U.S. bonds in the Social Security Trust Fund and, in the decade prior to 2040, by gradually selling the U.S. treasury bonds that were accumulated by the Trust Fund from the mid-1980s to 2030. The U.S. government bonds that have accumulated in the Social Security Trust Fund are backed by the full faith and credit of the U.S. government and have the same degree of safety as U.S. government bonds held by households and business firms.

After 2040, when the Trust Fund runs out of bonds, the chief actuary estimates that payroll tax revenue will be sufficient to finance a monthly benefit equal to about 70% of that scheduled under the current benefit formula. This post-2040 benefit will be a bit larger (after adjusting for inflation) than today's benefit because the growth of real, inflation-adjusted wages between now and 2040 will make the scheduled (inflation-adjusted) benefit in 2040 about 50% larger than today (70% of 1.5 is greater than 1).

Nevertheless, if nothing is done before 2040, the abrupt 30% drop in the monthly benefit that would occur when the Trust Fund runs out of bonds would be extremely undesirable. Steps can and should be taken as soon as possible to ensure that there will never be such an abrupt, large drop in the Social Security monthly benefit.

The 2040 problem is shown in the two graphs of Figure 5.4. The top graph shows projected total benefits that will be paid out under Social Security's current benefit formula (line *BF*) and projected total payroll tax revenue that will be coming in under Social Security's current tax rate (line *TG*). The bottom graph shows the amount accumulated in the Trust Fund. Total outgoing benefits rise not only with total wage incomes (because the formula links scheduled benefits to wage histories) but also with the number of retirees. Because of the retirement of the large number of baby boomers, but also because retirees are expected to live longer, outgoing benefits are projected to rise more rapidly than incoming taxes. From 2000 until about 2020, taxes exceed benefits, but after 2020 taxes are below benefits. Still, from 2020 to about 2030, incoming taxes plus interest on the U.S. government bonds held by the Trust Fund will exceed outgoing benefits, so these benefits can be paid, and the amount in the Trust Fund will keep increasing. But after 2030, taxes plus interest will become less than scheduled benefits—to pay these scheduled benefits, the Trust Fund will have to exchange (redeem) its bonds for cash from the U.S. Treasury to supplement taxes plus interest. This will cause the bonds in the Trust Fund to decline from a peak in 2030 to zero in about 2040.

It should be emphasized that Social Security will impose a cash-flow burden on the U.S. Treasury starting in 2020. Prior to 2020, each year the payroll tax that the Treasury collects exceeds the benefits that it pays retirees, so it enjoys a cash surplus each year due to the Social Security program. After 2020, the payroll tax that the Treasury collects is less than the benefits it pays retirees, so it suffers a cash burden from the Social Security program; it must come up with additional cash each year due to Social Security. Thus, from the Treasury's perspective, the key year will be 2020, not 2040, because that's when Social Security will switch from providing the Treasury with a cash surplus each year to imposing a cash burden each year.

After 2040, if tax rates are unchanged, benefits actually paid out will have to be cut abruptly by 30% in order to equal incoming taxes (assuming that the Social Security Trust Fund is not permitted to borrow funds).

Slowing Benefit Growth and/or Raising Payroll Tax Growth

To prevent this abrupt benefit cut after 2040, the government can slow benefit growth and raise payroll tax growth beginning in 2010. Look at how this would alter Figure 5.4. In the top graph, the growth path of the benefits line would rotate down from *BF*, for example to *BG*, and the taxes line would rotate up from *TG*, for example to *TF*, so that in 2040 benefits paid out would be *less* than taxes coming in (instead of *greater* than taxes) by the amount *FG*. Social Security would still be providing the Treasury with a

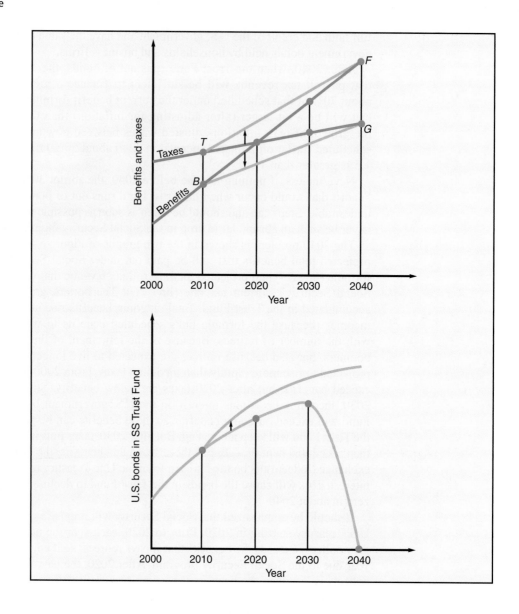

cash surplus instead of imposing a cash burden. In the bottom graph, starting in 2010, the Trust Fund would grow faster; instead of peaking in 2030, it would still be growing in 2040.

Slowing benefit growth and raising payroll tax growth are a repeat of what Congress and the president did in the mid-1980s. With bipartisan support providing political cover for both parties, Congress approved the key recommendation of a bipartisan commission headed by Alan Greenspan: Build up government bonds in the Social Security Trust Fund by raising payroll tax growth and slowing future benefit growth, thereby running annual surpluses for several decades and investing the surpluses in interest-earning U.S. government bonds. To slow future benefit growth, Congress scheduled a gradual increase in the full benefits age beginning in 2000 from 65 to 66 by 2005 and to 67 by 2022.

By 2008, the Social Security Trust Fund had accumulated over $2.3 trillion in interest-earning U.S. government bonds, nearly four times annual benefits paid; according to the chief actuary, it is on track to reach nearly five times annual benefits in 2015. If this accumulation had not occurred, then around 2020 Congress would have had to cut the monthly benefit because in that year tax revenue will become less than benefits due under the current Social Security benefit formula. However, with this accumulated sum earning interest, payroll taxes plus interest income will exceed benefits due until about 2030; then the fund itself can be drawn down over the next decade by gradually exchanging the U.S. bonds for cash from the U.S. Treasury, so that there is no need to make the monthly benefit smaller than currently scheduled until about 2040. Thus, the building up of the Social Security Trust Fund since the mid-1980s (and the gradual raising of the retirement age) has succeeded in pushing back the year that the monthly benefit must be cut from 2020 to 2040—a postponement of two decades.

It shouldn't be surprising that mitigating the 2040 problem requires sacrifice. An important source of the 2040 problem is that people are living longer. Consider an individual facing the prospect of living longer. The prospect itself is a blessing, but preparing for it involves sacrifice. A sensible individual would strike a compromise between saving more while working, working to an older age, and reducing consumption in retirement. Let's consider how Social Security might do the same.

Ways to Raise Tax Growth

Payroll tax revenue can be increased in three different ways. First, the payroll tax rate (the percentage) can be raised; this would impose an additional tax burden on low- and moderate-income workers as well as high-income workers. Second, the payroll tax ceiling ($102,000 in 2008) can be raised; this would impose a 12.4% tax on newly taxed payroll (note that it would automatically raise benefits to which high-income workers are entitled because the benefit formula links the benefit to the ceiling). Third, payroll above the ceiling can be taxed. Since 1994, Medicare has taxed all payroll above the Social Security ceiling at a combined (employer plus employee) rate of 2.9%. One option would be to tax payroll above the ceiling an additional 3%; alternatively, instead of a flat 3%, the rates could be raised in steps from 1% to 5% as income above the ceiling increases.

Ways to Slow Benefit Growth

In order to slow benefit growth, Social Security could encourage people to work to an older age. Today, most people work at jobs that are physically less demanding than years ago, and they remain healthy enough to work to an older age. Of course, some people still work at physically demanding jobs or develop poor health at an early age. In the early 1980s, Congress scheduled a gradual increase in the full benefit age, beginning in 2000 from 65 to 66 and then after a 10-year delay from 66 to 67. One option would be to reduce or eliminate the delay in setting the FBA at 67, so that 67 is reached sooner, and then continue to increase the FBA until it reaches 68. Congress has not scheduled any increase in the earliest eligibility age which is still 62. We saw that in the United States and other countries many workers choose to retire as soon as they reach the Social Security EEA. One option to help slow benefit growth would be to schedule—with advanced warning of perhaps five years—an increase in the EEA from 62 to 63 (and perhaps eventually to 64).

If benefit growth must be reduced, the burden can be placed mainly on affluent retirees or spread across all retirees. Placing the burden mainly on the affluent can be accomplished by modifying the benefit formula to achieve a gradual reduction in the replacement rate of high earners. This seems reasonable in light of the trend of increasing inequality in favor of high earners. Today, as noted earlier, the benefit formula is governed by three brackets—90%, 32%, and 15%. The first dollars of a retiree's average indexed monthly earnings are converted into a monthly benefit at a 90% rate, then the next dollars at a 32% rate, and the next dollars at a 15% rate. Gradually reducing the third rate from 15% to, say, 10% would offset some of the increasing inequality that has favored high earners.

Instead, the burden can be spread across all retirees by having Social Security switch from wage indexing to price indexing. The current Social Security benefit formula uses **wage indexing**: It automatically raises a new retiree's initial monthly benefit at the same rate as wages rise in the economy, so that the replacement rate—the ratio of the initial benefit to the preretirement wage—stays fairly constant over time. The replacement rate for the average worker is currently about 40%. By contrast, under **price indexing** the replacement rate would decline continuously as time passes because wages generally rise faster than prices (wage growth exceeds price growth by an amount roughly equal to productivity growth). Price indexing would implement a permanent freeze in the inflation-adjusted Social Security benefit, so as inflation-adjusted wages rise over time, the replacement rate would decline.

Progressive indexing is a compromise between wage indexing and price indexing. Wage indexing would be retained for low-income workers, while price indexing would be used for high-income workers, and middle-income workers would be subject to an average of the two. With progressive indexing, the largest burden would be born by high-income retirees and the least burden by low-income retirees.

Making Each Generation Self-Sufficient

A more fundamental change in Social Security would be to gradually switch from a workers-support-retirees system to an each-generation-self-sufficient system. As indicated in Table 5.1, this can be done in two different ways: collectively or individually. Thus, starting from the northeast cell in Table 5.1, it would be possible to move either straight down to the southeast cell—collective self-sufficiency—or to the southwest cell—individual self-sufficiency. We consider each in turn.

It is important to emphasize our earlier point that breaking out is hard to do. Switching would appear very attractive to workers if they did not have to continue supporting retirees who contributed under the old system. If workers are told that they can send their payroll tax to either their own individual investment account or to their own generation's investment account, so that bonds and stocks would accumulate for their own benefit, the proposal sounds attractive. The problem is that the proposal involves diverting payroll taxes that would have gone to current retirees. To switch without reneging on obligations to current retirees, workers must make additional contributions above current payroll taxes.

Is there any way out of this dilemma? A false escape is borrowing. Understandably, workers might ask, "Can't we divert our payroll tax to our own individual or generational account and borrow to meet our obligation to current retirees?" Borrowing does indeed postpone bearing a burden—but it does not escape it. Whoever must pay the interest will bear the burden. So if workers divert their payroll taxes and the government borrows to pay current retirees, workers in the future will have to pay additional taxes to finance the interest payments that the government will owe on its borrowing. Thus, there is no permanent escape for workers through government borrowing.

Collective Self-Sufficiency

Under collective self-sufficiency, each generation would pay payroll taxes into the Social Security Trust Fund, which would use the revenue to buy financial assets (government bonds and perhaps also corporate bonds and stocks) for that generation of workers. When that generation retired, the Trust Fund would sell their financial assets and use the proceeds to pay that generation's benefits. Total benefits paid to a generation of retirees would equal total proceeds from the sale of bonds and stocks accumulated by that generation.

Thus, in any given year, the Trust Fund would be selling financial assets for retirees and buying financial assets for workers. For example, the Trust Fund might sell $100 billion of bonds for retirees to pay benefits and use the $300 billion of payroll tax revenue to buy bonds for workers. An observer would see that the Trust Fund had collected $300 billion in payroll tax revenue, paid $100 billion in benefits, and increased its holding of bonds by $200 billion.

How would each individual retiree's benefit be determined? One option would be to give each retiree a share of the total benefits equal to the share of his generation's payroll taxes that he paid. Another option would be to give a low-income retiree a share greater than he paid, and the reverse for a high-income retiree. Thus, with a collective system, Congress could implement partial redistribution (as it does under the current Social Security program). Also, with a collective system, Congress could give each retiree an inflation-protected annuity—a benefit payment adjusted annually for inflation for as long as the retiree lives (as it does under the current Social Security program).

Individual Self-Sufficiency: Individual Investment Accounts

Under individual self-sufficiency, each individual would pay payroll taxes into his own individual Social Security investment fund and purchase financial assets (government bonds, corporate bonds, and corporate stocks). When that individual retired, the individual would sell his bonds and stocks and use the proceeds to withdraw retirement benefits. Each retiree's benefits would equal total proceeds from the sale of that individual's bonds and stocks, so each individual would receive back whatever his own portfolio accumulated.

Each individual would decide whether to buy an annuity at retirement. Any part of the retiree's portfolio that is not used to buy an annuity can be left as a bequest to his heirs when he dies. Although each worker would be required to pay a payroll tax, he would rightly regard it as his own personal saving, so the tax should have no negative effect on his work effort. This approach would make each individual independent of the next generation and of the government for his own retirement. His retirement benefits would depend on the fate of his own investment portfolio.

Everyone agrees that it is a good thing for individuals to accumulate funds in their own investment accounts. The disagreement is over whether such accounts should be part of Social Security or "on top of" Social Security. One side believes such accounts should be separate from Social Security: Social Security should remain a workers-support-retirees defined-benefit plan, and individuals should be encouraged through tax advantages to build their own individual investment funds as a supplement to Social Security. The other side believes such defined-contribution accounts should be part of Social Security.

Combinations and Compromises

Rather than choose one of the "pure" approaches just discussed, the U.S. Congress may consider various combinations and compromises that include elements of different

In 2005 President George W. Bush proposed permitting each worker to decide whether to stay with the current Social Security program or divert 4 percentage points out of the 6.2%—hence, about two-thirds—of his payroll tax to his own newly established individual investment account and, in return, receive a lower regular Social Security benefit upon retirement. Under the proposal, the government would borrow to replace the diverted revenue in order to maintain benefits for current retirees, so in the future, additional taxes would be needed to finance the interest payments the government would owe on its borrowing. The majority of Republicans in Congress supported the president's proposal, while most Democrats (and a few Republicans) opposed establishing individual investment accounts as part of Social Security and borrowing to maintain the benefits of current retirees. President Bush was unable to secure passage by Congress of his proposal.

pure approaches. For example, Congress might decide to enact several of the measures discussed in the section "Treating the 2040 Problem," such as raising the retirement age; taking a step toward collective self-sufficiency by increasing the buildup of the Social Security Trust Fund enough to prevent the complete drawing down of bonds in the Trust Fund; and establishing individual investment accounts using a small percentage of payroll tax and some borrowing. Thus, if no pure solution can command a majority in Congress (as well as obtain a signature from the president), the challenge will be to find some combination and compromise that can be enacted into law and make a significant improvement in the prospects of Social Security.

Summary

There are four ways to prepare for retirement: workers can support retirees individually or collectively or each generation can be self-sufficient individually or collectively. When workers support retirees collectively, the workers' rate of return approximately equals the sum of the growth rate of the labor force and the growth rate of wages. When workers are self-sufficient, the rate of return equals the marginal product of capital. It is likely that the rate of return will be several points higher when workers are self-sufficient than when workers support retirees. Also, the capital stock of the economy will be higher when workers are self-sufficient than when workers support retirees. However, once a system of workers-support-retirees is in place, breaking out is hard to do, because during the transition it requires double saving: Workers must save to support retirees while also saving to provide for their own retirement.

Under the U.S. Social Security program, workers support retirees collectively: Payroll taxes from workers are sent to retirees as benefits. Each worker's benefit upon retirement depends on the worker's wage history. The benefit formula enacted by Congress gives a higher replacement rate to low-income workers than to high-income workers; the replacement rate for the average worker is roughly 40%. Each retiree receives a benefit that is automatically adjusted each year for inflation and continues as long as the person lives. Payroll taxes have caused little reduction in the work of heads of households, but payroll taxes together with the 50% spousal benefit may have reduced the market work effort of spouses who would have been second earners. Evidence from several countries, including the United States, suggests that many workers choose to retire at whatever age the Social Security program designates as the youngest age at which benefits are available; thus Social Security influences retirement. It seems likely that Social Security reduces private saving, because workers expecting Social Security benefits at retirement recognize that they do not have to save as much as they would have if there were no Social Security program.

If there is no reform, Social Security will face a serious problem around 2040 when the bonds in the Trust Fund have been drawn down to zero and payroll tax revenue is projected to be about 70% of scheduled benefits; either benefits will be cut from $100 to $70 (an abrupt 30% cut), or taxes will be raised from $70 to $100, or the difference will be split at $85. To avoid facing these options in 2040, payroll tax growth has to be raised and benefit growth slowed, as soon as possible. A more fundamental change would be to gradually shift Social Security from a workers-support-retirees system to an each-generation-self-sufficient system. Whether this is done collectively (with a larger buildup of bonds in the Trust Fund) or individually (with the establishment of individual investment accounts), during the transition, workers would need to double-save and continue to support retirees while saving for their own retirement.

Key Terms

rate of return, *100*
marginal product of capital (mpk), *103*
defined-benefit plan, *106*
replacement rate, *106*
annuity, *106*
defined-contribution plan, *106*
pay-as-you-go (PAYGO), *109*
Social Security Trust Fund, *111*

Federal Insurance Contribution Act (FICA), *112*
payroll tax ceiling, *112*
Old Age, Survivors, and Disability Insurance (OASDI), *113*
earliest eligibility age (EEA), *113*
average indexed monthly earnings (AIME), *113*

primary insurance amount (PIA), *113*
progressive benefit formula, *113*
full benefits age (FBA), *114*
social security wealth, *116*
present value of the benefits, *117*
wage indexing, *122*
price indexing, *122*
progressive indexing, *122*

Questions

1. If workers support retirees, $BR =$ _____. Then $B/W =$ _____. But L/R has been (*rising, falling*) because retirees have been living _____; so if t stays constant, B/W will (*rise, fall*); to keep B/W constant, t must be (*raised, lowered*).

2. Suppose Social Security begins in period 1 with a payroll tax rate of 20%. The wage grows 20% per period, and the number of workers grows 20% per period. Complete the table.

Period	Workers	Wage	Tax/Worker	Total Taxes	Retirees	Benefit
1	100	$10,000	$_____	Omit	Omit	Omit
2	___	$_____	$_____	$_____	_____	$_____

3. For a worker who pays T_1 and later receives a benefit B_2, the rate of return is defined as $r^* =$ _____, so in this table, $r^* =$ _____%.

4. Starting with r^*'s definition, use algebra to derive a relationship between r^*, g_w, and g_L.

5. If each generation is self-sufficient, then $r^* =$ mpk because each person uses his saving to buy a _____ from a firm that buys a $100 _____ that raises firm revenue $6 per year so the mpk is __% per year and the saver is paid $r^* =$ _____ %.

6. It is estimated that when workers support retirees, r^* would be _____ %, and when each generation is self-sufficient, r^* would be _____ %.

7. "Breaking out is hard to do" because workers must save _____. Explain.

8. Complete the following table.

	Collective Workers Support Retirees	Each Individual Self-Sufficient
Rate of return r^*	_____ = __%	_____ = __%
Capital and output of economy	(*higher, lower*)	(*higher, lower*)
Individual has control	(*yes, no*)	(*yes, no*)
Risk of variation of r^*	(*high, low*)	(*high, low*)
Benefit depends on	_____ "defined _____"	_____ "defined _____"
Redistribution from high-W to low-W	(*some, none*)	(*some, none*)
Benefit is inflation-protected annuity (as long as retiree lives)	(*yes, no*)	(*yes, no*)

9. If the United States stays with a workers-support-retirees system, it faces a 2040 problem. Explain the problem using Figure 5.4, and tell what would happen after 2040.

10. Without changing the workers-support-retirees system, what can be done between now and 2040 to reduce the 2040 problem: (*a*) with taxes and (*b*) with benefit growth. Give specific options for (*a*) and (*b*).

11. A more fundamental change would be to make each generation self-sufficient.

    a. Explain how collective self-sufficiency could be achieved.

    b. Explain how individual self-sufficiency could be achieved.

12. Switching from the current system to generational self-sufficiency involves a difficult transition. Why?

13. Explain why borrowing postpones but does not eliminate the burden of this transition.

14. Go online and read about the debate in 2005 over President Bush's proposal to reform Social Security. Give the main specifics of his proposal. What arguments did the president and his supporters make? What arguments did opponents make?

Appendix

Social Security *Your Rate of Return When You Work for 40 Years and Retire for 20 Years*

In the text of this chapter the rate of return was defined only for the case where there are just two stages of life—(1) the work stage and (2) the retirement stage—so $r^* = (B_2/T_1) - 1$. Suppose you want to calculate the rate of return you will get under Social Security when you work for 40 years and pay a payroll tax each year, and then retire for 20 years and receive a benefit each year. How would you calculate your r^*?

There is a way to view the rate of return r^* that will let you calculate it if you work for 40 years and are retired for 20 years. Begin with $r^* = (B_2/T_1) - 1$, add 1 to both sides so $(1 + r^*) = B_2/T_1$, then multiply both sides by T_1, and divide by $(1 + r^*)$ to obtain:

$$T_1 = \frac{B_2}{(1 + r^*)}$$

Thus, the rate of return r^* is the percentage that makes the two sides equal when your tax is T_1 and your benefit is B_2. In our text numerical example, $\$100 = \$150/(1 + r^*)$, so $r^* = 50\%$ makes the two sides equal. Another way to say this is that if the future benefit B_2 is "discounted" (divided) by $1 + r^*$, the discounted benefit will equal the tax T_1. In terms of the concept of *present value* explained in Chapter 4:

The rate of return equals the value of the discount rate that would make the present value of the benefit equal the tax.

This way of viewing r^* can be applied to the case where you pay tax each year for the 40 years that you work and receive a benefit each year for the 20 years you are retired.

The rate of return is the discount rate that would make the present value of your benefits equal to the present value of your taxes.

Thus, your rate of return is the numerical value of r^* that makes

$$\sum_{1}^{40} \frac{T_i}{(1 + r^*)^i} = \sum_{41}^{60} \frac{B_i}{(1 + r^*)^i}$$

where T_i = the tax you pay each year you work from year 1 to year 40

B_i = the benefit your receive each year you are retired from year 41 to year 60

$\sum_{1}^{40}$ = the sum over the 40 years you work (years 1 to 40)

$\sum_{41}^{60}$ = the sum over the 20 years you are retired (years 41 to 60)

If you had a numerical estimate, with the help of the Social Security Administration, of the tax T_i that you will pay each year you work for 40 years and the benefit B_i that you will receive each year you are retired for 20 years, then r^* would be the only unknown in the equation. Unfortunately, there is no way to just solve for r^*. You must find it by trial and error. You pick a number for r^* (say, 2.0%) and compute the left side by adding 40 numbers, then the right side by adding 20 numbers, and see if the two sides are approximately equal. If they are, then 2.0% is your estimated rate of return. If they aren't equal, pick another number for r^* and try again. Of course, this would be very time-consuming.

Fortunately, computer programmers have written a *rate of return computer program* that will perform the repeated trial-and-error process in a split second. If you have access to a rate of return computer program, all you have to do is enter the 40 numbers for your 40 tax payments and the 20 numbers for your 20 benefits, press a button, and you'll see the numerical value of your r^*—the value that makes the left side (the present value of your taxes) equal the right side (the present value of your benefits).

Finally, here's the general formula. If you work until year R (from year 1 to year R) and are retired from year $R + 1$ to year J, then your rate of return is the numerical value for r^* that makes

$$\sum_{1}^{R} \frac{T_i}{(1 + r^*)^i} = \sum_{R+1}^{J} \frac{B_i}{(1 + r^*)^i}$$

In our example, R was 40 and J, 60. The rate of return computer program is ready to handle any numerical value of R and J.

Chapter **Six**

Health Insurance

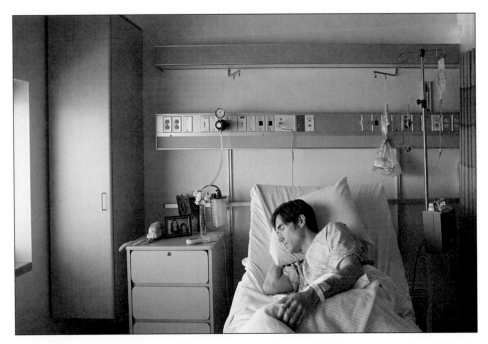

Jupiterimages/Imagesource

What role should the government play in the provision of health insurance? What would happen if the government played no role and left the provision of health insurance completely to the private sector? Alternatively, what would happen under various specific kinds of government intervention? What in fact has happened under actual government interventions? This chapter addresses these questions.

For most goods and services, consumers pay the full price of anything they buy. However, most consumers of medical care—patients—pay only a portion of the price charged by the providers of medical care—doctors and hospitals. In some cases, consumers pay nothing. An insurer—either a private company or the government—often pays a large share of the price, sometimes 100%. In this chapter, we analyze why that is so, evaluate the impact of health insurance, and consider public policies for improving its performance.

HEALTH INSURANCE IN THE UNITED STATES

There have been great advances in medical care over the past half century, but they have come at considerable cost:

From 1960 to 2007, spending on medical care in the United States rose from 5% to 16% of GDP.

The United States devotes a much larger share of GDP to medical care than other countries:

Economically advanced countries on average spend about 10% of GDP on medical care.

No other country spends over 12% of GDP.
Britain only spends about 8% of GDP.

The United States' high and rising medical share of GDP should prompt an examination of whether incentives are in place to induce an optimal balancing of the benefits of medical care against its costs and to promote efficiency in the delivery of medical care.

It is important to recognize that the health and longevity of a population depends on much more than medical care. Diet, exercise, lifestyle, tobacco, alcohol, drugs, income, education, climate, geography, and genetics are all important determinants of health and longevity. Although the United States spends a much higher percentage of its GDP on medical care than other countries, the health and longevity of the U.S. population is not always better than other countries. This does not necessarily imply that higher medical care spending is unhelpful. It may mean that poor performance on other determinants of health and longevity may be overwhelming the benefits from more medical care.

The majority of people in the United States—roughly 60%—have health insurance coverage through private insurance; most of these obtain their private insurance at their workplace. About 90% of people with private insurance have coverage through their workplace; the other 10% buy insurance individually. Private health insurance plans vary considerably: Some cover virtually all medical services and pay virtually the entire bill; others exclude many medical services and pay only a limited portion of the bill. It is therefore misleading to simply characterize a person as uninsured or insured—the degree of insurance matters and varies greatly among the insured.

Roughly 25% of the population have health insurance coverage through the government—roughly half of these (the elderly) are covered by Medicare and half (the poor) by Medicaid. But a significant minority—roughly 15% of the population (over 45 million people)—are uninsured. Some turn down the opportunity to be insured, but others are not given the opportunity at an affordable price. The uninsured are virtually always given hospital care for medical emergencies, but they then bear a substantial financial burden and impose a large cost on others who end up paying a large share of the bill for their hospital episode. The uninsured often avoid or delay medical care until it is too late or very costly, and they generally obtain less care than the insured. Some insured people discover, during a costly medical episode, that their insurance plan won't pay because the episode is related to a preexisting condition—a medical condition that the patient had prior to joining the insurance plan. Insured people sometimes discover that their plan will not pay for certain medical services or it will pay only a limited amount for particular services, so that they must pay a large share of the price of the services they received.

The challenge for public policy is to improve the efficiency and equity of medical care and health insurance without impeding incentives for continuing innovation and progress in the quality of medical care.

PRINCIPLES OF HEALTH INSURANCE

The Genesis of Health Insurance

What would happen if the government played no role in health insurance? There would still be health insurance, because entrepreneurs would start private companies to sell health insurance. So why not leave health insurance to the private sector? After all, most economists argue that the government should play no role for most goods and services because the free market does a very satisfactory job. To decide whether government should intervene, let us first investigate what would happen if we left health insurance to the free market.

Imagine that you live in a society without health insurance, and you must pay your own medical bills. In this society, most people have good health and have no trouble paying their modest bills, but a few people are not so lucky; they require a hospital episode and get hit with a huge medical bill. Assume that at the beginning of each year, no one knows whether a hospital episode is coming, so even the majority, who end up fine, worry about being blindsided by a huge medical and financial blow. Often you find yourself asking, "What will I do if I'm hit with a huge medical bill?"

Suppose you hear that someone has started a health insurance company. If you buy *insurance* by paying a **premium** (the price of the insurance) to this company, the company will pay your entire medical bill. Suppose you, and everyone else, have a 5% chance that a hospital episode will hit you with a $61,000 bill and a 95% chance that your medical bill will only be $1,000. What is the most you would be willing to pay for the insurance? There's no right or wrong answer. Your answer depends on how *risk-averse* you are. If you're very worried (averse to a risk) about the hospital bill, you'll pay a lot for insurance; if you're not that worried, you'll pay less.

Starting a Health Insurance Company

Now imagine that you've just graduated from college in this society, and you decide to start a health insurance company. But can you make money selling health insurance? There are many factors to consider as you crunch the numbers.

Initially you assume that insurance won't change anyone's medical bill—5% will still have a $61,000 bill and 95% will still have a $1,000 bill—and that no one has inside information about her own health prospects, so everyone assumes her chances are 5% and 95%, respectively. For every 100 people who buy your insurance, 5 people are likely to incur a $61,000 bill, and 95 people, a $1,000 bill. Hence, your expected total bill from hospitals and doctors for your enrollees will be

$$5(\$61,000) + 95(\$1,000) = \$305,000 + \$95,000 = \$400,000$$

To obtain premium revenue of $400,000 from your 100 enrollees, you must charge a premium of $4,000 per enrollee. As long as you charge a premium of at least $4,000 and enrollees are willing to pay your premium, for every 100 persons you will take in at least $400,000 in revenue, thereby covering your expected cost of $400,000.

Let's redo the calculation using a concept from statistics: **expected value**. What is the expected value—the average, or *mean,* value—of the medical bill per enrollee? If a person has a 5% chance of incurring a $61,000 medical bill and a 95% chance of incurring a $1,000 medical bill, then the expected value of the person's medical cost (the expected medical cost) is

$$.05(\$61,000) + .95(\$1,000) = \$3,050 + \$950 = \$4,000.$$

As long as your premium is at least $4,000, it looks like you'll make a profit.

However, there are some complications that will reduce your profit. First, there's some risk that your medical bills will be more than $400,000 per 100 enrollees. You can't be sure that *exactly* 5% of your enrollees will have a $61,000 medical bill. If you flip a coin a million times, you can be sure that heads will come up very close to 50% and tails, 50%. But if you only flip the coin 10 times, it is quite possible for heads to come up much higher or lower than 50%. In statistics this is called the *law of large numbers*. You have to make sure that you operate on a large enough scale—enroll enough people—so that the law of large numbers will get your percentages close to 5% and 95%.

Second, even though people are willing to pay a lot more than $4,000 to buy insurance, this doesn't mean you will be able to charge as much as they would pay. The price that you will be able to charge depends on whether you have competition from other insurance companies. If you're the only insurance company, you can charge a lot more than $4,000. However, if you can make a substantial profit selling health insurance at this high price, others are bound to start rival insurance companies. To attract enrollees away from you, these companies may charge less than you're charging, and you'll have to cut your premium to retain enrollees. Of course, the other companies can't cut their premium below their expected cost. As long as you operate efficiently—that is, keep your operating cost to a minimum—you'll be able to match their premium, retain a solid market share, and make enough revenue to cover all your costs (including your own compensation). Competition will force you to charge an **actually fair premium**—a premium that just covers the expected cost of your enrollees. In the example above, the actuarially fair premium would equal the expected value of the medical cost per person, $4,000.

Third, you will incur costs operating the insurance company. You'll need to pay employees to sign up enrollees, process the medical bills, and pay the hospitals and doctors, and you'll need to compensate yourself for your time and effort. You'll need to rent office space or perhaps construct your own office building, which may require borrowing money to finance the construction. You'll need to advertise. These operating costs will cut down your profit. You will need to figure out your operating costs per 100 enrollees to make sure that your revenue will cover all your costs. You'll have to charge more than $4,000 to cover these costs.

Price Equals Expected Medical Cost

Would you charge everyone the same premium? Immediately you realize that it would be very useful to get some medical information about each enrollee. Before you enroll someone, why not require the person to answer questions about health history? You may not always get accurate information, but for our example, let's assume that you do. Suppose that a high-expected-cost person has a 9% chance of incurring a $61,000 medical bill. Then, as indicated in Table 6.1, the high-cost person's expected medical cost is

$$.09(\$61,000) + .91(\$1,000) = \$5,490 + \$910 = \$6,400.$$

Suppose a low-expected-cost person has only a 1% chance of incurring a $61,000 medical bill. Then, as indicated in Table 6.1, the low-cost person's expected medical cost is

$$.01(\$61,000) + .99(\$1,000) = \$610 + \$990 = \$1,600.$$

TABLE 6.1
Expected Medical Bills

	Chance of a $61,000 Medical Bill	Chance of a $1,000 Medical Bill	Expected Medical Bill
High-cost person	9%	91%	$6,400
Low-cost person	1	99	1,600

The premium that you charge each person must cover the expected medical cost of that person plus the operating cost per person. Ignoring the operating cost, you must charge each person a price that covers her expected medical cost. With competition from other insurance companies, you will not be able to charge any higher. Thus, in a competitive insurance market, each person will be charged a price P equal to her expected medical cost (EMC). For person i:

$$P_i = \text{EMC}_i$$

Thus, the price charged to a person will vary with the person's expected medical cost, but the price will not vary with the person's income. Throughout this discussion we often refer to a person who has a high *expected* medical cost as simply a high-cost person.

Suppose your conscience bothers you about setting $P_i = \text{EMC}_i$ for each enrollee because you realize that it is often a matter of luck, not behavior or effort, that determines whether a person has a high or low expected medical cost. You feel guilty about charging the high-cost person a higher price than the low-cost person. Instead, you would rather charge them the same price. For example, instead of charging the high-cost person $6,400, and the low-cost person, $1,600, you would rather charge each $4,000 (the average of $6,400 and $1,600). What will happen if you do this? Some of your competitors will offer low-cost persons a price of only $1,600, and you will lose your low-cost enrollees. Left with only high-cost enrollees, you will have to raise your price to $6,400 to break even.

Now suppose your conscience bothers you about setting the same price regardless of the person's income. You decide to charge a price below medical cost for a low-income person and make it up by charging a price above medical cost for a high-income person. What will happen? Some of your competitors will offer your high-income enrollees a price equal to their expected medical cost, and you will lose your high-income enrollees. Left with only low-income enrollees, you will have to raise your price to their expected medical cost to break even.

As long as some insurance companies don't let conscience interfere with making a profit, each person will end up being charged a price equal to her expected cost. Note we're simply assuming that some insurance companies are as interested in profit as companies making other goods and services. A normal profit motive is enough to cause each person to be charged a price equal to her expected medical cost.

Our conclusion—that in a competitive individual insurance market each person will be charged a price equal to that person's expected medical cost—has important implications. If everyone had roughly the same income and expected medical cost, things would work fine. But in fact there is significant variation in income and expected medical cost across individuals. Some people have low incomes and high expected medical costs. They may be charged a premium that is so high relative to their income that they can't afford insurance. A person with a huge expected medical cost due to a chronic costly illness will either be charged a huge premium or simply be rejected.

Moral Hazard and Price Responsiveness

There's another problem to watch out for when you're deciding which premium to charge called **moral hazard**: the use of more medical care by insured people because they know that their insurer will pay part or all of their bill. They may order more medical care when they are sick. They may even take less care to stay healthy (through diet and exercise) if they know that insurance will cover their medical care. Suppose insurance causes every enrollee to use 20% more medical care. For every 100 enrollees, 5 will use $73,200, not $61,000, and 95 will use $1,200, not $1,000. For every 100 enrollees, your total medical bill will be 20% greater—instead of $400,000, it will be $480,000:

$$5(\$61,000) + 95(\$1,000) = \$305,000 + \$95,000 = \$400,000$$

$$5(\$73,200) + 95(\$1,200) = \$366,000 + \$114,000 = \$480,000$$

The expected value of the medical bill of an enrollee will be 20% greater—instead of $4,000, it will be $4,800.

$$.05(\$61,000) + .95(\$1,000) = \$3,050 + \$950 = \$4,000$$

$$.05(\$73,200) + .95(\$1,200) = \$3,660 + \$1,440 = \$4,800$$

Why is this expansion in use called *moral hazard?* One possible reason is that it may strike some people as immoral for a person to use more medical care just because insurance will cover it. But this behavior is familiar to economists. Whenever the price of something is cut, people naturally demand more of it. Economists usually don't call their behavior immoral, but they simply note that demand has some price responsiveness—people respond to a cut in price by demanding more. For each person, the effective price of using additional medical care has been cut to zero when the insurance company pays the entire bill; not surprisingly, the typical person will expand use in response to this cut in the price. To economists, *moral hazard is simply price responsiveness.*

Economists have used various techniques to try to estimate the magnitude of price responsiveness—specifically, the **price elasticity** for different kinds of medical care.

The price elasticity is defined as the ratio of the percentage increase in the quantity demanded to the percentage reduction in the price.

To estimate actual price elasticity, economists use econometric analysis—statistical analysis of data generated by actual behavior in society. The researcher observes changes in price, either over time or across individuals at a point in time, and tries to measure how much quantity changed. Of course, things other than price might have caused quantity to change, so the researcher must try to control for changes in other relevant variables, such as income or medical condition. These studies have found differing estimates, but the studies suggest that the price elasticity for most medical care is not zero—the price patients must pay often has some effect on how much they use.

A different source of evidence on price elasticity was provided by an ambitious study conducted in the 1970s called the RAND Health Insurance Experiment.[1] Individuals were randomly assigned different prices for medical care—the administrators of the experiment would reimburse some individuals a high percentage and

---

[1] A comprehensive account and analysis of this experiment is given in Joseph Newhouse, *Free for All? Lessons from the RAND Health Insurance Experiment* (Harvard University Press, 1993).

others a low percentage, thereby varying the out-of-pocket price faced by different individuals. The random assignment helped control for other factors, thereby isolating the impact of the price on the quantity demanded. The price elasticity varied according to the particular medical service, but for the average medical service:

The study estimated a price elasticity of 0.2: a 50% reduction in the price a person faced raised the quantity the person demanded by 10%.

The demand for medical care is inelastic—its price elasticity is less than 1.0—but it is *not* zero: What patients must pay does have some effect on how much medical service they demand.

Adverse Selection and Asymmetric Information

When setting up your health insurance company, you must also be aware of adverse selection: Instead of a random sample selecting to enroll, a biased sample with higher medical cost is likely to enroll. Thus far we've assumed that no one knows, at the beginning of the year, whether his bill will end up $61,000 or $1,000, so that there is no bias in the mix of persons who decide to buy insurance. You charge them all the same premium because their health prospects look the same to you. However, suppose people have accurate "inside information" about their health prospects: Some people know they are likely to have a hospital episode, while others know they probably won't. Because buying insurance is voluntary, there will be a bias in the mix of people who decide to buy your insurance. Instead of just 5% of your enrollees incurring a hospital episode, you'll discover at the end of the year that a higher percentage go to the hospital. Therefore, if you think people know more about their hospital prospects than you do, you'd better charge a higher premium.

Suppose you charge a higher premium in anticipation of a biased mix of enrollees. Your higher price is likely to make your mix of enrollees even more biased. At the higher price, some people who are confident that they won't have a hospital episode will decide to take their chance and go without insurance; the people who keep enrolling despite your higher price will be the ones who, with inside information, know they are very likely to have a hospital episode. So at the end of the year, it may turn out that even your higher premium is not high enough to cover the medical bills of your enrollees. Next year you may feel that you have to charge an even higher price, which will cause even greater bias in who decides to enroll. It is even possible that this problem will be so severe that there is no premium that you can charge in order to make a profit.

This problem was illustrated nicely in a 1970 article by Nobel prize–winning economist George Akerlof on the market for "lemons," used cars that have hidden serious defects (a lemon's nice appearance conceals its acid taste). The seller of the used car knows whether it's a lemon, but the buyer doesn't. Potential buyers suspect that if someone is offering to sell a used car at a reasonable price, it's probably a lemon. Thus, potential buyers are cautious about purchasing any used car, so there is a market failure: Used cars without defects are not sold to buyers who would have been glad to pay a reasonable price if they were sure they weren't lemons. The source of the problem is the *asymmetry of information* between the buyer and the seller.

Catastrophic Insurance

Let's return to the moral hazard problem—or, as economists say, the price responsiveness problem. To focus on this problem, assume that all persons have identical health prospects—everyone's expected medical cost is the same. Also, assume there is no adverse selection problem (there is no inside information). If insurance pays the entire bill so that medical care is free to patients, price-responsive patients will demand 20% more medical care. How does the 20% expansion of use by the 95% strike you? It should strike you as wasteful. The main purpose of insurance is to prevent a huge burden like $61,000. But a side effect of the insurance is to induce the 95% to expand their use by 20%—from $1,000 to $1,200—solely because the insurance makes additional medical care free to them. Of course, this additional medical care is not free to society—producing this additional medical care absorbs resources that could have been used to make other goods and services. As a consequence of inflating their use of medical care, people end up paying a premium that is 20% higher ($4,800 instead of $4,000).

This is just like the waste induced by splitting the bill at a restaurant. Suppose ten people go to a restaurant and agree in advance that, instead of individual checks, each will pay one-tenth of the total bill. Each person realizes that if she inflates her order, it will hardly affect the amount she pays. For example, if she orders wine A that has a price $10 higher than wine B, it will raise her share of the bill by only $1. So each person inflates her order. In the end, of course, each person feels the effects of the wasteful overordering because each must pay one-tenth of a highly inflated bill, and each person concludes that it would have been better to use individual checks.

There is a way to achieve the main purpose of insurance—preventing a huge burden on the 5%—without inducing wasteful expansion by the 95%: catastrophic insurance. Thus far we've assumed that insurance always pays the entire bill for every person. Under **catastrophic insurance**, the insurance company will pay the entire medical bill *above a threshold*—for example, $5,200. The person will have to pay the first $5,200 of a hospital bill—hence, under this catastrophic insurance policy, the patient will have a **deductible** of $5,200. The strategy behind catastrophic insurance should be obvious. The 95% won't inflate their use because they'll bear the full burden of their own ordering. The insurance will be restricted to the 5%, reducing their burden from $61,000 to $5,200 plus the premium.

If your insurance company sold catastrophic insurance, what premium would you have to charge to be able to pay the excess of any medical bill over $5,200? For 95% of your enrollees who incur a $1,000 medical bill, you won't have to pay anything. The 5% with a hospital episode will each incur a $73,200 bill (after paying the first $5,200, additional medical care will be free to the 5% so they will use 20% more than $61,000), of which you will pay $73,200 − $5,200 = $68,000. Thus, the expected value of your payment per enrollee is

$$.05(\$68,000) + .95(\$0) = \$3,400$$

so $3,400 is what you must charge to each customer (plus the amount needed to cover operating costs).

Consider three insurance coverage choices shown in Table 6.2: none, complete, or catastrophic. "None" would be too risky for most people—they would have a 5% chance of bearing a $61,000 burden. "Complete" entails a $4,800 burden.

TABLE 6.2
Catastrophic Insurance versus Complete Insurance

Insurance Coverage	Premium	Out-of-Pocket Burden 5% Chance	Out-of-Pocket Burden 95% Chance	Total Burden 5% Chance	Total Burden 95% Chance
None	$ 0	$61,000	$1,000	$61,000	$1,000
Complete	4,800	0	0	**4,800**	**4,800**
Catastrophic	3,400	5,200	1,000	**8,600**	**4,400**

"Catastrophic" entails a 95% chance of a $4,400 burden (a $3,400 premium and $1,000 out of pocket) and a 5% chance of an $8,600 burden (a $3,400 premium and $5,200 out of pocket). Some people would prefer complete, but other people would prefer catastrophic. Why, then, don't we see more people with catastrophic insurance? As we explain shortly, one reason is that there is a tax advantage to having your medical bills paid by an insurance company rather than by you, out of pocket, using your after-tax income.

X% Insurance

Now consider insurance that pays a specific percentage ($X\%$) of any medical bill and requires the patient to pay the remaining percentage ($100\% - X\%$). For example, assume the insurance plan pays 75% and requires the patient to pay 25%. We'll call this "75% insurance." The patient **cost-sharing rate** (25%) is sometimes called the **coinsurance rate**. With 75% insurance, the insurer reimburses the patient 75% of the medical bill, so the reimbursement rate (subsidy rate) is 75%. Thus, $X\%$ insurance means that the patient receives a reimbursement rate of $X\%$.

We can analyze the impact of 75% insurance using a supply and demand diagram as shown in Figure 6.1. The suppliers of medical care are doctors, hospitals, medical technology firms, drugs companies, and so forth; as indicated by the positively sloping supply (S) curve, the higher the price that the suppliers receive, the greater the quantity of medical care they will supply. The demanders of medical care are patients guided by their doctors. Their demand curve without insurance is D: If they must pay a price of $100, they would demand 100 units of medical care (point O); if they must pay a price

FIGURE 6.1
X% Insurance
X% insurance shifts up the demand curve.

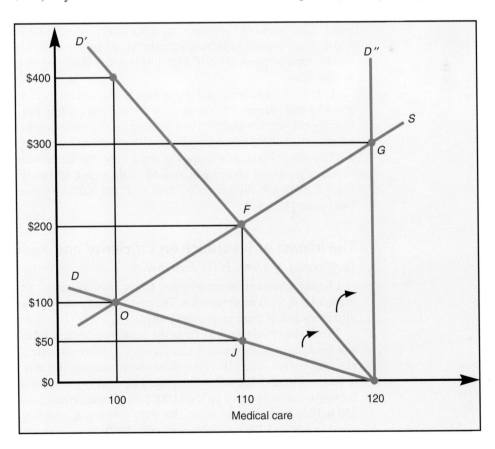

of $50, they would demand 110 (point J). Thus, starting from a price of $100, a 50% cut in the price that they must pay would raise their demand 10%; as noted earlier, this is what the RAND experiment estimated—an elasticity of 0.2 (10% ÷ 50% = 0.2). With no insurance, S and D intersect at point O, so the price is $100 and the quantity of medical care is 100 units.

The 75% insurance causes the demand curve to rotate upward (clockwise), pivoting around the point (120, $0), so that each point on the new D' curve is four times higher than the point directly below it on the original D curve. Why? Consider the point (100, $400) on the new D' curve. If medical providers charged a price of $400, the insurance company would pay 75%, or $300, and patients would pay 25%, or $100, so the out-of-pocket (effective) price to patients would be $100, and patients would therefore demand a quantity of 100, just as they did when they faced a price of $100 without insurance.

The new D' curve intersects the S curve at a point F which has a higher price and quantity than point O—for example, (110, $200) as shown. The price charged by the suppliers of medical care has been bid up from $100 to $200 due to the rotation upward (clockwise) of the demand curve; the subsidy has increased consumer demand (shifting up the demand curve), resulting in a higher price and quantity. But note that the out-of-pocket price faced by patients is 25% of $200, or $50, indicated at point J. This fall in the out-of-pocket price from $100 (at point O) to $50 (at point J) induces patients to expand their use—in this example, from 100 to 110.

It is worth taking a moment to consider what would happen if the insurance had been 100%. The higher the subsidy rate, the more the demand curve rotates upward (clockwise) toward the vertical position D'', so at first glance it might seem that the market would move to where a vertical demand curve (D'') that goes straight up from point (120, $0) would intersect the supply curve—point G. With straight-line supply and demand curves, as shown, intersection of supply with this vertical demand curve would occur at point G (120, $300). But rather than stop at G, price would continue to rise. Why?

As long as the subsidy rate is less than 100%, patients prefer to buy from the medical provider that charges the lowest price for a given quality. But what happens when the subsidy rate reaches 100%? Then patients don't care about the price. Any provider can raise its price above another provider without fear of losing any customers. In fact, with a 100% subsidy rate, raising quality is the only way for providers to attract consumers, so providers would compete by raising quality, cost, and price—without any apparent limit. A 100% subsidy gradually "explodes" the market, like a rocket launching upward from point (120, $0).

The Impact of Insurance on Efficiency and Redistribution

Inefficiency If There Is No Externality

In Chapter 1, we explained why any tax or subsidy causes an efficiency loss (a *BAD* triangle) *if* there is no externality. The price subsidy due to insurance causes a standard efficiency loss if there is no externality.

To see the efficiency loss from the insurance price subsidy, redraw points F and J and the S curve from Figure 6.1 in Figure 6.2. Through point J draw the marginal benefit (MB) curve. The MB curve shows how many dollars this sick person would have to be given to keep her utility the same if she had to give up that unit of medical care. If the consumer had to give up the 110th unit of medical care, she would have to be given $50 to keep her utility the same. But if the 110th unit were not produced, the resources saved would be $200—the marginal cost (MC)—so she could be given $50, and other

FIGURE 6.2

***X*% Insurance and Efficiency**

X% insurance decreases efficiency if there is no externality but may increase efficiency if there is an externality.

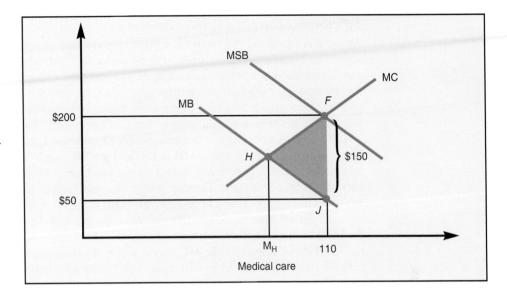

people could be given $150 of resources making them better off. As long as MB is less than MC, other people could be made better off while keeping the sick person's utility the same by cutting another unit of medical care, giving the sick person her MB and giving other people MC – MB. By cutting medical care from 110 to M_H (where MB intersects MC), the gain to other people (while keeping sick people's utility constant) would be the area of the triangle *FJH;* the efficiency loss from not cutting medical care from 110 to M_H equals the area of the triangle *FJH.*

Now notice something important about Figure 6.2. The size of the triangle area—the efficiency loss—depends on how steep the MB curve is. If the MB curve is steep, then the area of the triangle—the efficiency loss—would be small. What would make the MB curve steep? Suppose sick people judge that cutting medical care even slightly below what they obtain with insurance would cause a sharp drop their utility. Then they would need a large payment to compensate (to keep their utility constant) for even a slight reduction in their medical care, therefore their MB curve would be steep, and the efficiency loss from insurance would be small.[2]

Even if the efficiency loss from insurance were large, this does not mean that citizens should oppose insurance. Insurance redistributes resources and utility from the healthy to the sick. In theory, this redistribution could be accomplished without generating an efficiency loss by giving sick people cash income rather than a price subsidy. However, if the most practical way to redistribute resources is through an insurance price subsidy, then citizens should support use of the insurance price subsidy if they judge that the social benefit from the redistribution outweighs the efficiency loss. In judging the best numerical magnitude for *X*%, citizens should balance the social benefit of redistribution against the efficiency loss.

[2] A technical point: The MB curve in Figure 6.2 is the *compensated* demand curve which shows how much the quantity demanded decreases when price increases, but income also increases enough to keep the person's utility constant (despite the price increase which would have lowered utility). Because income also increases, the compensated demand curve—the MB curve through *J*—is steeper than the ordinary demand curve through *J* (which connects *J* and *O* in Figure 6.1), so the efficiency-loss triangle is *smaller* than the triangle that would be formed by the ordinary demand curve in Figure 6.1. This chapter's appendix provides further analysis.

Efficiency If There Is a Positive Externality

As we also explained in Chapter 1, a price subsidy may increase efficiency if there is a positive externality; in that case, it is a "corrective" subsidy. Suppose other people care about whether a patient gets a unit of medical care. Other people may care due to self-interest—for example, if a person gets a flu shot, she won't spread the flu to other people. Other people may also care simply due to compassion—they feel better when sick people get help, even sick people they don't personally know.

For example, consider the last unit produced with the 75% subsidy (the 110th) in Figure 6.2, where the patient's MB is $50 and the MC is $200. Suppose other people care about the sick person and would be willing to pay $150 to make sure the sick person gets that 110th unit. Then the marginal *social* benefit (MSB) of the 110th unit, as shown in Figure 6.2, would be $200, not $50; when the patient consumes the 110th unit, the patient benefits $50 (MB), and other people benefit $150. If this is so, then the MSB of the 110th unit would equal the MC. The socially optimal quantity is where the MSB curve intersects the MC curve, so the socially optimal quantity of medical care for sick people would be 110 units. This is exactly what patients would consume with 75% insurance. Thus, 75% insurance would be exactly what is needed to avoid any inefficiency and achieve the efficient quantity of medical care.

Optimal Redistribution from the Healthy to the Sick

Insurance engineers a redistribution of resources and utility from the healthy to the sick. When the healthy help to buy medical care for the sick by paying X% of the cost, they have less left to spend on their own consumption, so their utility falls. Like any other redistribution of income, the donor's utility falls and the recipient's utility rises. Economics cannot declare a particular degree of redistribution to be optimal, deficient, or excessive. Economics and medical science can illuminate the trade-off between the well-being of the sick and the healthy and try to measure it in order to provide useful information to policy makers and citizens. Then policy makers and citizens, armed with this information, will have different preferences about how much redistribution from the healthy to the sick should occur.

Citizens' preferences concerning the redistribution of resources from the healthy to the sick may be complex. One citizen may prefer a large redistribution whenever the recipient is young and the prospect for full recovery is good, but a small redistribution when the recipient is old and frail and recovery is very doubtful. A citizen may prefer a large redistribution when the recipient has a painful disease that medical care can cure, but a small redistribution when the recipient has a painless disease that medical care is unlikely to cure. A citizen may support a large redistribution if she knows the sick person or receives a direct appeal for help from the sick person (an "identified" sick person), but the citizen may support a small redistribution if she doesn't know the sick person and doesn't receive a direct appeal for help from the sick person (an "unidentified" sick person). As medical care advances over time and becomes more effective, most people are likely to prefer a larger redistribution from healthy to sick.

Suppose that medical care becomes so effective that even after a very large percentage of the income of the healthy (M% of GDP) has been redistributed to the sick, more medical care would still be beneficial to the sick. What if the benefit of medical care for the sick is only exhausted when most of the income of the healthy has been redistributed? A similar question could be asked of citizens of wealthy countries concerning redistribution of income to poor people in poor countries. How much redistribution would a citizen prefer? Once again citizens' preferences will be complex, and economics cannot declare a particular degree of redistribution to be optimal, deficient, or excessive.

Limitation of Price and Supply by the Insurer

In Figure 6.1, the suppliers of medical care—doctors, hospitals, medical technology firms, drug companies—are assumed to respond freely to any clockwise rotation of the demand curve caused by insurance, so that the market would go to the intersection of supply and demand. With no insurance, the quantity and price of medical care would be at point O (100, $100); with 75% insurance, at point F (110, $200); and with 100% insurance, at point G (120, $300) but with the price continuing to rise above $300, as explained above.

If insurance is 100% so that patients pay 0%, the insurer—the government or a private insurance company—would not want to let the suppliers go freely up their supply curve to point G and then continue straight up without any stopping point. If the suppliers move freely up to point G, the insurer must pay the suppliers an amount $E = P \times Q = \$300 \times 120 = \$36,000$; when suppliers continue to raise their price above $300, the insurer's expenditure will rise above $36,000. The insurer will surely try to prevent this from happening. But how? The insurer can refuse to pay a price greater than P^*—for example, $100 (the price that would have occurred in the market with no insurance at point O).

What happens if the insurer limits the price to $P^* = \$100$? As shown in Figure 6.3, with $P = \$100$, the suppliers will supply only $Q = 100$, and they will receive only the amount $E = P \times Q = \$100 \times 100 = \$10,000$. With 100% insurance, the patient pays 0% so demand is 120. The result is a *shortage*—excess demand—of 20 units of medical care. Rather than being simply turned down, patients will probably be put on a *waiting list* for the 20 units, so in Figure 6.3, the waiting list is 20. As also shown in Figure 6.3, the magnitude of excess demand can be reduced if insurance switches from 100% to 75%, so that the demand curve is D' instead of D''. With 75% insurance, patients must pay 25%, and at $P = \$100$, patient demand is 115, not 120; the shortage (excess demand) is 15, not 20 (the waiting list is 15, not 20).

Thus, the insurer may provide 100% insurance, but if so, the insurer won't allow the suppliers to respond freely to patient demand—to climb up their supply curve until the vertical patient demand curve D'' is reached and then continue to raise P. The insurer will find a way to limit the supply. One way is to limit the price the insurer will pay suppliers.

It is sometimes asked how in a country like Britain, where medical care is free to the patient and where the government, who is the insurer, pays 100%, so much less is spent on medical care than in a country like the United States, where the patient often pays a percentage of the bill. In Britain, health spending is only 8% of GDP, while it is 16% in the United States. The answer can be seen in Figure 6.3. The numbers in Figure 6.3 are not the actual numbers in Britain or the United States, but the numerical example in the figure illustrates why expenditure in Britain is smaller than in the United States despite Britain's "free care." In Britain, the patient demand curve is the vertical D'', but the government limits price to $100 and quantity to 100, so expenditure is only $10,000 and the waiting list is 20. In the United States, patient demand is D' (because patients pay 25%), there is no price limit, and insurance companies allow the suppliers to satisfy patient demand by moving up their supply curve to point F where $P = \$200$ and $Q = 110$. There is no waiting list, and expenditure $E = P \times Q = \$200 \times 110 = \$22,000$ (insurers bear 75% of the burden, $16,500, and patients bear 25% of the burden, $5,500).

FIGURE 6.3
Price Control
A price ceiling results
in waiting lists.

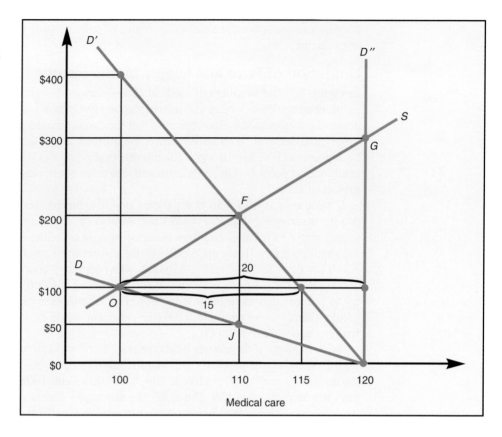

FEATURES OF HEALTH INSURANCE MARKETS

Let's now examine several distinctive features of health insurance markets that we need to grasp before we can consider the role that government might play in health insurance.

Patients, Doctors, and the Principal-Agent Problem

The patient often doesn't know which medical care option would be best. Hence, she must rely on her physician for advice and help in decision making. The patient (the principal) hires the doctor to act as her agent—an expert on whom the patient relies. The problem is that the doctor's motivations may not always coincide with the patient's. After all, a doctor's earnings are affected by her decisions. Hence, the patient-doctor relationship presents a principal-agent problem.

To simplify, there are two opposite risks for the patient. Suppose that the more service a doctor provides, the more the doctor is paid. This is called **fee for service (FFS)**. Under FFS, there is a risk that the doctor will advise her patients to accept more service than would really be best for them. On the other hand, suppose the doctor is prepaid a fixed sum for the patient for the year, regardless of how much service is provided. This is called *capitation*. Under capitation, there is a risk that the doctor will advise patients to accept less service than would really be best for the patients. Medical provider organizations that charge capitation have been called **health maintenance organizations (HMOs)**.

Thus, with FFS there is a risk that doctors will do too much, but with an HMO there is a risk that doctors will do too little. Each patient will have a different preference.

A patient who worries that too much will be done might prefer an HMO, while a patient who worries that too little will be done might prefer FFS. There is no perfect solution to the principal-agent problem between patients and their doctors.

Fortunately, there are at least three constraints on doctors to prevent them from deviating too much from what is best for patients. The first is ethics. Most doctors know it would be morally wrong to sacrifice the best interests of their patients for their own financial gain. The second is malpractice suits. Doctors know that patients may sue for medical malpractice. The third is reputation and long-run financial gain. If an FFS doctor develops a reputation of doing too much—for example, recommending surgery when it is unnecessary—eventually patients may avoid this doctor, hurting the doctor financially. Similarly, if an HMO develops a reputation of doing too little—for example, failing to recommend surgery when it is necessary—eventually patients may avoid this HMO, hurting its doctors financially.

Regulation by Insurers

Thus far we've assumed that the insurer passively pays a fraction of whatever bill the patient incurs, but insurers have become active rather than passive. Because they are paying a large share of the bill, they have an incentive to try to limit their expenditures. They do this in a variety of ways. The insurance company may inform its enrollees and medical providers that there will be a set of restrictions and conditions. If there are relatively few large insurance companies, they may be able to exercise market power over both enrollees and providers. The insurers may try to regulate, influence, or "manage care" rather than simply letting fee-for-service providers and patients do whatever they want.

First, the insurance company may pay only an "allowable charge" for each service (a charge the insurer will allow), even if the doctor or hospital charges a higher price. Either the patient will have to pay the difference in price, or the doctor or hospital will accept the allowable charge instead of the initial price. The insurance company may try to reach agreements with doctors and hospitals to accept the company's allowable charge instead of the initial price and to refrain from billing the patient for the difference. The insurance company may develop a preferred provider organization (PPO) or network, a list of providers that have agreed to accept its allowable charges and refrain from additional billing of patients. Patients who "go outside the network" will have to bear the financial consequences.

Second, the insurance company may refuse to pay for medical care that it judges to be unnecessary. It may decide that procedure B, which costs less than procedure A, should have been used for the patient, and it will therefore not pay for procedure A, or pay only its allowable charge for procedure B. For certain procedures, the insurance company may refuse to pay unless the procedure was certified in advance. It may refuse to pay for costly drug A when cheaper drug B is available.

Of course, there are limits to the restrictions and conditions an insurer can impose. If an insurance company is too restrictive, potential enrollees might choose another insurance company, and doctors and hospitals might inform patients that they will not adhere to the conditions dictated by that insurer and advise patients to seek coverage from another insurance company. Nevertheless, if there are relatively few large insurance companies, they may succeed in imposing restrictions and conditions on enrollees and providers.

Employer-Provided Health Insurance

Thus far we have assumed that insurance is sold to individuals or to individual families. In fact, most people obtain their insurance through their employer. Why?

Once again, imagine you're running an insurance company. You can sell insurance person by person, enrolling one person (or family) at a time, or you can go to an employer and, in a single deal with that employer, enroll a hundred employees. Obviously, you'll enjoy a huge cost saving by enrolling a hundred people in a single transaction, but of course, you give up something as well. You'll have to agree to enroll all employees without asking individual health questions.

Why would an employer want to provide health insurance? First, because there is an important tax advantage. If an employer pays an employee cash wages, both the employer and employee owe payroll taxes, and the employee owes income tax. For example, on $10,000 of wages, the employer must withhold 7.65%, or $765, for the employee's payroll tax and also pay an employer's payroll tax of $765. If the employee is in a 15% income tax bracket, the employee will owe $1,500 of income tax (and roughly this amount will be withheld from her paycheck by the employer). By contrast, if the employer instead buys the employee health insurance for $10,000, then no tax is owed—either payroll or income tax. This tax advantage has been part of U.S. tax law for more than half a century and has surely stimulated the spread of employer-provided health insurance. It has also encouraged the spread of insurance with high premiums but low patient cost-sharing and discouraged the spread of catastrophic insurance—insurance with low premiums but high patient cost sharing for normal medical bills.

Even without the tax advantage, there is a second reason many employers would probably want to offer health insurance: Many employees like getting their health insurance taken care of at their workplace. Why? Because if a person buys insurance individually, she will usually have to write a large check to pay the premium. If the employer takes care of insurance, the person usually does not know or feel its cost. Hence, an employer who offers health insurance coverage is more attractive to many potential employees. Of course, an employer who buys health insurance won't be able to pay as much in wages and salaries. However, employers get a group discount (insurers, like other firms, give group discounts for buying in bulk because the sales cost per unit sold is lower), so it is still a good deal for most employees to have their employer buy the insurance rather than buying it on their own. Many employees rightly prefer a compensation package with health insurance. Workplace health insurance is especially attractive to employees having a health problem and who would be charged a high premium (or possibly rejected) if they had to buy insurance on their own. Even healthy individuals must pay a premium that covers the high cost of selling insurance to individuals one by one. Finally, the employer's benefit office provides the useful service of investigating alternative insurance companies, scrutinizing plan options, and selecting a small number of plans.

Who Bears the Burden of Employer-Provided Health Insurance?

It is likely that workers, not employers, end up bearing the burden of employer-provided health insurance. This section explains why.

Suppose initially that employers don't provide health insurance and the cash salary of a worker is $50,000, as shown in Figure 6.4. The demand curve for labor depends on the worker's marginal revenue product—the additional revenue that the worker will generate for the firm. The higher the worker's marginal revenue product, the more the employer is willing to pay to employ the worker. If the 100th worker's annual marginal revenue product is $50,000, the most that the employer will pay the worker is $50,000. The height of the D curve indicates the maximum amount the employer is willing to pay for each worker.

FIGURE 6.4

The Burden of Employer-Provided Insurance
Workers bear the burden of employer-provided health insurance.

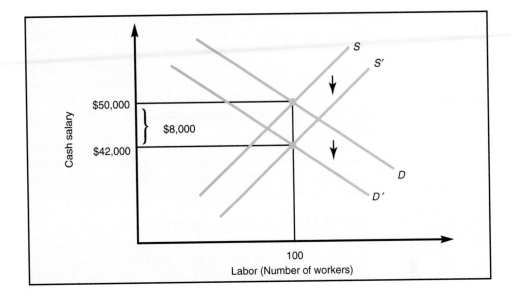

Now suppose that the employer provides $8,000 of health insurance with the job. In the supply-demand diagram, plotting cash salary on the vertical axis, the employer's demand for labor curve will shift down $8,000. For example, if the employer was previously willing to pay a cash salary of $50,000 for the 100th worker, now it will be willing to pay a cash salary of $42,000, because it is also paying $8,000 for health insurance—for a total compensation of $50,000.

The key question is this: What happens to the supply curve when a job provides $8,000 worth of health insurance? Perhaps the most likely response is shown in Figure 6.4: The *S* curve shifts down by $8,000. With no insurance, the 100th worker was willing to take the job for a cash salary of $50,000. With insurance given by the job, the 100th worker might be willing to take the job for a cash salary of $42,000. If so, the *S* curve shifts down $8,000. And if that happens, the *SD* intersection remains at 100 workers while the cash salary drops by $8,000, from $50,000 to $42,000. In this case, the worker has borne the entire burden of health insurance: The worker's cash salary has fallen by $8,000, while the employer's total compensation has remained $50,000. This case is shown in Table 6.3.

It should be noted, however, that the *S* curve might not shift down by $8,000. If workers value health insurance less than cash salary, the supply curve would shift down by less than $8,000, and cash salary would fall less than $8,000. Conversely, if workers value the employer-provided insurance more than $8,000, the supply curve would shift down by more than $8,000, and cash salary would fall more than $8,000. Although it is therefore possible that the worker's burden differs from $8,000, it seems reasonable to conclude that the worker bears most of the cost of insurance.

TABLE 6.3

Cash Salary and Health Insurance for an Employee

Option	Employee's Compensation		Employee's Purchase of Insurance	Employee's Burden from Insurance
	Cash	Insurance		
1	$50,000	$ 0	$8,000	$8,000
2	42,000	8,000	0	8,000

However, if workers, not employers, bear most of the cost, why do employers worry about rising health insurance premiums? The answer is that while workers bear the burden of a premium increase in the long run, employers bear it in the short run. If insurers raise their premiums by more than expected, employers usually still pay the wage increase that they promised; so in the short run, employers bear the burden of the unexpected premium hike. Gradually over time, employers respond to the unexpected premium rise by slowing the growth of cash wages below what it otherwise would have been.

In conclusion, workers, whether they realize it or not, have a direct stake in slowing the growth in insurance premiums; the faster the rise in premiums, the slower the rise in workers' cash wages and salaries. However, premiums must be raised if medical expenditures rise. So what determines the rate of growth of medical expenditures?

Rising Medical Expenditures

Rising medical expenditures are due to the continuous upward shifting of both demand and supply curves for medical care. What causes a shift up of the demand curve? Suppose everyone had 100% insurance that paid the entire medical bill. As noted earlier, the medical market would "explode": There would be no resistance by consumers to any rise in medical prices, and suppliers would be happy to continuously raise prices. Even short of this extreme case, the closer that insurance is to 100% and the more services that are covered, the greater should be the rise in the medical expenditures. Imagine a new medical technology that would improve quality but would also raise cost by $1,000 for treating a patient with a particular condition. If insurance paid 100%, all patients with this condition and their doctors would definitely demand the new technology, and it would be supplied and used. If insurance paid 80%, most patients and doctors, but not all, would demand it, so the rise in medical expenditures would be a bit less. Hence, the lower the percentage paid by insurance, the slower should be the rise in medical expenditures.

So what determines the percentage paid by insurance? Most insurance is provided by employers, and employer-provided insurance is stimulated by the tax advantage noted earlier. Recall that all employer expenditures for health insurance premiums, in contrast to cash wages, are excluded from payroll taxes and from the personal income tax of employees. Note further that there is no limit on the amount of employer expenditure that is excluded. This is one reason that catastrophic insurance—despite its appeal in the earlier example—is uncommon and the percentage of medical bills paid by insurance companies is high. Suppose that there is a limit on the amount excluded; above that limit, there would be no tax advantage to giving additional compensation in the form of more insurance rather than cash wages. It seems likely that this would result in a smaller percentage of medical bills paid by insurance companies and hence a slower growth in medical expenditures. We return to this point when we consider public policy.

What causes the supply curve to shift up? New technology, equipment, procedures, and medications are continuously being introduced into health care. While some of these innovations reduce cost, many raise cost while improving the quality and effectiveness of medical care. The height of the supply curve reflects cost, so cost-raising innovations shift up the supply curve.

THE ROLE OF GOVERNMENT

With this background on the principles of insurance and the features of health insurance markets, we turn to the role government might play in health insurance.

Recall the analysis of individually purchased insurance from the beginning of this chapter. We saw that in a competitive insurance market—even without the problem of adverse selection—each household would be charged a premium equal to its expected medical cost, so households with low income and high expected medical costs would be unable to afford insurance. With adverse selection driving premiums still higher (because high-cost households buy insurance, while many low-cost households do not), the number of uninsured households would be even larger.

A system of employment-provided health insurance has several appealing features. A high-cost household is charged (through a reduction in its cash salary) the same amount as a low-cost household; adverse selection is less of a problem (low-cost people seek employment and are then automatically assigned insurance coverage); and insurance comes automatically with the job rather than having to be obtained by searching the individual market. An employment-based insurance system almost certainly results in a smaller number of uninsured people than a system based entirely on individually purchased insurance.

However, a system of employment-provided insurance also has serious shortcomings. Retirees are usually not covered by this system (though some employers continue to buy coverage for former employees who have retired). Unemployed people are usually not covered (though some employers buy coverage for former employees who have been laid off). Businesses with primarily low-wage workers often provide no coverage because employees cannot afford the corresponding cuts in cash wages that employers would require to afford the insurance. Workers in families with a health problem often experience *job lock*—they are afraid to switch to a more productive job or risk a period of unemployment while they search for such a job because their new insurance policy may refuse to cover preexisting health conditions.

Medicaid and the State Children's Health Insurance Program

Poor people cannot afford medical care without help. The main government program for helping poor people (whether young or old) pay for medical care is Medicaid, enacted in 1965, the same year as the Medicare program for retirees. Since 1997, Medicaid has been supplemented by another government program, the State Children's Health Insurance Program (SCHIP, pronounced *s-chip*), which extends coverage to children in near-poor families. In contrast to Medicare, which is run by the federal government, Medicaid and SCHIP are federally mandated but administered by the state governments. They are financed by a combination of federal and state general revenues (not a payroll tax); the federal government bears more of the cost for low-income states than high-income states. Medicaid and SCHIP are *not* government-provided medical care. The medical care is provided by private sector hospitals and doctors, and Medicaid and SCHIP pay the hospitals and doctors for treating low-income people. The prices that hospitals and doctors can charge are regulated, and there is little or no patient cost sharing. To qualify for Medicaid or SCHIP, a person must meet both an income and an assets test: Income must be sufficiently low, and assets (resources) must also be sufficiently low; the exact dollar number varies across states.

Medicaid also assists many retirees who earned substantial income earlier in life but who became poor in old age because of large financial burdens from medical problems and the cost of a nursing home. Once people have used up most of their savings paying for these costs and have therefore become poor, they qualify for Medicaid. Hence, Medicaid pays the fees of nursing homes for many elderly people who were not poor when they were younger (Medicare does not pay nursing home fees). For these elderly, Medicaid also pays the patient cost sharing that Medicare imposes for hospitals, doctors, and drugs. The cost of Medicaid has risen at a rapid rate, and efforts are continuously being made to try to devise methods to slow cost growth while still ensuring access to medical care for poor people.

Alternative Public Policies for Working Families

A variety of public policies have been proposed to improve health insurance coverage for working people and their children. In this section we consider several of them.

Consumer-Driven Health Care and Health Savings Accounts

Advocates of consumer-driven health care contend that the free market can work in health care if each consumer bears more of the cost of her own medical care.[3] They would like to see more consumers choosing catastrophic insurance with substantial patient cost sharing for normal medical bills. Advocates contend that if consumers pay most of the price of medical care most of the time, they will monitor the health care market the way consumers do for other goods and services. One way to try to induce a switch to catastrophic insurance would be to remove the tax advantage for insurance with high premiums and low patient cost sharing. Another would be to introduce a tax advantage for catastrophic insurance.

A tax advantage for catastrophic insurance was enacted in 2003 as part of the Medicare Modernization Act, though it has nothing to do with Medicare. Here is how it works. If a family obtains an insurance policy with at least a $2,000 deductible—so the family must bear the first $2,000 of medical expenses out of pocket—then it will be given a tax advantage. The tax advantage is that the employer can deposit an amount up to the deductible ($2,000) into an account for the employee called a health savings account (HSA) and no tax (income or payroll) must be paid on this $2,000 compensation, either when it is deposited or when it is used by the employee to pay medical bills. Any funds not used can accumulate in the HSA tax-free. HSA funds will only be taxed if withdrawn to finance nonmedical expenditures. It is too early to know whether this new tax advantage will gradually cause many employers and individuals to shift from high-premium insurance to catastrophic insurance.

Responsible Health Insurance

A plan called *responsible health insurance (RHI)* has been proposed by economists Mark Pauly, Patricia Danzon, Paul Feldstein, and attorney John Hoff.[4] Other health policy analysts have proposed some or all of its components; recently, Massachusetts enacted a health insurance plan that contains one key element of RHI. As explained below, RHI would cover all people of working age (and their children) regardless of income, so it would replace Medicaid (and SCHIP) for nonelderly low-income people.

RHI has three elements: (1) a requirement (mandate) that each household obtain insurance; (2) a refundable tax credit; and (3) provision of fallback (last-resort) insurance.

The prevention of free riding is the rationale given by the RHI authors for an individual mandate. With a mandate, a person would no longer have the option of being a *free*

[3] An exposition of this approach by economists is given in John Cogan, R. Glenn Hubbard, and Daniel Kessler, *Healthy, Wealthy, and Wise: Five Steps to a Better Health Care System* (American Enterprise Institution Press, 2005).

[4] Mark Pauly, Patricia Danzon, Paul Feldstein, and John Hoff, *Responsible National Health Insurance* (American Enterprise Institute Press, 1991).

TABLE 6.4

Proposed Tax Credit by Household Income for a Family of Four

Household Income	Tax Credit
$ 0	$ 8,000
50,000	6,000
100,000	4,000
150,000	2,000

rider who escapes paying for insurance but then receives substantial resources from society upon becoming seriously ill. The Massachusetts plan contains this element. Advocates of a requirement contend that practical methods can be devised to enforce it for most of the population, while critics doubt it can be adequately enforced.

The tax credit helps households afford insurance. The tax credit would vary inversely with the household's income, as shown in Table 6.4 with numbers given just for illustration for a family of four. The credit would be the same whether the household purchased insurance on its own, split the cost of insurance with an employer, or obtained insurance from an employer. A household would claim its health insurance tax credit on its annual income tax return. The credit would be *refundable*: A low-income family that owed no tax would receive a U.S. Treasury check equal to the credit; a family that owed a tax less than its credit would receive a check equal to the difference.

Under the RHI plan, the current tax exclusion would be terminated. Under the exclusion, an employer's contribution for an employee's health insurance does not appear on the employee's annual W-2 form (which shows wage income subject to income tax) and is excluded from that individual's annual taxable income. Under RHI, any employer contribution for health insurance would be reported on the employees' W-2 forms as taxable income.

Reporting these contributions on W-2 forms and in employees' taxable income would serve another important goal: It would educate employees about the magnitude of the cost of their health insurance. Currently, many employees are unaware of how much their employer pays for their health insurance. Moreover, many mistakenly assume that their employer bears the cost. W-2 form inclusion would unmask the huge hidden cost of health care for all employees to see. This should have two effects. First, more employees would support their employers' efforts to find a health insurance policy that limits the premium, even if this involved more patient cost sharing and some selectivity in what is covered. Second, more employees would politically support governmental policies that try to achieve health sector cost containment.

One important feature of RHI would provide an incentive for cost containment in the health sector: A household's tax credit would *not* vary with the household's actual insurance premium or actual health expenditure. Thus, an individual who obtains insurance plan A with a premium $1,000 larger than plan B would bear an additional $1,000 burden. Even if the employer purchased the insurance, the premium's inclusion on the W-2 form and in the employee's taxable income would serve as a reminder of the individual's stake in holding down the premium.

Fallback or last-resort insurance is essential to ensure that every household can satisfy the individual requirement. The RHI authors recommended that the government contract with private insurers to sell fallback insurance at an affordable premium to all households that want to buy such insurance. An alternative approach would be to have Medicare be the fallback insurer.

An Employer Mandate or an Employer Play-or-Pay Option

Since the majority of working Americans are covered by employer-provided health insurance, why not require all employers to provide insurance to all employees?

An employer mandate has been a central element of health insurance proposals by four presidents: Nixon, Ford, Carter, and Clinton. In the early 1970s, Republican Presidents Nixon and Ford proposed an employer mandate as an alternative to the liberal Democrat proposal for universal government insurance. In the context of that period, their proposal was deemed relatively conservative because it relied on private insurance rather than government insurance. By the end of the 1970s, Democratic President Carter had been persuaded to support the employer mandate. By this time many conservatives were becoming wary of putting a requirement on private employers. In the 1980s, Republican Presidents Reagan and Bush opposed an employer mandate as an unacceptable imposition by government on private firms, and most conservatives opposed Democratic President Clinton's proposal for an employer mandate. Today, most conservatives, including President Bush, oppose an employer mandate.

One problem with an employer mandate has always been its application to small businesses with mostly low-wage employees. Representatives of these businesses contend that they cannot afford health insurance; they say that, unlike businesses with high-wage workers, low-wage workers can't afford to accept lower wages to enable businesses to afford insurance. Also, if a small business has just a few employees with high-cost medical problems, then the insurance company may charge the company a high premium.

Consequently, advocates of an employer mandate usually recommend subsidies to small businesses with low-wage employees to help those businesses afford insurance and comply with the mandate. Representatives of small businesses, however, are usually skeptical whether the subsidies will prove adequate.

Instead of requiring employers to provide insurance for their employees, the government might offer each employer the option of **play-or-pay**. Under play-or-pay, the employer must either "play"—provide health insurance—or "pay" a tax that would help finance government efforts to cover the uninsured.

Government Reinsurance

The premium charged by a private insurer must be high enough to cover the costs incurred by the minority of patients with huge medical bills. Suppose the government makes a commitment to reimburse any private insurer X% of the amount by which a patient's medical bill exceeds a high threshold. This commitment would reduce the expected financial burden that the private insurer must bear, and competition among private insurers would reduce the premium they charge enrollees; lower premiums would make private insurance more affordable to more employers and individuals.

A government commitment to reimburse private insurers for X% of the amount by which a patient's medical bill exceeds a high threshold is called **government reinsurance** of the private insurance firms. Of course, the government would have to increase taxes to obtain the revenue needed to reimburse private insurance firms X%, so government reinsurance would reduce premiums but raise taxes. Note that the numerical value of X% must be set significantly less than 100%, so that each private insurer retains a strong incentive to try to limit the patient's huge medical bill by monitoring the services and prices charged by hospitals and doctors to the patient.[5]

[5] Katherine Swartz, *Reinsuring Health: Why More Middle-Class People Are Uninsured and What Government Can Do* (Russell Sage, 2006).

Government Insurance

Government insurance would replace private insurance. Everyone would be covered by government insurance regardless of income, health, or employment. The federal government would pay most or all of each medical bill. This has been called a single-payer plan because the government, rather than many private insurance companies, would be the single payer of all medical bills. The private sector—business firms and households—would pay taxes to the government instead of premiums to private insurance companies.

Although medical providers—doctors and hospitals—would remain in the private sector, the government—as the primary payer of medical bills—would have the power to exercise some control over prices charged, services supplied, technology used, and medical practices utilized. Congress would determine whether government regulation would be heavy or light, rigid or flexible, macro or micro. Earlier in this chapter we examined ways that private insurance companies, which now pay most of each medical bill, currently attempt to regulate medical care. Government would use many of the same techniques as it already does under Medicare and Medicaid.

The government might pay each person's entire medical bill, or it might require patient cost sharing. Patient cost sharing might be independent of a patient's income; for example, the patient might have to pay 15% regardless of income until the patient's burden reaches $4,000, after which the government pays the rest. Patient cost sharing could also vary with income; for example, a low-income patient might pay 5% until the burden reaches 2% of income, while a high-income patient might pay 25% until the burden reaches 4% of income, after which the government pays the rest. Government could use the previous year's federal income tax returns to implement income-related patient cost sharing.

Advocates of government insurance make several arguments:

1. It would be a simple way to get everyone covered.
2. It would be a fairer system because everyone is covered regardless of income, health, or employment.
3. The government's leverage as the primary payer of most medical bills would give it the ability to hold down prices and payments to providers.

Opponents of government insurance also make several arguments:

1. Taxes would have to increase substantially.
2. Government would overregulate medical providers, thereby impeding the introduction of new technologies, procedures, and medications.
3. Government would overrestrict supply, generating queues and excessive waiting times.
4. The majority of households are currently satisfied with their employer-provided private insurance, so such insurance should be retained, not replaced.

Medicare for Retirees

As longevity increases and medical technology advances, the cost of Medicare for retirees is projected to increase dramatically. The Congressional Budget Office projects a rise in Medicare expenses over the next half century that is much larger than the rise in Social Security benefits; Social Security is projected to rise by 2% of GDP, but Medicare is projected to rise by 6% of GDP. Unless something is done to curtail the projected rise in Medicare costs, federal taxes will therefore have to be raised by about

6% of GDP over the next half century to cover the rise in Medicare costs (currently federal taxes are roughly 20% of GDP).

How Medicare Works

Enacted in 1965, Medicare is health insurance for retirees provided by the federal government. Prior to the enactment of Medicare, many retirees were uninsured because they faced high premiums in the individual market because of their expected high medical costs. The qualifications for receiving Medicare and the method of financing are generally similar to Social Security. For example, 10 years of work are required to earn coverage. Coverage by Medicare begins at age 65 (even if a person starts Social Security at age 62). Part A of Medicare for hospital care is financed by a payroll tax—1.45% on the employer and 1.45% on the employee—and the total of 2.9% is withheld by the employer and sent to the government; the payroll tax applies to the entire wage income of each employee (in contrast to the payroll tax for Social Security which applies only up to a wage ceiling—$102,000 per employee in 2008). Part B of Medicare for physician care is financed 75% by general tax revenues and 25% by monthly premiums paid by retirees; these monthly premiums are collected by reducing the retiree's monthly Social Security benefit (so some retirees may not even be aware of their monthly premium payment). Medicare requires some patient cost sharing but permits retirees to obtain private insurance to cover this cost sharing (so-called medigap coverage); many low-income retirees qualify for Medicaid, which then pays most or all of their Medicare patient cost sharing. Medicare negotiates or regulates fees that it pays to hospitals and doctors.

Government Insurance for Retirees

If there were no Medicare today, consider the situation of a newly retired individual. When the person retires and leaves workplace health insurance, she faces private health insurance companies as an individual. Health insurance firms have a financial incentive to avoid high-cost individuals and attract low-cost individuals. If the individual retiree applies for insurance, the insurance company requires the individual to supply information on medical history. A person expected to be high cost would either be offered insurance at a high premium or rejected. By the time individuals reach the age of retirement, many have discernible health problems—in fact, a health problem may be the reason why the individual retired. Even if a retiree is initially judged low or moderate cost by the insurance company and therefore offered insurance at an affordable premium, what happens if the retiree later develops a costly health problem? Ideally, the insurance policy would be *guaranteed renewable* so that the insurer agrees to continue offering coverage without an unreasonable increase in the premium due to the onset of a costly medical problem. Although some insurers would offer guaranteed renewable insurance, others would not, and some retirees would find their insurance discontinued once they developed a costly health problem. With Medicare, when people reach age 65, they are given health insurance by the government that lasts for the rest of their life, regardless of what happens to their health or income.

Medicare Regulation of Hospital and Doctor Fees

Initially Medicare simply paid hospitals and doctors whatever fees they charged, but in the 1980s, Medicare began regulating fees, first of hospitals and later of doctors. Hospitals were required to classify each patient as belonging to one of roughly five hundred diagnostic-related groups (DRGs), and Medicare set the fee that it would pay for a patient in each DRG. Later, Medicare established a resource-based relative value scale (RBRVS) for doctor fees, setting the fee it would pay for each service according to its cost (including medical school training).

A Medicare Voucher

It has been proposed that retirees be given a Medicare voucher that they can use to buy insurance from private companies. With a voucher system, Medicare would provide *premium support* rather than be the insurer. Advocates say a voucher system would accomplish two objectives. First, Congress would get better control over its Medicare expenditure; its expenditure would equal the voucher amount set by Congress *times* the number of retirees. Second, retirees would have a choice among insurance companies and plans so insurers would have to compete for retirees.

As we discussed earlier, competition by health insurers for individual enrollees has serious problems. Such a competition tends to result in each individual being charged a premium equal to her expected medical cost—and if that expected cost is very high, a simple refusal to provide insurance. Because older people often have documented medical problems, premiums would on average be high and might vary dramatically across individuals. It might be possible to contain these problems by varying the amount of premium support according to the individual's health status (called *risk adjustment*) and income, or by imposing regulations on how much insurers can vary premiums (or reject individuals). However, it is unclear whether this can be done satisfactorily for the majority of elderly people.

Medicare Prescription Drug Coverage

When Medicare was enacted in 1965, it did not cover prescription drugs. In the next decades, effective but expensive prescription drugs were developed by pharmaceutical companies, and Medicare's omission became more important. As a result, many retirees became increasingly concerned about Medicare's omission.

There were two sources of resistance to having Medicare cover prescription drugs. First, the cost of coverage would require either an increase in taxes or in premiums for retirees. Second, pharmaceutical companies generally opposed coverage, because they feared that it would lead to Medicare's setting prices for drugs, just as it had for hospitals and doctors. The Medicare Modernization Act of 2003 finally added prescription drug coverage to Medicare (part D), but with the compromise that private insurance companies, not Medicare, would directly interact with drug companies and patients, thereby making it less likely that Medicare would set prices. Medicare's prescription drug program actually began in 2006.

Medicare requires the private insurance companies to utilize a patient cost-sharing schedule. While poor patients get their cost sharing paid by Medicaid, nonpoor retirees are prohibited from getting their cost sharing paid by a private (medigap) insurer, because the aim is to keep most retirees concerned about drug prices. In 2008, under the standard schedule, patients are required to pay the first $275 of prescription drug costs, 25% of drug costs between $275 and $2,510, 100% of costs between $2,510 and $5,726 (this range of $3,216 where patients get no help is called the *doughnut hole*), and, finally, 5% of any drug costs above $5,726. Why did Congress leave a doughnut hole? To hold down the federal budget cost of the drug coverage.

Income-Related Patient Cost Sharing

Medicare's current cost sharing for drugs does not vary with a patient's income. Another way to limit budget cost of the Medicare prescription drug program would be to make each patient's cost-share vary with the patient's income using each patient's previous year federal tax return. Income-relating patient cost sharing can be done at low cost with today's computer technology. Each Medicare recipient would use a "Medicard" to purchase drugs. The pharmacy would be paid by the government, and the patient would be sent a bill every month. The patient would be charged a percentage that would vary inversely with the patient's income as reported on the preceding year's federal tax return. The government would contract with private firms to process the bills and collect cost sharing from households.

It might be feasible to use income-related cost sharing for other services covered by Medicare. Every retiree covered by Medicare would receive a Medicard to use at the doctor's office or hospital the way she uses a credit card at a department store. The household would then be billed a percentage that depends on its income as reported on its most recent federal tax return. Once the household's financial burden reaches a designated percentage of its income, it would not be billed again that year, so Medicare would limit every household's financial burden to its ability to pay. The government would contract with private firms—insurance companies and credit card companies—under competitive bidding to process medical bills and to bill and collect from patients.

Advocates of income-related patient cost sharing contend that it would promote equity and efficiency. Patients are asked to contribute to financing their own medical costs according to their ability to pay, so that the subjective burden is comparable but tolerable for patients at all income levels. At the same time, each patient is given an incentive to weigh the benefit of any service against its cost.

Opponents of income-related patient cost sharing make several arguments. First, they point out that the prices of most goods and services in our society are not varied according to the consumer's income. Second, trying to link patient cost sharing to patient income adds administrative complexity; also, using the preceding year's tax return may not always be equitable. Third, some conservatives philosophically oppose varying price with income, and some liberals fear that doing so ("means-testing" Medicare) might weaken political support for Medicare among the affluent.

Rationing

The word rationing in this section means limiting the use of medical care other than by raising the price to patients. Rationing involves denying some medical care to some people who want the care and would obtain some benefit from the care. The rationale given for such rationing is that the benefit, though positive, is judged by society to be not worth the cost.

Imagine that it becomes possible to give each very old person who is about to die one additional year of life but at a medical cost of $1 million per person. How should public policy respond to this prospect?

Perhaps the simplest option would be to have the government provide the extra year of life "free" to each person when the time arrives. If the extra year of life is provided free and is not painful, most people will request it, and the citizenry will bear the cost through taxes. Perhaps the tax per person needed to raise $1 million per recipient would be judged tolerable by the citizenry. If so, suppose that the medical cost of an extra year of life were $10 million per recipient. Clearly, there is some sufficiently large medical cost at which many citizens would judge that the benefit is not worth the cost. Then what?

If this were a typical good rather than an extra year of life, most economists would recommend charging a price equal to the cost of the good and letting each consumer decide whether to buy it at that price. It is possible to imagine conditions under which

Current Research Should Some Medical Care Be Rationed?

In their 2005 book, *Can We Say No? The Challenge of Rationing Health Care* (Brookings Institution Press), economist Henry Aaron of the Brookings Institution and physician William Schwartz contend that the United States will either have to deny some medical care to some people who would obtain some benefit from the care or to accept a significant slowdown in the improvement of our nonmedical standard of living. Their new book revises and updates their earlier 1984 book that examined rationing in the British health care system and contrasted it with the U.S. health care system. They begin their new book by writing, "The good news is that modern medicine works miracles. The bad news is that it breaks banks—public and private." Beneficial but costly medical advances are likely to continue at a rapid pace, making it possible for us to spend an increasing share of our GDP on medical care that gives some medical benefit to more people, thereby leaving a decreasing share of our GDP for nonmedical goods and services. They contend that if we want to avoid this slowdown in the growth of nonmedical consumption, we must be willing to "limit the provision of care that is worth less than it costs to people who are well insured—that is, to ration care." Aaron and Schwartz concede that rationing care is painful (their 1984 book called rationing "the painful prescription") and that "the steps necessary to ration health care may prove more objectionable than the cost of paying for it." They write that "health care can be rationed efficiently or inefficiently," and argue that if there is to be rationing, it is important that it be done efficiently and equitably in a way that maximizes the overall benefits that can be achieved from a limited amount of resources.

Aaron and Schwartz examine concrete examples of how particular kinds of medical care have been rationed under the British health care system and try to assess whether these same methods can or should be attempted in the United States. They conclude: "The choices are clear. We can simply pay the enormous bill for all beneficial medical care whatever the cost. Or we can ration. . . . Rationing will inevitably be controversial and difficult to implement, but like bitter but efficacious medicine, it can be good for our nation's health."

this might be an acceptable solution for an extra year of life for a very old person. Assume for a moment that everyone earned the same income during the work stage of life and that everyone would die on her 100th birthday without the $1 million medical service. Assume each person's income is high enough that anyone willing to save enough during the work stage of life would be able to accumulate an additional $1 million by age 100, which could be used to buy one more year of life. It would then be up to each person in the work stage of life to decide whether to save enough or not. Of course, some who arrive at their 100th birthday without having saved the extra $1 million will regret it. But the citizenry might respond: "You were told what would happen at age 100, and you made your choice—now you must accept the consequences."

Of course, people in the work stage of life earn very different incomes. Individuals differ in the exertion and luck they have in their career, in the health of their family, and in numerous other ways. Given these differences, most citizens would probably find it unacceptable to have an extra year of life provided only to persons willing and able to pay $1 million for it. At the same time, most citizens would probably judge that it was not worth raising taxes by the amount required to buy another year of life for every very old person.

If we shift from this hypothetical option about an extra year of life to the actual numerous medical conditions and options that will face retirees, the basic problem remains: The citizenry is unlikely to be willing to pay enough taxes to finance the provision of every medical service that can provide retirees some medical benefit.

One option is for Medicare to develop a system of rationing for such costly services and to try to make it as equitable and cost effective as possible. Suppose that a person age 65 and a person age 100 are afflicted with the same life-threatening illness and that for the same cost—say, $1 million—each can be cured. Suppose that once cured, the 100-year-old is likely to live to 101, and the 65-year-old, to age 85. If there is only enough tax revenue to treat one of them, most citizens would probably prefer saving the 65-year-old rather than the 100-year-old. Rather than provide treatment on a first-come, first-serve basis regardless of age until funds run out, the citizenry might prefer that Medicare give younger retirees priority over very old retirees for this medical service. Thus, it seems likely that the citizenry will have to confront difficult Medicare choices in the years ahead. For further analysis of this topic, see the box, "Should Some Medical Care Be Rationed?"

Health Insurance in Other Countries: An International Perspective

What do other countries do about health insurance? Most high-income countries utilize a larger role for government in health insurance than the United States. Many of these countries finance most medical care through taxes rather than private insurance premiums (this is one reason that taxes as a percentage of GDP average about 40% in economically advanced countries but about 30% in the United States). Most of these countries achieve close to universal insurance coverage in contrast to the United States. However, some countries have substantially longer waiting times for obtaining medical care than the United States and have less of the latest medical technology. In this section we take a brief look abroad.

Under Britain's system—the National Health Service (NHS), established in the mid-1940s—the role of government is maximized: The government runs and operates the health care system. Medical care is free and everyone is covered by the NHS. Hospital administrators, physicians who are specialists, and nurses are salaried employees of the government. Physicians who are general practitioners (GPs) are the "gatekeepers" of the system. The government pays GPs according to the number of people—potential patients—for whom they are responsible (capitation payment); they are *not* paid according to how much medical service they actually provide patients. Persons seeking medical care must first see a GP, who either treats them or evaluates their problem and decides whether they can see a specialist.

The system is financed by taxation. Spending for medical care is determined by the government budget process. Britain spends about half as much of its GDP on medical care as does the United States (8% for Britain versus 16% for the United States). With medical care free and supply limited by the budget process, patient demand exceeds supply for many services. As a consequence, the system is characterized by rationing which takes the form of long waits for nonemergency services such as elective surgery; demanders (patients) cannot get as much as they want as soon as they want it. Government planners set priorities for allocating the limited budget for new medical technology and facilities. Doctors evaluate patients and set priorities for use of the limited hospital resources and medical technology. The affluent have the option of paying the full cost of services in a small private sector. With medical care free to patients, the degree of rationing is determined by the level of taxes: The higher the taxes, the greater the supply of medical services, the less severe the rationing. Apparently, British voters are unwilling to pay higher taxes to reduce the current level of rationing.

In Canada the role of government in health insurance is less than in Britain but still substantial—similar to the role government plays in health insurance in several Western

European countries. The Canadian government provides health insurance to everyone (implemented through its provincial governments with financial assistance from the national government)—its system was established in the early 1970s. Medical care is free to patients and financed by taxation. The government pays the fees charged by physicians and hospitals. In contrast to Britain, hospitals and physicians remain in the private sector, and physicians are generally paid a fee for service rather than by salary or capitation. But there is substantial government regulation of physician fee schedules and hospital rates, budgets, and operations. Thus, in contrast to Britain, the Canadian government does *not* run and operate a national health service. It is the single payer of the fees charged by medical providers, and it imposes substantial regulation on the private health sector. Hence, the Canadian system is sometimes referred to as a *single-payer system*. Through its regulation, the government limits supply, and with medical care free to patients, demand often exceeds supply. Therefore, there is substantial rationing of nonemergency medical services, evidenced in wait lists and in the fact that some wait-listed Canadians seek and obtain elective surgery in the United States. The degree of rationing is determined by the level of taxes and the degree to which regulation limits supply.

As countries advance economically, they become able to afford better health care for a larger share of their population. An example of this is Taiwan. In the mid-1990s, after several decades of impressive economic growth, Taiwan adopted universal government insurance financed largely by taxes. Prior to its adoption a significant portion of the population had no health insurance. Universal coverage does not mean medical care is free to patients. Under Taiwan's government insurance, patients are charged a moderate copayment for doctor office visits; preventive services, such as annual checkups, are free. There is 10% patient cost sharing for hospital care until the patient reaches a burden equal to 10% of Taiwan's per capita income—once this burden ceiling is reached, the government pays the rest. Poor people, however, are exempt from patient cost sharing. The replacement of multiple insurers by a single insurer—the government—has reduced administrative costs and given the government more leverage to implement regulation of hospital and doctor fees.

Summary

If the government played no role in health insurance, private insurance firms would be established by entrepreneurs and would offer health insurance that many consumers would buy in order to avoid the risk of being hit with a huge medical bill. If insurance is sold to individual households (not employers), each household would be asked to provide information about its health, and insurers would charge each household a price equal to its expected medical cost. Insurance reduces the price of medical care to patients and therefore increases their demand for medical care; this consequence of insurance has been called moral hazard, but economists view it as a standard response to a cut in price. People who know they are more likely to need medical care are more likely to buy insurance and because of this adverse selection, insurers need to charge a higher price to cover the cost of people who actually enroll; this higher price may, in turn, induce even more adverse selection. Catastrophic insurance covers only medical costs above a high threshold; it protects people against a huge financial burden while giving them an incentive to care about the cost of routine medical care.

Insurance affects efficiency and redistribution. If there is no externality, insurance that pays *X*% of each patient's medical bill causes an efficiency loss; it would have been better in theory (though it may not have been practical) to give the sick person cash income rather than a price subsidy through insurance. Citizens should support use of the insurance price subsidy if they judge that the social benefit of redistribution from the healthy to the sick outweighs the efficiency loss. If there is a positive externality—that is, if other people experience utility when sick people get medical care—then an insurance price subsidy equal to the positive externality would increase efficiency. Insurance redistributes resources and utility from the healthy to the sick; economics cannot declare a particular degree of redistribution to be optimal, deficient, or excessive.

If insurers (private firms or government) impose a price ceiling by paying less than the market-clearing price, then the result will be waiting lists and delays in obtaining service.

Patients rely on doctors as their agents to help them make medical decisions; under fee for service, there is a risk that doctors will do too much, while under capitation (used by health maintenance organizations), there is a risk that doctors will do too little. Insurers—private and government—perform some regulation by paying less than doctors and hospitals charge and refusing to pay for some medical care they judge unnecessary or ineffective. A key feature of private insurance in the United States is that it is sold mainly to employers rather than to individual households. Selling to large employers reduces sales cost per person covered; in return, insurers agree to cover all employees without health restrictions. Employees end up bearing most of the burden of employer-provided insurance because employers pay lower cash salaries when they buy insurance. Rising medical expenses are driven by new technology raising costs and insurance raising demand.

The U.S. system of mainly employer-provided private insurance covers many but not all households. Low-income families and children have received government assistance through Medicaid and the State Children's Health Insurance Program. Various new public policies have been proposed for working families. Under the strategy of consumer-driven health care, households would be given a tax incentive to buy high-deductible catastrophic insurance that would keep them paying routine medical bills and therefore keep them cost-conscious in choosing medical care; contributions to a fund to pay their routine bills called a health savings account would be tax-free. Under the responsible health insurance plan, households would be required to obtain health insurance, a refundable tax credit would help them afford it, and fallback (last-resort) insurance would make sure they can obtain insurance at a reasonable premium. Under an employer mandate, employers would be required to provide insurance for their employees; under an employer play-or-pay plan, employers would either have to provide insurance or pay a tax to help cover the uninsured. Under government reinsurance, government would reimburse private insurers $X\%$ of the amount by which a patient's medical bill exceeds a high threshold; this would enable private insurers to charge lower premiums and should therefore increase the number of households that can afford insurance. Under government insurance that replaces private insurance, all households would be covered, government would pay a large share (there might be some patient cost sharing) of all medical bills, taxes would be levied to fund the program, and regulation of medical care provided would try to limit price increases but might result in wait lists.

Medicare, enacted in 1965, is government insurance for retirees. Without government insurance many retirees would have difficulty obtaining private insurance at an affordable premium because older people often have high expected medical costs. Medicare is financed by a payroll tax, general revenue, and contributions from retirees. Drug coverage was recently added. Medicare regulates doctor and hospital fees.

Medicare expenditures are expected to grow as a share of GDP because there will be more old people living longer and medical costs keep rising. Proposals for Medicare reform include vouchers, income-related patient cost sharing, and some rationing.

Compared to the United States, other economically advanced countries generally have more government involvement in health insurance, finance a larger share of their medical care through taxes, cover more of their population, have more regulation of fees of providers, and have longer wait lists.

Key Terms

premium, *133*
expected value, *133*
actuarially fair
 premium, *134*
moral hazard, *136*
price elasticity, *136*
adverse
 selection, *137*

catastrophic
 insurance, *138*
deductible, *138*
cost-sharing rate, *139*
coinsurance
 rate, *139*
fee for service
 (FFS), *144*

health maintenance
 organizations
 (HMOs), *144*
play-or-pay, *152*
government reinsurance,
 152
single-payer plan, *153*
rationing, *156*

Questions

1. Suppose that private insurance firms sell health insurance to individuals (not employers). Then each individual would be charged a price P for insurance equal to her_____.

	Chance of a $45,750 Medical Bill	Chance of a $750 Medical Bill	Expected Medical Bill
High-cost person	9%	91%	$_____
Low-cost person	1%	99%	$_____

   a. The high-cost person would be charged $P = \$$_____.
   b. The low-cost person would be charged $P = \$$_____.

2. Suppose that private insurance firms sell health insurance to employers for $3,000 per worker; then each worker's cash wage will be (*unchanged, reduced $*_____).

3. Explain moral hazard and adverse selection.

4. Suppose the government pays 80% of the patient's medical bill so the patient pays 20%. The supply-demand diagram below shows the impact on the price and quantity of medical care. Note that with no insurance, D and S intersect at $P = \$100$, $Q = 100$ and $E = P \times Q = \$10,000$; if $P = \$0$, $D = 200$.

   a. With 80% insurance, D' and S intersect at $P = \$250$, $Q = 150$; of the $250, the patient pays $_____ and the government pays $_____.
   b. With 80% insurance, $E = \$$_____ and taxpayers must pay $_____.

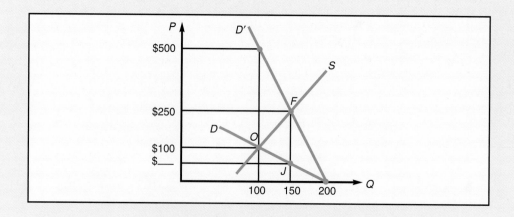

5. With income-related patient cost sharing, the government would pay 80% for a patient of average income, more than 80% for a patient with (*low, high*) income,

and less than 80% for a patient with (*low, high*) income. This could be done by giving everyone a government credit card for medical care and billing each patient a percentage based on the patient's i_____ t_____ from the last year which the government has collected.

6. If the government pays 100% instead of 80% of each patient's medical bill there would be a new demand curve D″.

   a. Draw D″ on your diagram.

   b. Suppose taxpayers and the government want E to be only $10,000 so government imposes a price control of P* = $100. Then the suppliers (doctors, medical technology firms, drug firms) are only willing to supply Q = _____. But with P = $100, D is (*greater, less*) than Q; show this in the diagram. Many patients would be unhappy because there would be a w_____ l_____. How many patients would be unhappy? _____.

   c. With P* = $100, if the government makes patients pay 20% (so insurance pays 80% instead of 100%) then the w_____ l_____ would be (*shorter than, the same as*) with 100% insurance because patient demand would be (*less, the same*). Also, switching from 100% insurance to 80% insurance would (*increase, decrease*) taxes.

7. If there is no externality, use a diagram to explain the efficiency loss due to the insurance price subsidy.

8. If there is a positive externality, use a diagram to explain why there may be no efficiency loss due to the insurance price subsidy.

9. Using a diagram, explain who bears the burden of employer-provided insurance.

10. Explain the strategy of consumer-driven health care and health savings accounts.

11. Explain the responsible health insurance plan.

12. Describe:

    a. An employer mandate.

    b. An employer play-or-pay option.

    c. Government reinsurance.

13. Give the pros and cons of replacing private insurance with government insurance.

14. Discuss these possible reforms of Medicare:

    a. A Medicare voucher.

    b. Income-related patient cost sharing.

    c. Rationing.

15. Go online and read about the health insurance plans of the Democratic and Republican candidates for president in the 2008 election. Describe, compare, and evaluate the two plans.

16. *Appendix Question:* Consider Figure 6A.1. With insurance the patient pays price P_L, chooses point _____, and her demand for medical care is _____. If price rises from P_L to P_H, the budget line would rotate, the person would move from _____ to _____, and her utility would (*rise, fall*). The person would move (*up, down*) her (*ordinary, compensated*) demand curve to _____. But suppose that as price rises from P_L to P_H the person is given additional _____ so her utility stays _____. Then she moves to _____. This move is called the _____ *effect*. The person moves (*up, down*) her (*ordinary, compensated*) demand curve from _____ to _____. The compensated demand curve is (*steeper, flatter*) than the ordinary demand curve.

As the person moves up her ordinary demand curve, utility (*falls, stays constant*). By contrast, as the person moves up her compensated demand curve, utility (*falls, stays constant*). The MB curve shows how many dollars the consumer would have to be given to keep her utility _____ if she had to _____ that unit of medical care. So the MB curve is the _____ demand curve, not the _____ demand curve. Hence, the area of the efficiency loss triangle is (*smaller than, the same as*) the area of the triangle formed using the ordinary demand curve.

Appendix

Health Insurance

This appendix explains why the MB curve in Figure 6.2 is the *compensated* demand curve (D_c) and is *steeper* than the ordinary demand curve (D_o).

Figure 6A.1 is an indifference-curve/budget-line diagram applied to the good "medical care." Before reading further, review the appendix to Chapter 1 which gives an introduction to the indifference-curve/budget-line diagram.

Each point in Figure 6A.1(a) indicates a particular quantity of medical care and a particular expenditure on other goods. Any two points that give the person the same

FIGURE 6A.1
If insurance is removed, the person chooses less medical care.

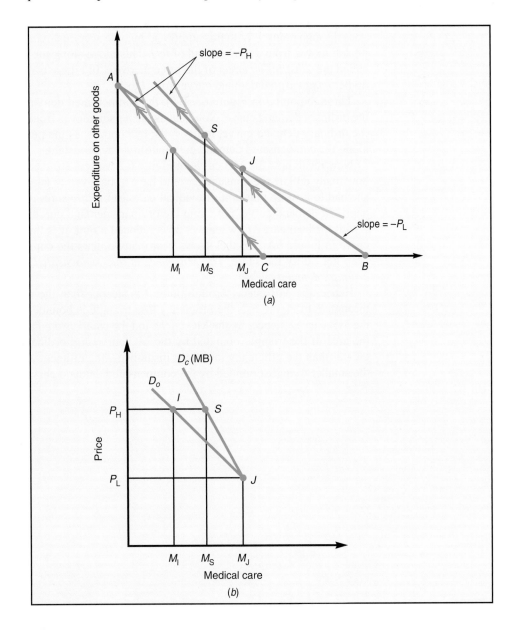

utility lie on the same indifference curve. With insurance, the out-of-pocket price to the consumer is low, P_L, and the person can afford to buy any point on the budget line *AB* (the slope of the budget line is equal to $-P_L$). The person chooses the point on the budget line with the highest utility—the point that is tangent to an indifference curve. As drawn, the person chooses point *J* with quantity of medical care M_J. Figure 6A.1(*b*) shows the corresponding point *J* with price P_L plotted on the vertical axis. With insurance, the price is P_L and the person demands quantity M_J.

In Figure 6A.1(*a*), if the price rises from P_L to P_H, the budget line would rotate down (clockwise) to *AC,* the person would move from point *J* to point *I,* and her utility would fall. In Figure 6A.1(*b*) the person would move up her ordinary demand curve D_o to point *I.*

But suppose that as the price rises from P_L to P_H in Figure 6A.1(*a*), the person is given additional income so that she can stay on the indifference curve that goes through point *J.* The additional income moves the budget line out parallel to *AC* until it goes through point *S.* With this additional income accompanying the price increase, the person moves from *J* to *S* instead of to *I.* This move along the original utility curve is called the *substitution effect* of the price increase. In Figure 6A.1(*b*), the person moves up her *compensated* demand curve from *J* to *S.*

Through point *J* in Figure 6A.1(*b*), the compensated demand curve is steeper than the ordinary demand curve. Note that as the person moves from point *J* to point *I* along the ordinary demand curve, utility falls; by contrast, as the person moves from *J* to *S* along the compensated demand curve, utility stays constant.

Now recall how the MB curve in Figure 6.2 was constructed. The MB curve shows how many dollars the consumer would have to be given to keep her *utility the same* if she had to give up that unit of medical care. But *utility stays constant* along the *compensated* demand curve, not along the ordinary demand curve. So starting from point *J* with medical care M_J, whenever *M* is reduced a unit, it is the compensated demand curve in Figure 6A.1(*b*) that shows how many dollars the consumer must be given to keep her utility the same. *The MB curve is the compensated demand curve, not the ordinary demand curve.*

Hence, the MB curve through point *J* is steeper than the ordinary demand curve through *J.* In Figure 6.2, the efficiency loss triangle is bounded by the MC curve and the MB curve—hence, by the MC curve and the *compensated* demand curve D_c. Thus, the area of the triangle bounded by the MC curve and ordinary demand curve D_o is greater than the efficiency loss from insurance—the efficiency loss equals the area of the smaller triangle bounded by the compensated demand curve D_c.

Chapter **Seven**

Tax Incidence and Inefficiency

SuperStock / Alamy

Taxes are necessary to raise the revenue needed to finance government programs, such as national defense and Social Security. Taxes also impose burdens on people and efficiency losses on the economy. The aim of tax policy should be to try to distribute these burdens fairly (equitably) and to minimize the efficiency losses on the economy.

This chapter has two parts. The first part analyzes who bears the burden from a particular tax—that is, the "incidence" of the tax. The second part analyzes the inefficiency (efficiency loss) to the economy that results from particular taxes.

INCIDENCE: WHO BEARS THE BURDEN?

People, Not Firms, Ultimately Bear All Tax Burdens

A variety of taxes are levied on business firms—payroll taxes, corporate income taxes, and sales taxes. In response, firms may do some or all of the following: raise product prices, passing some burden onto consumers; reduce wages, passing some burden onto workers; reduce dividends, passing some burden onto stockholders; reduce executive compensation, passing some burden onto managers. Hence, people, in their role as consumers, workers, stockholders, and managers will ultimately bear the burden of taxes levied on business firms. The purpose of incidence analysis is to determine which people bear how much of the burden from particular taxes.

In this chapter we use the supply-demand diagram to analyze the incidence of tax burdens and explain how the tax burden is divided between suppliers (sellers) and demanders (buyers). Two examples are a tax on gasoline and a payroll tax. For the gasoline tax, the suppliers are gas station firms and the demanders are drivers. When we show how much of the burden falls on the suppliers—business firms—it should be understood that these firms then pass the burden onto the workers, managers, and owners, who ultimately bear the burden. For the payroll tax, the suppliers of labor are the workers and the demanders are business firms. When we show how much of the burden falls on the demanders—the firms—it should be understood that the firms then pass the burden onto consumers, managers, and owners, who ultimately bear the burden.

The Distribution of the Burden Depends on the Relative Elasticities

A Tax on Gasoline

Figure 7.1(a) shows the effect of a tax on gasoline in a competitive market governed by demand and supply. Price is set in the competitive market, and given the market price, each firm decides how many gallons to supply and each driver decides how many gallons to demand. Hence, firms and drivers are "price takers." The lower the price, the greater the quantity demanded by the buyers (drivers). The higher the price, the greater the quantity supplied by the sellers (gas station operators). The market will go to the intersection point: In the absence of a tax, the price would be $3.50 per gallon.

The height of the supply curve equals the marginal cost (MC). Suppliers (sellers) compare the cost that they will actually have to pay to supply another unit—their marginal cost—to the price they will get for it. As long as their MC is less than the price, they will make more *profit* by supplying another unit. For example, when the price is $3.50 a gallon, station operators keep supplying gasoline as long as the MC is less than $3.50; the cost of supplying the last unit must be just under $3.50.

Consider the effect of a $1.00 per gallon tax. Assume the tax is levied on the station operators—they are legally required to make the payment to the government; the drivers are not required to pay.[1] The effect of a $1.00 tax per gallon would be to shift up the supply curve by $1.00, because the tax would increase the marginal cost that the station operators have to pay by $1.00. The market would therefore move to the intersection of the D curve with the new S' curve, so the amount of gasoline bought and sold would fall. As drawn in Figure 7.1(a), the price paid by the drivers would rise from $3.50 to

---

[1] Under U.S. tax law the check must be written by the first entity to refine, distribute, or wholesale gasoline; in this chapter we simplify by assuming that the supplier who writes the check is the station operator.

FIGURE 7.1

(*a*) The supply curve shifts up and most of the burden is born by buyers. (*b*) The supply curve shifts up and most of the burden is born by sellers. (*c*) The demand curve shifts down and the distribution of the burden is exactly the same as in Figure 7.1(*a*) (most of the burden is born by buyers). (*d*) The tax wedge shows the distribution of the tax burden between buyers and sellers.

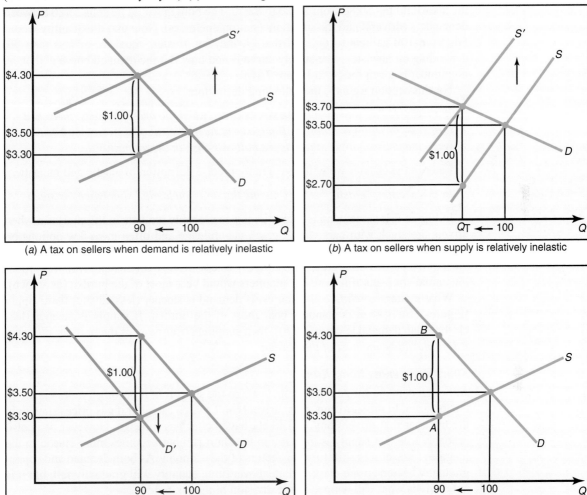

(*a*) A tax on sellers when demand is relatively inelastic

(*b*) A tax on sellers when supply is relatively inelastic

(*c*) A tax on buyers when demand is relatively inelastic

(*d*) The tax wedge shortcut

$4.30 per gallon, and the quantity demanded would fall from 100 to 90 gallons. Note also that the tax revenue equals the area of the rectangle with the base 90 and the height $1.00, so the tax revenue equals $90.

Who bears the burden of the $1.00 per gallon tax? Without the tax, drivers would have paid $3.50 per gallon. With the tax, they pay $4.30. So drivers bear a burden of $0.80 per gallon. Without the tax, station operators would have received and kept $3.50 per gallon. With the tax, they receive $4.30 per gallon from the drivers but must pay $1.00 per gallon to the government, so they keep $3.30 per gallon. Hence, suppliers bear a burden of $0.20 per gallon. As drawn in Figure 7.1(*a*), the burden of the $1.00 per gallon tax is split 80/20 between demanders (drivers) and suppliers (station operators).

In Figure 7.1(*a*), the demand curve is steep and the supply curve is flat. Suppose instead that the demand curve is flat and the supply curve steep as shown in Figure 7.1(*b*). Then, as drawn, the $1.00 tax would cause the price paid by drivers to rise only $0.20 from $3.50 to $3.70, and the price kept by station operators after paying the tax would fall $0.80 from $3.50 to $2.70. The burden would be split 20/80 between demanders (drivers) and the suppliers (station operators). Note that the quantity would fall from 100 gallons to Q_T, and that Q_T may be greater, equal to, or less than 90, depending on how steep the supply curve is and how flat the demand curve is [hence, no number is given for Q_T in Figure 7.1(*b*)].

For this section we have the following definition:

If a curve is flat, we say it is elastic *because when the price changes, there is a large response in the quantity. If a curve is steep, we say it is* inelastic *because when the price changes, there is a small response in the quantity.*

Later in the chapter we will give a more precise definition of elastic and inelastic.

In this section, "elastic" simply means flat and "inelastic" simply means steep.

In Figure 7.1(*a*), demand is inelastic; this is probably realistic in the short run when drivers are stuck with cars with a given gas mileage and often have few options on commuting to work. With demand less elastic than supply in Figure 7.1(*a*), drivers bear most of the burden. In Figure 7.1(*b*), supply is less elastic than demand which is probably unrealistic—but if it were so, suppliers would bear most of the burden (as shown).

What matters is *relative* elasticities. If demand is steeper (less elastic) than supply [Figure 7.1(*a*)], then demanders bear most of the burden. If supply is steeper (less elastic) than demand [Figure 7.1(*b*)], then suppliers bear most of the burden. *Whoever is less elastic bears most of the burden.*

Short Run versus Long Run

Although demand for gasoline is inelastic in the short run, it becomes more elastic in the long run. In the short run, most drivers can't switch cars, but if gas prices stay high, the next car that drivers buy will likely have better gas mileage. However, it is also probably true that supply is inelastic in the short run but becomes more elastic in the long run as resources shift to other sectors of the economy. As both demand and supply gradually become more elastic (flatter) over time, quantity will gradually fall, but it is not obvious what will happen to the division of the tax burden.

The Distribution of the Burden Doesn't Depend on Who Writes the Check

We have assumed that the gas station operator, not the driver, is legally required to write a check to the government for the gasoline tax. What would happen if the government legally required drivers, not station owners, to write the checks for the gasoline tax? It is likely that many drivers would forget, either accidentally or on purpose, to send a check for the full amount that they owed the government. But suppose, unrealistically, that drivers were perfectly honest and kept every gas station receipt. What would happen?

The answer is shown in Figure 7.1(*c*), where we assume the *D* and *S* curves are exactly as in Figure 7.1(*a*) (demand steep and supply flat). If the driver must send the government a check covering $1.00 per gallon, then the demand curve shifts down $1.00. For example, at a price of $3.30, drivers will now demand the quantity that they would have demanded before at a price of $4.30 because they realize that when they pay the station operator $3.30 they will also have to pay the government another $1.00 for a total of $4.30. When *D* shifts down to *D'*, the price at the pump will fall to $3.30. Station operators will receive $3.30 per gallon, and consumers will bear a burden (including the tax) of $4.30 per gallon [as in Figure 7.1(*a*), quantity will fall from 100 to 90 and tax revenue will equal $90]. But this is exactly the same result as in Figure 7.1(*a*). It doesn't matter for the division of the burden who writes the check (pays the tax).

The Tax Wedge Shortcut

Here's a shortcut for finding the division of the tax burden between buyers and sellers. Instead of shifting up the supply curve [Figure 7.1(*a*)] or shifting down the demand curve [Figure 7.1(*c*)], simply insert a vertical *tax wedge* equal to the amount of the tax (labeled *BA* and equal to $1.00 in this example) between the original demand and supply curves, as shown in Figure 7.1(*d*). Just start at the *D/S* intersection point, and move left until the vertical gap between *D* and *S* (the tax wedge) equals the amount of the tax ($1.00). This tax wedge diagram shows how much quantity falls, how much burden the demanders bear (the rise in price along the *D* curve), and how much burden the suppliers bear (the fall in price along the *S* curve). Note also that tax revenue equals the area of the tax wedge rectangle, because the height of the rectangle is the tax per unit ($T = \$1.00$) and the base of the rectangle is the number of units, 90, so tax revenue equals $90. The *tax wedge shortcut* makes it clear that the only thing that matters for the division of the burden is the relative steepness of the two curves: Whoever has the steeper (less elastic) curve bears most of the burden.

A Sales Tax

Now consider a 6% sales tax as shown in Figure 7.2. A 6% sales tax collected from the seller raises the seller's marginal cost 6% and therefore shifts up the supply curve 6% from *S* to *S'*; every point on the *S'* curve is 6% higher than the point directly below it, so the *S'* curve is slightly steeper than the *S* curve. Note that a percent-of-price tax, which is also called an *ad valorem tax,* makes the new supply curve slightly steeper

FIGURE 7.2
A Sales Tax
A sales tax shifts up the supply curve.

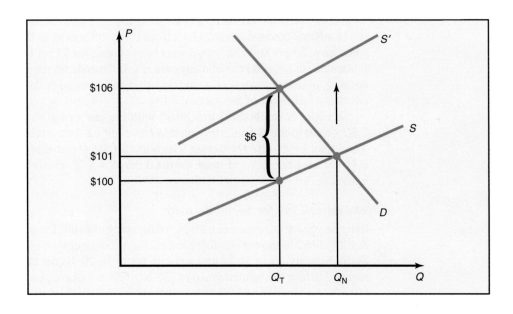

than the original supply curve. By contrast, a dollars-per-unit tax, such as the gasoline tax, makes the new supply curve parallel to the original supply curve.

With the 6% sales tax, when you buy an item with a sticker price of $100, $6 of sales tax is added, and you pay $106; the seller keeps $100 and sends $6 to the government. With the tax in effect, people buy the quantity Q_T. With no tax, they would have bought the quantity Q_N. What burden did the tax impose on you and other consumers? You need to know what you would have paid had there been no tax. Figure 7.2 shows your burden if demand is steep and supply flat; without the sales tax, you would have paid $101 (and the quantity with no tax would have been Q_N), so the tax made you pay $5 more ($106 instead of $101). Your burden due to the tax is $5, and the seller's burden is $1 (without the tax, the seller would have kept $101; with the tax, the seller keeps $100).

A Tax on Wage Income

Figure 7.3(*a*) shows a competitive market for labor. Employers are demanders and workers are suppliers. In the absence of a wage tax, the wage per hour would be $15.

If a wage (payroll) tax of $4 per hour is levied on workers (suppliers) so that they must send a check for $4 per hour to the government, the supply curve would shift up $4 to S'. At a wage of $16 an hour, for example, workers would now supply the same labor that they would have supplied at a wage of $12 when there was no tax. The labor market would therefore move to the intersection of the D curve with the new S' curve. As drawn, the wage paid by employers would rise from $15 to $16 an hour (and the quantity of labor would fall from 100 to 95 hours). Workers would receive $16, pay a tax of $4, and keep $12.

If instead the tax is levied on employers (demanders) so that they must pay the government $4 per hour, then as shown in Figure 7.3(*b*), the demand curve would shift down $4 to D'. At a wage of $12 an hour, for example, employers would now demand the same labor they would have demanded at a wage of $16 when there was no tax. The labor market would therefore move to the intersection of the S curve with the new D' curve. As drawn, the wage paid by employers would fall from $15 to $12 (and the quantity of labor would fall from 100 to 95 hours). Employers would pay a wage of $12 and a tax of $4.

In both cases, workers keep $12 an hour, and the cost to the employer (wage plus tax) is $16 an hour (and the quantity falls from 100 to 95 hours). In both cases, workers bear a burden of $3 per hour, and employers bear a burden of $1 per hour. The division of the burden doesn't depend on who pays the tax. It depends on the relative elasticities, and because, as drawn, supply is steep (inelastic) and demand is flat (elastic), the suppliers (workers) bear most of the burden.

We could have obtained this result with the tax wedge shortcut shown in Figure 7.3(*c*). Start at the *D/S* intersection and move left until the vertical gap between D and S is $4 per hour—the tax wedge. The wage on the D curve is $16 so employers bear a $1 per hour burden. The wage on the S curve is $12, so workers bear a $3 per hour burden.

The Payroll Tax for Social Security

Imagine you are an employee earning a daily wage of $100. The payroll tax rate for Social Security is 6.2% on your employer and 6.2% on you the employee, so your employer owes Social Security tax of $6.20 and you owe tax of $6.20. Under the law, your employer is required to take the amount you owe ($6.20) right out of your paycheck—so you receive $93.80—and send the $6.20 on your behalf along with the employer's $6.20—a total of

FIGURE 7.3
(*a*) The supply curve shifts up and most of the burden is born by workers. (*b*) The demand curve shifts down and the distribution of the burden is exactly the same as in Figure 7.3(*a*) (most of the burden is born by workers). (*c*) The tax wedge shows the distribution of the wage tax burden between workers and employers.

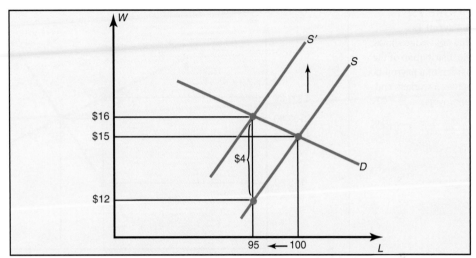

(*a*) A wage tax on workers when supply is relatively inelastic

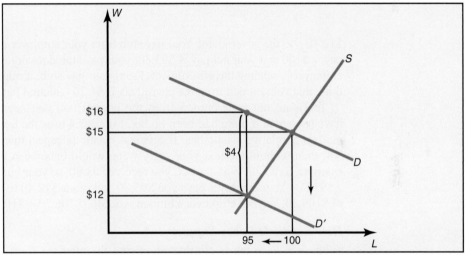

(*b*) A wage tax on employers when supply is relatively inelastic

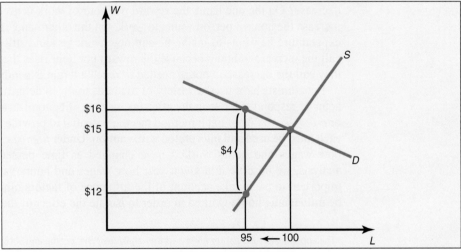

(*c*) The tax wedge shortcut

FIGURE 7.4

A Payroll Tax

The tax wedge shows the distribution of the burden of a payroll tax between workers and employers.

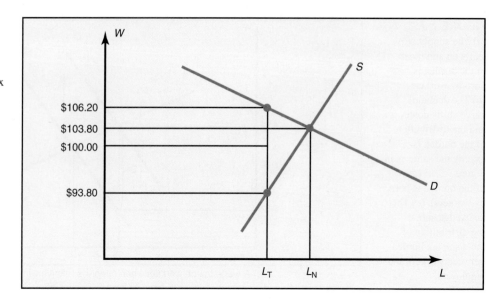

$12.40—to the government. Your pay stub from your employer indicates that your gross pay is $100 and your net pay is $93.80; your pay stub does not indicate how much your employer is sending the government. From your pay stub, it might be natural for you to think that your burden from the payroll tax is $6.20—natural but incorrect.

To figure out your burden from the payroll tax, you need to know what would have happened if there had been no tax. Figure 7.4 uses the tax wedge shortcut. What matters is relative elasticities. If S is less elastic (steeper) than D as drawn in Figure 7.4, then without the tax, your daily wage would have been greater than $100—for example, $103.80. With the tax, you receive $93.80, so your burden is $10.00 ($103.80 − $93.80). Your employer pays you $93.80 and sends $12.40 to the government, a total of $106.20, so your employer's burden is $2.40 ($106.20 − $103.80).

How Elastic Is Labor Supply?

Suppose a wage tax is eliminated, raising the after-tax (net) wage w_n that a worker receives. Will the number of hours a person wants to work (supply) increase or decrease? On the one hand, the reward per hour of work is greater; this would tend to increase the hours a person wants to work. On the other hand, if the person has a target expenditure he wants to make, he can now work less and still achieve it. Economists call the increase in hours because the reward per hour rises the *substitution effect*, and they call the decrease in hours needed to reach a target expenditure the *income effect*.[2]

Economists have used a variety of methods to try to determine how workers would actually respond to a rise in the after-tax wage w_n. Economists analyze *time-series* data or *cross-section* data. Each method has the potential to provide useful information, but each must be used and interpreted with caution. Under *time-series* analysis, we observe how wages and hours worked have changed as time passed. Under *cross-section* analysis, we observe in a given year how wages and hours vary across persons. It is important to try to take account of the influence of factors other than wages that may be influencing hours worked in order to isolate the effect of the wage on hours.

---

[2] The appendix to this chapter gives a further analysis of the income and substitution effects by using an indifference-curve/budget-line diagram.

Based on empirical studies using time-series and cross-section data analysis, economists have found that it is important to distinguish between *primary* earners and *secondary* earners. If one person in a household earns substantially more wage income than anyone else, that person is the primary earner and anyone else who works is a secondary earner. Economists have generally found that most *primary* earners would not change their hours of work in response to the elimination of tax on wage income, but that *secondary* earners would sometimes increase their hours—particularly by deciding to work rather than not work. There are fixed costs that must be incurred when a person decides whether or not to work. For a secondary earner, it is often the cost of arranging for child care. If the after-tax wage increases, it may pay to incur this cost; hence, eliminating a tax on wage income may cause some secondary earners to decide to work.

From these econometric studies, the following rough estimate has emerged. If the after-tax wage of a primary earner increases 10%, hours of labor supplied increases only about 1%. Another way to say this is that the elasticity for primary earners is only about 0.1 (1%/10%), where the *elasticity* is defined as the ratio of the percentage change in hours supplied (1%) to the percentage change in the after-tax wage (10%). Hence, the labor supply of primary earners is very inelastic. By contrast, if the after-tax wage of a secondary earner increases 10%, hours of labor supplied increases about 5%. In other words, the elasticity for secondary earners is about 0.5 (5%/10%). Hence, labor supply is not as inelastic for secondary earners as for primary earners. For primary earners, the S curve in Figure 7.4 is nearly vertical so that primary earners bear nearly the entire burden of the combined (employer plus employee) 12.4% payroll tax for Social Security.

A Tax on Capital Income

Figure 7.5 shows a competitive market for saving. Firms (borrowers) are demanders and households (lenders) are suppliers. Firms borrow saving, invest in machinery, and from the return on machinery, they pay the savers (lenders) interest income (*capital income*). On the vertical axis is the rate of return r. As drawn, the saving supply curve has a positive slope—the higher the rate of the return, the more the households save. In the absence of a tax, the rate of return would be 4%. Consider the last $100 saved at the intersection point. A firm borrows the $100 and uses it to make an investment in a

FIGURE 7.5
A Capital Income Tax on Savers
The supply curve shifts up.

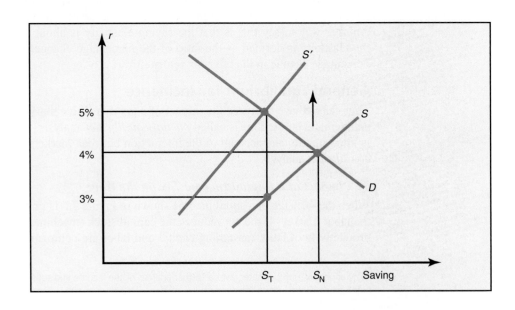

machine that costs \$100. The machine generates additional revenue of \$4 per year—a rate of return of 4% on the \$100 investment. The saver is paid \$4 interest—a rate of return of 4% on the \$100 of saving.

Figure 7.5 shows the effect of a tax levied on the capital income that savers earn. Consider a 40% tax on capital income. Suppose a person saves \$100. If he earned interest income of \$5 before tax, he must pay a tax of \$2 (40% of \$5) and therefore would keep \$3. Hence, a 40% tax implies that if he earns a 5% return before tax, he would receive a 3% return after tax. According to the S curve in Figure 7.5, people would save S_T if there were a 3% return and no tax; with a 40% tax, they would save S_T if they earned a 5% return before tax, so they could keep 3% after tax. Hence, this tax would shift up the saving supply curve to S' because it would now take a before-tax return of 5%, not 3%, to induce people to save S_T. Because the tax is 40%, the height of each point on S is 60% of the height of the point above it on S', so S' is not parallel to S—S' is slightly steeper than S. With the relative elasticities as drawn, the 40% capital income tax causes the market rate of return to rise from 4% to 5%; the savers send 2% to the government and keep 3% after tax. Savers bear a 1% burden, and borrowers bear a 1% burden.

How Elastic Is Saving Supply?

Suppose a tax on capital income is eliminated, raising the after-tax return r_n a saver receives. Will the person's saving increase or decrease? As in the case of labor supply, there are two opposing tendencies. On the one hand, the reward to a dollar of saving is greater; this would tend to increase a person's saving. On the other hand, if the person has a target expenditure he wants to make, he can save less and still achieve it. Economists call the increase in saving when the reward to a dollar of saving increases the *substitution effect;* they call the decrease in saving needed to reach a target expenditure the *income effect.*[3]

As in the case of labor supply, economists have used a variety of methods to try to determine how saving would actually respond to a rise in the after-tax return r_n. Using either time-series or cross-section analysis, some economists have found that saving is inelastic, while other economists have found a positive elasticity. Although there is a wide variation of estimates from econometric studies, the average estimate is roughly the following: If the after-tax return increases about 33% (for example, from 3% to 4%; an increase of 1% starting from 3% is a 33% increase), saving increases about 10%. Another way to say this is that the saving elasticity is about 0.3 (10%/33%), where the elasticity is defined as the ratio of the percentage change in saving (10%) to the percentage change in the after-tax return (33%).

General Equilibrium Tax Incidence

Thus far we have analyzed the impact of a tax in a single market with a single supply and demand curve. This is called *partial equilibrium* analysis. Sometimes, however, it is important to take account of the interaction between markets. This is called *general equilibrium* analysis.

The Impact of a Capital Income Tax on the Wage

When the 40% tax on capital income shown in Figure 7.5 is imposed, what happens in the labor market? If the tax reduces the capital stock (machinery), this will reduce the productivity of labor (assuming capital and labor are complements in the production

---

[3] The appendix to this chapter gives a further analysis of the income and substitution effects using an indifference-curve/budget-line diagram.

FIGURE 7.6
**The Impact on
Workers of Taxing
Savers**
The tax on savers
reduces the wage.

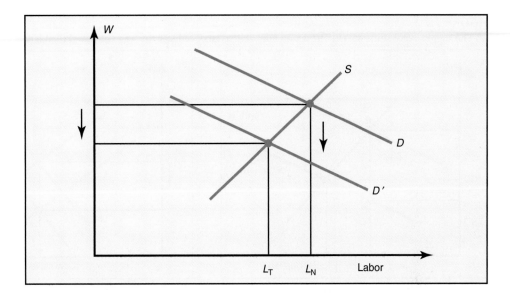

FIGURE 7.6
The Impact on Workers of Taxing Savers
The tax on savers reduces the wage.

process) and shift down the labor demand curve as shown in Figure 7.6. As a consequence, the wage will fall. Thus, perhaps surprisingly, workers bear some burden from a capital income tax.

The Impact of a Progressive Wage Tax on the Low-Skilled Wage

Consider an economy with two kinds of labor—low-skilled and high-skilled. The demand for labor reflects the productivity of each kind of labor, so the demand curve for high-skilled labor is higher than the demand curve for low-skilled labor. Initially assume that there are no taxes and there is the same number of workers of each skill level. Figure 7.7(*a*) shows that the wage for high-skilled labor is $30, and Figure 7.7(*b*), that the wage for low-skilled labor is $10.

Consider a progressive wage tax that levies a tax on a worker equal to $X\%$ of his wage in excess of $20. At first glance, it might seem that low-skilled workers with a wage of $10 would be unaffected because they are exempt from paying the tax. However, general equilibrium analysis shows that low-skilled workers will bear some burden due to this tax. Why?

In the high-skilled labor market shown in Figure 7.7(*a*), the progressive wage tax shifts up the supply curve of labor just as it did in Figure 7.3(*a*); this moves the market from point *O* to point *F*, thereby reducing the quantity of high-skilled labor. The before-tax wage will rise above $30, but the after-tax wage will fall below $30, so high-skilled workers, not surprisingly, bear some burden from the progressive wage tax.

In the low-skilled labor market shown in Figure 7.7(*b*), the demand curve will shift down and the supply curve will shift right, moving the market from point *O* to point *G*, thereby reducing the wage of low-skilled labor. Why will the demand curve shift down? The decrease in the quantity of high-skilled labor will reduce the productivity of low-skilled workers (assuming high-skilled and low-skilled workers are complements in the production process) and shift down the labor demand curve. Why will the supply curve shift right? When fewer workers choose to become high-skilled because of the lower after-tax wage received by high-skilled labor, more workers remain low-skilled. As a consequence of both shifts, the low-skilled wage will fall.

FIGURE 7.7

(*a*) The supply curve shifts up. (*b*) The tax on high-skilled labor reduces the wage of low-skilled labor.

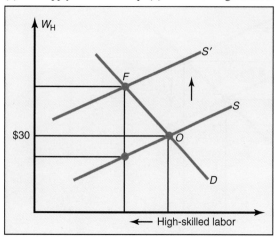

(*a*) A wage tax on high-skilled workers

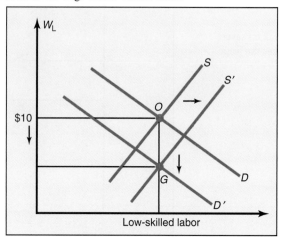

(*b*) The impact on low-skilled workers
of taxing high-skilled workers

Thus, perhaps surprisingly, low-skilled workers will bear some burden from the progressive wage tax.

The Corporate Income Tax

Suppose a tax is imposed on capital invested in one sector of the economy but not elsewhere. For example, because of the corporate income tax, capital invested in corporations is taxed more heavily than capital invested in noncorporate business firms. At first glance it might seem that only investors in the taxed sector would be harmed by the tax, but this is not so in the long run.

Suppose without the tax financial investors (savers) earn a 4% rate of return in both the corporate and noncorporate sectors. A corporate tax reduces the after-tax return below 4%. With noncorporate business firms still earning 4%, financial investors will gradually shift capital (funds) into these firms; the shift right of the supply of capital curve to the noncorporate sector will drive down the rate of return below 4%. In the final equilibrium, capital in both the corporate and noncorporate sectors will earn an after-tax return below 4%. Clearly, then, financial investors in both sectors will be burdened by the tax on corporate capital.

Furthermore, if the lower after-tax return reduces saving and investment as shown in Figure 7.5, it will reduce the wage as shown in Figure 7.6 so some burden may fall on workers.

INEFFICIENCY

Most taxes impose an efficiency loss on the economy. Let's explain what this inefficiency means. Imagine that $100,000 worth of your favorite mix of goods has been produced and is sitting waiting for you to take it home. As you arrive with your truck you see 10% of the goods—$10,000 worth—get loaded onto a van, driven to a cliff, and dumped into the ocean far below. Only $90,000 worth of goods is left for you. "What a waste!" you cry out as you think about how you could have enjoyed consuming the lost $10,000.

Now imagine that you are promised $100,000 of your favorite goods, but when you arrive, you find that the mix of goods has been changed and is no longer your favorite mix. You judge that the changing of the mix has the same effect on you as dumping $10,000 of your favorite goods in the ocean, leaving you with only $90,000 of your favorite goods. Economists say that this changing of the mix has caused an **efficiency loss** of $10,000—and you should think of it as equivalent to dumping goods you could have enjoyed into the ocean.

A tax usually causes an efficiency loss by causing an unfavorable change in the mix of goods. For example, a tax on a particular good usually causes less of that particular good to be produced and consumed and more of the untaxed goods to be produced and consumed. A tax on labor income causes less work and therefore, less goods that are produced from work, and causes more of the good called "leisure"—hence the mix of goods shifts toward leisure. A tax on capital income causes less saving and more goods consumed in the present, but less goods consumed in the future—the mix of goods shifts toward present goods and away from future goods.

There are at least four other equivalent terms for the efficiency loss from a tax: the *deadweight loss* from the tax, the *welfare loss* from the tax, the *welfare cost* of the tax, and the *excess burden* of the tax.

Economists do more than simply identify the existence of an efficiency loss from a particular tax. We try to estimate the magnitude of the efficiency loss. The magnitude is important. Consider two different taxes that raise the same total tax revenue. Suppose the first tax causes an efficiency loss of $15,000, while the second causes an efficiency loss of $5,000. The first should be thought of as causing $15,000 of your favorite goods to be dumped in the ocean, the second only $5,000. Clearly, you should prefer that the second tax, not the first, be used to raise the required revenue, unless there are other reasons to prefer the first tax.

There is another way to think about the efficiency loss from a tax. A tax changes the mix of goods (how many units of good A, how many units of good B, and so on) and results in a particular pattern of well-being (utility) among individuals. Starting from that original mix and pattern of utility, would it be possible to change the mix and distribute this new mix among individuals, so that some are better off (achieve higher utility) while none are worse off (experience lower utility)? If the answer is yes, then we say that the tax has caused an efficiency loss. Then we ask: How much better off could people have been with this new mix? Suppose the answer is that they could have been made $15,000 better off—that is, changing the mix and distributing it would have had the same effect on their well-being (utility) as distributing $15,000 to them. Then we say that the efficiency loss from the tax is $15,000.

Whether the efficiency loss from taxes is small or large may influence how much to spend on government programs. Suppose it turns out that all taxes cause large efficiency losses. Then we should reconsider whether the government program is really worth imposing the taxes. If the tax causes 10%—$10,000 out of $100,000—to be dumped in the ocean, maybe the government program is good enough to justify the efficiency loss, but if the tax causes 40%—$40,000 out of $100,000—to be dumped in the ocean, maybe the government program is not good enough to justify the efficiency loss. The magnitude of the efficiency loss from taxes should influence the magnitude of government spending that is chosen.

It should be emphasized that inefficiency is not the only criterion that should be used to judge particular taxes. One tax might cause a larger efficiency loss than another tax, but it might still be preferred by citizens because they regard it as a fairer or a more administratively feasible tax. Efficiency is only one criterion for judging taxes, but it is an important one.

The Efficiency Loss from a Tax on a Good

In Figure 7.8, a $4 tax on a good has resulted in 100 units being produced and consumed; consumers pay $20 per unit and producers keep $16 per unit. Assume that the good has *no* externality (negative or positive). Then it's wasteful—inefficient—that the 101st unit was not produced and consumed. Why? Because the marginal benefit (MB) to the consumer of the 101st unit—the maximum amount that the consumer would be willing to pay for that unit (thereby keeping his utility constant)—equals the height of the *D* curve (the height of point *B*, $20), while the marginal cost (MC) equals the height of the *S* curve (the height of point *A*, $16). The MB would have exceeded the MC, and the net gain to society would have been *BA*, $4. It's also wasteful that the 102nd unit wasn't produced because MB would still have exceeded MC, and so on until the 110th unit where MB finally equals MC.[4]

The sum of the net gains that *could* have occurred by increasing the quantity of the good from 100 to 110 equals the area of the shaded triangle: ½(base × height) = ½($4 × 10) = $20. The (vertical) base of the triangle equals the tax per unit *T*, and the (horizontal) height equals the change in quantity, ΔQ. The triangle shows the net loss in society's welfare due to the tax:

$$\text{Efficiency loss} = \text{area of triangle} = \tfrac{1}{2}T(\Delta Q)$$

It is clearly appropriate that the triangle is labeled *BAD*.

We noted above that one equivalent term for the efficiency loss from a tax is the excess burden of a tax. Now we can explain why. The direct burden of the tax is the tax revenue paid by the private sector to the government. Since the tax per unit is $4, and the number of units is 100, tax revenue equals $4 × 100 = $400; tax revenue equals

---

[4] A technical point: The MB curve in Figure 7.8 is the compensated demand curve as explained in the appendix to Chapter 6.

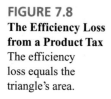

FIGURE 7.8
The Efficiency Loss from a Product Tax
The efficiency loss equals the triangle's area.

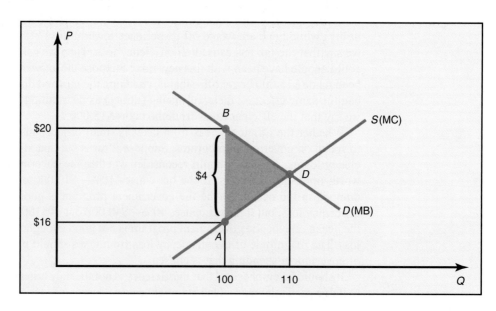

the area of the rectangle in Figure 7.8. It is often assumed that this is the entire burden of the tax, but it is not so. The tax causes the quantity to be less than socially optimal. This *BAD* triangle burden is in excess of the rectangle direct burden. The total burden of the tax is the revenue rectangle plus the *BAD* triangle. Note that in this example the ratio of the excess burden to the direct burden is $20/$400 = 5%. Thus, when $100 of revenue is raised, there is an additional burden of $5, so the total burden is $105.

Suppose the tax were twice as great—$8 instead of $4. How much greater would the efficiency loss be? In Figure 7.8, if the tax were $8, then the quantity would be only 90 (not shown), and the area of *BAD* triangle would be four times as great. Why? Because the base of the triangle (the tax) would be twice as great ($8 instead of $4), *and* the height of the triangle (the reduction in the quantity) would *also* be twice as great (20 instead of 10), so the area, ½(base × height), would be four times as great. Thus:

> *The efficiency loss from a tax is proportional to the square of the tax: If the tax is doubled, the efficiency loss quadruples.*

Look again at Figure 7.8. Imagine the *D* and *S* curves were steeper (less elastic). Then for a particular tax wedge ($4), the efficiency loss triangle would be smaller. Clearly, both elasticities (*D* and *S*) matter for the efficiency loss. Thus:

> *The less elastic (steeper) the* D *and* S *curves, the smaller the efficiency loss from a tax.*

Thus far in this chapter, elastic has simply meant "flat" and inelastic has meant "steep." It will now be necessary to give more precise definitions. In contrast to some other economics textbooks, we define elasticity *e* so that it is a *positive number*.

The **elasticity of demand** *e is defined here as the ratio of the percentage* increase *in quantity demanded (%ΔQ) over the percentage* decrease *in the price (%ΔP):*

$$e \equiv \%\Delta Q / \%\Delta P$$

For example, if quantity demanded increases 5% when the price decreases 10%, then the elasticity of demand is 0.5. Note that we have defined the elasticity of demand *e* so that *e* is positive because a decrease in price causes an increase in quantity demanded. If the elasticity *e* is greater than 1, we say that demand is *elastic,* and if the elasticity *e* is less than 1, we say that demand is *inelastic*. The larger the *e,* the more elastic the demand; the smaller the *e,* the less elastic the demand.

As shown in the footnote[5], if the supply curve were horizontal in Figure 7.8, the area of the triangle would equal

$$L = ½t^2 e P Q$$

where *t* is the tax rate (*t* equals *T/P*) and *e* is the demand elasticity.[6] According to this formula, if the tax rate *t* doubles, the efficiency loss *L* quadruples; also, the lower the elasticity *e,* the smaller the efficiency loss. Since tax revenue *R* equals *tPQ,* then *L/R* = ½t²ePQ/tPQ = ½te. The ratio of efficiency loss *L* to tax revenue *R* equals

$$L/R = ½te$$

---

[5] The area of the triangle $L = ½T(\Delta Q)$. By definition $e = (\Delta Q/Q)/(\Delta P/P)$, so $\Delta Q = e(\Delta P/P)Q$. Since $\Delta P = T$, $\Delta Q = e(T/P)Q = etQ$. Then $L = ½T(etQ) = ½(T/P)(etPQ) = ½t(etPQ) = ½t^2 ePQ$.

[6] If the supply curve has a positive slope as shown in Figure 7.8, then the formula is more complicated and includes the elasticity of supply as well as the elasticity of demand. A technical point: The *e* in the formula is the compensated demand elasticity, as explained in the appendix to Chapter 6.

For example, if $e = 0.5$ and $t = 20\%$, the formula says $L/R = 5\%$: For every $100 of revenue raised, there is an efficiency loss of $5.

Optimal Commodity Taxation

Suppose initially that all commodities (goods) are taxed at the same rate under a sales tax, but different goods have different demand elasticities. The efficiency loss of raising a target amount of revenue can be reduced by varying the tax rate across goods—specifically, setting higher tax rates on inelastic goods and lower tax rates on elastic goods. This is called the *Ramsey inverse elasticity rule* (Ramsey was the economist who discovered it nearly a hundred years ago).

But trying to vary tax rates inversely with elasticities has four drawbacks. First, it is not easy to determine each good's elasticity. Second, it would encourage wasteful lobbying of politicians by producers seeking lower rates for their own goods. Third, it would raise the compliance cost of retailers and the administrative cost of government auditors. Fourth, it would result in a pattern of tax rates many citizens would find unfair, because necessities have inelastic demand and would therefore be taxed at high rates while luxuries have elastic demand and would therefore be taxed at low rates. Because of these drawbacks, it is probably not worth trying to vary tax rates inversely with elasticities. So setting the same tax rate for all goods may not be best in theory but may be sensible in practice.

The Efficiency Loss from a Tax on Wage Income

Figure 7.9 shows a market supply-demand diagram for labor. In Figure 7.9, suppose employers pay workers a wage of $16 an hour, equal to the worker's **marginal revenue product of labor (MRPL)**, which is the amount of additional revenue generated by another hour of work. Each worker pays a tax of $4 and keeps $12. In response to the after-tax wage of $12, workers choose to supply 20,000 hours of labor in a year, because the market consists of 10 workers and each worker chooses to supply 40 hours per week for 50 weeks—hence, 2,000 hours per year. Then it's wasteful—inefficient—that an additional hour beyond 20,000 was not supplied and used by a firm to produce output. Why?

FIGURE 7.9
The Efficiency Loss from a Wage Tax
The efficiency loss equals the triangle's area.

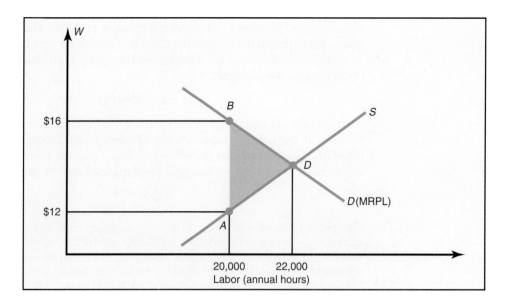

The dollar amount that the worker would need to be compensated to keep his utility constant if he worked an additional hour equals the height of the labor supply S curve (the height up to point A, \$12). This hour of work would have produced an MRPL equal to the height of the D curve (the height of point B, \$16), so the "surplus" marginal product (the vertical gap between D and S, which is BA, \$4) could have been distributed to others, making them better off. It's also wasteful that all the additional hours from 20,000 to 22,000 were not worked—22,000 is where the height of the S curve finally equals the height of D (the MRPL).[7]

The sum of the net gains to society that *could* have occurred by increasing the quantity of hours from 20,000 to 22,000 equals the area of the shaded triangle: ½(base × height) = ½(\$4 × 2,000) = \$4,000. The base (vertical) of the triangle equals the tax per hour T, and the height (horizontal) equals the change in hours ΔH. The triangle shows the net loss in society's welfare due to the tax:

$$\text{Efficiency loss} = \text{area of triangle} = \tfrac{1}{2}T(\Delta H)$$

The total burden of the tax is the revenue rectangle plus the BAD triangle. The area of the revenue rectangle is \$4 × 20,000 = \$80,000. In this example the ratio of the excess burden to the direct burden is \$4,000/\$80,000 = 5%. Thus, when \$100 of revenue is raised, there is an additional burden of \$5, so the total burden is \$105.

As in the case of the tax on a good, *the efficiency loss is proportional to the square of the tax*: If the tax were doubled, the base and the height of the triangle would double, so that its area—equal to the efficiency loss—would quadruple.

Look again at Figure 7.9. Imagine the S and D curves were steeper (less elastic). Then for a particular tax wedge (\$4), the efficiency loss triangle would be smaller. Once again:

The less elastic (steeper) the D *and* S *curves, the smaller the efficiency loss from a tax.*

The **elasticity of labor supply** ε *is defined here as the ratio of the percentage* increase *in hours supplied (%ΔH) over the percentage* increase *in the wage (%ΔW):*

$$\varepsilon \equiv (\%\Delta H)/(\%\Delta W).$$

For example, if hours supplied increases by 5% when the wage increases by 10%, then the elasticity of labor supply ε is 0.5.

As shown in the footnote[8], if the demand curve in Figure 7.9 were horizontal, the area of the triangle would equal

$$L = \tfrac{1}{2}t^2\varepsilon WH$$

where t is the tax rate (t equals T/W) and ε is the labor supply elasticity.[9] According to this formula, if the tax rate t doubles, the efficiency loss L quadruples; also, the lower the elasticity ε, the smaller the efficiency loss. Since tax revenue R equals

---

[7] A technical point: The S curve in Figure 7.9 is the compensated supply curve. An explanation is given in the appendix to this chapter.

[8] The area of the triangle $L = \tfrac{1}{2}T(\Delta H)$. By definition $\varepsilon = (\Delta H/H)/(\Delta W/W)$, so $\Delta H = \varepsilon(\Delta W/W)H$. Since $\Delta W = T$, $\Delta H = \varepsilon(T/W)H = \varepsilon tH$. Then $L = \tfrac{1}{2}T(\varepsilon tH) = \tfrac{1}{2}(T/W)(\varepsilon tWH) = \tfrac{1}{2}t(\varepsilon tWH) = \tfrac{1}{2}t^2\varepsilon WH$.

[9] If the demand curve slopes down as shown in Figure 7.9, then the formula is more complicated and includes the demand elasticity as well as the supply elasticity. A technical point: The ε in the formula is the compensated labor supply elasticity as explained in the appendix to this chapter

tWH, then $L/R = \frac{1}{2}t^2\varepsilon WH/tWH = \frac{1}{2}t\varepsilon$. The ratio of efficiency loss L to tax revenue R equals

$$L/R = \frac{1}{2}t\varepsilon$$

For example, if $\varepsilon = 0.4$ and $t = 25\%$, the formula says $L/R = 5\%$: For every $100 of revenue raised, there is an efficiency loss of $5.

The Efficiency Loss from a Tax on Capital Income

Figure 7.10 shows the efficiency loss from a tax on capital income. The efficiency loss equals the area of the triangle BAD. With a 40% tax on the saver's interest income, the total amount saved by all savers is $100,000. The last $100 saved enables the borrowing firm to buy a machine that raises its net revenue $5 per year, and the firm pays the saver $5 of interest income; the saver pays $2 tax (40% of $5) and keeps $3. The tax drives a wedge between the firm's 5% return on the machine and each saver's after-tax return of 3%.

Starting from total saving by all savers of $100,000, it would be possible to increase saving by $100 and make everyone better off. Each saver only needs to receive a 3% return to keep his utility constant. Why? Because the saver received only $3 after taxes on the last $100 he saved, yet he was still willing to save this last $100. However, the $100 machine generates a return of 5%. Hence, 3% can be given to the saver, and the remaining 2% can be distributed to everyone else making them better off. Each additional $100 of saving from $100,000 to $120,000 generates a return on the machine that exceeds the return that savers require to keep their utility constant; this surplus is the vertical distance between the D curve and the S curve. The sum of the surpluses from $100,000 to $120,000 equals the area of the triangle BAD. Thus, the area of the triangle measures the efficiency loss from the tax on capital income. With these numbers, the area is $\frac{1}{2}(2\% \times \$20,000) = \$200$, so the efficiency loss is $200.[10] The steeper the S and D curves in Figure 7.10, the smaller the efficiency loss.

---

[10] A technical point: The S curve in Figure 7.10 is the compensated supply curve. An explanation is given in the appendix to this chapter. An alternative analysis of the efficiency loss from a tax on capital income that applies Figure 7.8 to the demand and supply of a good called retirement consumption is given in Martin Feldstein, "The Welfare Cost of Capital Income Taxation," *Journal of Political Economy* 86, no. 2 (April 1978), pp. S29–S51.

FIGURE 7.10
The Efficiency Loss from a Capital Income Tax
The efficiency loss equals the triangle's area.

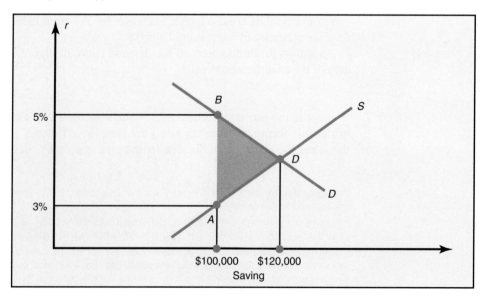

A Lump-Sum Tax and the Marginal Tax Rate

Instead of these taxes, consider a **lump-sum tax**—a tax for which the amount owed doesn't vary with the taxpayer's behavior (i.e., how much the person works and earns, how much the person consumes and saves, and so on). For example, a tax of $1,000 per person regardless of the person's income or consumption is a lump-sum tax. A lump-sum tax doesn't necessarily have to be the same amount for each taxpayer, but the amount owed must be based on some attribute of the taxpayer that can't be affected by the taxpayer's behavior. Most citizens would judge a lump-sum tax to be unfair, so it is seldom used. But it is important to understand why a lump-sum tax would have no efficiency loss.

None of the *BAD* triangles in figures 7.8 through 7.10 would occur if only lump-sum taxes were levied. Once a person has paid his lump-sum tax, in Figure 7.8 there would be no wedge between the price he pays for a good and the marginal cost of its production; in Figure 7.9, there would be no wedge between the wage that he receives and his marginal revenue product; in Figure 7.10, there would be no wedge between the return the saver receives and the return the machine generates.

Large lump-sum taxes, of course, could impose large *direct* burdens on taxpayers. But there would be no *excess* burden—no efficiency loss—resulting from having a person face a wedge when making a behavioral decision. It's a shame that lump-sum taxes don't pass the fairness test because they obtain a perfect score on the efficiency test.

Look back at Figure 7.9 in which each worker chooses to supply 2,000 hours per year if the after-tax wage is $12; recall that there are 10 workers in this market so that the total number of hours supplied is 20,000. In deciding to work the 2,000th hour, but not the 2,001st hour, what does each worker consider? What matters is not the tax that the worker has paid up to this point on wage income from the first 2,000 hours. What matters is the tax that would be paid on the 2,001st hour. To see this, imagine the worker must pay the same tax on the earnings from 2,000 hours but no further tax starting with the 2,001st hour. Then there would be no tax wedge in Figure 7.9 and no *BAD* triangle.

What matters, then, for efficiency is not the **average tax rate (ATR)**—the ratio of total taxes paid to total income earned (T/Y). Instead, what matters is the **marginal tax rate (MTR)**—the ratio of the additional tax to additional income earned ($\Delta T/\Delta Y$) from another hour of work. A lump-sum tax may have a high ATR, but its MTR is zero so its efficiency loss is zero.

Consider a proportional income tax under which each person pays a tax rate of 25% on all income earned. Then every person, regardless of income, faces a marginal tax rate of 25% and experiences a 25% wedge between the marginal revenue product he generates and the after-tax wage he keeps. For example, a worker who generates $16 keeps $12, and a worker who generates $32 keeps $24; hence every person has a *BAD* triangle with a 25% tax wedge.

Now suppose the proportional income tax is converted to a progressive income tax under which a person's income up to $50,000 is taxed at a 0% rate (the first $50,000 of income is exempt from tax) and income above $50,000 is taxed at a 50% rate. Then for every person who makes less than $50,000, the marginal tax rate is 0%, there is no tax wedge, and there is no *BAD* triangle. But for every person who makes more than $50,000, the marginal tax rate is 50%, and there is a 50% tax wedge with its corresponding *BAD* triangle. Converting the proportional income tax to the progressive income tax reduces inequality in after-tax incomes, decreases the efficiency loss for people making less than $50,000, but increases the efficiency loss for people making more than $50,000.

The Revenue-Rate Curve

Consider a tax on wage income. As the tax rate t increases from 0%, tax revenue (tWH) increases. However, when the tax rate reaches 100%, presumably no one would work, and revenue would fall to zero (because H would be zero). Thus, the relationship between tax revenue and the tax rate—the **revenue-rate curve**—is shown in Figure 7.11. Clearly, there is some tax rate between 0% and 100% that maximizes tax revenue; in the figure, we indicate this *revenue-maximizing rate* as t_m. The shape of the revenue-rate curve, with revenue equal to zero at tax rates of 0% and 100% and the maximum revenue at a tax rate somewhere in between, has long been known by economists, and practical policy makers have long recognized that at some point (t_m) raising the tax rate further is counterproductive in that it yields less revenue. The tax rate t should be set somewhere between 0 and t_m but not above t_m.

What is the numerical value of t_m? Is it high or low? Is it higher or lower than the current tax rate on wage income? Here economists disagree. The majority of economists believe that t_m is high, closer to 100% than 0%, so that the current tax rate on wage income, which is below 50% (including both income and payroll tax rates), is substantially lower than t_m. The majority view is drawn in Figure 7.11. If the majority is correct, then starting from the current tax rate, if the rate is increased, revenue will increase, and if the rate is decreased, revenue will decrease.

However, a minority of economists, sometimes called *supply-siders,* believe that t_m is low, closer to 0% than 100%, and that the current tax rate on wage income is greater than t_m. If the minority is correct, then starting from the current tax rate, if the rate is increased, revenue will decrease, and if the rate is decreased, revenue will increase—a tax rate cut will "pay for itself"—so that when the tax rate is cut, there is no need to cut government spending. Several decades ago economist Arthur Laffer contended that the current tax rate is greater than t_m in Figure 7.11. Because of this, some began to refer to the revenue-rate curve as the "Laffer curve." However, this confuses the issue. All economists agree about the shape of the revenue-rate curve. The disagreement is over *Laffer's hypothesis* that the current tax rate is greater than

FIGURE 7.11
The Revenue-Rate Curve
The income tax rate that maximizes revenue is less than 100%.

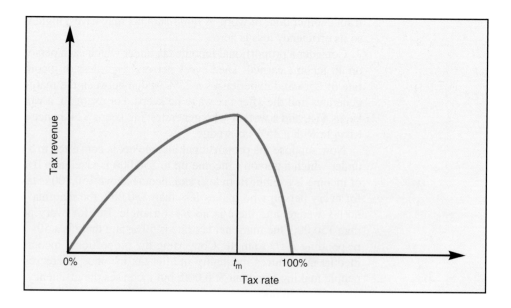

the revenue-maximizing rate t_m. Thus, we will refer to Laffer's hypothesis and not use the phrase "Laffer curve."

How should the disagreement be settled? Here a mistake in logic is often made. If the tax rate is cut in 2008, the key question is whether tax revenue in 2008 is greater or less than *it would have been in 2008* if the rate had not been cut. The issue is *not* whether tax revenue in 2008 is greater or less than it was in 2007. It is easy to compare revenue in 2008 and 2007—the data are readily available—and it is almost always the case that revenue grows from one year to the next, just as GDP usually grows. An example will clarify. Suppose revenue in 2007 was $100 billion, and if the tax rate were held constant, suppose somehow we know with certainty that revenue in 2008 would have been $105 billion. Suppose the tax rate is cut in 2008, and revenue is $102 billion. Then the tax rate cut has caused revenue in 2008 to be less than it would have been ($102 billion versus $105 billion)—revenue decreases relative to what it would have been in 2008, even though revenue is greater than it was in 2007 ($102 billion versus $100 billion).

Thus, we must compare actual tax revenue in 2008 to *hypothetical* tax revenue in 2008—what revenue would have been had the tax rate been held constant. We cannot know with certainty what would have happened had the tax rate been held constant, because it wasn't held constant—it was cut. Anyone attempting to answer the key question must make an estimate of what the revenue would have been in 2008 if the tax rate had stayed constant, so that it can be compared to actual revenue in 2008. Thus, a test of Laffer's hypothesis depends on the accuracy of the estimate of a hypothetical—what would have happened had the tax rate stayed constant.

Summary

This chapter has two parts. The first part analyzes who bears the burden from a particular tax—that is, the incidence of the tax. The second part analyzes the inefficiency (efficiency loss) to the economy that results from particular taxes.

The first part on incidence makes several points. People, not firms, ultimately bear all tax burdens. The distribution of the burden of a tax depends on relative elasticities. If demand is steeper (less elastic) than supply, then demanders bear most of the burden; if supply is steeper (less elastic) than demand, then suppliers bear most of the burden; whoever is less elastic bears most of the burden. The distribution of the burden doesn't depend on who (demanders or suppliers) writes the check (pays the tax) to the government. The analysis is applied to a tax on wage income and a tax on capital income (income from saving). Using general equilibrium analysis, it is shown that a tax on capital income imposes some burden on labor, and a progressive wage tax imposes some burden on low-wage workers who are exempt from the tax.

The second part on inefficiency makes several points. All taxes (except a lump-sum tax) distort behavior resulting in a change in the mix of goods and services or work versus leisure that reduces welfare. This loss in welfare is called the efficiency loss from the tax. The dollar magnitude of the efficiency loss is equal to the area of a *BAD* triangle. For a tax on a good, the *BAD* triangle is formed by the *S* and *D* curves for the good. Although levying the same tax rate on all goods doesn't minimize efficiency loss, it may be sensible in practice. For a tax on labor income, the *BAD* triangle is formed by the *S* and *D* curves for labor. For a tax on capital income, the *BAD* triangle is formed by the *S* and *D* curves for saving. What matters for the efficiency loss is the marginal tax rate. A switch from a proportional income tax to a progressive income tax that raises the same revenue reduces inequality in after-tax incomes, decreases the efficiency loss from low-income people, but increases the efficiency loss from high-income people. The revenue-rate curve has a peak (maximum) for tax revenue at a tax rate t_m that is less than 100%; hence, the tax rate should be set somewhere between 0 and t_m. Most economists (but not supply-siders like Laffer) estimate that t_m is probably higher than the current tax rate for most U.S. taxes; this implies that, starting from the current tax rate, raising the rate would increase tax revenue and cutting the rate would reduce tax revenue.

Key Terms

elastic, *170*
inelastic, *170*
efficiency loss, *179*
elasticity of
    demand, *181*

marginal revenue product
    of labor (MRPL), *182*
elasticity of labor
    supply, *183*
lump-sum tax, *185*

average tax rate
    (ATR), *185*
marginal tax rate
    (MTR), *185*
revenue-rate curve, *186*

Questions

1. What determines how much burden consumers bear from a tax on the sellers of good X? Draw and refer to two diagrams in your explanation.

2. Suppose the price of gasoline that drivers pay at the pump is $4 and stations pay a tax of $1 to the government and keep $3. Draw a diagram to show this.

   Then there is a tax switch: The tax on stations is ended, and drivers are required to keep receipts and pay the government a $1 tax for each gallon they consume. On the same diagram, show what happens to the pump price. What is the impact of the switch on drivers? On stations?

3. With a 7% sales tax, the consumer buys an item for $100 and pays $107 at the cash register. How much burden does the 7% sales tax impose on the consumer? Draw a diagram and refer to it in your explanation.

4. Suppose a worker's two-week paycheck states that his gross wage income was $1,000. How much will he see has been taken out for Social Security? How much has his employer also contributed to Social Security? How much burden has the payroll tax imposed on him? Draw a diagram, put numbers on it, and refer to it in your explanation.

5. How elastic is the supply of labor?

6. How elastic is the supply of saving?

7. Using two diagrams, explain how a tax on capital income burdens workers.

8. Using two diagrams, explain how a tax on high-skilled labor burdens low-skilled workers.

9. Consider a tax of $T per unit on good X. With two diagrams show how the efficiency loss from the tax varies with the elasticities.

10. If a tax is doubled, the efficiency loss is __ times as great. Explain with a diagram.

11. Using a diagram, explain the efficiency loss from a tax on labor income.

12. Using a diagram, explain the efficiency loss from a tax on capital income.

13. Draw and explain the revenue-rate curve, and comment on Laffer's hypothesis.

14. Derive the formulas $L = \frac{1}{2}t^2eWH$ and $L/R = \frac{1}{2}te$. Explain your derivation.

15. *Appendix questions:*

   a. Draw an indifference-curve/budget-line diagram to show the effect of removing a wage tax on labor supply. Directly below, draw another diagram that shows the ordinary labor supply curve and the compensated labor supply curve. Explain.

   b. Draw an indifference-curve/budget-line diagram to show the effect of removing a tax on interest income on saving. Directly below, draw another diagram that shows the ordinary saving supply curve and the compensated saving supply curve. Explain.

Appendix

Tax Incidence and Inefficiency

In the appendix to Chapter 1, we introduced the indifference-curve/budget-line diagram. Before reading this appendix, review the appendix to Chapter 1.

A TAX ON LABOR INCOME USING AN INDIFFERENCE-CURVE/BUDGET LINE DIAGRAM

We now use an indifference-curve/budget-line diagram to analyze the effect of removing a wage tax on labor supply. We assume that a person gets utility (subjective well-being) from two goods: leisure and after-tax income. Each hour that a person works earns him after-tax income but sacrifices an hour of leisure. We assume that the person is offered a job with a specific after-tax wage but that he is given a choice about how many hours to work per year—that is, how many hours of labor to supply per year. The person can vary his annual hours of labor supply by varying his hours per day, days of work per week, and/or vacations. Of course, employers usually do not give an employee completely free choice over the number of hours—but many employers do give some choice.

Figure 7A.1(*a*) shows the indifference-curve/budget-line diagram. Leisure (hours) is plotted horizontally, and after-tax income (dollars) is plotted vertically. With 365 days in a year and 24 hours in a day, there are 8,760 hours in a year. We define any hour that the person is not working in the market place to be an hour of *leisure* (so "leisure" includes time sleeping, caring for children, doing home chores or repairs, etc.). Suppose the person works 40 hours per week for 50 weeks, 2000 hours, and takes a 2-week vacation. Then the person "consumes" 8,760 − 2,000 = 6,760 hours of leisure in the year.

As shown in the diagram, the maximum possible hours of leisure per year is 8,760 hours, so point *M* is a point on the person's budget line (a point he could choose). Suppose the after-tax wage is $12 (because the before-tax wage is $16 and the wage tax is $4). If the person worked 2,000 hours, he would earn $24,000 after taxes and would enjoy 6,760 hours of leisure, so another point on the person's budget line is point *A*. The person can choose any point on his budget line, the line from *M* through *A* to point *N*. Starting at point *M*, for each hour of leisure the person gives up in order to work, he gains $12 of after-tax income. Thus, the slope of the person's budget line *NAM* is –$12. The person can choose any point on his budget line. We assume the person chooses the point on his budget line that maximizes utility—that reaches the highest indifference curve—so the person chooses point *A*. Point *A* has 6,760 hours of leisure (2,000 hours of market work) and an after-tax income of $24,000.

Now suppose the tax is removed for all workers and the after-tax wage rises above $12. The removal of the tax may reduce the market wage—assume it reduces it from $16 to $15. Then the after-tax wage rises from $12 to $15, and in the diagram the person's budget line becomes steeper (because the slope changes from –$12 to –$15), and he moves from point *A* to point *B*, which is the point on the steeper budget line that reaches the highest indifference curve. As drawn, point *B* is directly above ("north of") point *A*, but this need not be so; point *B* might be either northeast or northwest of point *A* rather than directly north. As drawn, the removal of the tax and the rise in the after-tax wage from $12 to $15 do not cause this person to change his annual hours

FIGURE 7A.1

Taxes and Labor Supply

If a wage tax is removed, the person moves from *A* to *B* if there is no compensation and to *s* if there is compensation.

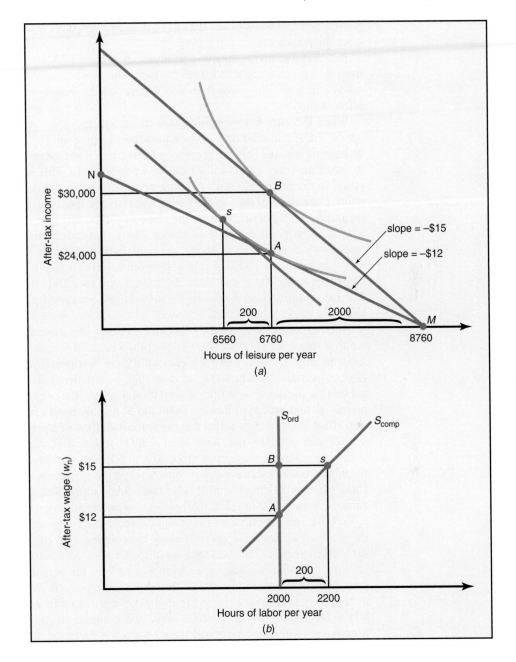

(a)

(b)

of leisure—his hours remain 6,760—so his annual hours of work remain 2,000; but with the after-tax wage $15 instead of $12, his after-tax income at point *B* is $30,000 (instead of $24,000 at *A*). When the person moves from point *A* to point *B*, his utility increases because he reaches a higher indifference curve.

Figure 7A.1(*b*) shows what happens to this person's labor supply when the tax is removed and the after-tax wage rises from $12 to $15. In this figure [in contrast to Figure 7A.1(*a*)], annual hours of *labor* (not *leisure*) are plotted horizontally, and the after-tax *wage* (not *after-tax income*) is plotted vertically. The person's labor supply remains at 2,000. Thus, the person's *ordinary labor supply curve* (S_{ord}) is vertical (*completely inelastic*): When the after-tax wage rises, there is no change in the hours of labor the person chooses to supply.

It is useful to divide the move from *A* to *B* in Figure 7A.1(*a*) into two parts: A move from *A* to point *s*, and a move from *s* to *B*. The move from *A* to *s* is called the *substitution effect,* and the move from *s* to *B* is called the *income effect*. Let's explain each effect in turn.

When the after-tax wage increases (from $12 to $15), each hour of leisure has a "price" of $15 instead of $12—the person must give up $15 instead of $12 to enjoy an hour of leisure. This higher price of leisure in itself gives the person an incentive to *substitute* other goods for leisure by working more. This is called the *substitution effect*. In the diagram, the move from point *A* to point *s* is the substitution effect. At point *A,* the slope of the indifference curve (strictly speaking, the slope of a tangent to the indifference curve) is –$12, the slope of the budget line when the after-tax wage is $12. From point *A,* move northwest along that indifference curve until its slope reaches –$15 at point *s*. Clearly, the substitution effect in itself would reduce leisure—as drawn, by 200 hours annually from 6,760 to 6,560—hence, it would increase labor supply by 200 hours annually, from 2,000 to 2,200. Note an important point: *The substitution effect holds the person's utility constant* because the person moves along the original indifference curve.

Another way to describe the substitution effect—the move from *A* to *s*—is to imagine that when the after-tax wage rises from $12 to $15, instead of letting the person move to point *B* and achieve a higher utility, we "compensate" for this utility-raising effect by simultaneously taking away enough income from the person to shift his budget line parallel southwest from *B* until it is tangent to the original indifference curve at point *s*, so that instead of moving from *A* to *B*, he only moves from *A* to *s*. The substitution effect is sometimes called the *compensated* effect of a price increase.

In Figure 7A.1(*b*), the move from *A* to *s* is plotted in the labor supply diagram. When the after-tax wage rises from $12 to $15 but we simultaneously *compensate* for this by taking away enough income to keep the person on the original indifference curve (thereby holding his utility constant), labor supply would increase by 200 hours annually from 2,000 to 2,200 (corresponding to the reduction of leisure from 6,760 to 6,560). We call the curve joining points *A* and *s* the *compensated labor supply curve* (S_{comp}). As the after-tax wage rises along the compensated labor supply curve, the person's utility remains constant because of the simultaneous removal of income.

When the after-tax wage rises from $12 to $15, the person doesn't actually move from point *A* to point *s;* he moves from point *A* to point *B*. Why does he end up at *B* instead of *s*? Because the rise in the after-tax wage makes the person richer and enables him to reach a higher indifference curve and a higher utility. It is as though, starting from point *s* with the slope of –$15, the person was given income that moves his budget line parallel in a northeast direction until it reaches point *B*. The move from *s* to *B* is called the *income effect*. Note that the move from *s* to *B* in itself would increase leisure (assuming leisure is a normal good)—as drawn, by 200 hours annually from 6,560 to 6,760. *The income effect raises the person's utility* because it moves the person to a higher indifference curve.

For this person, it just happens that the income and substitution effects have exactly the same magnitude (200) and exactly offset each other, so the person keeps leisure constant (6,760) by moving from *A* to *B* when the after-tax wage rises.

Consider another person for whom point *B* would be north*west* (instead of directly north) of point *A* (the substitution effect to the left would be larger than the income effect to the right). That person would *decrease* leisure moving from *A* to *B* (hence, *increase* labor) when the after-tax wage rises, so the person's ordinary labor supply curve would have a positive slope (instead of being vertical). Consider another person for whom point *B* would be north*east* (instead of directly north) of point *A* (the substitution effect to the left would be smaller than the income effect to the right). That person would *increase* leisure (hence, *decrease* labor) when the after-tax wage rises, so the person's ordinary labor supply curve would have a negative slope (instead of being vertical).

A TAX ON CAPITAL INCOME USING AN INDIFFERENCE-CURVE/BUDGET-LINE DIAGRAM

We now use an indifference-curve/budget-line diagram to analyze the effect of removing an interest income tax on saving. Suppose there is a 40% tax on interest income, the before-tax interest rate is 10%, and the after-tax interest rate is 6%. We assume that a person gets "utility" (subjective well-being) from two "goods": present consumption (C_0) and future consumption (C_1).

Figure 7A.2(a) shows the indifference-curve/budget-line diagram. Present consumption (C_0) is plotted horizontally, and future consumption (C_1) is plotted vertically. Suppose at the beginning of period 0, the person earns $1,000 of after-tax wage income. One extreme option for the person would be to consume $1,000 in period 0 and $0 in period 1. Starting at this extreme option, for each $100 of C_0 he forgoes by saving, he can consume $106 of C_1 because the after-tax interest rate is 6%, so the slope of the budget line is –1.06. The person chooses the point on his budget line that maximizes utility—that reaches the highest indifference curve. In this example, the person chooses C_0 = $500, S_0 = $500, and C_1 = $530 (because interest is $50, tax is $20, so $530 can be spent in period 1).

Now suppose the tax is removed for all savers and the after-tax interest rate rises above 6%. The removal of the tax may reduce the market interest rate—assume it reduces it from 10% to 9%. Then the after-tax interest rate rises from 6% to 9%, and in the Figure 7A.2(a) the person's budget line becomes steeper (because the slope changes from –1.06 to –1.09) and he moves from point *A* to point *B*, which is the point on the steeper budget line that reaches the highest indifference curve. As drawn, point *B* is directly above (north of) point *A*, but this need not be so; point *B* might be either northeast or northwest of point *A* rather than directly north. As drawn, the removal of the tax and the rise in the after-tax interest rate from 6% to 9% do not cause the person to change his saving in period 0 (S_0)—his saving remains $500 and his consumption (C_0) remains $500. But with the after-tax interest rate 9% instead of 6%, his interest is $45, so his future consumption (C_1) is $545 at point *B* (instead of $530 at point *A*). When the person moves from point *A* to point *B*, his utility increases because he reaches a higher indifference curve.

Figure 7A.2(b) shows what happens to this person's saving when the tax is removed and the after-tax interest rate increases from 6% to 9%. In Figure 7A.2(b) [in contrast to Figure 7A.2(a)], *saving* (not present consumption) is plotted horizontally, and the after-tax *interest rate* (not future consumption) is plotted vertically. This person's saving remains $500. Thus, this person's *ordinary saving supply curve* (S_{ord}) is vertical (*completely inelastic*): When the after-tax interest rate rises, there is no change in the person's saving.

It is useful to divide the move from *A* to *B* in Figure 7A.2(a) into two parts: a move from *A* to *s*, and a move from *s* to *B*. The move from *A* to *s* is called the *substitution effect*, and the move from *s* to *B* is called the *income effect*. Let's explain each effect in turn.

FIGURE 7A.2

Taxes and Saving
If a capital income
tax is removed, the
person moves from
A to *B* if there is
no compensation
and to *s* if there is
compensation.

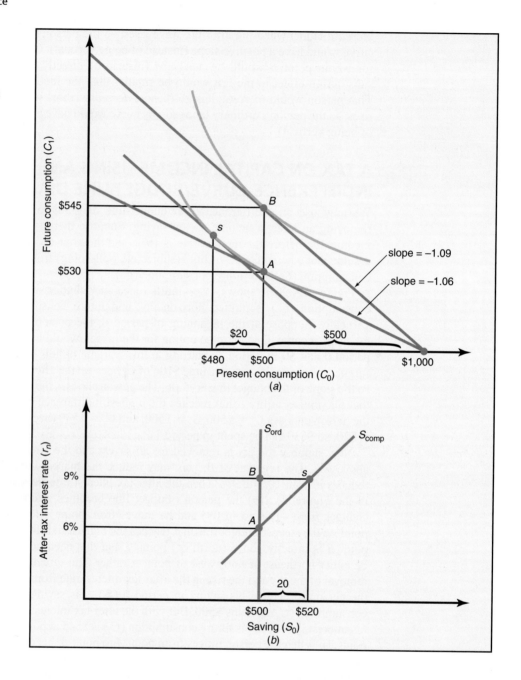

When the after-tax interest rate increases (from 6% to 9%), each $1.00 of present consumption has a "price" of $1.09 of future consumption instead of $1.06—the person must give up $1.09 of future consumption instead of $1.06 to enjoy $1.00 of present consumption. This higher price of present consumption in itself gives the person an incentive to *substitute* future consumption for present consumption. In the diagram, the move from point *A* to point *s* is the substitution effect. At point *A,* the slope of the indifference curve (strictly speaking, the slope of a tangent to the indifference curve) is –1.06, the slope of the budget line when the after-tax interest rate is 6%. From point *A,* move northwest along that indifference curve until its slope reaches –1.09. Clearly, the substitution effect in itself would reduce present consumption—as drawn, by $20 from $500 to $480—hence, it would increase saving by $20, from $500 to $520. Note an important point: *The substitution effect holds the person's utility constant* because the person moves along the initial indifference curve.

Another way to describe the substitution effect—the move from *A* to *s*—is to imagine that when the after-tax interest rate rises from 6% to 9%, instead of letting the person move to point *B* and achieve a higher utility, we "compensate" for this utility-raising effect by simultaneously taking away enough income from the person to shift his budget line parallel southwest from *B* until it is tangent to the original indifference curve at point *s*, so that instead of moving from *A* to *B*, he only moves from *A* to *s*. The substitution effect is sometimes called the *compensated* effect of a price increase.

In the bottom panel of the diagram, the move from *A* to *s* is plotted in the saving supply diagram. When the after-tax interest rate rises from 6% to 9%, we simultaneously *compensate* for this by taking away enough income to keep the person on the initial indifference curve (thereby holding his utility constant); saving would increase by $20 from $500 to $520 (corresponding to the reduction in present consumption from $500 to $480). We call the curve joining points *A* and *s* the *compensated saving supply curve* (S_{comp}). As the after-tax interest rate rises along the compensated saving supply curve, the person's utility remains constant because of the simultaneous removal of income.

When the after-tax interest rate rises from 6% to 9%, the person doesn't actually move from point *A* to point *s*; he moves from point *A* to point *B*. Why does he end up at *B* instead of *s*? Because the rise in the after-tax interest rate makes the person richer and enables him to reach a higher indifference curve and a higher utility. It is as though, starting from point *s* with the slope of −1.09, the person was given income that moves his budget line parallel in a northeast direction until it reaches point *B*. The move from *s* to *B* is called the *income effect*. Note that the move from *s* to *B* in itself would increase present consumption (assuming present consumption is a normal good)—as drawn, by $20, from $480 to $500. *The income effect raises the person's utility* because it moves the person to a higher indifference curve.

For this person, it just happens that the income and substitution effects have exactly the same magnitude ($20) and exactly offset each other, so the person keeps present consumption constant ($500) by moving from *A* to *B* when the after-tax interest rate rises.

Consider another person for whom point *B* would be north*west* (instead of directly north) of point *A* (the substitution effect to the left would be larger than the income effect to the right). That person would *decrease* present consumption moving from *A* to *B*—hence, *increase* saving—when the after-tax interest rate rises, so the person's ordinary saving supply curve would have a positive slope (instead of being vertical). Consider another person for whom point *B* would be north*east* (instead of directly north) of point *A* (the substitution effect to the left would be smaller than the income effect to the right). That person would *increase* present consumption—hence, *decrease* saving—when the after-tax interest rate rises so the person's ordinary saving supply curve would have a negative slope (instead of being vertical).

THE EFFICIENCY LOSS FROM A TAX ON A GOOD

In the discussion of Figure 7.8 it was noted in a footnote that the *D* curve in the diagram used to construct the *BAD* triangle is the *compensated* demand curve, not the ordinary demand curve. Here we explain why.

Starting from 100 units (the quantity of the good resulting from the tax), the amount a consumer would willing to pay for another unit—the consumer's marginal benefit (MB)—is $20, while the marginal cost (MC) of producing the unit is $16. If the 101st unit is produced, hypothetically it would be possible to take $20 from the consumer for that unit so his *utility stays constant*, give $16 to the producers so their utility stays constant, and distribute the $4 surplus to other people making them better off; hence, the net gain in welfare from the 101st unit would be $4. Then do the same thing for the 102nd unit, distributing the surplus which is now slightly less than $4 to other people; and so on for additional units as long as the MB is still greater than the MC, stopping at intersection point *D* (110 units), where the MB equals the MC so that there would be no surplus to distribute on an additional unit. During this hypothetical process, consumers would be compensated so that their utility would stay constant. Thus, the MB curve used to draw the *BAD* triangle that measures the efficiency loss from the tax on a good is a curve along which the *utility of consumers remains constant*.

The MB curve looks like a demand curve, but utility does not stay constant along an *ordinary* demand curve. An ordinary demand curve shows how a consumer's demand increases as the price falls—but as the consumer "slides down" an ordinary demand curve, the consumer's utility increases. To keep the consumer's utility constant as the price falls, we must compensate for the price cut by taking away just enough income from the consumer, so that his utility stays constant despite the price cut. This decrease in income would cause the consumer to demand less of the good (assuming it is a normal good). This curve, which is therefore steeper than the ordinary demand curve, is called the *compensated demand curve*. Along the compensated demand curve, the consumer's utility stays constant. *Thus it is the compensated demand curve (not the ordinary demand curve) that should be used to construct the BAD triangle that measures the efficiency loss from the tax.*

THE EFFICIENCY LOSS FROM A TAX ON LABOR INCOME

In the discussion of Figure 7.9 it was noted in a footnote that the *S* curve in the diagram used to construct the *BAD* triangle is the *compensated* supply curve, not the ordinary supply curve. Here we explain why. Recall that in Figure 7.9 there were 10 workers in the market, each supplying 2,000 hours in response to an after-tax wage of $12, for a total supply of 20,000 hours.

Starting from 20,000 hours—the quantity resulting from the tax—the amount a worker would need to be paid to be willing to work the 20,001st hour is $12, while the marginal revenue product of an hour of labor (MRPL) is $16. If the 20,001st hour is worked, it would be possible to compensate the worker $12, so that the worker's *utility stays constant*, and then distribute the $4 surplus product to other people making them better off; hence, the net gain in welfare from the 20,001st hour would be $4. Then do the same thing for the 20,002nd hour, distributing the surplus which is now slightly less than $4 to other people; and so on, stopping at intersection point *D* (22,000 hours). During this hypothetical process, workers would be compensated so that their utility would stay constant. Thus, the curve we need to construct the *BAD* triangle is a curve along which the *utility of workers remains constant*.

The curve looks like a supply curve, but utility does not stay constant along an *ordinary* supply curve. An ordinary supply curve shows how a worker's labor supply increases as the after-tax wage rises—but as the worker "climbs up" an ordinary supply curve, the worker's utility increases. To keep the worker's utility constant as the after-tax wage rises, we must compensate for the wage increase by taking away just enough income from the worker so that the worker's utility stays constant despite the wage increase. This decrease in income would cause the worker to choose less leisure, hence more work, so the worker would choose a higher labor supply. This curve, which is therefore flatter than the ordinary supply curve, is called the *compensated labor supply curve*. Along the compensated supply curve, workers' utility stays constant. *Thus it is the compensated supply curve (not the ordinary labor supply curve) that should be used to construct the* BAD *triangle that measures the efficiency loss from the tax.*

THE EFFICIENCY LOSS FROM A TAX ON CAPITAL INCOME

In the discussion of Figure 7.10 it was noted in a footnote that the S curve in the diagram used to construct the *BAD* triangle is the *compensated* supply curve, not the ordinary supply curve. Here we explain why.

Starting from $100,000 dollars (the quantity of saving resulting from the tax), the after-tax interest rate a saver would need to be paid to be willing to save the $100,001st dollar is 3%, while the rate of return of a dollar invested in a machine is 5%. If the $100,001st dollar is saved and invested in a machine, it would be possible to compensate the saver 3%, so that the saver's utility stays constant, and then distribute the rest of the surplus return (2%) to other people, making them better off; hence, the net gain in welfare from the $100,001st dollar saved would be 2%. Then do the same thing for the $100,002nd dollar, distributing the surplus which is now slightly less than 2% to other people; and so on, stopping at intersection point D ($120,000). During this hypothetical process, savers would be compensated so that their utility stays constant. Thus, the curve we need to construct the *BAD* triangle is a curve along which the *utility of savers remains constant*.

The curve looks like a supply curve, but utility does not stay constant along an ordinary supply curve. An ordinary supply curve shows how a person's saving supply increases as the after-tax interest rate rises—but as the saver climbs up an ordinary supply curve, the saver's utility increases. To keep the saver's utility constant as the after-tax interest rate rises, we must compensate for the interest rate increase by taking away just enough income from the saver, so that the saver's utility stays constant despite the interest rate increase. This decrease in income would cause the person to choose less present consumption, hence more saving, so the person would choose a higher saving supply than without this decrease in income. This curve, which is therefore flatter than the ordinary supply curve, is called the compensated saving supply curve. Along the compensated supply curve, savers' utility stays constant. *Thus it is the compensated supply curve (not the ordinary saver supply curve) that should be used to construct the* BAD *triangle that measures the efficiency loss from the tax.*

Chapter **Eight**

Income Taxes

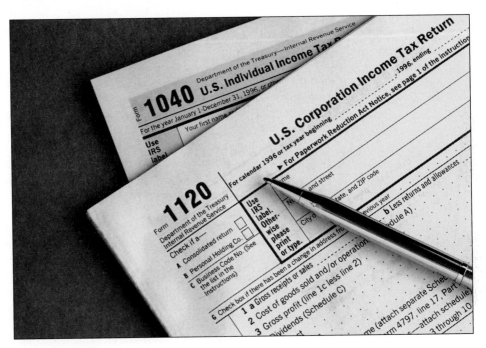

Royalty-Free/CORBIS

Once a year, most U.S. households file an annual federal income tax return (a form called the 1040) sometime between January 1 and April 15 when it is due. The tax return reports all income that the household earned in the preceding calendar year and indicates the amount of tax that the household owes on that income.

It is sometimes said that a household "pays" its income tax when it files its return, but this is incorrect. The typical household has been paying its income tax as it earns income throughout the year because each person's employer has been withholding tax from each employee's paycheck and periodically sending the withheld tax to the government (the Internal Revenue Service of the U.S. Treasury).[1] When a household files its tax return, it reports all income earned in the preceding year and computes the tax it should have paid for the preceding year. If the amount that has already been withheld is less than what the household should have paid, it includes a check for the difference with its tax return. Conversely, if the amount withheld is greater than what

---

[1] Also households with investment income have been required to make quarterly payments of estimated taxes on this income.

TABLE 8.1

Tax Revenue from the Major Federal Taxes for Two Years

Source: Congressional Budget Office.

	1999		2005	
	% of GDP	% of Federal Revenue	% of GDP	% of Federal Revenue
Household income taxes	9.6%	48%	7.5%	43%
Payroll taxes (social insurance)	6.7	34	6.5	37
Corporate income taxes	2.0	10	2.3	13
Excise taxes	0.8	4	0.6	3
Estate and gift taxes	0.3	1	0.2	1
Customs duties (tariffs)	0.2	1	0.2	1
Other revenues	0.4	2	0.3	2
Total	20.0%	100%	17.5%	100%

it should have paid, the household requests a refund of the difference and will receive a check from the U.S. Treasury within a month or two of filing its return. Thus, filing a tax return involves an adjustment for any difference between what the household has already paid and what it should have paid.

The household income tax (called the "individual" income tax, whether it applies to single persons or married couples) raises about 45% of all federal government revenue—more revenue than any other federal tax. Table 8.1 shows tax revenue from the major federal taxes for two years when the economy was not in recession, 1999 and 2005.

In 1999, federal revenue was 20.0% of GDP; the individual income tax was nearly 10% of GDP and provided 48% of federal revenue. In 2005, after several rounds of household income tax cuts between 2001 and 2003, federal revenue was 17.5% of GDP; the individual income tax was 7.5% of GDP and provided 43% of federal revenue.

The payroll tax, which is a labor income tax, is the second most important source of federal revenue. The corporate income tax is third. In contrast to most other economically advanced countries, the U.S. federal government does not have a broad-based consumption tax such as a retail sales tax or value-added tax; it has a set of **excise taxes**—taxes on particular commodities such as gasoline, alcohol, and tobacco—that contribute a small share of federal revenue. Estate and gift taxes and customs duties (tariffs) also contribute a small share.

In the United States, state governments rely primarily on sales taxes and income taxes, while local governments rely primarily on property taxes. We discuss state and local public finance in Chapter 10.

MECHANICS OF THE U.S. INCOME TAX

Determining Your Income Tax

Imagine you and your spouse are both employed in the year 2008. Assume the only investment income you have is interest income; you have no dividends or capital gains from corporate stocks. On or before April 15, 2009, you file a 2008 income tax return (a 1040) for the income you both earned from January 1 through December 31, 2008. You add up your income for 2008, make certain subtractions, and follow 1040 instructions to determine the tax you owe for 2008.

During 2008, your employers have withheld income tax from each of your paychecks and sent the withheld tax in your names to the Internal Revenue Service (IRS) of the U.S. government's Department of the Treasury, so the IRS has already collected

TABLE 8.2
Determining a Family's 2008 Income Tax

Total income (wage income plus investment income)	$100,000
Adjustments	−4,000
Adjusted gross income (AGI)	$ 96,000
Personal exemptions	−14,000
Itemized deductions (or the standard deduction)	−12,000
Taxable income	$ 70,000
Tentative tax	$ 10,188
Credits	−2,000
Tax	$ 8,188
Withholding	−7,000
Payment (or refund)	$ 1,188

most of your 2008 income tax. Suppose you owe $8,188 in tax for 2008, but your employers have already withheld $7,000 from your paychecks. Then when you mail in your 1040 tax return, you should include a check for $1,188 to the U.S. Treasury. Suppose instead that your employers have withheld $9,000. Then on your 1040 tax return, you should request a refund of $812; a few weeks later you would receive a check for $812 from the U.S. Treasury.

Now let's look at Table 8.2 to see how you determine your 2008 tax. You add up your household's wage income plus investment income to get your household's **total income** of $100,000. You are allowed to subtract a few adjustments ($4,000), resulting in your **adjusted gross income (AGI)** of $96,000.

You subtract your **personal exemptions**, one for each member of your household. Imagine you and your spouse have two children; then you get four personal exemptions. Each exemption is $3,500 in 2008 (the exemption is automatically adjusted with inflation each year), so four exemptions are $14,000.

You choose between a set of **itemized deductions** and the **standard deduction**; naturally, you choose whichever is larger. The standard deduction is $10,900 in 2008 (the standard deduction is automatically adjusted with inflation each year). Your itemized deductions are shown in Table 8.3.

Because your total itemized deductions ($12,000) exceeds the standard deduction ($10,900), you choose the itemized deductions. Subtracting your personal exemptions ($14,000) and your itemized deductions ($12,000) from your AGI ($96,000) yields your taxable income ($70,000). Out of your $100,000 of total income, the first $30,000 ($4,000 + $14,000 + $12,000) is not subject to tax—or, equivalently, it is taxed at a 0% rate. Thus, the adjustments, personal exemptions, and the standard or itemized deductions mean that the first X dollars (in your case, $30,000) of a household's income are taxed at a 0% rate.

How do you proceed from your taxable income of $70,000 to your tentative tax of $10,188? If some of your investment income is from capital gains and dividends—for example, $5,000—then you would divide your $70,000 of taxable income into

TABLE 8.3
Itemized Deductions

State and local income and property tax payments	$ 9,000
Home mortgage interest payments	1,000
Charitable contributions	2,000
Medical expenses in excess of 7.5% of AGI	0
Total	$12,000

two parts—$65,000 and $5,000—and compute tax on each part separately because Congress has set a maximum tax rate on capital gains and dividends of 15%, while the maximum tax rate on other taxable income is 35%.

Assume that your investment income consists solely of interest income, which is taxed just like wage income. Then there is no need to divide your $70,000 into two parts. You look up your tax in the 1040 tax table: Next to $70,000 of taxable income is $10,188 of tentative tax (the word *tentative* is not in the table—we explain our use of *tentative* in a moment). But how does the preparer of the table—the U.S. Treasury—arrive at your tentative tax? Congress has enacted the tax schedule shown in Table 8.4. For married couples filing jointly in 2008, the first $16,050 of taxable income is taxed at a 10% rate; taxable income from $16,050 to $65,100 is taxed at a 15% rate; and so on (the bracket dollar numbers are automatically adjusted with inflation each year):

Thus, your tentative tax is calculated this way:

$$.10(\$16,050) + .15(\$65,100 - \$16,050) + .25(\$70,000 - \$65,100) =$$

$$.10(\$16,050) + .15(\$49,050) + .25(\$4,900) =$$

$$\$1,605 + \$7,358 + \$1,225 = \$10,188$$

But $10,188 is only your tentative tax, not your final tax, because you can still subtract tax credits to which you are entitled. Because you have two children and the child tax credit is $1,000 per child, you can subtract $2,000. Note that having two children reduces your final tax in two ways. First, it gives you two personal exemptions ($3,500 per child). Second, it gives you two child tax credits. Your tax for the year is therefore $8,188.

It is now time for a confession. If you look on your 1040 tax return, you will not see the phrase "tentative tax" anywhere. On your 1040 you will see the word *tax,* not tentative tax, to indicate the amount you find from the tax table. But the word *tax* is misleading. It seems to imply that this is what you pay—that there is no hope left for paying a smaller amount. That's not true! Tax credits reduce the tax you must pay for the year, just as exemptions or deductions do. Humbly, we recommend to Congress that it instruct the IRS to put the phrase "tentative tax" on the 1040 and use the word *tax* for the final tax after the subtraction of tax credits.

Now let's return to Table 8.2 and your final tax of $8,188. Remember that you have already paid most of it because your employer and your spouse's employer have been withholding income tax from your paychecks in your names and sending it to the IRS; the IRS has already collected $7,000 from you and your spouse. Hence, when you file your tax return, you should include a check to the U.S. Treasury for $1,188.[2]

---

[2] Suppose instead that the IRS has already collected $9,000 from your household; then on your tax return you would request a refund of $812, and several weeks later, you would receive a U.S. Treasury refund check of $812.

TABLE 8.4
Tax Schedule
Married couple
in 2008

Taxable Income	Tax Rate
$0 to $16,050	10%
$16,050 to $65,100	15
$65,100 to $131,450	25
$131,450 to $200,300	28
$200,300 to $357,700	33
Over $357,700	35

TABLE 8.5

Tax as a Percentage of Income

Total income	$100,000
Adjusted gross income (AGI)	$ 96,000
Taxable income	$ 70,000
Tax bracket (marginal tax rate)	25.0%
Tentative tax	$ 10,188
Tentative tax as a percent of taxable income	14.6%
Final tax	$ 8,188
Final tax as a percent of taxable income	11.7%
Final tax as a percent of AGI	8.5%
Final tax as a percent of total income	8.2%

The last $100 of income you earned is taxed at a 25% rate, and if you or your spouse would work more or earn more interest, the next $100 of income you earn (and every $100 after that until you reach the next tax bracket) would be taxed at a 25% rate. So your **marginal tax rate (MTR)** is 25%, and you can say you are *in a 25%* **tax bracket**. From Table 8.4 you can see that at higher incomes, the tax rate rises to 28%, then 33%, and finally 35%.

Table 8.5 shows your tax as a percentage of your income. Your tentative tax ($10,188) is 14.6%, not 25%, of your taxable income ($70,000), because your first $16,050 of taxable income is taxed at 10% and your taxable income from $16,050 to $65,100 is taxed at 15%. Your final tax ($8,188) is 11.7%, not 14.6%, of your taxable income ($70,000), thanks to the tax credits. Your final tax ($8,188) is 8.5% of your adjusted gross income ($96,000) and 8.2% of your total income ($100,000). So although you are in a 25% tax bracket facing a marginal tax rate of 25% on your wage and interest income, your final tax is 8.2% of your total income. If you are asked the percentage of your income you pay in tax, you should answer 8.2%—even though you might also note that you are in a 25% tax bracket, so that on the last $100 you earned you paid $25.

Suppose that you had $5,000 of investment income from corporate stocks—dividends or capital gains (if you buy stock for $2,000 and later sell it for $3,000, your capital gain is $1,000). In 2003, Congress enacted a maximum tax rate for dividends and capital gains of 15%. To determine your tentative tax, you would subtract your $5,000 of dividend and capital gains income from your $70,000 of taxable income, obtaining $65,000; you would apply the rates in Table 8.4 to your $65,000 and apply a maximum rate of 15% to your $5,000 of capital gains and dividends, and then add the taxes on the two components to get your total tentative tax. Thus, your maximum marginal tax rate on dividend and capital gains income is 15%, even though your marginal tax rate on wage and interest income is 25%. It is more accurate to say that you are in a (25%, 15%) tax bracket: You would pay 25% on the next $100 of wage or interest income, but only a maximum of 15% on the next $100 of capital gains or dividend income.

The Alternative Minimum Tax

The **alternative minimum tax (AMT)** replaces the regular income tax for a subset of high-income households. The AMT was enacted several decades ago after it was discovered that some very affluent households managed legally to pay little or no income tax due to deductions, exemptions, and credits. The intent of the AMT is to make every very high-income household pay at least a minimum amount of tax even if that household would owe little or no regular income tax. A household must pay whichever

Case Study   A Brief History of the Top Income Tax Rate

In the early 1960s the top income tax rate was over 90%! It should be emphasized that only a tiny number of very rich people were subject to the top rate, and only on the top portion of their income (most of their income was subject to much lower tax rates), and that more than half of capital gains income was excluded from taxation.

The United States was not the only country with a top tax rate over 90% at that time. In the early 1960s, four working-class lads from Liverpool, England, exploded on the world music scene. The four Beatles were soon earning huge incomes, and to their shock, they found themselves subject to huge income taxes. One of them, George Harrison, wrote a song with an angry lead guitar riff for the Beatles' *Revolver* album; the song, called "Tax Man," begins:

> Let me tell you how it will be,
> There's one for you nineteen for me,
> 'Cause I'm the Tax Man,
> Yea, I'm the Tax Man.

According to Harrison, the Beatles were subject to a top tax rate of 95%, because out of the last 20 British pounds they earned, the tax man took 19, leaving them with only 1 (19 ÷ 20 = 95%). Go online to get the rest of the lyrics to "Tax Man," listen to Harrison and the Beatles sing it, and hear Harrison play his angry guitar.

Back in the United States, the top rate was cut to 70% in the 1960s, 50% in the early 1980s under President Reagan, and 28% under the Tax Reform Act of 1986 enacted with bipartisan support. The 1986 act was a compromise: The Democrats accepted President Reagan's proposal to lower the top tax rate from 50% to 28%, and in return, the president and other Republicans accepted the Democrats' proposal to include all capital gains in taxable income and tax it at the same rate as labor income.

At the 1988 Republican convention, Vice President George H. W. Bush, the nominee for president, said to thunderous applause, "Read my lips: No new taxes." But in 1990, faced with continuing huge federal budget deficits, President Bush compromised with the Democratic Congress. Democrats agreed to accept his proposal to limit the growth in domestic spending, and he agreed to accept their proposal to raise the top rate from 28% to 31% while keeping the maximum tax rate on capital gains at 28%. Although his acceptance of 31% displeased many conservatives, this compromise was the first step in the successful bipartisan effort during the 1990s to bring down huge budget deficits and eventually achieve a surplus by the end of the decade with the help of a booming economy.

The next step came in 1993 when Democratic President Bill Clinton and a Democratic Congress raised the top rate to 39.6% while keeping the maximum tax rate on capital gains at 28%. In the November 1994 election, the Republicans won control of both houses of Congress for the first time in many decades and in 1997 (with President Clinton's reluctant acceptance) reduced the maximum tax rate on capital gains from 28% to 20%.

With the election of Republican George W. Bush in November 2000 and the continued control of Congress by Republicans, the top tax rate was cut from 39.6% to 35% in 2001, and the top tax rate on capital gains and dividends was cut to 15% in 2003.

In the 2008 election, the Democrats pledged to increase the top rate several percentage points while the Republicans pledged to oppose such an increase.

is larger: its regular income tax or its AMT. The AMT does not permit the exemptions, deductions, and credits of the regular income tax; instead, in order to restrict its application to high-income households, the AMT has a single large exemption. Under current law, in contrast to the regular income tax which is automatically indexed for inflation, the dollar amounts of the AMT exemption and of its tax brackets stay fixed over time unless Congress specifically votes to raise them.

It would be easy for Congress to make sure the AMT remains restricted to the very affluent by **indexing** the AMT—automatically raising the exemption and tax brackets each year as average household income increases in the economy. Thus far Congress has not indexed the AMT; the moment that Congress passes a law to index the AMT, the Congressional Budget Office (CBO) will be required to announce a huge increase in its official estimate of future federal budget deficits—an announcement that would get headlines and embarrass Congress and the president. The CBO is required by Congress to make its official estimate of future federal budget deficits based on current law. According to current law, the AMT exemption and tax brackets are fixed dollar amounts, so the CBO has been required to estimate that the AMT will collect a huge amount of tax revenue in future years as household incomes rise. This official estimate of huge future AMT revenues has reduced the CBO's official estimate of future budget deficits. The moment the AMT is indexed by law, the CBO's official estimate of future AMT revenues will fall drastically, and its official estimate of future budget deficits will rise sharply. It is politically attractive for Congress and the president to compel the CBO to keep overestimating future AMT revenues and underestimating future budget deficits.

Another option would be to terminate the AMT and replace the lost revenue by raising the top tax rates on labor and capital income—raising the tax rate on labor income and interest income above 35% and the top rate on capital gains and dividends above 15%. Terminating the AMT, of course, might permit some very affluent households to pay little or no income tax due to deductions, exemptions, and credits. However, it would obviously eliminate the AMT threat to the middle class, and raising the top tax rates would maintain the tax burden on most of the very affluent.

Different Tax Schedules for Married Couples and Single Persons

Under the U.S. income tax, Congress has set a more severe tax schedule for singles than for married couples. Why did Congress set different schedules?

Suppose that the tax schedule shown in Table 8.4 applied to singles as well as couples (it actually applies only to couples). Consider two single persons deciding whether to get married. Look back at Table 8.4 and suppose each person's taxable income is $65,100 (the taxable income at the top of 15% tax bracket). Each dollar of their taxable income would be taxed either 10% or 15%, and no dollar would be taxed 25%. But if they married, $65,100 of their $130,200 would be taxed 25%. Marriage would push them into a higher tax bracket. Clearly, they would pay more total tax if they married than if they remained single.

Congress has reduced the marriage penalty by setting a more severe tax schedule for singles. The initial tax rate is 10%, but it jumps to 15% sooner (at a lower income threshold) and then jumps to 25% sooner. With the two U.S. tax schedules, marriage can raise or lower the taxes of two individuals depending on their incomes; for some there is a marriage penalty, while for others there is a marriage bonus.

Note that if the U.S. income tax had one tax rate (instead of progressive rates), there would be marriage neutrality for everyone: If every dollar of income were taxed at the same rate, then clearly two persons would always pay the same total tax whether they married or remained single.

CONCEPTS UNDERLYING THE INCOME TAX

Having examined the basic facts, numbers, and mechanics of the income tax, let's turn to the underlying concepts.

Ability to Pay

A basic justification for the income tax is that it taxes households according to their ability to pay. Consider two households. The first has $40,000 of labor income and $20,000 of capital (investment) income; the second has $60,000 of labor income and no capital income. Since both have the same total income, $60,000, it seems reasonable to conclude they have the same ability to pay tax, even though the sources of their income differ.[3] Consider two other households. Suppose the first household plans to consume a lot (and save little), while the second plans to consume little (and save a lot). These plans do not seem to affect the household's ability to pay tax this year. A household's total income, therefore, seems like a better measure of its ability to pay tax than its labor income alone, its capital income alone, or its consumption.

Proportional, Progressive, Regressive

One important feature of an income tax is how much more tax a high-income household than a low-income household owes. It is useful to apply these definitions—proportional, progressive, regressive—to an income tax schedule. The schedule describes how a household's (tentative) tax varies with its taxable income. Suppose high-income household H has twice the taxable income of low-income household L. If the schedule says H must pay a tax that is twice as great as L, then the tax schedule is called **proportional**; if H's tax is more than twice L's, then the schedule is called **progressive**; and if H's tax is less than twice L's tax, then the schedule is called **regressive**. An equivalent way to say this follows:

> *Looking across households in a given year, if the ratio of tax to taxable income stays constant as taxable income rises, the schedule is proportional; if the tax/income ratio rises, the schedule is progressive; and if the tax/income ratio falls, the schedule is regressive.*

It is evident from Table 8.4 that the U.S. income tax schedule is progressive. For example, as shown in Table 8.6, consider household L with taxable income $16,050, whose tax is $1,605 or 10% of taxable income; and household H, with twice as much taxable income, $32,100, whose tax equals $1,605 + .15($16,050) = $4,013, so H's tax is 12.5% of taxable income. With the rising bracket rates shown in Table 8.4, tax as a percent of taxable income rises—hence, the schedule is progressive.

Consider two simpler tax schedules. Under the first, every household must pay a tax equal to 10% of its entire taxable income. Clearly, this schedule is proportional—every household's tax as a percentage of taxable income would be the same (10%). Under the second, every household must pay a tax equal to 20% of its taxable income above $20,000; hence, each household pays a 0% rate on the first $20,000 and a 20% rate on income above $20,000; so with rising rates (0% then 20%), the tax is progressive. As shown in Table 8.7, if L has taxable income of $25,000, it must pay .20($5,000) = $1,000, and if H has taxable income of $50,000 it must pay .20($30,000) = $6,000; so L's tax is 4% of its taxable income, and H's tax is 12% of its taxable income. Because H's percent is greater than L's, the tax schedule is progressive.

According to a study by the Congressional Budget Office for the year 2001, the ratio of federal income tax to household income was 16.3% for the top 20% (i.e., the top

---

[3] Note, however, that gifts or inheritances received by a household are currently exempt from the household's income tax even though these inflows increase the household's ability to pay. A proposal to include gifts and inheritances received under the income tax is discussed in the section, "The Estate Tax."

TABLE 8.6
Progressive Taxation

	Taxable Income	Tax	Tax as a % of Taxable Income
L	$16,050	$1,605	10.0%
H	32,100	4,013	12.5

TABLE 8.7
Progressive Taxation

	Taxable Income	Tax	Tax as a % of Taxable Income
L	$25,000	$1,000	4%
H	50,000	6,000	12

quintile) of households, but 10.4% for all households. Thus, the tax to income ratio for the federal income tax was roughly 60% higher (16.3%/10.4% = 1.6) for the top 20% than for the average household.

Comprehensive Income

Most economists use the following definition of **comprehensive income**:

> *A household's comprehensive income equals its consumption plus its increase in wealth (saving). Equivalently, a household's comprehensive income equals the maximum it could consume in a given year while holding its wealth constant.*[4]

Saving is defined as the increase in wealth; hence, saving equals comprehensive income minus consumption.

As shown in Table 8.8, suppose you begin the year on January 1 with $10,000 in your bank account and $10,000 of corporate stock, so your **assets** are $20,000. You've borrowed $5,000, so your **liabilities** (debt) are $5,000. Then your **wealth**—*defined as assets minus liabilities*—is $15,000. During the year, you receive $1,000 of interest from your bank and $1,000 of dividends from corporate stock; you earn $38,000 of wage income, consume $36,000, and save $4,000 in your bank account (raising your bank account to $14,000). Assuming that your corporate stock is still worth $10,000, your increase in wealth is $4,000, and your wealth at the end of the year is $19,000. Then according to the definition of comprehensive income above (consumption plus increase in wealth), your income equals your consumption ($36,000) plus your increase

[4] This is sometimes called the Haig-Simons definition of comprehensive income after the two economists who proposed it to evaluate income taxation nearly a century ago.

TABLE 8.8
Wealth Calculation

Jan. 1 Assets	$20,000
Bank account	10,000
Corporate stock	10,000
Jan. 1 Liabilities (debt)	5,000
Jan. 1 Wealth	$15,000
Sources of income, Jan. 1–Dec. 31	$40,000
Interest	1,000
Dividends	1,000
Wage income	$38,000
Uses of income, Jan. 1–Dec. 31	$40,000
Consumption	36,000
Increase in wealth	$ 4,000
Dec. 31 Assets	$24,000
Bank account	14,000
Corporate stock	10,000
Dec. 31 Liabilities (debt)	5,000
Dec. 31 Wealth	$19,000

in wealth ($4,000), so your income is $40,000.[5] Equivalently, you could have consumed $40,000 this year while holding your wealth constant at $15,000 (instead of increasing it by $4,000 to $19,000); this is another way to see that your comprehensive income is $40,000. Note that the sum of your wage income ($38,000), interest ($1,000), and dividends ($1,000) is also $40,000, so there is no conflict in this example between the economist's definition of income which is based on uses of income and the conventional definition which is based on sources of income.

If you borrowed this year, the inflow would not increase your comprehensive income. Why not? Suppose you borrowed $3,000. If you consumed the $3,000, then your wealth would decrease $3,000, because by definition wealth equals assets minus debt, and your debt has increased $3,000. If you instead invested the $3,000 in stocks and bonds, your consumption would stay the same, your assets (stocks and bonds) would increase $3,000, but your debt would increase $3,000 so your wealth would stay constant.

The current U.S. income tax differs from a comprehensive income tax. Let's consider some examples.

Gifts or Inheritances Received by a Household

If you receive $5,000 this year in a gift ($3,000) from your parents and an inheritance ($2,000) from your grandparent who died, the inflow of $5,000 will raise either your consumption or your wealth $5,000, or it will enable some combination of consumption and increase in wealth that sums to $5,000. Hence, the inflow is a component of your comprehensive income, but currently it is exempt from your U.S. income tax.

The Exclusion from Tax of Employer-Paid Health Insurance

If your employer pays you $10,000 that you use to buy health insurance, you must pay income tax on the $10,000; for example, if you're in a 25% tax bracket, you must pay $2,500 in tax, and will then have $7,500 available for health insurance. However, if your employer takes $10,000 and buys you health insurance, you do *not* have to pay income tax on the $10,000. This exclusion of employer-paid health insurance from your taxable income provides you a tax saving that depends on your tax bracket; if you're in a 35% tax bracket, exclusion of $10,000 of health insurance reduces your tax $3,500; if you're in a 15% tax bracket, $1,500.

Why is employer-paid health insurance excluded? One argument is that the exclusion encourages greater health insurance coverage. But as we explain in the section below on credits versus deductions, a refundable tax credit may be a better way to encourage health insurance.

The Deferral of Tax on Contributions to Certain Retirement Accounts

If your employer pays you $10,000 that you save in your bank account, you must pay income tax on the $10,000; for example, if you're in a 25% tax bracket, you must pay $2,500 in tax, and will then have $7,500 available for your bank account. But if your employer takes $10,000 and contributes it to your pension fund or a 401(k) retirement plan, or if you contribute to your pension fund or 401(k) for your retirement or to a regular individual retirement account (IRA), you can **defer** (postpone) paying tax until you retire and withdraw the funds.[6]

---

[5] Taxes you pay are counted as part of your consumption on the assumption that taxes are your expenditure on consumption of public services.

[6] With a regular IRA, the advantage of tax deferral is available only to middle-income households: High income households are excluded, and low-income households that owe no income tax have no benefit.

Why is tax on your income that is contributed to these accounts deferred until you withdraw it at retirement? One argument is that the deferral encourages greater saving for retirement. Again, a refundable tax credit may be a better way to encourage saving for retirement.

Exclusion of Capital Income in Roth IRAs

If you save in a Roth individual retirement account, there is no deduction in the year you save (in contrast to a regular IRA), but all capital income earned will be excluded from taxation in future years (in contrast to regular saving), and there will be no tax when funds are withdrawn. The Roth IRA exclusion provides an incentive to save for retirement.

Exclusion of Interest from State and Local Bonds

The state and local interest exclusion is a form of aid to state and local governments because they are able to pay a lower interest rate and still attract savers. As discussed in Chapter 10, cash grants from federal to state or local governments may be a better way to provide aid.

The Deferral of Tax on Unrealized Capital Gains

Return to Table 8.8 and make just one change: Suppose that during the year the market value of your corporate stock rises $1,000—from $10,000 to $11,000. Then Table 8.8 becomes Table 8.9 (changed numbers are indicated in boldface). You've had a **capital gain** of $1,000. Your wealth has increased by $5,000—$4,000 in your bank account and $1,000 in your corporate stock. Your income equals your consumption ($36,000) plus your increase in wealth ($5,000)—so your income is $41,000. The sum of your wage income ($38,000), interest ($1,000), dividends ($1,000), and capital gain ($1,000) is also $41,000. Thus, you get the correct answer for your income ($41,000) when you include your capital gain of $1,000; therefore, your capital gain is a component of your income.

TABLE 8.9
Wealth Calculation

Jan. 1 Assets	$20,000
Bank account	10,000
Corporate stock	10,000
Jan. 1 Liabilities (debt)	5,000
Jan. 1 Wealth	$15,000
Sources of income, Jan. 1–Dec. 31	**$41,000**
Interest	1,000
Dividends	1,000
Wage income	38,000
Capital gain	**$ 1,000**
Uses of income, Jan. 1–Dec. 31	**$41,000**
Consumption	36,000
Increase in Wealth	**$ 5,000**
Dec. 31 Assets	**$25,000**
Bank account	14,000
Corporate stock	**11,000**
Dec. 31 Liabilities (debt)	5,000
Dec. 31 Wealth	**$20,000**

Suppose you sell the stock for $11,000 on December 31 and deposit the $11,000 in your bank account. The only thing that would change in Table 8.9 is the bottom block; the new bottom block is shown in Table 8.10.

Thus, it doesn't matter whether you sell your stock on December 31 or not: Your income would be $41,000, and you would need to add your capital gain of $1,000 to your wage income ($38,000), interest ($1,000), and dividends ($1,000) to get the correct answer for your income—$41,000. Hence, whether or not you realize your capital gain (i.e., sell your stock for cash), your income is $41,000, and your capital gain of $1,000 is a component of your income.

Yet under the U.S. income tax, only **realized capital gains** are subject to income tax. Tax on an **unrealized capital gain** is deferred until the stock is sold. Why is tax on an unrealized capital gain deferred? One reason given is that tax must be paid in cash, but an unrealized capital gain doesn't generate any cash for paying tax. Another reason given is that it is not always possible to know the market value of all corporate stock.

The Taxation of Nominal rather than Real Capital Income

Initially suppose the government levies no income tax, there is no inflation, and the interest rate is 4%. A saver who puts $100 in the bank at the beginning of the year would be able to buy 4% more goods at the end of the year, so the real return to saving is 4%.

Now suppose inflation is raised permanently to 8% (due to a permanent increase in the growth rate of money by the central bank). If inflation is 8% higher (8% instead of 0%), historical experience shows that eventually the **nominal interest rate**—the interest rate actually paid—will also be roughly 8% higher (12% instead of 4%), so that the **real interest rate** (the nominal interest rate minus the inflation rate) will be roughly the same (4%).[7] A saver who puts $100 in the bank at the beginning of the year will be able to buy 4% more goods at the end of the year (the saver would need $108 to buy the same goods, so $112 will let the saver buy 4% more goods). With no tax, inflation would not affect the real return to saving—it would remain 4%.

Ideally what should be taxed is real (inflation-adjusted) income, not nominal income. Only interest in excess of what is needed to keep up with inflation should be taxed. Whether inflation is 0% or 8%, the saver should be taxed on $4 of real interest income.

However, under the current U.S. income tax, the household is taxed on nominal interest income—if inflation is 0%, the household is taxed on $4, but if inflation is 8%, the household is taxed on $12. Table 8.11 shows how this improper taxation of nominal interest income affects the after-tax real return to saving. *Assume the tax rate is 25% throughout this example in all three rows of the table.*

---

[7] When inflation is high, nominal interest rates are high (this is called the Fisher effect after the economist who observed and explained it nearly a century ago). For example, in the late 1970s inflation was roughly 10% in the United States, and most nominal interest rates were double-digit (above 10%), while today inflation is roughly 3%, and most nominal interest rates are single digit (below 10%).

TABLE 8.10
Wealth Calculation

Dec. 31 Assets	$25,000
Bank account	**25,000**
Corporate stock	**0**
Dec. 31 Liabilities (debt)	5,000
Dec. 31 Wealth	$20,000

TABLE 8.11
Taxation of Nominal Interest Income

	p	i	$i - p$	Tax Rule	t	$i - t$	$i - t - p$
1	0%	4%	4%	25% tax on i	1%	3%	3%
2	8	12	4	25% tax on i	3	9	1
3	8	12	4	25% tax on $i - p$	1	11	3

In row 1, with no inflation ($p = 0\%$), the saver who puts $100 in the bank earns $4 interest ($i = \$4/\$100 = 4\%$), pays $1 tax ($t = \$1/\$100 = 1\%$), and has $103 to spend. At the end of the year the saver can buy 3% more goods than at the beginning of the year; the after-tax return is 3% ($i - t - p = 4\% - 1\% - 0\% = 3\%$).

In row 2, with inflation 8% higher ($p = 8\%$ instead of 0%), the nominal interest rate would be roughly 8% higher ($i = 12\%$ instead of 4%), so a saver who puts $100 in the bank would earn $12 interest, pays $3 tax ($t = \$3/\$100 = 3\%$), and has $109 to spend. At the end of the year the saver can buy only 1% more goods than at the beginning of the year); the after-tax real (inflation-adjusted) return is only 1% ($i - t - p = 12\% - 3\% - 8\% = 1\%$).

In row 3 there is also 8% inflation, but the 25% tax rate is applied to real, not nominal, interest income. The saver really shouldn't have to pay tax on $12, because $8 of the $12 is needed just to keep up with 8% price inflation at the stores. Only $4 should be taxed. In the table, the tax should be 25% of ($i - p$), not of i. If this were done, then the saver would pay $1 tax ($t = \$1/\$100 = 1\%$) and have $111 to spend, so the after-tax real return would be 3% ($i - t - p = 12\% - 1\% - 8\% = 3\%$), the same as in row 1.

The current U.S. income tax gives the same treatment to capital gains. What should be taxed is real (i.e., inflation-adjusted) capital gains, not nominal capital gains. Only a rise in the value of stock in excess of what is needed to keep up with inflation should be taxed. The example for interest income in Table 8.11 is easily reinterpreted for capital gains. Suppose a household buys stock for $100 on January 1. On December 31, if inflation is 0%, it sells the stock for $104; if inflation is 8%, it sells the stock for $112. In either case it should be taxed only on $4—its real capital gain (in excess of inflation). But under the current U.S. income tax, it is taxed on nominal capital gains, $12. The impact on the after-tax real rate of return is exactly as shown in Table 8.11. With taxation of nominal capital gains in row 2, the after-tax real return would be only 1%, while with taxation of real capital gains in row 3, the after-tax real return would be 3%, the same as in row 1.

Why doesn't Congress change the U.S. income tax so that real capital income, not nominal capital income, is taxed? Most economists think that it should. However, economists point out that the adjustment for inflation should be made not only when a household receives interest but also when a household pays interest (for example, after it borrows to buy a house or car)—thus, only real (inflation-adjusted) mortgage interest payments, not nominal mortgage interest payments, should be given an itemized deduction. Congress is probably reluctant to reduce the amount borrowers can deduct because this would be unpopular. Maybe this is why Congress has chosen to ignore inflation when it comes to capital income.

Credits versus Deductions

Suppose the aim is to encourage or reward a household for spending on category X. One way is to give a household a tax deduction for its spending on X. Suppose households H and L each spend $1,000 on X and therefore get a tax deduction of $1,000.

TABLE 8.12

Tax Deduction for Spending

	Spending on X	Deduction	Tax Bracket	Tax Saving
H	$1,000	$1,000	35%	$350
L	1,000	1,000	15	150

As shown in Table 8.12, if H is in a 35% tax bracket, the $1,000 deduction reduces its tax by $350; if L is in a 15% tax bracket, the $1,000 deduction reduces its tax by $150. Thus, a deduction automatically gives a larger tax reduction to the household in the higher tax bracket.

> *With a tax deduction, Congress has no control over the size of the assistance or how assistance varies with household income—both are determined by the household's tax bracket.*

Another way is to give a household a tax credit for spending on X as shown in Table 8.13. The credit rate is set by Congress. Suppose the credit rate is set at 25% of the amount spent on X for all households (top block). Then the credit would reduce H's tax by $250 and L's tax by $250.

Instead, Congress could vary the credit rate with household income. For example, it could set the credit rate at 35% for H and 15% for L (middle block); this would have the same effect as the tax deduction because H's tax would be reduced by $350 and L's by $150. Or it could set the credit rate 15% for H and 35% for L (bottom block), so H's tax would be reduced by $150 and L's by $350.

> *With a tax credit, Congress controls both the size of the assistance and how assistance varies with household income.*

Consider a household with total income so low that it owes no income tax. Is there any way to encourage or reward such a household for spending on X? Not with a tax deduction or a regular tax credit. A tax deduction doesn't help you if your income would not have been taxed. And a regular tax credit can help you only if you would have owed some tentative tax that can be reduced.

However, there is a policy instrument that can encourage or reward a low-income household for spending on X: a **refundable tax credit**. Suppose Congress enacts a 25% refundable tax credit for spending on X. Then if a low-income household (that would owe zero income tax) spends $1,000 on X, it would file a tax return indicating its expenditure on X, and several weeks later it would receive a refund from the U.S. Treasury for $250. Congress has enacted very few refundable tax credits, but one is extremely important: the Earned Income Tax Credit (EITC), a refundable tax credit for low-income workers. We examine the EITC in Chapter 12, where we also consider the possibility of other refundable tax credits to assist low-income households.

TABLE 8.13

Tax Credit for Spending

	Spending on X	Credit Rate	Credit	Tax Saving
H	$1,000	25%	$250	$250
L	1,000	25	250	250
H	1,000	35	350	350
L	1,000	15	150	150
H	1,000	15	150	150
L	1,000	35	350	350

Encouraging Home Ownership

Consider the example of encouraging home ownership. The instrument that Congress has chosen is a tax deduction for mortgage interest payments, which is one of the itemized deductions on the 1040 return. If a household borrows from a bank (i.e., takes out a mortgage) to buy a house, it can deduct its monthly interest payments. Note that a household's monthly mortgage payment to the bank consists partly of interest and partly of repayment of the principal; only the interest is deductible; and the bank will send a statement at the end of the year noting the total interest. For example, if the household makes a total of $2,000 of home mortgage interest payments in a year, it can take an itemized tax deduction of $2,000 on its tax return.

As shown in Table 8.14, this policy instrument gives much larger assistance to high-income households than low-income households. Suppose high-income household H buys a high-priced home, takes out a large loan, and has monthly interest payments that total $20,000. If H is in a 35% tax bracket, its tax is reduced by $7,000. By contrast, suppose low-income household L buys a low-priced home, takes out a smaller loan, and has monthly interest payments that total $4,000. If L is in a 15% tax bracket, its tax is reduced by $600.

Another property of this policy instrument is that it favors the household that borrows over the household that saves in advance to buy a home.

Consider instead a refundable tax credit for buying a home. Congress could vary the credit with the price of the home or the income of the household—however it desires. Consider a home-buyer refundable tax credit that is $10,000 if the household's income is below $50,000 and that phases down gradually to $0 as household income rises to $150,000; the home-buyer credit would not depend on the price of the home or how much the household borrowed. What would be the effect of Congress' replacing the home mortgage interest deduction with this home-buyer refundable tax credit? More low-income households would be eligible for more assistance, so there would probably be an increase in home ownership among low-income households. High-income households would buy less expensive homes and take out smaller mortgages, and some high-income households would choose to be renters rather than homeowners. Note that the phaseout schedule would impose an implicit marginal tax rate on home buyers of 10%, because a household that raises its income from $50,000 to $150,000—by $100,000—would have its credit reduced from $10,000 to $0—by $10,000—so the implicit marginal tax rate due to the phaseout would equal $10,000/$100,000, or 10%.

Of course, Congress could instead design the credit so that it gives roughly the same pattern of assistance as the current tax deduction. To do this, Congress would need to explicitly vary the tax credit directly with the price of the home, or the amount borrowed, and directly with household income. Hence, the credit would be larger, the higher the price of the home or the amount borrowed, and the higher the income of the household. With the credit, unlike the current deduction, Congress can vary its assistance however it desires.

TABLE 8.14
Encouraging Home Ownership

	Mortgage Interest Payment	Tax Bracket	Tax Saving
H	$20,000	35%	$7,000
L	4,000	15	600

Should a Deduction or Credit Have a Ceiling or a Floor?

Consider the example of encouraging or rewarding contributions to charities (spending on X, where X is a charity). Under the current U.S. income tax, if a household chooses to itemize deductions, then all of its contributions to charity are deductible—there is no ceiling or floor. If the household is in a 35% tax bracket, then for every $100 contribution, its tax would be reduced by $35.

It would be possible for Congress to put a limit (ceiling) on the amount that would be deductible. For example, if Congress set a ceiling of $10,000, then contributions in excess of the ceiling would not result in any further tax reduction. One advantage of a ceiling is that it limits the loss in tax revenue to the government. Another advantage is that it prevents any household from obtaining a deduction that some would consider "too large."

The disadvantage of a ceiling is that it removes the price incentive at the margin for the household to make additional contributions. Consider a household in a 35% bracket whose taxable income would still be in the 35% bracket if it gave $10,000 to charity. Suppose that if the U.S. income tax did not have a charitable deduction (or credit) provision, this household would give $10,000 to charity. Suppose Congress now enacts a charitable deduction, but with a $10,000 limit. The household recognizes that its $10,000 contribution would reduce its tax $3,500, but contributions above $10,000 would not reduce its tax. Thus, it is doubtful that Congress' enactment of the deduction with a $10,000 limit would cause the household to raise its contribution much above $10,000. It is true that the deduction raises the income of the household $3,500, and this income effect may cause the household to raise its charitable contributions a bit above $10,000, but there is no price incentive at the margin.

By contrast, consider the actual U.S. charitable deduction which has no limit. The household recognizes that for each $100 it gives, its tax is reduced $35, so at the margin it always has a price incentive of 35% to give more—any $100 contribution costs the household only $65 (because its tax is reduced $35). This price incentive is likely to result in a larger increase in the household's contribution above $10,000.

There is a way for Congress to lose less tax revenue but retain a price incentive at the margin. Instead of a ceiling, Congress could enact a floor. For example, suppose there would be no tax deduction for the first $10,000 contributed, but above $10,000 additional contributions would be deductible without limit. Then the government would lose no tax revenue on the first $10,000 the household contributes. But the household would recognize that once it has given $10,000, each additional $100 contribution would reduce its tax $35.

The floor could be set as a percentage of income (either total income or AGI); for example, charitable contributions in excess of 4% of the household's income might be deductible. Ideally, the floor for each household should be set at the amount the household would have given had there been no deduction, but a percentage of income should come closer to this ideal than a same dollar amount for high- and low-income households.

Thus, a floor rather than a ceiling seems an attractive design, but it also has a disadvantage. The government cannot know for certain how much each household would have given without the deduction. Suppose the floor is mistakenly set too high; for example, set at 4% of income when the household would only have given 2% of income. Then the household would not raise its contribution above 2% of income.

Particular Deductions, Exemptions, and Credits

Let's consider several important itemized deductions, exemptions, and credits under the U.S. income tax.

The Deduction for State and Local Tax Payments

Advocates of an itemized deduction for state and local tax payments contend that these are involuntary payments that reduce the ability of a household to pay federal income tax. Suppose households A and B each earn $50,000 of income but live in two different states; household A pays $8,000 in state and local taxes, while B pays $2,000. Advocates say it's fair to tax A on income of $42,000 and B on income of $48,000 because they differ in their ability to pay federal income tax.

Opponents of this deduction contend that A is consuming $8,000 of public services, while B is consuming only $2,000; for example, if the taxes are property taxes that finance their children's public schools, A's children are consuming higher-quality public education than B's children. Moreover, the difference in tax payments may be voluntary; for example, A may have chosen to live in its community because of a high-quality public school, while B may have chosen to live in its community because of its low property tax. Finally, the deduction causes excessive spending by state and local governments because every $100 spent costs local taxpayers less than $100 due to the reduction in their federal income tax.

The Deduction for Home Mortgage Interest Payments

Advocates for a deduction for home mortgage interest payments contend that there is an external benefit to the community when a household owns its home rather than rents; for example, it takes better care of its home, and this benefits its neighbors. However, as explained in the section above on credits versus deductions, a refundable tax credit for a home purchase (whether financed by a mortgage or not) may be a fairer and more efficient way to encourage home ownership.

The Deduction for Medical Expenses in Excess of 7.5% of AGI

Medical expenses that cost an excess of 7.5% of a household's adjusted gross income and are borne by the patient (not an insurance company) impose an exceptional involuntary burden on the household. These expenses also cause a reduction in ability to pay federal income tax on a household that has suffered medical hardship. Again, a refundable tax credit may be better.

Personal Exemptions and the Child Tax Credit

Advocates of personal exemptions and the child tax credit point out that a household with more children has more necessary expenses and therefore less ability to pay federal income tax. The personal exemption ($3,500 in 2008) and the child tax credit ($1,000) reduce the tax that a household must pay.[8] The tax reduction from the exemption varies directly with the household's tax bracket (for example, it's $350 for a household in the 10% tax bracket and $875 for a household in the 25% tax bracket), while the tax reduction from the credit is the same ($1,000) for most households (except that the credit is nonrefundable, so the household's benefit is limited to the amount of tax it would otherwise have owed, and the credit phases down for high-income households).

Opponents note that the number of children is a voluntary choice; having more children is a form of consumption, and like other consumption, it should not reduce the federal income tax an adult should have to pay.

---

[8] The personal exemption and the child tax credit phase down for high-income households.

ISSUES IN TAXING CAPITAL INCOME

Let's consider several interesting issues in taxing capital income.

Retirement Saving Incentives

Under a comprehensive income tax there should be no tax deduction for saving, and capital income should be taxed in the year it is earned. The current U.S. income tax gives an incentive to saving for retirement. The incentive is given in one of two ways: Either a tax deduction is given for saving in the year it occurs, or capital income is exempt from tax as it is earned. A tax deduction is given when a household saves through a 401(k) plan at the workplace or in a regular individual retirement account (IRA). Note that a deduction for saving in a regular IRA is one of the adjustments made in going from total income to adjusted gross income (AGI) on the 1040 tax return. A tax exemption is given for capital income earned on saving in a Roth IRA.

Capital Gains

On the one hand, the current U.S. income tax is easier on capital gains than a comprehensive income tax would be, because taxation is deferred until the stock is sold (i.e., until the gain is realized). Suppose the market value of your stock increases 10% this year from $10,000 to $11,000 and 10% next year from $11,000 to $12,100 when you sell it. Under a comprehensive income tax, you would be taxed this year on the $1,000 of unrealized capital gain and taxed next year on the $1,100; if the tax rate on capital gains is 15%, you would pay $150 this year and $165 next year. Under the current U.S. income tax, this year you would pay no tax, but next year you would be taxed on the two-year capital gain of $2,100, so you would pay $315. Although the total tax over the two years, $315, is the same, deferring this year's $150 lets you earn interest on it.

On the other hand, the current U.S. income tax is harder on capital gains than a comprehensive income tax would be, because it taxes nominal instead of real capital gains. Suppose the market value of your stock increases 10% this year from $10,000 to $11,000 when you sell it, but inflation this year is 10%. A comprehensive income tax would tax only a capital gain in excess of inflation, so you would pay no tax. The current U.S. income tax would tax you on your nominal capital gain of $1,000.

Thus, whether the current U.S. income tax is easier or harder on capital gains than a comprehensive income tax would be depends on which effect dominates.

Business Income

When you add up your income to obtain your total income, one of the items you must add is your business income. If you are a sole proprietor of a business, your profit is your business income; if you are a partner in a business, your share of the profit is your business income. Profit, in turn, equals sales revenue minus the costs incurred to generate the revenue. Thus, you deduct costs incurred in your business from your revenue to obtain your business income.

What are your deductible business costs? Several are obvious. If you paid any employees, their compensation is a deductible cost. If you bought materials used up this year, that expense is deductible. If you borrowed money, the interest that you paid is deductible (*note:* the principal of the loan was excluded from taxable revenue so the repayment of the principal should not be a deductible cost). But suppose you bought a machine at the beginning of this year for $1,000 and you plan to use it for five years. Then a simple estimate of the cost of using the machine for the goods or services you produced this year is $200 (one-fifth of the purchase price), so each year you should be allowed to deduct $200. The cost of the wearing out of machinery is called **depreciation.** Under straight-line depreciation, you deduct $200 in each of the five years you use the machine. But suppose you're not sure how long your machine will last? The IRS provides you with asset lives for categories of machines which prescribe how many years you must "write off" (or depreciate) your machine.

The Corporate Income Tax

Suppose you incorporate your business—your business becomes a corporation. The owners of a corporation become shareholders, and they receive the important benefit of **limited liability,** which means they are not personally responsible for the debts of the corporation; the corporation is a legal entity separate from its individual owners. Nevertheless, it can be argued that the business income you earn in your corporation should be attributed to you and included in your household income for taxation, just as it would be if your business were a sole proprietorship or a partnership. If the corporation paid out all profit as dividends to its shareholders, then all corporate income would be included in the household income of shareholders.

Most corporations, however, do not pay out all profit as dividends. Some corporations pay no dividends at all. Most retain a substantial portion of profit to finance investment in machinery and technology or to make portfolio investment (in bonds or stocks). Thus, if your household is taxed only on the dividends you receive, your business income (profit) that is retained and reinvested would escape household tax—in contrast to business income in proprietorships or partnerships. In theory, the proper thing to do would be to attribute (impute) all profit, whether paid out as dividends or retained, to shareholders and have each shareholder pay household tax on it.

However, shareholders might object that they are not receiving cash with which to pay the tax on profit that is retained in the corporation. Although the same might be said of business income retained in a proprietorship or partnership, it can be argued that the choice to retain rather than pay out business income is clearly in the control of the proprietor or the partner. By contrast, shareholders in a corporation, especially a large one, often have little or no control over the share of profit that is paid out and the share that is retained. The argument, then, is similar to the argument about postponing tax on unrealized capital gains. Households who have not received any cash complain that it is unfair to be required to pay tax.

A Separate Corporate Income Tax

An alternative way to prevent retained profit from escaping taxation is to have a separate tax on corporate income that the corporation, not shareholders, must pay. The corporation clearly has the cash if it retains the profit. This has been the approach taken by many countries, including the United States: a separate corporate income tax.

A separate corporate income tax does not adjust its rate to the income of each shareholder. The current U.S. corporate income tax rate is 35%.[9] By contrast, consider business income earned by two sole proprietorships: one whose owner is in a 15% tax bracket, the other in a 35% tax bracket. Each owner's business income would be taxed at the appropriate bracket rate. By contrast, the tax rate for a corporation (35%) is not adjusted according to the tax brackets of its owners. Thus, a corporate income tax is an imperfect method of taxing the business income of shareholders.

---

[9] The first dollars of a corporation's income are taxed at a lower rate, but most corporate income is subject to the 35% rate.

Although a separate corporate income tax succeeds in taxing profits that are retained, it causes profits that are paid out as dividends to be taxed twice. First the corporation pays a tax on all profit (whether the profit is destined to be retained or paid out), and second the individuals who receive dividends from the corporation pay taxes on their dividend income.[10] Congress could eliminate this double taxation of dividends by permitting corporations to deduct dividends the way they are permitted to deduct interest payments before applying the corporate tax rate to compute their corporate income tax. Congress has chosen not to let corporations deduct dividends.

Another justification for a corporate income tax is that the corporate legal form confers a benefit on its owners that is not enjoyed by owners of proprietorships and partnerships—namely, limited liability. It is argued that it is therefore fair and appropriate to levy a separate corporate income tax. Of course, there is still another expedient rationale for a corporate income tax: Corporations have the ability to pay substantial taxes.

Finally, there is a rationale that is based on a fallacy. Some citizens mistakenly think that a separate corporate income tax reduces the tax burden on people by placing the burden on business firms. *But it is people, not business firms, who ultimately bear the burden of all taxes.* If a tax is levied on corporations, particular people will bear the burden: If corporations reduce dividends or stock prices fall, stockholders will bear a burden; if managers or employees receive less compensation, they will bear a burden; if corporations raise prices, consumers will bear a burden; if financial investors shift funds out of corporations to unincorporated business firms, owners of incorporated firms will receive a lower return and bear a burden. Thus, a corporate income tax does not reduce the tax burden on people. Instead, it shifts the tax burden from certain groups of people to other groups of people.

Determining a Corporation's Income Tax

How does a corporation determine its income tax? Business income equals sales revenue minus the cost of goods sold this year. We discussed the elements of cost in the section, "Business Income." Compensation (cash wages and salaries plus fringe benefits such as purchase of health insurance coverage or contributions to pensions) to employees, expense on materials (intermediate product) used up making the final product, interest paid to creditors (note once again that dividends are not deductible as a cost), and the depreciation of capital goods are all costs of goods sold this year. The corporate tax rate is then applied to this income. Like the household income tax, there are tax brackets. Large corporations are in a 35% tax bracket. Applying the rates yields the corporation's tax.

Who bears the burden of the corporate income tax? In the short run, after-tax profit would fall, reducing dividends and the price of corporate stock so the owners of corporate capital would bear a burden. In the long run, financial investors would direct less funds into corporations and more funds into unincorporated business, so the return to capital elsewhere would be driven down; hence, owners of capital throughout the economy, not just in the corporate sector, would bear a burden. Economists therefore usually assume that owners of capital bear the burden of the corporate income tax.[11] But if the lower

---

[10] Note that labor income is also taxed twice—once by the payroll tax and once by the individual income tax.

[11] It is possible that corporate managers and employees would receive less pay than they otherwise would have; if so, they would bear some burden. Also, corporations might be able to pass on some of the tax to consumers by raising prices.

after-tax return reduces saving and investment, it will reduce the productivity of labor and the wage (see Figure 7.6) so some burden may fall on workers.

Under the U.S. corporate income tax, a U.S. multinational corporation is taxed on its income wherever that income is earned. A U.S. corporation with a factory located abroad, however, is usually taxed by the foreign government on the income generated within its borders. To avoid double taxation, the U.S. corporate income tax gives a U.S. corporation a foreign tax credit for taxes paid to foreign governments. For example, if a U.S. corporation earns $100 million abroad and the foreign government levies a 25% tax on this income ($25 million), then although its tentative U.S. corporate income tax is 35% ($35 million), it obtains a foreign tax credit of $25 million so that it only has to pay the U.S. government $10 million. A further advantage is also given: deferral of tax until repatriation. This corporation does not have to pay the U.S. government $10 million until the income earned abroad is returned—repatriated—to the United States.

The Estate Tax

Although the estate tax is not a tax on capital income, it is discussed here because it is a tax on the capital (wealth) that a person holds at death, and the argument is sometimes made that the estate tax is a double tax on capital income that has already been taxed under the income tax.

When a person dies, should the person's bequest—the estate (i.e., wealth) that will be given to heirs—be subject to taxation? Most agree that as long as the person's spouse is alive to receive the bequest, there should be no tax. However, suppose the spouse has already died, so that the bequest would go to children, grandchildren, and/or other individuals named by the person in a will. Should the estate of such a deceased person be subject to taxation? Should the amount of tax depend on the wealth of the deceased person or the income of the heirs (i.e., recipients)? If there is an estate tax, should it apply only to the largest estates, or should it apply to a substantial share of estates?

Taxing a person's wealth after the person dies raises a more basic question. Why not tax the person's wealth annually or at least periodically (say, every five years) while the person is alive? Why tax a person's wealth only at death? Opponents of the estate tax have called it the "death tax," and they say that death should not be a taxable event. Few opponents of the estate tax support annual or periodic taxes on a person's wealth while the person is alive. Most opponents of the estate tax also oppose taxing wealth because they believe that holding wealth should not be a taxable event—during life or at death. Should it?

Levying an estate tax leads to levying a tax on the giving of gifts before a person dies, because without a gift tax an older person would have an incentive to give away her estate to heirs before she dies. The United States, since 1976, has a unified transfer tax that coordinates the taxation of a person's estate at death with gifts given to heirs prior to death.

The U.S. Estate and Gift Tax

Under the U.S. estate tax, a person's gross estate includes all property owned by the person who died—such as stocks, bonds, and housing—minus any debt outstanding, plus gifts given during the person's lifetime. To help preserve family businesses and farms, these are valued at less than their fair market value. Then certain deductions are allowed before obtaining the taxable estate. The amount given to a spouse is deductible; no matter how large the estate, there is no tax if it is given to a spouse. The amount given to charity during life and at death is deductible; no matter how large the estate, there is no tax if it is given to charity. Annual gifts of up to $12,000 per recipient are deductible, so only the amount of a gift in excess of $12,000 per recipient is subject to the estate tax.

Roughly 99% of all estates are exempt from the federal estate tax because a very large tax credit eliminates all but the very largest estates—estates valued above $2 million in 2008, which are roughly the top 1%—from being taxed, so the U.S. estate tax is a very progressive tax. Most family businesses and farms are exempt from tax. Above the exemption, estate tax rates rise gradually to a maximum over 40%, but because of the $2 million exemption, the tax paid is generally less than 20% of the value of the estate. Congress has scheduled an increase in the exemption to $3.5 million in 2009 and then the complete repeal of the estate tax in 2010.

By taxing the top 1% of estates, the U.S. estate tax raises about 1% of federal tax revenue, or about 0.2% of GDP (because federal revenue is roughly 20% of GDP); for example, if federal tax revenue were 20.0% of GDP in a given year, then without the estate tax, federal revenue would be 19.8% of GDP.

Taxing Gifts and Inheritances Received under the Income Tax

Some reformers propose taxing gifts and inheritances received under the income tax either as a substitute for or a complement to taxing large estates. According to this perspective, the recipient should pay tax according to the recipient's income—the higher the income, the higher the tax the recipient must pay. This can be implemented simply by including any gift or bequest received as a component of the recipient's income on the annual income tax return. Currently under the income tax, an inheritance—a gift or bequest received—is not counted in the recipient's income even though it clearly raises a recipient's ability to pay tax, consume, and save. The change would remedy this omission.

Note that a bequest (or even a gift given while the donor is alive) may be a large sum that pushes the recipient into a higher tax bracket for that year; but note also that this is true for other kinds of income (for example, realized capital gains from the sale of stock bought many years ago at a much lower price).

If only financial gifts were taxed, donors might give nonfinancial gifts. To prevent this, large nonfinancial gifts might be subject to tax—to implement this, the recipient might be required to report the value of large nonfinancial gifts, such as a home, a car, a painting, expensive clothing or jewelry, and other consumer durables.

Should Wealth Be Taxed Annually or Periodically?

Why not tax wealth annually or periodically (say every five years) rather than only at death? It can be argued that wealth is even a better measure of ability to pay than income. Consider two households with $60,000 of income. Suppose the first household has $400,000 of financial wealth (stocks, bonds, and a savings account that sum to $400,000), while the second household has no financial wealth (no stocks or bonds, and nothing in its savings account). Despite their equality of income, the first household with $400,000 of financial wealth has a greater ability to pay tax than the second household with no financial wealth.

Nevertheless, few countries tax households annually or even periodically on their wealth. There are a number of reasons for this:

- Some components of wealth are hard to measure. Although the prices of corporate stocks traded daily are easily measured, shares of ownership in other businesses are not. Also, the market value of nonfinancial assets, such as a home, a car, a painting, or expensive jewelry, is difficult to measure; the past purchase price (even adjusted for intervening inflation) may provide a poor measure.

- The date on which wealth is measured may not reflect average wealth over the year or the period. Wealth is a stock which is measured at a moment in time. But with fluctuations in the stock market, wealth on one day may differ substantially from wealth on another day. By contrast, income is a flow measured over the entire year. A wealth tax could require a household to compute its wealth on several specific dates and take the average, but this would raise the cost of complying with the tax.

- A wealth tax encourages a household to consume rather than save; the more you spend down your wealth, the lower your wealth tax. The tax discourages the accumulation of real capital in the economy and therefore reduces workers' productivity and wages.

ISSUES IN TAXING LABOR INCOME

Let's consider several interesting issues in taxing labor income.

Household Taxation, Progressivity, and the Second Earner

To work or not to work: that is the question facing a potential second earner. The answer is affected by the income tax. Why?

Household taxation plus progressivity creates a dilemma for a potential second earner in a household. What is the dilemma? Call the person in a household with the highest income the "first earner." Suppose the first earner in family H earns income high enough to place the household in the top tax bracket—35%. Now consider the dilemma of a potential second earner. If the second earner goes to work, the second earner's first $100 earned will be taxed $35 (and the rest of her earnings will also be taxed 35%). Thus, the second earner immediately faces the marginal tax rate achieved by the first earner. This can be discouraging for the potential second earner who might therefore decide that it doesn't pay to go to work.

Given household taxation, the source of the second earner's dilemma is progressivity. Suppose instead that the income tax were proportional with all household income (no exemptions or deductions) taxed at the same rate. The marginal tax rate facing the second earner would be independent of how much income the first earner earns. So the second earner dilemma is a consequence of progressivity.

One way to reduce the second-earner dilemma while preserving progressivity would be to institute a second-earner deduction. A 10% second-earner deduction (up to a maximum of $3,000) was in effect in the United States from 1981 to 1986; on the first $30,000 of the second earner, 10% would be deductible; for example, if the second earner made $30,000, then $3,000 would be deductible, so the household's taxable income would increase $27,000, not $30,000. If the first earner put the household in a 35% tax bracket, then with the 10% deduction, the second earner's tax would be .35($27,000) = $9,450 instead of .35($30,000) = $10,500, a tax saving of $10,500 − $9,450 = $1,050. The 10% deduction would reduce the second earner's tax by 10% (from 35% to 31.5%). If the second-earner deduction were 40%, then a similar calculation shows that the marginal tax rate facing the second earner would be reduced by 40%—for example, from 35% to 21%. More generally, if the second earner's deduction were D%, then the marginal tax rate facing the second earner would be reduced by D%.

The second-earner dilemma can be eliminated while preserving progressivity by taxing each individual rather than each household. With individual taxation, every earner would be a "first earner." Even if the rate schedule were progressive, the first

$100 earned by each individual would be taxed at the lowest rate in the schedule, regardless of the income earned by the individual's spouse.

However, taxing individuals instead of households has a shortcoming. Given progressivity, two married couples with the same income would now pay different taxes: The household with income earned by one individual would pay more tax than the household with income earned by two individuals. Consider two couples each with $100,000 of income. In couple A, one spouse earns $100,000, the other earns $0. In couple B, each spouse earns $50,000. With household taxation, the two couples pay the same tax because income is the same. But with individual taxation and progressive rates, couple A pays more tax than couple B.

Another concern is that, with individual taxation, household investment income and itemized deductions would need to be assigned to each spouse. If there were no rule preventing it, a high-earning spouse in a happy marriage (with no divorce on the horizon) might transfer the ownership of stocks, bonds, and bank accounts to the low-earning spouse, so that the investment income would be taxed at that spouse's lower rate, while ownership of the house would remain with the high-earning spouse, so that spouse could take the mortgage interest and property tax deductions, thereby achieving a greater tax saving. To prevent this, Congress could adopt a rule assigning 50% of a household's investment income and itemized deductions to each spouse.

A Labor Income Tax

An income tax is levied on a household's entire income—the sum of income from labor and income from capital. Let's consider a proposal to exclude capital income (i.e., interest, dividends, capital gains) from the income tax and therefore tax only labor income.

Note that the tax rate on labor income would have to be set higher than the income tax rate to raise the same revenue. For example, in the typical household, suppose that for every $100 of income, $80 is labor income and $20 is capital income. An income tax rate of 20% raises $20 of tax revenue. Then the labor income tax rate would have to be set at 25% to raise the same $20 of revenue (because 25% of $80 equals $20).

What arguments can be given for excluding capital income from tax? First, it can be argued that a person shouldn't be taxed more when she saves than when she consumes; but taxing capital income—income from saving—would do this. Second, excluding capital income probably induces the average household to save more. Third, a capital income tax causes an efficiency loss by reducing the return received by the saver below the return actually generated by the investment. Fourth, it can be argued that capital income has already been taxed at the business level through the corporate income tax or through other business taxes that we discuss in Chapter 9, so that the capital income a household receives is really after-tax income, and taxing it would be double taxation.

What arguments can be given against excluding capital income from tax? First, it would strike many citizens as unfair to tax one kind of income but not another because both contribute equally to a household's ability to consume. Suppose household K has $100,000 of capital income but no labor income, and household L has the reverse. They have the same ability to consume. Would it be fair to tax L but not K?

Second, the exclusion may not increase saving. If a person has a *target* expenditure she wants to make in the future, the exclusion means that she doesn't have to save as much to reach this target. Also, excluding capital income from tax requires raising the tax on labor income, so each person pays more tax during the work stage of life, which reduces the ability of a worker to save. Although the empirical evidence cited in Chapter 7 appears to contradict this, it is possible there are flaws in these studies. Third, the efficiency loss from a capital income tax may be small if the supply of saving is inelastic with respect to the return that the saver receives. Fourth, even if it is true that capital income has already been taxed at the business level, so has labor income through the payroll tax, so taxing the household on its labor income is also double taxation. *If* capital income is taxed more heavily at the business level than labor income, perhaps it should be taxed more lightly at the household level; but then lighter taxation, not exclusion, would be warranted.

The Payroll Tax

The payroll tax that finances Social Security and Medicare is a labor income tax with particular features. The payroll tax is levied on each employee's wage and salary income. Half the payroll tax is levied on the employer and half on the employee, but the employer is required to send both halves to the government. As explained in Chapter 7 (Figure 7.4), workers bear most of the burden of both halves. For Social Security, the tax is levied on an employee's annual wage income up to a ceiling ($102,000 in 2008 and is automatically increased each year in line with wage income in the economy) at a tax rate of 6.2% on the employer and 6.2% on the employee for a combined rate of 12.4%. For Medicare, an employee's entire wage income is taxed (there is no ceiling) at a tax rate of 1.45% on the employer and 1.45% on the employee for a combined rate of 2.9%. Thus, wage income below the ceiling is taxed at a combined rate of 12.4% + 2.9% = 15.3%.

The payroll tax for Social Security is regressive. An employee's wage income is taxed at a combined flat rate of 12.4% up to the ceiling and a 0% rate above the ceiling. Moreover, the payroll tax excludes capital income. As household income rises, the ratio of payroll tax to household income falls for two reasons: the decline in the rate from 12.4% to 0% and the exclusion of capital income, which generally rises as a percentage of household income.

The payroll tax for Medicare is also regressive, though less regressive than the payroll tax for Social Security. An employee's entire wage income is taxed at a combined flat rate of 2.9%. However, the payroll tax excludes capital income, which makes the ratio of payroll tax to household income fall as household income rises.

Under the U.S. tax system, therefore, it might be said that labor income is double-taxed: once under the household income tax and once under the payroll tax. What really matters is the total tax rate on labor income. If an employee's wage income is taxed 15% under the income tax and 15.3% under the payroll tax, then the total tax rate on the employee's labor income is 30.3%.

Summary

The household income tax raises over 40% of all federal revenue—more revenue than any other federal tax. To compute its income tax, a household adds its wage income and investment income (such as interest and dividends) to obtain its total income, makes a few adjustments to obtain its adjusted gross income, subtracts personal exemptions, subtracts either the standard deduction or a set of itemized deductions to obtain its taxable income, applies the tax rates in the tax tables to obtain its tentative tax, and subtracts tax credits to obtain its tax. An affluent household pays whichever is larger: its regular tax or its alternative minimum tax. Different tax schedules apply to married couples and single persons; when two persons marry, some incur a marriage penalty, others enjoy a marriage bonus, and still others are unaffected.

A basic justification for the income tax is that it taxes households according to their ability to pay. A household's total income seems like a better measure of its ability to pay tax than its labor income alone, its capital income alone, or its consumption. If graduated tax rates are utilized, then the household income tax will be progressive: As we move from low- to high-income households, the ratio of tax to income will rise. On the other hand, if a single rate applies to all income, the income tax will be proportional: As we move from low- to high-income households, the ratio of tax to income will stay constant. Economists generally define a household's comprehensive income as its consumption plus the increase in its wealth. The U.S. income tax, however, differs from this definition by excluding gifts and bequests received by the household, deferring tax on unrealized capital gains, excluding employer-paid health insurance, deferring tax on contributions to pension funds, and taxing nominal rather than real (inflation-adjusted) capital income.

Either a tax credit or a tax deduction can be used to encourage or reward a household for spending on X. With the tax credit, Congress can vary the credit by household income however it desires and set the credit rates low or high. By contrast, with a tax deduction, Congress has no control over how the tax benefit varies with household income or the size of the tax benefit: Automatically, the tax benefit varies directly with the tax bracket of the household, and the size of the tax benefit equals the household's tax bracket rate times the amount spent on X. Under the current income tax, itemized deductions include state and local tax payments, home mortgage interest payments, and out-of-pocket medical expense in excess of 7.5% of AGI; the personal exemption and the child tax credit reduce tax owed according to the number of children.

An income tax entails taxing both capital income and labor income. Issues that arise in taxing capital income include incentives for retirement saving, treatment of capital gains, the measurement and taxation of business income and corporate income, and an estate tax on accumulated wealth. Issues that arise in taxing labor income include the effect on a potential second earner, the difference between a labor income tax and an income tax, and the effects of a payroll tax.

Key Terms

excise taxes, *200*
total income, *201*
adjusted gross income
 (AGI), *201*
personal exemptions, *201*
itemized deductions, *201*
standard deduction, *201*
marginal tax rate
 (MTR), *203*
tax bracket, *203*
alternative minimum
 tax (AMT), *203*
indexing, *204*

marriage penalty, *205*
marriage bonus, *205*
ability to pay, *205*
proportional, *206*
progressive, *206*
regressive, *206*
comprehensive
 income, *207*
saving, *207*
assets, *207*
liabilities, *207*
wealth, *207*
defer, *208*

capital gain, *209*
realized capital gain, *210*
unrealized capital
 gain, *210*
nominal interest rate, *210*
real interest rate, *210*
refundable tax credit, *212*
depreciation, *217*
limited liability, *217*
foreign tax credit, *219*
bequest, *219*
unified transfer tax, *219*
inheritance, *220*

Questions

1. Fill in the blanks of the 1040 Income Tax Return for this family of four (assume none of the income is capital gains or dividends):

_____	$50,000
− Adjustments	$ 50
= _____ (____)	$49,950
− _____ (4 × $3,500)	$14,000
− _____or _____	$10,900
= _____	$_____
Tentative ____	$_____
− _____	$ 2,000
= _____	$_____
− _____	$ 800
= _____	$_____

2. Fill in all the percentages in the table. Then show how the tentative ____ in question 1 is calculated:

Taxable Income	Tax Rate
$0 to $16,050	____%
$16,050 to $65,100	____%
$65,100 to $131,450	____%
$131,450 to $200,300	____%
$200,300 to $357,700	____%
Over $357,700	____%

3. For the family above, the tax is _____ % of its taxable income and _____% of its total income.

4. If a household with $357,700 of labor income earns another $10,000 of labor income, the household's tax will increase $_____; but if that household earns $10,000 of dividends or capital gains, the household's tax will increase $_____.

5. List four important itemized deductions:

   a. _____

   b. _____

   c. _____

   d. _____

6. Explain how you would determine whether a tax schedule is proportional, progressive, or regressive?

7. The U.S. income tax differs from a comprehensive income tax for each of the following. Explain the difference for each one:

   a. Capital income when there is inflation.

   b. Receiving a cash gift or an inheritance.

   c. An employer's purchase of health insurance for an employee.

8. According to George Harrison, the Beatles faced a MTR of _____%. Explain why by referring to the lyrics from his song "Tax Man."

9. Explain the difference between a deduction and a credit. Use an example where H and L each spend $100 on category X (H, 35% bracket; L, 15% bracket; credit rate 25%).

10. Explain the ability-to-pay argument for an income tax.

11. How is a corporation's income tax computed?

12. Why does the estate tax include gifts given in past years by the deceased?

13. What percentage of those who die owe U.S. estate tax?

14. What is the potential second-earner problem, and how can it be reduced?

15. Go online and read about the different tax reform plans of the Democratic and Republican candidates for president in the last election. Describe, compare, and evaluate the two plans.

Chapter **Nine**

Consumption Taxes

Ryan McVay/Getty Images

A **consumption tax** is a tax that imposes a burden on a household according to its consumption spending. A retail sales tax (RST) is one example of a consumption tax. Under a 6% RST, a consumer who buys a good priced at $100 pays a tax of $6 to the retailer for a total payment of $106; the retailer in turn pays $6 in tax to the government. A person is burdened by a sales tax according to how much he has spent on consumer goods.

The most important and widespread consumption tax around the world today is not the RST but the value-added tax (VAT). Many countries levy a VAT ranging from 5%

to 20%, and the VAT provides an important share of their tax revenue. It is not immediately obvious that a VAT is a consumption tax, but we will see shortly that economic analysis leads to the conclusion that a VAT is a consumption tax.

Although both the RST and the VAT are general consumption taxes, in practice each tax exempts many services and often exempts certain categories of goods, such as food or medicine. There are also consumption taxes on particular goods, such as gasoline, alcohol, and tobacco, with the rationale of either discouraging pollution, paying for transportation infrastructure, or discouraging unhealthful consumption. It would be possible to levy a tax on the annual consumption of a household; each household would compute its consumption by subtracting its saving from its income (such a tax has yet to be enacted and implemented). This chapter examines and analyzes various consumption taxes.

The U.S. federal government does *not* levy either a retail sales tax or a value-added tax. Both the RST and the VAT have been proposed for the U.S. federal government, and the pros and cons of enacting one of these taxes will be seriously considered and debated in the coming years. In the United States, most state governments and some local governments levy a retail sales tax.

A RETAIL SALES TAX

A **retail sales tax (RST)** is a percentage tax on the sale of consumer goods by retailers. In principle, investment goods are supposed to be exempt from the tax, so that the retail sales tax is a consumption tax. In practice, it is sometimes difficult to avoid taxing some investment goods. For example, suppose the sale of a personal computer is subject to the retail sales tax. This is appropriate if it is used by a household for non-business purposes, because such use can be considered consumption. But if it is used by a business, then it is really an investment good that is contributing to the production of output by the business.

The tax is levied on business firms—retailers. As we know from Chapter 7, if we assume that demand is inelastic relative to supply, most of the burden falls on the consumers through higher prices. In fact, most consumers probably assume that they are bearing the whole burden, because the tax is shown separately at the cash register. When a consumer buys an item with a sticker price of $100 in a state with a 6% retail sales tax, at the cash register a $6 tax is added and shown on the receipt, and the consumer must pay $106 to buy the good. Recall from Chapter 7 that the consumer is bearing the whole burden *if* the price would have been $100 in the absence of a retail sales tax; but it is possible that without the tax, the price would have been, say, $101; if so, then the consumer's burden is $5 and the retailer's burden is $1. When economists call the retail sales tax a consumption tax, they are assuming, quite plausibly, that most of the burden falls on consumers rather than on retailers.

Given the assumption that most of the burden of a retail sales tax falls on consumers, a retail sales tax is *regressive* with respect to *income*: As we move from low- to high-income households in a given year, the ratio of tax burden to *income* generally falls. The reason is that as we move from low- to high-income households, the ratio of household consumption to household income generally falls, because higher-income people usually save a larger fraction of their income than low-income people do.

Table 9.1 illustrates this point. As we move from the $20,000-income household to the $100,000-income household, the tax/income ratio falls from 20% to 15%, because the consumption/income ratio falls (from $16,000/$20,000 = 80% to $60,000/$100,000 = 60%).

TABLE 9.1
Burdens from a 25% Retail Sales Tax

Income	Consumption	Tax	Saving	Tax/Income
$ 20,000	$16,000	$ 4,000	$ 0	20%
100,000	60,000	15,000	25,000	15

Note that in this example, consumption is the amount that the household spends *excluding* the sales tax. Including the sales tax, the $100,000 household spends $75,000 and the $20,000 household spends $20,000. Thus, the tax equals 20% of the amount each person spends including the tax ($15,000/$75,000 = 20% and $4,000/$20,000 = 20%). Economists say that 25% is the **tax-exclusive rate**—the percentage that the consumer would actually see on the sales receipt, which is the rate that is applied to the sticker price—while 20% is the **tax-inclusive rate**.

A VALUE-ADDED TAX

A **value-added tax (VAT)** is a percentage tax on the value that is added at each stage of production. Table 9.2 shows how a 10% value-added tax works. The top block of Table 9.2 shows how the VAT applies to the production of a consumption good—bread. The farmer grows wheat and sells it to the miller, who then grinds it into flour and sells it to the baker, who then uses the flour to bake bread and sells the bread to the consumer. With a VAT, tax is collected at each stage of production. At each stage, value added is defined as sales minus purchases, so the farmer pays $3 of tax (10% of $30), the miller pays $4 of tax (10% of $40), and the baker pays $3 of tax (10% of $30), for a total of $10. Note that the total value added is $100, which is equal to the value of the final product (the bread) sold to the consumer.

One way for the miller to compute his VAT would be to take $70 of sales, subtract $30 of purchases to get $40, and then take 10% to get $4. More generally,

$$T = t(S - P)$$

$$\text{Miller: } \$4 = .1(\$70 - \$30)$$

where t is the tax rate, S is sales revenue, and P is purchases. This is called the **subtraction method**.

Another way for the miller to compute his VAT would be to take 10% of his $70 of sales to get a tentative tax of $7, but then subtract a tax credit equal to 10% of his $30 of purchases which is $3, so that his final tax is $7 − $3 = $4. More generally,

$$T = tS - tP$$

$$\text{Miller: } \$4 = .1(\$70) - .1(\$30)$$

TABLE 9.2
A 10% VAT

	A Consumption Good (Bread)			
	Purchases	Sales	Value-Added	VAT
Farmer	$ 0	$ 30	$ 30	$ 3
Miller	30	70	40	4
Baker	70	100	30	3
Total	$100	$200	$100	$10

where tS is the tentative tax and tP is the tax credit. This is called the **credit-invoice method**. Of course $t(S - P) = tS - tP$, so the two methods give the same result.

However, the two methods differ in appearance. The subtraction method makes the VAT appear similar to a corporate income tax, which also involves a subtraction from sales revenue before applying a tax rate. With the corporate income tax, the cost of goods sold (labor compensation, etc.) is subtracted from revenue. With the VAT, purchase from other firms is subtracted from revenue. If a country were considering replacing its corporate income tax with a VAT, it might seem natural to institute a subtraction-method VAT.

A Subtraction VAT

Several steps would be required to convert a corporate income tax to a subtraction VAT. Recall from Chapter 8 how a corporation determines its income tax. Business income (profit) equals sales revenue minus the cost of goods sold this year. Cost of goods sold this year includes compensation to employees, expense on materials (intermediate product) used up making the final product, interest paid to creditors, and the depreciation (wearing out) of investment goods. The corporate tax rate is then applied to this income.

Similarly, with a VAT, sales revenue is added and expense on materials is subtracted, but to convert the corporate income tax to a subtraction VAT, these changes must be made: No subtraction is permitted for compensation to employees, interest to creditors, or depreciation of investment goods; but a subtraction is permitted for the purchase of investment goods this year. The VAT rate is then applied to this tax base.

The credit-invoice method makes the VAT appear similar to a sales tax because its first step is to apply a tax rate to sales revenue to obtain tS (after computing its tentative tax tS, the firm is allowed to reduce its tax by taking a tax credit equal to tP). If a country initially taxed all firms (not just retailers) on their sales—such a sales tax is called a **turnover tax**—it might seem natural to institute a credit-invoice VAT. Several decades ago many European countries had a turnover tax, and they found it natural to replace their turnover tax with a credit-invoice VAT. The credit-invoice method is used by many more countries than the subtraction method.[1]

COMPARING A VAT TO A RST

Compare the 10% VAT to a 10% retail sales tax. Under the 10% RST, no tax would be paid by the farmer or the miller, but the baker would pay a tax of $10 on his sales of $100. In both cases, $10 of tax would be built into the price that the consumer pays. With the VAT, the $10 is built in stages—$3 from the farmer, $4 from the miller, and $3 from the baker. With the RST, the $10 tax enters in the final stage from the baker. In both cases, the bread comes to the consumer with $10 of tax built into its price. The effect on the consumer would be the same.

Under a retail sales tax, an investment good (e.g., a machine) sold to a business firm is not taxed. A VAT would not tax an investment good sold to a business firm. True, a VAT would be levied on the early stages of production of an investment good. However, the business firm that buys the investment good would reduce the total VAT it owes by purchasing the good; increasing tP reduces T in either formula above, thereby undoing

[1] The two methods also differ in administration. Advocates of the subtraction method contend it is easier to administer. Advocates of the credit-invoice method contend it reduces tax evasion because auditors can cross-check buyer and seller by using the invoice.

the effect of the taxes on the investment good that were levied at the early stages of its production.

Under a RST, imported consumer goods are taxed at the same rate as domestically produced consumer goods in order to prevent imports from having an improper advantage. For the same reason, imports would be subject to the same VAT rate as domestically produced goods.

Under a retail sales tax, exported goods are not taxed—only domestic retail sales to domestic consumers are taxed. The same exclusion of exports from tax would be achieved by a VAT. Sales revenue from goods that are exported would be omitted from sales revenue S in either formula above used to compute the tax. True, a VAT would be levied on the early stages of domestic production of an exported good. However, the business firm that exports the good would reduce the total VAT it owes by omitting it from sales revenue S, thereby undoing the effect of the taxes on the export good that was levied at the early stages of its production.

Based on this analysis, most economists reach this conclusion:

> *A VAT is equivalent to a RST. Since the RST is a consumption tax, the VAT is a consumption tax: A consumer bears a burden from either a RST or a VAT according to his consumption spending.*

Because economic analysis suggests that a VAT is equivalent to a RST, it follows that a VAT is *regressive with respect to income,* just like a RST: As we move from low- to high-income households (in a given year), the ratio of tax burden to income generally falls. The reason is that as we move from low- to high-income households, the ratio of household consumption to household income generally falls because higher-income people usually save a larger fraction of their income than low-income people do.

Exemptions Under a RST or a VAT

A major issue for any RST or VAT is whether to exempt any categories of consumer goods and services (or tax certain categories at a lower rate). There are two arguments for exemptions. One argument is that fairness calls for exempting (or setting a lower rate on) goods like foods and medicines because these are "involuntary necessities," not "voluntary luxuries" like many other goods and services. Note that this argument could be made even if all consumers had the same income. Second, exemptions can reduce the regressivity of a RST or a VAT. If low-income households spend a higher percentage of their income on goods in category X than do high-income households, then exempting category X reduces regressivity. Exempting food and medicines would reduce regressivity.

There are three arguments against exemptions. First, if there are no exemptions, then the tax base would be as broad as possible, and a given target revenue would be raised with the lowest possible tax rate; a lower tax rate usually results in a lower efficiency loss from a tax (as we discussed in Chapter 7). Second, there is an administrative cost for retailers and tax auditors when goods must be separated into categories at the cash register so that some are taxed while others are exempt. Third, exemptions are not well targeted; for example, a food exemption forgoes revenue from the rich as well as the poor.

Exemptions of particular consumer goods can be achieved under a VAT. True, a VAT would be levied on the early stages of domestic production of a particular consumer good. However, the retailer that sells the particular consumer good to a consumer would reduce the total VAT that it owes by omitting it from sales revenue, thereby undoing the effect of the taxes on the consumer good that was levied at the early stages of its production.

A Household Rebate with a RST or a VAT

Another way to reduce the regressivity of a RST or a VAT is to have the U.S. Treasury mail a "rebate" check to all households to partially or completely offset their consumption tax burden. For example, each household might be mailed a $2,000 rebate check once a year (or, alternatively, a $500 check four times a year) from the U.S. Treasury to offset the first $2,000 of its tax burden from a RST or a VAT. To pay for the rebates, the government would have to set the tax rate higher, so that net tax revenue (i.e., gross tax revenue minus total rebates) remains constant despite the rebate.

   One issue is whether to vary the amount of the rebate with the number of adults and children in the household. If so, verification of each member (through Social Security numbers) would be needed in the same way it is needed for the federal income tax. Another issue is whether to vary the amount of the rebate with household income. This cannot be done if the RST or the VAT *replaces* the household income tax, because the government would no longer receive information on each household's income.[2] It can, however, be done if the RST or the VAT *supplements* the household income tax. The rebate would then be claimed as a refundable tax credit on the annual household income tax, and the amount of the credit could be varied with the household's income as reported on its income tax return. It would then be possible to phase out the rebate as household income rises, thereby making the RST or VAT, plus rebate, progressive.

THE FLAT TAX AND THE X TAX

Another way to reduce the regressivity of a VAT is to modify it so it becomes either the *flat tax* or the *X tax*. To obtain the **flat tax**, start with a VAT on firms and no income tax on households. Then permit firms to deduct wage income (which is not permitted under a standard VAT), but tax households on wage income above an exemption (e.g., $25,000) at the same rate used by the VAT. The name "flat tax" comes from the fact that wage income above the exemption is taxed at a single rate, rather than at graduated rates, and that the single rate is the same as the VAT rate. However, the exemption means that a 0% rate is applied to the first dollars earned up to the exemption (say, $25,000), so there are really two rates under the flat tax: 0% up to the exemption and the "single" rate above the exemption. It is the 0% rate up to the exemption that reduces regressivity.

   The **X tax** is the same as the flat tax except that wage income above the exemption is taxed at graduated bracket rates like the current U.S. income tax. The graduated rates achieve progressivity with respect to labor income but not capital income.

   Like many other tax reformers, advocates of the flat tax support broadening the tax base in order to enable a low tax rate; broadening the base means eliminating most or all household itemized deductions. It is important to understand that base broadening is a completely separate issue. It can be pursued with or without the flat tax or X tax.

   But why, many citizens ask, is a household taxed only on its labor income under the flat tax or X tax but not on its capital (investment) income? The answer given by advocates is that the flat tax, like a VAT, doesn't allow the firm to deduct capital income, so capital income is really being taxed at the level of the firm and shouldn't be taxed again at the level of the household (the wage income of the household is taxed because the firm is given a deduction for wage income). Nevertheless, upon hearing about how

[2] Under the "fair tax" proposal to replace income and payroll taxes with a national RST, the household rebate would not (and could not) be varied with a household's income.

the flat tax or X tax would be computed, some citizens have been puzzled or troubled by the fact that at the household level the flat tax or X tax would tax wage income but not capital income.

A HOUSEHOLD CONSUMPTION TAX

It would be possible to *replace* the household income tax with a household consumption tax: On the annual 1040 tax return, the household would report its consumption instead of its income and pay tax on its consumption instead of its income. Alternatively, it would be possible to *supplement* the household income tax with a progressive consumption tax on very high consumption; on the annual 1040 tax return, a very affluent household would report its consumption as well as its income and pay tax on its consumption above a very high exemption as well as on its income.

The household would arrive at its consumption in the past calendar year by *subtraction:* It would sum its cash inflows and then subtract nonconsumption cash outflows—*all saving would therefore be tax deductible in the year it occurs.* This subtraction would yield the amount of cash that must have been used for consumption; this amount would be subject to tax at the rates in the tax table.

Like the household income tax, the household consumption tax could have graduated (progressive) rates.[3] If the household consumption tax is intended to replace the income tax and raise roughly the same revenue from each income class (so that the replacement is *revenue neutral* and the consumption tax has *the same progressivity* as the income tax it replaces), then the consumption tax rates must be more graduated than the income tax rates. This is because as we move from low- to high-income households, the ratio of consumption to income falls (the affluent save a greater percentage of their income). The rates would also have to be higher than income tax rates to raise the same revenue, because the tax base, consumption, is smaller than income (saving is tax deductible). Thus, to raise the same revenue from the affluent, the top rate would have to be set higher than the current top income tax rate of 35%.

History of a Household Consumption Tax

The case for converting the household income tax to a household consumption tax was presented a half century ago in two books by two distinguished economists: Irving Fisher of Yale University and Nicholas Kaldor of Cambridge University; it was developed further in the U.S. Treasury's *Blueprints for Basic Tax Reform* in the mid-1970s. The past three decades have witnessed numerous articles and several books describing and analyzing a household consumption tax (also called a consumed income tax or expenditure tax). In 1995 a bill to convert the household income tax to a household consumption tax was introduced in the U.S. Senate; its sponsors were Senator Domenici, a Republican, and Senator Nunn, a Democrat, and the bill was called the Unlimited Savings Allowance (USA) Tax.

Making saving tax deductible is not a radical departure because, as we saw in Chapter 8, saving in certain retirement accounts is already tax deductible under the current income tax. The difference is that under a household consumption tax, *all* saving—whether for retirement or not—would be tax deductible.

---

[3] If Congress did not want the consumption tax to be progressive, it would be simpler to enact a retail sales tax or value-added tax.

Computing Household Consumption

The following example illustrates how a household would compute its consumption. Suppose a household earns $70,000 in salaries, receives $6,000 in interest and dividends, and sells stocks and bonds for $4,000, for a total cash inflow of $80,000. If the household increases its savings account balance by $8,000, buys new stocks and bonds for $12,000, and has $10,000 of tax withheld from its paychecks, its total nonconsumption cash out-flow is $30,000. Therefore, its consumption is $50,000 ($80,000 minus $30,000).

Several practical problems arise under a household consumption tax that do not exist under an income tax. For example, it would be too burdensome for a household to be taxed on its huge expenditure on a home in the year it is purchased; some method is needed to spread the tax over time. One option would be to treat the purchase of a home as a tax-deductible investment in the year of purchase but then require the household every year to add 5% of the market value of its home to its other consumption on its 1040 return (5% of the home's market value would be an estimate of its housing con-sumption that year); this option requires the household to provide an estimate of the market value of its home each year, so that the IRS would have to instruct households on how to make the estimate.

Several practical problems that arise under an income tax would be eliminated under a household consumption tax. Employee compensation is complex under an income tax: Should stock options be taxed as ordinary income or be given special capital gains treatment? Compensation is simple under a consumption tax: Only cash received by the household is counted in its cash inflows. A capital gain is complex under an income tax: Should an attempt be made to make up for the advantage of deferring tax until the year of sale? A capital gain is simple under the consumption tax: Only cash from the sale of stock is counted in its cash inflows. Finally, saving is complex under the income tax: Which savings vehicles—for example, IRA or 401(k) plan—should be granted a tax deduction? Saving is simple under the consumption tax: All saving is tax deductible.

A Progressive Consumption Tax on Very High Consumption

A more modest proposal than replacing the income tax with a consumption tax would be to introduce a progressive consumption tax on very high consumption as a supple-ment to the income tax. All households would remain subject to the income tax. How-ever, high-income households would also be subject to a progressive consumption tax which would be collected through the regular 1040 income tax return. Households with income of less than $500,000 would be exempt from the progressive consumption tax, and households with income above $500,000 would pay a consumption tax only on consumption above $500,000.

Two arguments can be given for instituting a progressive consumption tax on very high consumption: one traditional and one novel. The traditional argument is that insti-tuting such a tax would be less harmful to the economy than raising income tax rates on the very affluent. Raising income tax rates discourages saving and financial invest-ment, because it raises tax rates on interest, dividends, and capital gains. Less saving and investment mean less economic growth. A progressive consumption tax avoids such discouragement to saving and investment.

The novel argument for taxing very high consumption is that it generates a *negative externality*. According to this view, when the *very* affluent increase the size of their homes or the luxury of their possessions or vacations, unintentionally they raise the implicit standard against which the *merely* affluent unconsciously measure their own consumption; the merely affluent become less satisfied with their own consumption and feel a subtle pressure to consume more just to maintain their utility. In turn, when the merely affluent raise their consumption, unintentionally they raise the implicit standard against which the *almost* affluent unconsciously measure their own consumption. So it continues downward as each stratum unintentionally puts pressure on the one below it. This *cascading effect* begins at the top and rolls down the social strata. From this perspective, taxing very high consumption is exactly what is needed to internalize the externality—to reduce the very high consumption at the top before it generates a waterfall of disutility.[4]

REPLACING THE INCOME TAX WITH A CONSUMPTION TAX

Let's analyze the impact of replacing the income tax with a consumption tax.

Impact on Saving

Table 9.3 shows the impact on saving when an income tax is replaced by a consumption tax. We consider an economy with just two people, C and S. Each has $100,000 income, so with a 10% income tax, each pays $10,000 for a total of $20,000. C and S are extremists about consuming and saving: As shown in the top block, after paying income tax, C consumes the rest ($90,000), while S saves the rest ($90,000). Total saving is $90,000, all from S.

Suppose the income tax is replaced by a consumption tax that raises the same revenue ($20,000). Because S consumes nothing, all $20,000 of tax revenue must come from C. In the middle block, we assume that C continues to save nothing, so C pays $20,000 in tax and consumes $80,000. Hence, the government should set the consumption tax rate at 25% ($20,000/$80,000 = 25%). Total saving increases from $90,000 to $100,000, because S increases saving from $90,000 to $100,000.

The middle block shows that even if C continues to save nothing, total saving would increase (from $90,000 to $100,000). The reason is that replacement causes person S who saves to pay less tax ($0 instead of $10,000), and the person C who consumes to

---

[4] Robert H. Frank, *Luxury Fever: Why Money Fails to Satisfy in an Era of Excess.* The Free Press, 1999. *Falling Behind: How Rising Inequality Harms the Middle Class.* University of California Press, 2007.

TABLE 9.3
The Impact on Saving of Replacing the Income Tax with a Consumption Tax

	Income	Tax	Consumption	Saving
10% Income Tax				
Person C	$100,000	$10,000	$90,000	$ 0
Person S	100,000	10,000	0	90,000
Total	$200,000	**$20,000**	$90,000	$ 90,000
25% Consumption Tax				
Person C	$100,000	$20,000	$80,000	$ 0
Person S	100,000	0	0	100,000
Total	$200,000	**$20,000**	$80,000	$100,000
33% Consumption Tax				
Person C	$100,000	$20,000	$60,000	$20,000
Person S	100,000	0	0	100,000
Total	$200,000	**$20,000**	$60,000	$120,000

pay more tax ($20,000 instead of $10,000). So $10,000 has been shifted from C, who would have consumed it, to S who saves it. This *horizontal redistribution effect* raises total saving (it is "horizontal" because it is a shift between two people with the same income, not a shift from rich to poor).

The bottom block of the table shows that the increase in total saving would be even greater if C responds to the new tax incentive by doing some saving. Because S consumes nothing, C must pay $20,000 in tax. However, if C now pays $20,000 in tax, assume that C would consume $60,000 and save $20,000. Hence, the government should set the consumption tax rate at 33% ($20,000/$60,000 = 33%). Total saving increases from $90,000 to $120,000 because S increases saving from $90,000 to $100,000 (the horizontal redistribution effect), and C increases saving from $0 to $20,000 (the incentive effect).

Finally, replacing an income tax with a consumption tax should raise capital accumulation in the economy through the *postponement effect*. Consider the life cycle of an individual. The person's income rises over a work career until retirement when labor income ceases and only capital income continues to be earned, so there is a sharp drop in income at retirement. Hence, over his life cycle, the person's income tax increases until retirement when it drops sharply; a person pays more tax in a typical year when working than when retired. With a consumption tax, an individual who saves enough during his work years can avoid having to cut consumption in retirement. Hence, over his life cycle, a person who plans ahead pays roughly the same consumption tax in a typical year when either working or retired.

Thus, if the income tax is replaced by a consumption tax, the person will pay less tax during the work stage of life and more tax during the retirement stage; tax will be *postponed* to later in life. The reduction in tax during the work stage of life will enable the person to save more during this stage. Hence, persons will accumulate more capital during their life cycle, and, correspondingly, the economy will accumulate more capital due to this postponement effect.

Impact on Efficiency Loss

An income tax consists of a tax on capital income and a tax on labor income. As we saw in Chapter 7, the tax on capital income causes an efficiency loss in the choice between saving and consuming, while the tax on labor income causes an efficiency loss in the choice between work and leisure. We now show that replacing the income tax with a consumption tax removes the efficiency loss in the choice between saving and consuming but may increase the efficiency loss in the choice between work and leisure. Hence, the net impact on efficiency depends on which efficiency change is larger.

Look back at Figure 7.10 which shows the efficiency loss from a tax on capital income. The 40% tax on capital income tax drives a wedge between the firm's investment return on the machine of 5% and each saver's after-tax return of 3%. Starting from the saving chosen under the 40% tax, it would be possible to increase saving $100 and make everyone better off. Each saver only needs to receive a 3% return to keep his utility constant, but the $100 machine generates a return of 5%. Hence, 3% can be given to the saver, and the remaining 2% can be distributed to everyone else, making them better off. Each additional $100 of saving generates a return on the machine that exceeds the return that savers require to keep their utility constant until the intersection is reached, so the efficiency loss equals the area of the triangle.

If the income tax is replaced by a consumption tax, then the wedge between the investment return on a machine and the return the saver receives is eliminated. If the person takes $100 of income and saves it, there is no tax on the $100, and the person receives a 5% return that is equal to the firm's investment return on the machine of 5%. Thus, in choosing how much to save, the person correctly expects a return equal to the firm's investment return (5%) when there is a consumption tax, but correctly expects a return less than the firm's investment return when there is an income tax (a 3% return if the income tax rate is 40%). Under a consumption tax, there is no efficiency loss in the choice between saving and consuming.

However, the efficiency loss between leisure and work remains. Suppose you are considering giving up an hour of leisure and working another hour. An income tax reduces your after-tax wage income and, therefore, the consumption you can enjoy from working another hour. If you earn $100 of wage income and the income tax rate is 25%, then you can enjoy only $75 of consumption. Similarly, a consumption tax also reduces the consumption you can enjoy. Even though your $100 of wage income is not immediately taxed, when you go to the store and pay $100 at the cash register, if the sales tax is 33%, you will only obtain $75 of consumption because $25 is going for tax (the sticker price of the good is $75, so with a sales tax rate of 33% your tax is $25). Thus, a consumption tax, like an income tax, reduces the consumption you can enjoy when you sacrifice an hour of leisure, and therefore, it causes an efficiency loss.

Look back at Figure 7.9 where the employer pays the worker a wage of $16, equal to the marginal revenue product of labor (MRPL), which is the dollar value of the additional output the worker produces in an hour. With the 25% income tax, the worker paid a tax of $4 and kept $12. To raise the same $4 of tax with a consumption tax would require a consumption tax rate of 33%; the worker would use the $16 wage income to consume $12 and then pay $4 of consumption tax ($4/$12 = 33%). Thus, when each of the 10 workers works his 2,000th hour, he will be able to consume only $12, even though he has generated a marginal revenue product of $16.

Thus, like the income tax, the consumption tax drives a wedge ($4) between the MRPL the worker generates ($16) and the consumption he can enjoy ($12). To work the 2,000th hour, the worker requires only $12 to keep his utility constant, but he produces $16. It is wasteful that he didn't work another hour, receive $12 to hold his utility constant, and have $4 of marginal revenue product distributed to others, making them better off. The same reasoning applies for additional hours until his marginal disutility (measured in dollars) rises to equal his marginal revenue product. The area of the triangle in Figure 7.9 measures the efficiency loss from the 33% consumption tax.

But the consumption tax rate must be set above 33%, because the consumption tax must raise enough revenue to replace the revenue from not only the tax on labor income but also the tax on capital income. The tax wedge from the required consumption tax would be greater than $4, and the area of the efficiency loss triangle would be greater than shown in Figure 7.9 for the 25% labor income tax.

Thus, replacing the income tax with a consumption tax would eliminate the efficiency loss in the choice between saving and consuming but would increase the efficiency loss in the choice between leisure and work.[5]

Impact on the Distribution of the Tax Burden

A switch from the current progressive income tax to either a retail sales tax or a value-added tax that raises the same total tax revenue would cause a redistribution of the tax burden away from high-income households. The reason is straightforward. In a given

---

[5] Recall, however, the novel argument noted at the end of the section, "A Household Consumption Tax," in which very high consumption by the affluent generates a negative externality that cascades down the social strata. If this argument is accepted, then a tax on very high consumption might actually increase efficiency by internalizing an externality.

TABLE 9.4 Effective Federal Tax Rates, 2005

Income Category	Average Income		Effective Tax Rate (Percent)				
	Pretax	After-Tax	All Federal Taxes	Individual Income Taxes	Social Insurance Taxes	Corporate Income Taxes	Excise Taxes
Lowest quintile	15,900	15,300	4.3	−6.5	8.3	0.4	2.1
Second quintile	37,400	33,700	9.9	−1.0	9.2	0.5	1.3
Middle quintile	58,500	50,200	14.2	3.0	9.5	0.7	1.0
Fourth quintile	85,200	70,300	17.4	6.0	9.7	1.0	0.8
Highest quintile	231,300	172,200	25.5	14.1	6.0	4.9	0.5
All quintiles	84,800	67,400	20.5	9.0	7.6	3.1	0.8
Top 10%	339,100	246,300	27.4	16.0	4.8	6.1	0.4
Top 5%	520,200	369,800	28.9	17.6	3.5	7.4	0.3
Top 1%	1,558,500	1,071,500	31.2	19.4	1.7	9.9	0.2

Source: Congressional Budget Office.

year as we move from low- to high-income households, the ratio of consumption to income falls, because the affluent save a greater percentage of their income. Thus, either a RST or a VAT is regressive—the tax burden as a percentage of income falls as we move from low- to high-income households. By contrast, with the progressive income tax, the tax burden as a percentage of income rises as we move from low- to high-income households.

Tables 9.4 and 9.5 present data and estimates based on tax incidence analysis from a Congressional Budget Office (CBO) study.[6] The tables provide important information on the distribution of the federal tax burden and provide a background for appreciating how the distribution of the burden would change if the income tax were replaced with either a retail sales tax or a value-added tax. In both tables, U.S. households are ranked in order from lowest income to highest income. Each quintile contains 20% of the nation's households.

To allocate the tax burden to households, the CBO makes certain assumptions about the incidence of each tax by using the kind of analysis we presented in Chapter 7:

- Individual income taxes are fully borne by the households that pay them. In terms of our analysis of tax incidence in Chapter 7, the CBO assumes that the supply of labor and the supply of saving are completely inelastic (i.e., both have vertical supply curves), so the suppliers (i.e., households) bear the whole burden. Thus, the burden is simply what each household pays—none is shifted to the demanders.
- Payroll taxes are fully borne by workers. In terms of our analysis in Chapter 7, the CBO assumes that the supply of labor is completely inelastic.
- Corporate income taxes are borne by the owners of capital. In terms of our analysis in Chapter 7, the CBO assumes the supply of saving is completely inelastic.
- Excise taxes—taxes on commodities—are fully borne by consumers. In terms of Chapter 7, the CBO assumes supply is completely elastic (a horizontal supply curve).

In Table 9.4 the left column gives the average *pretax* income in 2005 for households in each income class. For the bottom quintile, the average pretax income is $15,900; for

[6] U.S. Congressional Budget Office, *Historical Effective Federal Tax Rates: 1979–2005,* December 2007.

TABLE 9.5   **Shares of Federal Tax Liabilities, 2005**

| Income Category | Share of Income | | Share of Tax Liabilities | | | | |
	Pretax	After-Tax	All Federal Taxes	Individual Income Taxes	Social Insurance Taxes	Corporate Income Taxes	Excise Taxes
Lowest quintile	4.0	4.8	0.8	−2.9	4.3	0.6	11.1
Second quintile	8.5	9.6	4.1	−0.9	10.1	1.4	14.4
Middle quintile	13.3	14.4	9.3	4.4	16.7	3.0	18.1
Fourth quintile	19.8	20.6	16.9	13.1	25.1	6.2	21.9
Highest quintile	55.1	51.6	68.7	86.3	43.6	87.8	34.1
All quintiles	100.0	100.0	100.0	100.0	100.0	100.0	100.0
Top 10%	40.9	37.4	54.7	72.7	25.8	81.6	21.2
Top 5%	31.1	27.8	43.8	60.7	14.4	74.9	13.5
Top 1%	18.1	15.6	27.6	38.8	4.0	58.6	5.5

Source: Congressional Budget Office.

the top quintile, the average pretax income is $231,300 (and for the top 1% the average pretax income is $1,558,500). Move one column to the right to see average *after-tax* income—average income after subtracting the burden of federal taxes. For the bottom quintile the average after-tax income is $15,300 compared to pretax income of $15,900; for the top quintile, the average after-tax income is $172,200 compared to pretax income of $231,300 (and for the top 1%, the average after-tax income is $1,071,500 compared to pretax income of $1,558,500).

The rest of Table 9.4 gives the **effective tax rate**—the tax burden that the household bears as a percentage of its income. For all federal taxes the effective tax rate *rises* from 4.3% for the bottom quintile to 25.5% for the top quintile and to 31.2% for the top 1%; thus, the federal tax system is progressive. For individual income taxes, the effective tax rate *rises* from −6.5% for the bottom quintile (because many low-income people, instead of paying income tax, receive the Earned Income Tax Credit by filing their income tax return) to 14.1% for the top quintile and to 19.4% for the top 1%; thus, the federal individual income tax is highly progressive. For corporate income taxes, the effective rate *rises* from 0.4% for the bottom quintile to 4.9% for the top quintile and to 9.9% for the top 1%; thus, the federal corporate income tax is highly progressive.

By contrast, for social insurance payroll taxes, the effective tax rate is 8.3% for the bottom quintile but 6.0% for the top quintile and only 1.7% for the top 1%; thus, the social insurance payroll tax is regressive. Similarly, for excise taxes, the effective tax rate *falls* from 2.1% for the bottom quintile to 0.5% for the top quintile and to 0.2% for the top 1%; thus, federal excise taxes are regressive.

In Table 9.5, look at the left column—Share of Income, Pretax. The bottom 20% of households receive 4.0% of the nation's pretax income, the top 20% of households receive 55.1% of the nation's pretax income, and the top 1% of households receive 18.1% of the nation's pretax income. Move one column to the right—Share of Income, After-Tax—the share of income after subtracting the burden from federal taxes. The top 20% of households receive 51.6% of the nation's after-tax income (compared to 55.1% of the nation's pretax income). A comparison of these two columns—the shares of the nation's pretax and after-tax income—for all income classes shows that the federal tax system makes the distribution of the nation's after-tax income less unequal than the distribution of the nation's pretax income.

The rest of Table 9.5 shows the distribution of federal tax burdens across income classes. For all federal taxes, the bottom 20% of households bear 0.8% of the nation's federal tax burden, while the top 20% of households bear 68.7% of the nation's federal tax burden (and the top 1% bears 27.6% of the federal tax burden). The top 20% of households bear 86.3% of the federal individual income tax burden, 43.6% of the federal social insurance payroll tax burden, 87.8% of the federal corporate income tax burden, and 34.1% of the federal excise tax burden (the top 1% bears 38.8% of the federal individual income tax burden, 4.0% of the federal social insurance payroll tax burden, 58.6% of the federal corporate income tax burden, and 5.5% of the federal excise tax burden).

Tables 9.4 and 9.5 imply that replacing the income tax with a retail sales tax, value-added tax, or flat tax would shift the distribution of the tax burden away from high-income households. The reason is simply that the federal income tax is a *highly* progressive component of the current federal tax system. As shown in Table 8.4, graduated income tax rates rise from 10% to 35% on labor and interest income (the income tax would be even more progressive if these rates also applied to dividends and capital gains, which currently have a 15% maximum rate).

As discussed earlier, it is true that the burden of the retail sales or value-added tax on low-income households can be substantially reduced or even eliminated by an adequate cash rebate. It is also true that the burden of the flat tax on low-income households is substantially reduced or even eliminated by the exemption of the first $25,000 of wage income from tax. However, these three taxes are inevitably less progressive on high-income households because they all have a single tax rate rather than rising tax rates.

Consequently, citizens who believe that too large a share of the tax burden is currently born by high-income households would like the redistribution that results from replacing the income tax with a RST, VAT, or flat tax. Conversely, citizens who believe the share of the tax burden currently born by high-income households is appropriate would not like the redistribution that results from replacing the income tax with a RST, VAT, or flat tax.

By contrast, replacing the progressive income tax by a *household* consumption tax with sufficiently graduated rates (instead of by a RST, VAT, or flat tax) could avoid a redistribution of the tax burden. The household consumption tax rates would have to be more graduated than the income tax rates to offset the fact that the ratio of consumption to income falls as we move from low- to high-income households. This is the only consumption tax that could be made as progressive as the current income tax. Replacing the income tax with an equally progressive household consumption tax could increase national saving without redistributing the tax burden away from affluent households.

A CONSUMPTION TAX VERSUS A LABOR INCOME TAX

It is sometimes asserted that a consumption tax is equivalent to a labor income tax (wage tax), but the claim of equivalence is incorrect. Although in some respects the two taxes are similar, in other respects they are different.

Similarities

An income tax—due to its taxing of capital income—reduces the reward to saving. By contrast, neither a labor income tax nor a consumption tax reduces the reward to saving. A numerical example illustrates this point.

Suppose you are considering devoting $1,000 of your gross (before-tax) labor income to saving for retirement. Assume the interest rate is 4% and there is no inflation. If there

TABLE 9.6
Saving under Three Different Taxes

	Initial Deposit	Interest Earned	Taxes Paid on Withdrawal	Retirement Consumption
Y tax (saving)	$ 850	$34	$ 5.10	$878.90
C tax (regular IRA)	1,000	40	156.00	884.00
W tax (Roth IRA)	850	34	0.00	884.00

were no tax, you would save $1,000 and earn $40 in interest—a 4% return—and consume $1,040 in retirement. Hence, with no tax, your reward for saving would be 4%.

Assume you are currently in a 15% income tax bracket and will remain in that tax bracket after retirement. If you want to consume rather than save, you must pay a tax of $150 so that you can consume $850. But if you save, you forgo consuming $850 this year in order to consume more than $850 in the future.

Row 1 in Table 9.6 shows what happens with ordinary saving under an income tax (Y tax). On your $1,000 of wage income you must pay $150 in tax, so you deposit $850 in your saving account; it earns $34 of interest on which you pay $5.10 in tax, so you consume $878.90 in retirement. Note that $878.90/$850 = 1.034, so your after-tax return is 3.4% (which is 85% of 4%). This income tax reduces your reward for saving from 4% to 3.4%.

Row 2 in the table shows what happens under a consumption tax (C tax), which is also the treatment that occurs under the current income tax with a regular IRA or 401(k) plan where tax is deferred until withdrawal.[7] On your $1,000 of wage income you pay no tax, so you deposit $1,000 and it earns $40; but you must pay a 15% tax on the entire withdrawal, leaving $884 for retirement consumption. Note that $884/$850 = 1.04, so your after-tax return is 4%, the same as if there were no tax. A consumption tax does not reduce your reward for saving—it stays at 4%.

Row 3 in the table shows what happens with a labor income (wage) tax, which is also the treatment that occurs under the current income tax with a Roth IRA where there is no deduction in the year of saving but then there is no further tax (because capital income earned is exempt from tax and there is no tax on withdrawal). On your $1,000 you must pay $150 in tax, so you deposit $850 in your saving account, it earns $34 of interest on which you pay no tax, and you consume $884 in retirement. Note that $884/$850 = 1.04, so your after-tax return is 4%, the same as if there were no tax. A labor income tax does not reduce your reward for saving—it stays 4%.

Thus, the C tax (regular IRA) and the W tax (Roth IRA) result in the same retirement consumption ($884), which is greater than retirement consumption under regular saving ($878.90). Under both the C tax and the W tax (both IRAs), the after-tax rate of return is 4%—the same as if there were no tax—whereas with ordinary saving under the current income tax with a tax rate of 15%, the after-tax rate of return is 85% of 4%, or 3.4%.

The equality of the reward for saving under the C tax and the W tax depends on you remaining in the same tax bracket in retirement (in this example, 15%). If your tax bracket will be lower in retirement, then the C tax will give you more retirement consumption than a W tax, because with a C tax taxation is deferred until retirement. If your tax bracket will be greater in retirement, then a W tax (Roth IRA) will give you more retirement consumption than a C tax (regular IRA), because with a Roth IRA there is no taxation in retirement.

---

[7] The regular IRA deferral is implemented on the 1040 as one of the adjustments (i.e., subtractions) from gross income to obtain adjusted gross income. Note that only middle-income households benefit from the regular IRA deduction: High-income households are excluded, and low-income households that owe no income tax have no benefit.

Differences

There are two important differences between a consumption tax and a labor income tax: (1) fairness and (2) capital accumulation. Let's consider each difference in turn.

First, fairness: Consider a lazy heir who inherits a fortune, never works a day in his life, and each year spends part of his fortune, thereby enjoying extravagant consumption. Under a labor income tax, the lazy heir owes no tax. Under a consumption tax, the lazy heir owes substantial tax each year. More generally, under a consumption tax, any household enjoying high consumption owes a high tax. Under a labor income tax, a household can enjoy high consumption yet owe no tax if it finances its consumption out of inheritance, wealth, or capital income. Most citizens would therefore regard a consumption tax as fairer than a labor income tax.

Second, capital accumulation: Under a consumption tax, a person pays tax throughout his life, including retirement. Under a labor income tax, a person pays tax only until retirement. To raise the same revenue, a labor income tax must therefore raise more revenue from a person during the work stage of life than a consumption tax does because the labor income tax will raise no revenue from the person once the person retires. A consumption tax *postpones* more of a person's lifetime tax to later in life than a labor income tax does. Under the labor income tax, the higher tax in the work stage of life reduces a worker's ability to save. With a labor income tax, therefore, a worker accumulates less capital during the work stage. Because worker saving finances investment in real capital, there will be less accumulation of capital in the economy.

WHICH TAX IS FAIREST?

Let's consider ways to think about fairness: (1) regressivity, (2) taxing what you take versus taxing what you make, and (3) the grasshopper and the ants.

Regressivity

We have seen that a consumption tax with a single rate (e.g., a retail sales tax or value-added tax) is regressive: As we move from low- to high-income households, the ratio of consumption to income falls so the ratio of tax to income falls. If a citizen regards regressivity as fair, then that citizen should regard a single-rate consumption tax as fairer than a progressive income tax. Conversely, if a citizen regards regressivity as unfair, then that citizen should judge a progressive income tax as fairer than a single-rate consumption tax.

We have also seen that this regressivity can be offset by giving each household an appropriately scaled cash rebate, so that consumption tax plus rebate is not regressive. Also, we have seen that an annual household consumption tax can use graduated rates (like the current income tax) and therefore be made progressive. Thus, a citizen who regards regressivity as unfair should realize that it is possible to offset the regressivity of a consumption tax and even to make a consumption tax progressive.

Taxing What You Take versus Taxing What You Make

A consumption tax burdens a household according to what it takes out of the economic "pie" for its own enjoyment, thereby subtracting what is left for others to consume or businesses to invest. By contrast, an income tax burdens a household according to what it "makes." According to standard economic theory, what a household earns usually reflects what it makes—its marginal product. A consumption tax advocate argues that it is fairer to tax a household according to what it enjoys rather than what it produces.

Consider a household that produces a lot but consumes a little. Such a household leaves a large share of what it produces for others to consume or businesses to invest (which in the future raises the productivity of other workers). Shouldn't such a household, asks the consumption tax advocate, be subject to a lower tax than the household that consumes as much as it produces, leaving nothing for others to consume or businesses to invest?

An income tax advocate would reply that a household's ability to pay is measured by its income, not its consumption. The household that earns a lot can afford to pay a high tax even if it consumes a little. Moreover, the household enjoys a feeling of security and peace of mind from the income that it saves. Consider two households that have the same consumption, but one has twice the income of the other; the household with twice the income enjoys the same consumption as the other but also enjoys a feeling of security.

The Grasshopper and the Ants

One of Aesop's best-known fables is "The Grasshopper and the Ants." The ants restrain their consumption of food in the summer, let the crop grow larger into the fall, and then store it for the winter. The grasshopper, on the other hand, consumes the entire crop in the summer, storing nothing for the winter (in the memorable Disney cartoon portrayal, the grasshopper sits around during the summer, playing the fiddle and singing, "O the world owes me a livin'!"). When winter comes, the grasshopper faces starvation while the ants have sufficient food.

Imagine two persons, Ant and Grasshopper, who earn the same wage in the summer. Ant consumes half his wage, saves the other half, and earns income on his saving, so he can consume more than half of his summer's wage in the winter. Grasshopper consumes his entire wage in the summer and has nothing left when winter comes.

What is the fair way to tax these two persons? They have the same opportunity: They earn the same wage and therefore have the same ability to consume and save. Shouldn't they pay the same tax? Under a labor income tax, they would pay the same tax, but under an income tax, Ant would pay more tax over the year: Ant and Grasshopper would pay the same tax in the summer because their wage is the same, but Ant would also pay a tax in the winter on his capital income from saving. Is it fair to tax Ant more than Grasshopper just because Ant makes a different choice—many would argue, a more responsible choice—about how to use his summer wage?

How would Ant and Grasshopper be treated under a consumption tax? Ant pays less tax in the summer than Grasshopper does, but Ant pays a tax in the winter while Grasshopper doesn't. Consider the numerical example in Table 9.7. Suppose Ant and Grasshopper each earn a summer wage of $1,000 and the consumption tax rate is 25%. In the summer Grasshopper consumes $800 and pays $200 in tax, while Ant consumes $400 and pays $100 in tax; Ant saves $500 which earns interest income of $250 because the interest rate r is 50%. In the winter, Ant consumes $600 and pays $150 in tax.

TABLE 9.7 **A 25% Consumption Tax on Ant and Grasshopper**

	Wage	Summer Consumption	Tax	Saving	Interest	Winter Consumption	Tax	PV of Taxes
Grasshopper	$1,000	$800	$200	$ 0	$ 0	$ 0	$ 0	$200
Ant	1,000	400	100	500	250	600	150	200

The present value of Ant's consumption taxes is $100 + ($150/1.50) = $200, the same as Grasshopper's. Thus, under a consumption tax, Ant and Grasshopper would pay the same present value of taxes over the year.

By contrast, under an income tax, Ant pays a higher present value of taxes than Grasshopper does over the year. Ant and Grasshopper pay the same income tax in the summer. Grasshopper pays no income tax in winter, but Ant pays income tax in winter on the interest income that he earns from his summer saving. Clearly Ant's present value of income taxes is higher than Grasshopper's.

Thus, a labor income tax or a consumption tax would levy the same present value of taxes on Ant and Grasshopper. By contrast, an income tax would levy a higher present value of taxes on Ant than on Grasshopper. Wouldn't Aesop think it unfair to tax Ant more than Grasshopper?

POLLUTION TAXES

As we saw in Chapter 2, pollution taxes are generally recommended by economists to reduce pollution. Recall that polluters will find it profitable to reduce pollution as long as the marginal abatement cost (i.e., the cost of reducing pollution another unit) is less than the tax. If the government sets the tax equal to the marginal damage to the environment, profit-seeking polluters will unintentionally achieve the socially optimal reduction in pollution; they will reduce pollution as long as the marginal abatement cost is less than the marginal damage. The optimal pollution tax will therefore improve society's welfare because the benefit of avoiding environmental damage will exceed the cost to the economy of reducing pollution.

A CBO study estimates that a tax of $100 per ton of carbon would reduce carbon about 15%. In the United States in 2005, about 1.70 billion tons of carbon were consumed, so a 15% cutback would have been about 0.25 billion tons and would have reduced carbon consumption to about 1.45 billion tons. A $100 per ton carbon tax would have generated pollution tax revenue equal to $100 per ton $\times$ 1.45 billion tons = $145 billion, which is about 1% of GDP (GDP was about $12,500 billion in 2005). Because federal tax revenue is about 20% of GDP, this tax would have contributed about 5% of federal tax revenue. Thus, if Congress uses a set of pollution taxes to reduce carbon emissions and other pollutants, the pollution tax revenue might be about 1% of GDP and contribute about 5% of federal revenue.

TRANSPORTATION TAXES

In theory, user fees (tolls) rather than taxes should be used to finance roads, bridges, and airports. A vehicle should be charged a toll equal to the wear and tear it imposes on a particular road plus the congestion cost it imposes on other drivers. A truck should be charged a higher toll than a car because it causes more damage to the road. The toll should be higher at peak hours than at off-peak hours, because at peak hours each vehicle imposes a higher congestion cost on other drivers. Similarly, each airplane should be charged a toll each time it uses an airport.

In practice, however, user fees are sometimes unfeasible or costly. Although highways and bridges can use tollbooths to collect tolls because entrances and exits are limited, urban streets cannot. Tollbooths require drivers to slow down and wait in line, thereby imposing a significant cost. Thus, instead of a toll, a gasoline tax has been used to collect revenue from drivers. A gasoline tax, in contrast to other taxes, focuses its burden on drivers who benefit from using roads. A gasoline tax, however, is inferior to a toll.[8] It does not vary according to the wear and tear each vehicle imposes on the road. It does not vary with the cost of maintaining one road versus another road. It does not vary according to peak versus off-peak hours. Thus, whenever possible, tolls should be used instead. Advances in technology have been making tolls more feasible and less costly. Tolls are now assessed electronically (e.g., "EZ Pass") on highways, reducing the waiting time at tollbooths. Some cities (e.g., Stockholm, Sweden) are experimenting with electronically assessing tolls on urban streets. As technology advances, the financing of transportation should be shifted from taxes to tolls.

HEALTH TAXES

Two different arguments can be given for taxing such products as tobacco and alcohol that are usually harmful to health when consumed excessively. The first is an externality argument. The second may be called an internality argument.

The externality argument is that the excessive user of the unhealthful product may impose costs on others. A smoker who contracts lung cancer or an alcoholic who damages his liver may not pay the full cost of his medical treatment. Smokers who buy their own health insurance directly from an insurance company are often charged a higher premium because they smoke, but smokers who obtain health insurance through their employer usually are not charged (through a reduction in cash salary) more than nonsmoking employees.

Perhaps surprisingly, it is not immediately clear that a smoker imposes a net cost on others. A person who dies before age 62 from lung cancer collects no Social Security or Medicare benefits despite years of paying payroll taxes. Thus, it is possible that smoking actually reduces the costs a person imposes on others. It also depends on how harmful secondary smoke is to others. Careful quantitative analysis is required to determine whether smoking imposes a net cost on others and, if so, how much.[9]

Excessive alcohol consumption can lead to drunk driving that severely harms other people. Thus, even though alcoholics who die before age 62 collect no Social Security or Medicare benefits, drunk driving imposes a large cost on others. Once again, careful quantitative analysis is required to measure the net cost to others.[10]

The internality argument is that the excessive user of the unhealthful product may impose costs on himself that he underestimates. Of course, a rational planner with perfect knowledge, foresight, and self-discipline would not underestimate. He would even take account of the fact that becoming addicted would make quitting hard in the future. However, it seems likely that many teenagers and young adults (and perhaps even older people!) are not rational planners with perfect knowledge, foresight, and self-discipline. A tax may help a young person make decisions that are in his best long-run interest—decisions for which he will be grateful when he is older.

The practical quantitative issue is to estimate the optimal taxes for tobacco and alcohol. This requires estimating the external cost; it also requires estimating the internal cost if the internality argument is accepted. The tax can be imposed on the

---

[8] As we saw in Chapter 2, a gasoline tax may be justified as a pollution tax. If so, ideally the tax should be varied according to the pollution generated by a particular grade of gasoline.

[9] Frank Sloan, Jan Ostermann, Gabriel Picone, Christopher Conover, and Donald Taylor, *The Price of Smoking.* The MIT Press, 2004.

[10] Philip Cook, *Paying the Tab: The Costs and Benefits of Alcohol Control.* Princeton University Press, 2007.

manufacturer or the retailer. It can be imposed by the federal government and/or state governments. What should be the tax on a pack of cigarettes, a can or bottle of beer, a bottle of wine, or a bottle of liquor? Studies such as those cited in the footnotes have tried to provide estimates. We note two points here. First, tobacco and alcohol taxes have not been indexed for inflation, so Congress and legislatures must vote explicitly to raise the taxes periodically to keep up with inflation. Because the external and internal costs rise with inflation, it would seem sensible to index tobacco and alcohol taxes for inflation. Second, tobacco taxes have been raised significantly in recent years, but alcohol taxes have not; it therefore seems likely that alcohol taxes are currently below the social optimum.

Summary

The U.S. federal government does *not* levy either of the two major consumption taxes: the retail sales tax (RST) or the value-added tax (VAT). By contrast, the national governments of most other countries levy a VAT. When economists call the RST a consumption tax, they are assuming, quite plausibly, that most of the burden falls on consumers rather than on retailers. A retail sales tax is regressive: As we move from low- to high-income households (in a given year), the ratio of tax burden to income generally falls. With a VAT, part of the tax is collected at each stage of production; at each stage, value added is defined as sales minus purchases. Because economic analysis suggests that a VAT is equivalent to a RST, it follows that a VAT is regressive just like a RST. Both a RST and a VAT are neutral between domestic and foreign goods. With both a VAT and a corporate income tax, sales revenue is added and expense on materials is subtracted. To convert the corporate income tax to a VAT, these changes must be made: No subtraction is permitted for compensation to employees, interest to creditors, or depreciation of investment goods; but a subtraction is permitted for the purchase of investment goods this year.

Under a RST or a VAT, regressivity can be reduced in either of two ways: exemptions of certain necessities or (preferred by economists) cash rebates to households. Another way to reduce the regressivity of a VAT is to modify it so it becomes either the flat tax or the X tax. To obtain the flat tax, start with a VAT on firms and no income tax on households, then permit firms to deduct wage income (which is not permitted under a standard VAT), but tax households on wage income above an exemption at a single rate. The X tax is the same as the flat tax except that wage income above the exemption is taxed at graduated bracket rates (like the current U.S. income tax).

It would be possible to replace the household income tax with a household consumption tax: On the annual 1040 tax return, due April 15, the household would report its consumption instead of its income. Alternatively, it would be possible to supplement the household income tax with a progressive consumption tax on very high consumption. A household would arrive at its consumption in the past calendar year by subtraction: It would sum its cash inflows and then subtract nonconsumption cash outflows—all saving would therefore be tax deductible. Like the household income tax, the household consumption tax would have progressive rates.

Replacing the income tax with a consumption tax that raises the same revenue would have several effects. It would raise national saving because within each income class the tax burden would be reduced on high savers and increased on low savers, each person would have an incentive to save, and workers would postpone more lifetime tax until retirement, thereby increasing their ability to save. It would eliminate the efficiency loss between saving and consuming but would increase the efficiency loss between leisure and work, so the net effect on inefficiency is uncertain. If the switch is to a RST or VAT without exemptions or cash rebates, it would cause a large redistribution of the tax burden away from high-income households onto middle- and low-income households; exemptions and rebates would reduce the redistribution. If the switch is to a progressive household consumption tax, redistribution would be avoided. A consumption tax is not equivalent to a labor income tax, because a consumption tax taxes the lazy heir who never works but enjoys high consumption, while a labor income tax does not. Under a labor income tax, all tax is collected in the work stage of life, and this higher tax reduces the ability of workers to save and, hence, reduces the accumulation of capital in the economy. It can be debated which is fairer: a consumption tax or an income tax. Three ways to look at fairness were discussed: regressivity, taxing what you take versus taxing what you make, and the grasshopper and the ants.

Finally, consumption taxes on a particular category of products can be used to discourage pollution, pay for transportation infrastructure, or discourage the excessive consumption of unhealthful products like tobacco and alcohol.

Key Terms

consumption tax, *227*
retail sales tax (RST), *228*
tax-exclusive rate, *229*
tax-inclusive rate, *229*

value-added tax
  (VAT), *229*
subtraction method, *229*
credit-invoice method, *230*

turnover tax, *230*
flat tax, *232*
X tax, *232*
effective tax rate, *239*

Questions

1. Show that a 20% retail sales tax is regressive by putting numbers in the following table.

Income		Consumption		Tax		Saving	Tax / Income
$ 24,000	=	_____	+	_____	+	$ 0	_____
$120,000	=	_____	+	_____	+	$30,000	_____

2. Present a table with a numerical example (for a farmer, miller, and baker), and use it to compare a 20% value-added tax with a 20% retail sales tax.

3. Give two ways to reduce the regressivity of a RST or a VAT.

4. If the federal income tax is replaced by a federal VAT or RST that raises the same revenue, explain what happens to the distribution of the tax burden.

5. Fill in the blanks in the table below.

	Income	Tax	Consumption	Saving
		15% Income Tax		
Person C	$100,000	_____	_____	$ 0
Person S	$100,000	_____	_____	_____
Total	$200,000	_____	_____	_____
		___% Consumption Tax		
Person C	$100,000	_____	_____	$ 10,000
Person S	$100,000	_____	_____	_____
Total	$200,000	_____	_____	_____

6. Your employer pays you $1,000. The income tax rate is 20%. The interest rate is 5%. Fill in the blanks in the table below.

	Initial Deposit	Interest Earned	Taxes Paid on Withdrawal	Retirement Consumption
Y tax (saving)	$ _____	$ _____	$ _____	$ _____
C tax (regular IRA)	$ _____	$ _____	$ _____	$ _____
W tax (Roth IRA)	$ _____	$ _____	$ _____	$ _____

What conclusion should be drawn from this table?

7. If the corporate income tax is converted to a subtraction VAT:
   a. What can the firm subtract that it couldn't before?
   b. This change would encourage the firm to increase its _____.
   c. List three things the firm can no longer subtract that it could before.

8. Explain the flat tax. How does the X tax differ?

9. Explain the household consumption tax and how it can be made progressive.

10. What is the impact on efficiency loss when the income tax is replaced with a consumption tax?

11. How does a consumption tax differ from a labor income tax?

12. "Tax what you take versus tax what you make." Explain.

13. "The Grasshopper and the Ants." What is the lesson for taxes?

14. Discuss transportation taxes and health taxes.

15. Go online and search for "The Fair Tax," a proposal to replace all federal taxes with a national sales tax. What do advocates say? What do opponents say?

Chapter **Ten**

State and Local Public Finance

Photodisc

State and local governments in the United States spend and tax about half as much as the federal government. State and local spending or tax revenue is about 10% of GDP; federal spending or tax revenue is about 20% of GDP. Thus, one-third of government spending or tax revenue is state and local, and two-thirds is federal.

Figure 10.1 shows the composition of state and local government spending and revenue for 2006 and 1965. Today about 35% of state and local government spending is for education, 20% for health (including the state share of Medicaid), 15% for public order and safety, 5% for transportation, and 5% for welfare. Since 1965 there has been a big

FIGURE 10.1
(*a*) **Components
of State and
Local Revenue**
(*b*) **Components
of State and
Local Spending**

Source: Bureau of Economic
Analysis NIPA tables,
www.bea.gov: Revenues
from Table 3.3; spending
from Table 3.16.

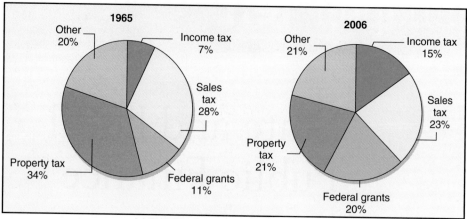

(*a*) State/local revenues (% of total revenue)

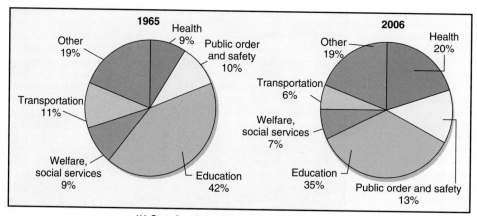

(*b*) State/local spending (% of total spending)

increase in the percentage devoted to health. Today, state and local governments together receive roughly 25% of their revenue from sales taxes, 20% from property taxes, 15% from income taxes, and 20% from federal grants. Since 1965 there has been a big increase in the percentage of revenue that comes from income taxes and from federal grants.

In Chapters 7 through 9 on taxation, we examined all the taxes used by federal, state, and local governments except the property tax. We postponed treatment of the property tax until this chapter because it is used almost exclusively by local governments. Most local governments obtain more than half their tax revenue from the property tax. The local property tax is levied on residences and businesses, and it is usually a flat percentage of the assessed property value of the residence or business. Later in this chapter, we devote a section to the analysis of the local property tax.

Federalism refers to the assignment of some government spending programs and taxes to the federal government, others to state governments, and others to local governments (towns, cities, counties, and school districts). Which level of government should do what? **Optimal federalism** refers to the particular assignment of programs and taxes to particular levels of government that best promotes the well-being of the citizenry. Political scientists have offered important reasons to explain why tasks should be divided among several levels of government rather than being concentrated in a single level of government. This chapter gives the perspective of economists on which programs and taxes should be assigned to which levels. The perspectives of both political scientists and economists should be considered in deciding what constitutes optimal federalism.

Our strategy for analyzing state and local public finance is as follows. In the first section of this chapter, we examine optimal federalism in a hypothetical society where all households have similar incomes. In order to decide which level of government should be assigned which tasks in such a society, we must understand the Tiebout process, local externalities, and scale economies. In the second section we examine optimal federalism in a more realistic society where households differ in income. It must be emphasized that in such a society the Tiebout process, local externalities, and scale economies *continue to be important*; but in addition, there is *also* a separation process that plays an important role in deciding which level of government should be assigned which programs and taxes.

OPTIMAL FEDERALISM WHEN HOUSEHOLD INCOMES ARE SIMILAR

In this section we assume unrealistically that all households throughout society have similar incomes, so that no one chooses to reside in one locality over another because of the income of its residents.

The Tiebout Process

Just as individuals differ about the mix of private goods that they prefer to consume, so they also differ about the mix of public goods. We know that one size doesn't fit all for private goods. The same is true with public goods. Even if people had the same income, some would prefer to spend more money to get a higher quality of public schools but not public parks, while other individuals would prefer the reverse. Because individuals with the same income differ in their preferences, it is better to offer them a variety of packages of public goods and taxes, rather than a uniform one size fits all.

A half-century ago, economist Charles Tiebout (pronounced *tee boo*) contended that just as firms compete to attract and retain consumers, local governments compete to attract and retain residents; this process—known as the **Tiebout process**—benefits individuals with varying preferences by offering them varying packages of public goods. Firms try to offer consumers an attractive package of quality and price. Similarly, local governments try to offer potential residents an attractive package of quality and taxes. Just as some firms try to attract consumers with particular preferences, some local governments try to attract potential residents with particular preferences. Just as some firms offer a high-quality, high-price product while others offer a low-price, low-quality product, some local governments offer a high-quality, high-tax package while others offer a low-tax, low-quality package. Tiebout contended that competition among local governments tends to satisfy the preferences of residents just as competition among firms satisfies the preferences of consumers.

This competitive process also promotes the efficient (least-cost) provision of public services of a given quality by local governments just as it does by private firms. If one local government produced a given quality of public education with unnecessarily high cost and hence high taxes, potential residents who prefer that quality would choose to live in another locality with the same school quality but lower cost and hence lower taxes. Hence, efficient localities would attract residents away from inefficient ones just as efficient firms attract consumers away from inefficient competitors.

Finally, the competitive process promotes innovation and experimentation by local governments, just as it does for private firms. Different local governments would try different mixes and types of services and taxes. Those perceived to be working would be copied by other localities, while those perceived to be failing would be discarded.

Under this process, homeowners pressure their local government to choose a desirable package of services and taxes and to provide services efficiently for two reasons. First, they consume the services and pay the taxes. Second, the better the job the local government does, the higher the home prices in the locality. This effect is called **capitalization**. Potential residents are willing to pay more for a home in a locality with a desirable service-tax mix that is provided efficiently. Thus, local homeowners have a financial stake in both monitoring their local government to ensure that it performs efficiently and in voting out officeholders who are poor managers. Such monitoring and voting should strengthen the Tiebout process.

In this description of the efficiency of the Tiebout process, it has been implicitly assumed that local residents will bear the entire burden of the local taxes that are levied to finance the local public goods, so that potential residents compare the full cost to the benefit. Just as a market competition for private goods promotes efficiency when consumers must pay a price equal to the full cost of each private good they buy, a marketlike competition for local public goods promotes efficiency when each resident must bear a tax burden equal to the full cost of each public good that she "buys."

Tax Exporting

Local government officials who are elected by local residents might be tempted to levy taxes that do not—or at least appear not to—burden local residents; that is, they may be tempted to export the tax burden to outsiders. For example, the local government might levy a tax on business firms in the community that are owned and managed by, and employ, nonresidents. The local government might levy a tax on the wages of nonresidents who work in the community or the purchases of nonresidents who shop in the community. Of course, such **tax exporting** could prove counterproductive for local residents. Discouraging businesses from locating in the community and nonresidents from working and shopping in the community could end up reducing the property value of homes in the community and reducing local job opportunities and wages for residents. Thus, local government officials might decide, after reflection, that they should not attempt significant tax exporting and should instead levy taxes that burden mainly local residents, just as the Tiebout process assumes. We discuss the possibility of tax exporting later in this chapter. Here we simply note that the Tiebout process works best when local public goods that benefit local residents are paid for by local taxes that burden local residents rather than nonresidents.

Tax Competition

A concern that has been raised about a competition among local governments is that it might result in a harmful **tax competition** to attract business firms. To attract firms and jobs, each local government might be driven to cut business taxes below other local governments, and the result might be a harmful *race to the bottom* that would eliminate local business taxes and place the entire local tax burden on residents, thereby resulting in an inadequate level of public services.

However the level of public services might still be adequate. Economic efficiency is promoted whenever those who benefit must weigh the full cost of providing the benefit. Suppose residents, not business firms, benefit from local public services. For example, think of schools. With residents bearing the entire local tax burden, they would weigh the benefit of local public services against their full cost. The level of public services that results from such a weighing might be socially optimal. A community with residents who have a strong preference for local public services would be willing to set relatively high taxes on residents to provide those services; a community whose residents have a weak preference for local public services would not. Each potential resident could then choose the community she prefers.

On the other hand, business firms do benefit from some local public services. For example, think of police and fire protection. It might indeed be harmful if firms that benefit from police and fire protection were not charged their share of the cost of providing those services.

To summarize: The Tiebout process implies that there is an advantage to letting local governments provide differing packages of public services and taxes. Through the Tiebout process, local governments engage in a marketlike competition for potential residents that benefits most households in society. Thus, if people had similar incomes, it would usually be best to let many public goods be provided by local governments, so that a variety can be offered across communities, and individuals can locate themselves in communities that best satisfy their individual preferences for particular public goods.

State Government for Local Externalities or Scale Economies

State government has a role to play when there are externalities or scale economies. Despite the Tiebout process, competition among local governments would not produce optimal outcomes in two cases: first, when there are externalities, and second, when there are economies of scale. In these cases, the state government can improve outcomes by intervening in either of two ways: first, by providing the service itself, or second, by giving a categorical matching grant to local governments.

Externalities

It is optimal to let each town government maintain neighborhood streets, but not optimal to let each town maintain its section of a major road that carries traffic through several localities. If one town fails to maintain its section, it imposes a cost on all the others. Similarly, it is optimal to let each town government maintain a small neighborhood park that is used primarily by town residents, but not optimal to expect one town to adequately maintain a large park that is used by many people who live outside the town (assuming it is unfeasible to charge user fees to the outsiders). Maintenance of a major road that carries traffic through several localities within a state should be made the responsibility of state or county government. So should maintenance of a large park or woods.

Scale Economies

Is it optimal for each local government to have its own university? No. There may be certain programs—science labs, athletic facilities, orchestras, and bands—where it is better to have a single university serving the residents of many towns. Is it optimal for each small town to have its own public hospital? No. Expensive technology would sit idle much of the time if each town's hospital were equipped to handle all kinds of medical problems. The state government or county government, not the government of a small town, should provide a large public hospital.

Categorical Matching Grants to Local Governments

A categorical matching grant may be optimal when there is a positive externality. Under a categorical matching grant, the city gets state funds only as a match for its own funds targeted for a particular service. Consider a sewage treatment plant that benefits residents of a particular locality but also residents of surrounding localities. Suppose it is estimated that for the typical sewage treatment plant the benefit to outsiders (residents of surrounding localities) equals the benefit to residents. Then the state government could establish a categorical matching grant under which the state would match, dollar for dollar, the funds raised by any locality for a sewage treatment plan. With this grant, a local government would have to bear only half the cost instead of the full cost of any treatment plant. This should induce local governments to construct a plant as long as the benefit to its own residents exceeds half the total cost. As a result, a locality would construct a plant whenever half the total cost (the locality's share) is less than the benefit to residents (which equals half the total benefit), and this is socially optimal for both residents and outsiders. Note that if it is estimated that outsiders receive twice the benefit that residents receive, then state government should provide a match of two dollars for every dollar raised by the local government. We will examine grants from higher governments to lower governments in the last section of this chapter.

OPTIMAL FEDERALISM WHEN HOUSEHOLD INCOMES DIFFER

Suppose more realistically that households in society differ in income. Most households probably want to live in a locality where most other residents have high incomes for two reasons. First, they believe that if most other residents have high incomes, neighborhoods are likely to be safe and the average educational performance of public school students will probably be above average for the society. Second, high-income residents are able to contribute substantial tax revenue to fund public services.

Conversely, most households probably prefer not to live in a locality where most residents have low incomes for two reasons. First, they believe that if most other residents have low incomes, neighborhoods may be unsafe and the average educational performance of other public school students will probably be below average for the society. Second, low-income residents are unable to contribute substantial tax revenue to fund public services.

Residential Location When Incomes Differ: The Separation Process

So what happens? Many high-income (i.e., affluent) people move away from large cities and establish suburban towns where most homes have high prices. They often get their town council to pass **zoning laws** that limit the construction of low-priced homes and rental apartments within their locality. A zoning law may require that a plot of land for a home must exceed a certain size or that the size of a home exceeds a certain square footage, or it may prohibit rental apartment buildings. Thus, this **separation process** can be summarized this way:

The affluent move away from the nonaffluent, the nonaffluent try to follow, but the affluent use zoning laws to maintain their separation.

Middle-income people who can't get into high-income suburbs establish their own suburbs and use zoning to maintain their separation from low-income people. Most low-income people remain in the cities, joined by some high- and middle-income people who prefer living near their city jobs or urban cultural attractions.

Of course, not every high-income suburbanite wants to maintain separation from all nonaffluent people. Some affluent people may feel it is wrong to try to separate from nonaffluent people and feel that their own children may benefit from experiencing some diversity in their school. Also, not every low-income household wants to live in a high- or even middle-income suburb despite the well-financed schools and other amenities.

Some low-income people may feel more comfortable living near other low-income people and having their children go to school with other low-income children.

In this chapter, we concentrate on separation motivated by differences in income. This is not to deny that some separation is motivated by differences in race, ethnicity, or religion. We focus on separation by income to illuminate the state and local public finance problems that would arise even if everyone were the same racially, ethnically, and religiously. Separation due to race, ethnicity, or religion adds further complexity. It should be emphasized that the Tiebout process still works in a society where income differs. Each high-income town competes with other high-income towns for high-income potential residents by varying the mix of public services and taxes and by trying to being efficient—producing a given quality of public services at minimum cost and, hence, minimum taxes. Similarly, middle-income towns compete for middle-income residents. Thus, the Tiebout process still generates a desirable mix of public services and taxes among towns competing for people of a particular income level.

Thus, two location processes operate simultaneously when household incomes differ in a society: *the separation process* and *the Tiebout process.*

Should a City Government Try to Tax Suburbanites?

At first glance it might seem that a city government can't tax high-income suburbanites, but it can. Many suburbanites work, shop, or get entertainment in the city. Thus, the city government can tax the wage income earned in the city by suburbanites—the tax can be withheld by businesses located in the city from employee paychecks. A city sales tax is partly borne by suburbanites who shop or get entertainment in the city. These are particular examples of *tax exporting*, where the aim is to export the tax burden to high-income suburbanites. Therefore, a city government does have the means to tax many suburbanites.

But should it? It depends on the elasticity of suburbanites' responses to city taxes. If the city levies a tax on the wage income earned in the city by suburbanites, some businesses may locate in the suburbs rather than the city, and some suburbanites may switch to jobs in the suburbs. If the city imposes a high sales tax, some suburbanites may shop in the suburbs, and some retailers may locate in the suburbs rather than the city. If the response is small—inelastic—then city residents may benefit because higher city revenue outweighs the slightly lower employment and wages, but if the response is large (i.e., elastic), then taxing suburbanites may turn out to be harmful for city residents.

Should a City Tax Economic Activity That Occurs within the City?

It is tempting for a city to use source-based taxation—to tax labor and financial capital employed in the city as well as goods purchased in the city regardless of where the workers, investors, and consumers reside. By contrast, under residence-based taxation the city would tax only workers and investors who reside in the city. Source-based taxation is appealing because it appears to be a way to extract revenue from outsiders—it appears to be a method of tax exporting. Also, it is relatively easy to collect source-based taxes: payroll, profit, and sales taxes on business firms located in the city.

However, source-based taxes can reduce the efficiency of the metropolitan economy. As we discussed, a tax on income earned in the city drives workers and businesses out of the city even if they are more productive in the city than in the suburbs. A tax on sales that occur in the city drives retailers and shoppers out of the city. Thus, it is probably more efficient to use residence-based taxation instead. Although residence-based taxation may discourage some people from living in the city, this is likely to cause less inefficiency than source-based taxes that discourage economic activity (working, investing, and shopping) in the city.

Despite the inefficiency of source-based taxation, it does succeed in shifting some of the city's tax burden to outsiders. However, it would clearly be better to achieve a redistribution of funds from outsiders to insiders without imposing significant distortions in the location of economic activity in the region.

Should a City Set a High Tax Rate on Affluent Residents?

It is tempting for low-income residents of a city to support high tax rates on affluent residents (through a progressive personal income tax or progressive residential property tax), but it may prove counterproductive. The higher the tax rate on affluent residents, the greater the number of affluent people who will move to the suburbs. Once again, the question is how elastic is this response. If the response is inelastic, then setting a high tax rate on the affluent may benefit the city's low-income residents. But if the response is elastic, then setting a high tax rate may reduce the number of affluent people sufficiently to reduce city revenue and hence public services for low-income residents.

The Role of State Government When People Separate by Income

State government has the capacity to redistribute income from high- to low-income localities because it can tax households wherever they reside within the state. This doesn't mean that the state must engage in geographic taxation where it taxes people in some geographic localities but not others. The state need only levy an income tax or a sales tax on all state residents and businesses. Under either tax, high-income people pay more dollars in tax than low-income people. The revenue raised can be channeled to low-income people throughout the state or to cities with a large population of low-income people. The mechanism is for the state to give grants to local governments according to criteria that favor low-income communities. State taxing and transferring through grants to local governments can achieve a net redistribution from high-to low-income people.

State Redistribution to Cities That Benefits High-Income Suburbanites

At first glance, it might seem that self-interested, high-income suburbanites should oppose any redistribution by state government, but this is not so. Most high-income suburbanites are affected by conditions in their city. Many work in the city. Many would like to go into the city to eat at restaurants; go to concerts, shows, and museums; attend professional sporting events; go shopping; and stroll in public parks. They have a stake in public safety in the sections of the city where they want to go and the routes to and from these city destinations.

Moreover, suburbanites benefit from the agglomeration economies that the city makes possible. **Agglomeration economies** are the gains in efficiency which come from having many firms and workers close to one another. A high density of firms within the same industry leads to lower shipping costs for the firms' inputs and outputs. A high density of firms in different industries enables a rapid transmission of a technological breakthrough in one industry to spread to another and enables efficient shopping by consumers. High density provides insurance protection against unemployment: Lose a job at one firm, and there is a good chance to find another from the many firms close by.

Suburbanites are harmed if low-income city residents can't contribute enough tax revenue to pay for adequate police and fire protection in the areas of the city where suburbanites work or want to visit (which we will call "center city"). If center city schools are underfunded, youngsters may drop out and become street criminals who prey on suburban visitors. If the city is littered with garbage because trash collection is underfunded, suburbanites won't want to visit.

Thus, it is in the self-interest of suburbanites to have the state government raise some revenue from them and transfer the revenue to cities to help fund police and fire protection, trash collection, schools, and parks in center city. But how can self-interested suburbanites ensure that these funds are used to expand center city services from which they benefit and not other services that benefit only city residents (e.g., police and fire protection in low-income city neighborhoods outside center city) or simply cutting the taxes of city residents in response?

The state government can give a categorical matching grant. Remember that under a categorical matching grant, the city receives state funds only as a match for its own funds targeted for a particular service. For example, for every dollar the city spends of its own funds for center city police and fire protection, the state might transfer a dollar to the city. The match need not be dollar for dollar; it might be two dollars for each dollar or fifty cents for each dollar.

State Redistribution That Benefits Low-Income City Residents

Low-income city residents benefit from having their state government tax high-income suburbanites through an income tax or a sales tax and having the funds transferred to their city. The state government is an instrument by which low-income city residents can extract revenue from high-income people who have moved out of the city to the suburbs.

As noted above, if the city itself tries to tax suburbanites through wage income or sales taxes, it may prove counterproductive if the response is elastic—city businesses may move to the suburbs and suburbanites may work and shop in the suburbs instead of the city. By contrast, the state government can redistribute revenue from suburbs to the city without generating this counterproductive relocation effect.

If, hypothetically, the state levied a geographic tax—taxing only suburban residents but not city residents—then high- as well as low-income city residents would benefit from the redistribution. But when the state actually levies an income or sales tax, city residents bear their share of the state tax burden in proportion to their income or consumption. Thus, it is not clear whether high-income city residents benefit more from their city's receipt of state funds than they lose from paying additional state taxes. It is almost certainly the case, however, that *low-income city residents* gain more from their city's receipt of state funds than they lose from the slight increase in the state taxes they pay.

A Strategy: Efficiency plus Redistribution

For many public finance problems, economists recommend a strategy of efficiency plus redistribution: Adopt policies that promote efficiency but compensate those who would lose from these policies by some redistribution from those who gain. Economists argue that such a strategy promotes fairness as well as efficiency and also has a chance of earning broad political support. How would this strategy apply to state and local public finance?

The strategy would call for avoiding taxes that distort behavior and cause substantial inefficiencies. It is understandable why low-income cities surrounded by affluent suburbs would be tempted to try to heavily tax businesses and suburban commuters and shoppers. However, this would be a mistake. Specifically, a city should avoid counterproductive taxes that drive away businesses and suburbanites (as workers or shoppers). In return, suburbanites should agree to politically support a reallocation to the city of a portion of the cash grants they would otherwise receive from the state—in

Case Study   Should Suburbs Help Their Central City?

In 2003, University of Pennsylvania economics professor Robert Inman provided an analysis and case study of whether Philadelphia's suburbs should help their central city, and if so, how. His study is relevant to the suburbs of most other cities as well.

In the Philadelphia metropolitan region, locally raised revenue pays for about three-fourths of local government spending, while grants from Pennsylvania pay for about one-fourth. Property taxes on residents and business firms account for more than half of local tax revenue, while income taxes account for more than a quarter. The central city of the region, Philadelphia, is the home of business firms and medical, educational, cultural, and entertainment centers that employ and serve suburbanites as well as city residents. The central city also has a large share of the region's poor people who cannot pay much in taxes but have the same needs for public services (in fact, a greater need for police protection). Consequently, tax rates must be set higher in Philadelphia than in more affluent suburbs to raise the same revenue. But these higher tax rates tend to drive affluent people and business firms out of the city, exacerbating its fiscal problem.

Faced with a large number of poor residents who need public services but can't pay much in taxes, the city levies a wage tax on the earnings of anyone who works in the city, regardless of where she resides. Some city workers take suburban jobs to escape the city's wage tax; to try to keep other workers from escaping, city businesses must raise wages; in turn

these higher business costs cause some city firms to relocate to the suburbs. As a result, employment and local tax revenue in Philadelphia decline.

In Pennsylvania, county governments are charged with providing welfare and services to poor people. Philadelphia is also a county. By contrast, the large city of Pittsburgh is part of Allegheny County, which includes the surrounding suburbs. As a result, Pittsburgh gets help from affluent suburbs in financing services for poor people; Philadelphia doesn't.

Clearly, the city of Philadelphia and its residents would benefit from a cut in its wage and business taxes *provided* that its suburbs replaced the lost revenue. How could its suburbs replace the city's revenue without a regional government? Through the state government. The state currently gives grants to Philadelphia and its suburbs. The state could reallocate some grant money from the Philadelphia suburbs to the city to replace revenue the city would lose by cutting its wage and business taxes.

The key question is whether Philadelphia's suburban residents would benefit from such a policy. Based on a quantitative econometric model of the Philadelphia region, Inman says that the answer is yes. In particular, a cut in the nonresident (i.e., commuter) wage tax would reduce the labor costs of city businesses, inducing them to expand output and employment. If the lost tax revenue is made up by suburban grants to the city implemented by the state government, then most suburbanites and city residents would benefit from the policy package.

effect, suburbanites should support a redistribution of funds from the suburbs to the city implemented by the state government. The case study described in the box above suggests that such a strategy can be "win-win," benefiting most suburbanites and city residents.

THE PROPERTY TAX

The most important source of tax revenue for local governments in the United States is the property tax; it accounts for more than half the tax revenue of most local governments.

We begin by explaining the mechanics of the property tax and how it distributes the tax burden across residents. Then we examine arguments for and criticisms of the property tax.

The Mechanics of the Property Tax

Under the property tax, the local government assigns an assessed value to each residential and business property, and the property owner annually pays a tax equal to a flat percentage of the property's assessed value. How is each property assigned an assessed value?

In theory the assessed value should equal the property's market value and should therefore be adjusted annually. In practice it is difficult to know the market value of a property that has not been sold for a long time. The best the tax agency can do is to make an estimate based on the prices of similar properties that have been sold recently. Thus, even when the local tax agency tries to assign an assessed value equal to the property's market value, there is bound to be a substantial divergence because of lack of information.

In many localities, moreover, the tax agency does not even try to make the assessed value equal to the market value. One reason is that market values generally rise in an economy that has some inflation, but properties are not reassessed very often. Another reason is that assessed values may sometimes be purposely set below market values in order to make property owners feel that they are getting a good deal from the local government. For example, if a property owner estimates that the property has a market value of $200,000 but the local tax agency assigns it an assessed value of only $100,000, the property owner may feel that she is getting a good deal and may therefore be less likely to complain of unfair treatment.

Of course, what really matters is the combination of the tax rate and the assessed value. If a local government generally assigns assessed values that are only half of market values—so that the assessment ratio (the ratio of assessed value to market value) is 50% on average in the locality—but it offsets this 50% assessment ratio by doubling the tax rate, then property owners pay just as much. Property owners should look at both the assessed value and the tax rate assigned by the local government, not just the assessed value, to decide whether they are getting a good or bad deal. In fact, property owners usually don't complain about their assessed value, which is often below market value; instead they complain about the property tax rate and the resulting tax.

The Distribution of a Residential Property Tax across Households

Assume initially that all homeowners in a locality are middle age. Suppose that, as we move from low- to high-income homeowners, property value rises at the same rate as income (so if H earns twice as much income as L, then H has twice as much property as L). Then the property tax would be proportional to income. Suppose instead that property value rises faster than income (so if H earns twice as much income as L, then H has more than twice as much property as L); then the property tax would be progressive with respect to income (H would pay more than twice as much tax as L). Conversely suppose that property value rises slower than income (so if H earns twice as much income as L, then H has less than twice as much property as L); then the property tax would be regressive with respect to income (H would pay less than twice as much tax as L).

It is important to recognize, however, that homeowners differ in age—they are in different stages of the life cycle. Consider the following typical life cycle: A young homeowner borrows to buy a home that has a property value that is high relative to the young worker's current income. As the worker advances to middle age, the worker's income rises relative to the home's value. When the worker retires, income falls and property value is high relative to the retired occupant's income.

How might stage of life cycle affect a resident's attitude toward a proposal to levy a high property tax to finance a high-quality public school system? The retired homeowner would not receive any direct benefit from the public school system (assume the children have moved away), and she has a high property value relative to current income, so if the retired homeowner considers only self-interest, she might well oppose the proposal. By contrast, the middle-age homeowner with children in the public schools is likely to support the proposal. Although a young homeowner would pay a tax that is high relative to current income, she will soon have children in the public schools, so despite the high tax, the young homeowner may support the proposal.

How might stage of life cycle affect a resident's attitude toward a proposal to switch from a property tax to an income tax that raises the same revenue from the locality? The retired homeowner and young homeowner would probably favor it because their current income is low relative to their property, while the middle-age homeowner would probably oppose it because current income is high relative to property.

Who Bears the Burden of a Residential Property Tax?

Economists have considered three different approaches to analyzing the burden of a residential property tax: traditional, benefit, and capital.

The Traditional Approach

According to the traditional approach, the property tax is a tax on a particular good—a home—and can be analyzed using a supply-demand diagram the same way we analyzed a tax on a good in Chapter 7. In the diagram, the vertical axis plots the price of a home. The suppliers are builders of new homes and owners of old homes, and the demanders are home buyers. With no tax, the price of a home is $250,000. If a property tax is levied, home buyers recognize that they will have to pay a tax annually. A tax on buyers shifts down the demand curve. The magnitude of the downward shift equals the present value of the taxes that the home buyer expects to pay while living in the home; for example, if the home buyer expects to pay $50,000 in property taxes while living in the home, then the buyer's demand curve should shift down $50,000; the price the buyer is willing to pay the builder should fall $50,000 to enable the buyer to afford $50,000 in property taxes.

As we saw in Chapter 7, the division of the burden between buyers and sellers depends on relative elasticities. In Figure 10.2(*a*), supply is steep (inelastic) and demand is flat (elastic); consequently, the $50,000 tax causes a $40,000 decrease in the price of a home from $250,000 to $210,000. In this case, $40,000 of the burden falls on home builders and owners, and only $10,000 of the burden falls on home buyers. In Figure 10.2(*b*), supply is flat (elastic) and demand is steep (inelastic); consequently, the $50,000 tax causes only a $10,000 decrease in the price of a home from $250,000 to $240,000. In this case, only $10,000 of the burden falls on home builders and owners, and $40,000 of the burden falls on home buyers.

Thus, according to the traditional approach, property taxes are partly capitalized into the price of the home—the imposition of a property tax reduces the price of a home because buyers anticipate the taxes they will have to pay, and this shifts down the demand curve for homes.

FIGURE 10.2
A Property Tax on Homes
Who bears the burden is determined by relative elasticities.

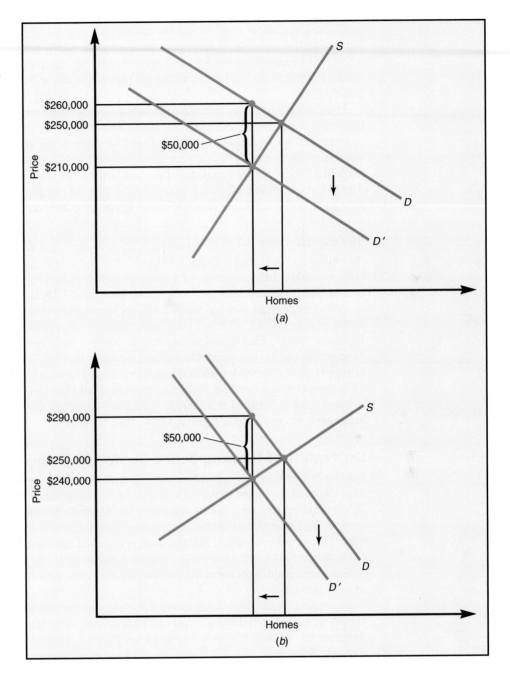

(a)

(b)

The Benefit Approach

According to the benefit approach, the traditional approach of a tax on a good ignores the benefit to home buyers from the public services that the tax finances. Suppose the tax finances public schools that home buyers' children will attend without charge. If home buyers value the benefit from a free public school as much as the tax that finances it, then the introduction of a property tax to finance a public school would leave the home buyers' demand curve unaffected. The tax alone would shift the demand curve down, but the benefit alone would shift it up. Hence, the demand curve would be unaffected, the home price would be unchanged, and home builders would bear no burden. In the example, if the home price stays at $250,000, the homeowner bears a $50,000 burden from the $50,000 property tax but receives an equal benefit from the free public schools. In effect, the tax makes the home buyer pay for the school benefit.

Thus, according to the benefit approach, property taxes are *partly capitalized* into the price of the home, but benefits of the public services that are financed by the property tax are *also partly capitalized* into the price of the home. The imposition of a property tax in itself would reduce the price of a home because buyers anticipate the taxes that they will have to pay, and this would shift down the demand curve for homes. The public services that the tax finances would raise the price of a home because buyers anticipate the benefits that they will enjoy from free public services.

The Capital Approach

According to the capital approach, individuals in the economy can accumulate capital (i.e., wealth) in different forms (e.g., savings accounts, stocks, bonds, land, buildings, homes, and other durables) and in different locations. A local property tax is a tax on accumulating capital in a particular form—a home. Individuals who view their home as an investment will channel their accumulation of capital away from forms and locations that are heavily taxed and into forms and locations that are lightly taxed. Note that as capital moves into forms and locations that are lightly taxed, the increase in supply should drive down the return earned by the owners of lightly taxed capital. Thus, property taxes end up burdening owners of all forms of capital in all locations.

Most economists think that there is some merit to each of the three approaches; some economists emphasize one approach more than the others.

Do Renters of Housing Bear a Burden from the Property Tax?

Individual homeowners are very aware of their property tax burden because of the large payment they must make each year to the tax collector of their local government. By contrast, renters who live in apartment buildings do not have to make such a payment to the tax collector. Some renters may therefore think that a local property tax imposes no burden on them. But the owners of rental apartment buildings are subject to the property tax and must make an annual payment. If the property tax on owners of apartment buildings causes the owners to raise rents, then renters would bear some of the burden.

According to the traditional approach, the property tax is a tax on a particular good—an apartment building—and can be analyzed using a supply-demand diagram the same way we analyzed a tax on a good in Chapter 7. In the diagram, the vertical axis plots the apartment rent. The suppliers are apartment owners and the demanders are renters. With no tax, the rent is $1,000 per month. If a property tax is levied, building owners recognize that they will have to pay a tax. A tax on owners shifts up the supply curve because it raises the cost to the owners. The magnitude of the upward shift equals the monthly tax per apartment. For example, if the building owners expect to pay $200 per month per apartment, then the supply curve should shift up $200.

As we saw in Chapter 7, the division of the burden between buyers and sellers depends on relative elasticities. In Figure 10.3(*a*), supply is steep (inelastic) and demand is flat (elastic); consequently, the $200 tax causes only a $50 increase in the rent. In this case, $50 of the burden falls on the renter and $150 on the building owner. In Figure 10.3(*b*), supply is flat (elastic) and demand is steep (inelastic); consequently,

FIGURE 10.3

A Property Tax on Apartment Buildings Who bears the burden is determined by relative elasticities.

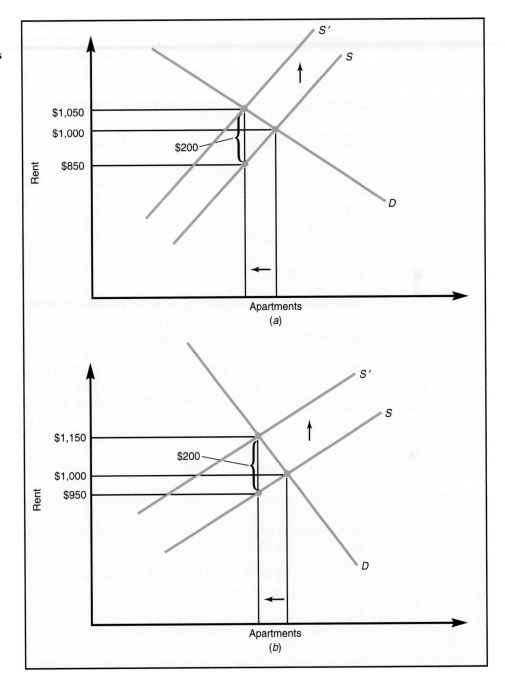

the $200 tax causes a $150 increase in the rent. In this case, $150 of the burden falls on the renter and $50 on the building owner.

However, according to the benefit approach, the renter's demand curve should also shift up by the amount of the benefit per apartment from the free public services that the renter will enjoy that are financed by the tax. If the benefit to the renter equals the tax, then in Figures 10.3(*a*) and 10.3(*b*), both supply and demand curves shift up the same amount, and the rent rises as much as the tax per apartment. Suppose the tax finances public schools that the renter's children will attend without charge. If renters value the benefit from a free public school as much as the tax that finances it, then the introduction of a property tax to finance a public school would raise the rent by the amount of the tax per apartment. The apartment owner would bear no burden. In effect, the tax makes the renter pay for the school benefit.

The Burden of a Property Tax on Land

Thus far we have assumed that the property tax falls on the value of structures—a home or an apartment building. However, the land itself on which the structure is built has property value. Prior to the building of a structure, vacant land can be sold or rented. Who bears the burden of a property tax on land? A key feature of land is that its supply is inelastic. If the land is sold, Figure 10.2(*a*) applies (*S* is steep) with land replacing homes on the *x* axis; the sellers of land bear most of the burden. If the land is rented, Figure 10.3(*a*) applies (*S* is steep) with land replacing apartments on the *x* axis; the landowners bears most of the burden.

The Burden of a Property Tax on Business Firms

As we saw in Chapter 7, it is usually important to consider the indirect (general equilibrium) effects of a tax in order to determine its burden. Suppose Tax Town levies a property tax on business firms but Free Town doesn't. The tax will reduce the after-tax return earned by firms in Tax Town, so firms will prefer to locate in Free Town, and the expansion of firms in Free Town will reduce their return. So business firms in both Tax Town and Free Town will earn a lower after-tax return, and hence business owners and investors in both towns, not just in Tax Town, will bear some burden.

As firms relocate from Tax Town to Free Town, the supply of goods and services will contract in Tax Town and expand in Free Town; the price of goods will rise in Tax Town and fall in Free Town, so consumers in Tax Town will bear some burden, but consumers in Free Town will receive some benefit. Also, firms relocating in Free Town will increase their demand for labor in Free Town, raising the wage of workers in Free Town. Firms leaving Tax Town will decrease their demand for labor in Tax Town, lowering the wage of workers in Tax Town. Thus, consumers and workers, not just business owners, are affected by a property tax on business firms.

Arguments for the Residential Property Tax for Local Governments

Several arguments can be given for having local governments rely on a flat rate residential property tax for financing local services.

First, a residential property tax doesn't discourage economic activity in the community in contrast to the following taxes: a tax on wage income earned or profits generated or sales transacted in the community. Second, it generates predictable revenue for each local budget cycle, because the total assessed value of residential property in the community is known in advance. Setting the tax rate determines the revenue; by contrast, the revenue that will be collected from an income or sales tax cannot be known in advance because income and sales are not known. Third, it is easy to administer because each resident is simply sent a bill; there is no need for the taxpayer to fill out a tax return or pay an accountant.

Fourth, the benefit a resident gets from several local public services varies directly with the value of the resident's property; when the police and fire departments protect all homes, they are protecting more value for the mansion than for the modest home, and the mansion resident would presumably pay more for protection than the modest homeowner. Fifth, property value roughly reflects ability to pay; the mansion resident generally can afford to pay more tax than the modest homeowner. Sixth, when local government uses a particular tax that is different from the tax used by the state or the federal government, it is easier for local residents to keep track ("Am I getting benefits from local services that outweigh my particular tax burden?"). The federal government uses the income and payroll tax, the state government uses sales and/or income tax, but neither uses the property tax.

Criticisms of the Residential Property Tax for Local Governments

Every tax imposes a burden, so it is not surprising that every tax has its critics. The residential property tax is no exception. What are the particular criticisms of this tax?

First, the property tax is often paid in a large sum once or twice a year (though some homeowners include a tax payment with each monthly mortgage payment, and the bank writes the large property tax check once or twice a year). By contrast, relatively small amounts of income and payroll tax are withheld from each paycheck, so the taxpayer usually does not have to write a large check to the government. Similarly, a relatively small amount of sales tax is collected at the cash register with each purchase. Of course, a household ends up paying a large sum annually for income, payroll, and sales taxes, but those payments are spread out in small amounts over the entire year rather than concentrated in a single payment. Note that it would be easy for local governments to bill homeowners quarterly or even monthly instead of annually—but few have chosen to do this.

Second, the property tax causes more of a cash-flow problem for some taxpayers than other taxes. Taxes must be paid with cash ("cash" here includes checks and credit cards). People receive income in cash and spend with cash, so a tax on income, payroll, or sales can be paid by withdrawing some of the cash from the transaction—withholding some cash from paychecks or collecting some cash at the cash register. By contrast, it is possible to own substantial property yet be short of cash. Some property owners complain that they don't have the cash to pay their tax. A homeowner cannot sell part of the home to get the cash to pay the tax. Although homeowners could borrow cash from a bank (secured by the property value of the home), borrowing usually isn't necessary to pay income or sales tax.

Third, the property tax is a substantial burden for some retirees who want to continue living in their home. Retirement causes a sharp drop in their income and cash inflow relative to the value of their property and the tax owed on it. If they can't come up with the cash, retirees may be forced to sell the home they have lived in for many years. For some of the elderly, their home is the only source of wealth, so the tax appears regressive because the tax they owe is a high percentage of either their income or total wealth. To mitigate this problem, some states have enacted **circuit breakers** which provide a refund through the state income tax to partially reimburse the taxpayer for a local property tax that is high relative to the taxpayer's income, but not all states do this.

Fourth, the property tax is based on a very rough estimate of the home's value. Because some homes are not sold for many years, the original purchase price is largely out of date as a measure of the home's current value. Some homeowners believe that their home's assessed value is too high relative to other homes. By contrast, the amount of income or payroll tax withheld is based on the actual paycheck. Similarly, the sales tax charged is based on the actual expenditure.

GRANTS FROM A HIGHER GOVERNMENT TO LOWER GOVERNMENTS

State governments give cash grants to local governments, and the federal government gives cash grants to state governments and to local governments. Grants from a higher government are an important source of revenue for lower governments; federal grants are important for state governments, and federal and state grants are important for local governments.

Purposes of Grants

There are three main rationales for grants from a higher government to lower governments:

1. The existence of a positive externality
2. Achieving a goal of the higher government
3. Redistribution

First, a program or project undertaken by one local or state government may benefit people in another locality or state—a positive externality may exist. To induce local or state governments to undertake projects with external benefits, the higher government can provide matching funds to the local or state government.

Second, a higher level of government may want a lower government to do more to achieve the higher government's goal by increasing its spending on activity X. To induce lower governments to spend more on activity X, the higher government can give grants for spending on X.

Third, the state or federal government is able to implement redistribution by taxing affluent suburbanites and transferring funds to low-income people in cities. The higher government can partly counter the effects of the separation process by which high-income people move away from low-income people. Also, the federal government can tax people in high-income states and transfer funds to people in low-income states.

Different Grants for Different Purposes

The most effective grant for increasing spending on activity X is an **open-ended categorical matching grant**. For every dollar the recipient itself spends on activity X, the higher level of government (the grantor) will add m dollars for X. *Open-ended* means there is no limit (ceiling). An open-ended categorical matching grant reduces the price faced by the recipient. For example, if m is 1, then to get a unit of X that has a price per unit of $20, the recipient puts up only $10 and the grantor puts up $10, so the price has been reduced 50% ($10/$20); if m is 3, then to get a unit of X with a price per unit of $20, the recipient puts up only $5 and the grantor puts up $15, so the price has been reduced 75% ($15/$20).[1]

By contrast, an **unconditional block grant** simply gives the recipient Z dollars to use however the recipient wants. Such a grant has only an income effect, not a price effect. When the recipient gets more income, it will spread the income among alternative spending and tax cut options including activity X, but it has no incentive to favor activity X. The unconditional block grant is a suitable instrument for redistributing

---

[1] More generally, the price reduction is $m/(1 + m)$; if $m = 1$, the price reduction is ½ (50%); if $m = 3$, the price reduction is ¾ (75%).

funds from high-income people in suburbs to low-income people in cities or from high-income states to low-income states, but it is a poor instrument for inducing an increase in spending on activity X.

A **conditional block grant** gives the recipient Z dollars to spend on activity X. If the recipient would have spent less than Z dollars on activity X without the grant, then this grant will increase what the recipient spends on X. However, suppose that the recipient would have spent more than Z dollars on X had there been no grant. Then the conditional block grant should increase spending on X by no more than an unconditional block grant. Why? Because the local government should simply cut its own funds for X by Z dollars, use the Z dollars of the grant for X, and then use the Z dollars it saves however it wants. Yet, surprisingly, some researchers have found that a conditional block grant sometimes increases spending on X more than an unconditional block grant. This has been called the **flypaper effect** because the money "sticks where it hits," and the recipient does not reallocate its own funds to other uses.

A **closed-ended categorical matching grant** has a limit. Once the ceiling is reached, there is no further matching by the grantor. If the recipient is initially below the ceiling, then this grant gives the recipient a price incentive to expand X until it reaches the ceiling. If the recipient would have reached the ceiling without the grant, then this closed-ended categorical matching grant should be no better than an unconditional grant in stimulating X—it has an income effect but no price effect. Unless there is a significant flypaper effect, the ceiling weakens the grant's impact on activity X.

For example, suppose without the grant, the recipient would have chosen 10 units of X at a price of $20 per unit, so that it would have spent $200 on X. Consider a dollar-for-dollar matching grant for X with a ceiling of $100. Then once the recipient uses 5 units and spends $100, it receives $100 from the grantor—the ceiling. For any additional units, it receives no match and must pay the full price per unit of $20. True, the grant has given the recipient $100; with this additional $100 of income, it may use a bit more of X. But it has no price incentive to do so.

So why does the grantor put a ceiling on the categorical matching grant? Because the grantor has its own budget constraint and wants to limit its own spending. But is there any way to limit its spending but still give the recipient a price incentive? The answer is by using an incremental open-ended categorical matching grant. With an **incremental matching grant**, the match begins only *after* the recipient has first spent Z dollars on the activity (the threshold); but then there is no ceiling. Thus, the grantor does not "waste" its money matching units the recipient would have bought anyway. The grantor conserves funds to get a price effect at the margin.

The incremental grant is clever, but it does have a problem. The incremental grant would work perfectly if the grantor knew how much each recipient would have bought without the grant and sets each recipient's threshold accordingly. But the grantor can't be sure how many units the recipient would have bought anyway. If the grantor accidentally sets the threshold higher than the recipient would have spent on its own, then the recipient may not respond at all to the grant. Thus, the lower the threshold is set, the more likely the recipient will respond, but the more funds the grantor will waste matching units that would have been bought anyway. Furthermore, no matter what criterion is used to set the threshold, some recipients will complain that it favors other recipients. Thus, devising a criterion for setting the threshold is a challenge facing the designer of an incremental grant.

Another purpose of a grant formula could be to equalize **fiscal capacity**, the ability of a community to finance public services. Consider two communities—H (high income) and L (low income). If they make the same **tax effort** by setting the same tax rate on income or property, H will raise more revenue per resident than L. A grant formula could target more dollars to L and less to H, so that if L sets the same tax rate as H, it will achieve the same revenue (tax plus grant) per resident as H does.

Summary

State and local governments spend and tax roughly half as much as the federal government (10% of GDP versus 20% of GDP). Education constitutes about 35% of state and local spending. In contrast to the federal government, the sales tax is an important revenue source for state government, the property tax for local government.

If household incomes were similar, there is an advantage to letting local governments provide differing packages of public services and taxes. Through the Tiebout process, local governments engage in a marketlike competition for potential residents that benefits most households in society. There would still be a role for state government in public services that involve externalities or economies of scale.

Household incomes differ, and most households probably want to live in a locality where most other residents have high incomes. Although the Tiebout process continues to work, there is also a separation process where the affluent move away from the nonaffluent, the nonaffluent try to follow, but the affluent use zoning to maintain their separation. The separation process and the Tiebout process operate simultaneously. If low-income cities try to tax affluent suburbanites, affluent residents, or business firms, it may drive them away and prove counterproductive for low-income city residents. An alternative strategy is to have the state government levy taxes and use grants to redistribute income from affluent suburbs to low-income cities. This strategy is analyzed in a case study of the city of Philadelphia.

The most important tax for local governments is the property tax which is levied on residences and business firms. Economists have considered three different approaches to analyzing the burden of a residential property tax: traditional, benefit, and capital. According to the traditional approach, a property tax is a tax on a good—a home—and the division of the burden depends on the relative elasticities of the supply and demand for homes. The benefit approach points out that people benefit from the public services financed by the property tax; this leads to the conclusion that home buyers bear the burden of paying for the public service from which they benefit. According to the capital approach, homes are just one form in which people accumulate wealth; hence, a property tax causes investors to divert their saving away from homes and into other forms of capital, thereby driving down the return to all forms of capital.

There are arguments for and against the residential property tax. Advocates note that it doesn't discourage economic activity in the community in contrast to other taxes; it generates predictable revenue; it is easy to administer and comply with; and it is a fair tax in that it roughly reflects ability to pay and the benefit derived from public services. Critics note that the property tax causes more of a cash-flow problem for some taxpayers than other taxes do; that it causes a substantial burden for some retirees; and that assessed values are poor measures of market values of homes and hence are an unfair basis for levying a tax.

There are three main purposes for grants from a higher government to lower governments: the existence of a positive externality, achieving a goal of the higher government, and redistribution. A matching grant provides more stimulus for activity X than a block grant because it has a price as well as an income effect.

Key Terms			
	federalism, *252*	source-based	unconditional block
	optimal federalism, *252*	taxation, *257*	grant, *268*
	Tiebout process, *253*	residence-based	conditional block
	capitalization, *254*	taxation, *257*	grant, *269*
	tax exporting, *254*	agglomeration	flypaper effect, *269*
	tax competition, *254*	economies, *258*	closed-ended categorical
	categorical matching	assessed value, *261*	matching grant, *269*
	grant, *255*	assessment ratio, *261*	incremental matching
	zoning laws, *256*	circuit breakers, *267*	grant, *269*
	separation	open-ended categorical	fiscal capacity, *269*
	process, *256*	matching grant, *268*	tax effort, *269*

Questions

1. If all households had the same income, why would economists recommend that each local government, rather than the state government, provide most public services?

2. Economists agree that it would be better to have some public services provided by a higher level of government. Give two examples.

3. Because households differ significantly in income, there is a separation process that influences where people live. Explain.

4. How can a city government tax suburban households? Why might it be counterproductive for a city to do this?

5. Why might it be counterproductive for low-income city residents to get the city government to levy high taxes on affluent city residents and businesses?

6. An alternative strategy for low-income city residents is to use a higher level of government. Explain.

7. Give two reasons why retired homeowners might object to the local property tax.

8. Use a diagram to explain the traditional approach about who bears the burden of a property tax.

9. How does the benefit approach modify this analysis?

10. Explain the capital approach to the burden of a property tax.

11. Do renters bear a burden from the property tax? Explain using a diagram.

12. Give several criticisms of a residential property tax.

13. Give a practical defense of the property tax.

14. What kind of grant is most effective for increasing the recipient's spending on activity X?

15. Go online to read about controversy over the property tax in a city near you. Give both sides of the argument, and explain the debate.

Appendix

State and Local Public Finance

Figure 10A.1 shows the effect of an open-ended matching grant (a matching grant with no ceiling or limit) from the state government to a local community for activity X and compares it to the effect of an equal unconditional block grant or a conditional block grant for activity X.

Assume a unit of X has a price of $20. Suppose the local community has an income of $2,000. If it spends its entire income on X, it can buy 100 units. The slope of the community's budget line is –$20. The budget line is *AB*. The community, like an individual, is assumed to have indifference curves for combinations of X and spending Y on other goods (review the appendix to Chapter 1 that introduces the indifference-curve/budget-line diagram). Without the matching grant, the community chooses point *O* and buys 20 units of X.

Suppose the state offers a dollar-for-dollar matching grant for activity X, so *m* is 1, and the price of X is reduced 50% from $20 to $10 (to get a unit of X, now the local community only has to put up $10, and the state puts up the other $10 to make $20). With the matching grant, the community's budget line rotates and gets flatter (its slope is –$10), so that it hits the *x* axis at 200; the new budget line is *AC*. Clearly, the price reduction will cause the community to choose a larger quantity of X—for example, as shown in the diagram, the community chooses point *M* ("matching"), raising X from 20 to 30 (in this example, the 50% reduction in price induces the community to increase its quantity of X by 50% from 20 to 30 units). The total matching grant from the state is $300 ($10 × 30).

Suppose instead that the state gave the community a $300 grant that the community could use for any purpose. This unconditional block grant of $300 would shift up the

FIGURE 10A.1
An Open-Ended Matching Grant
An open-ended matching grant induces the largest increase in activity X.

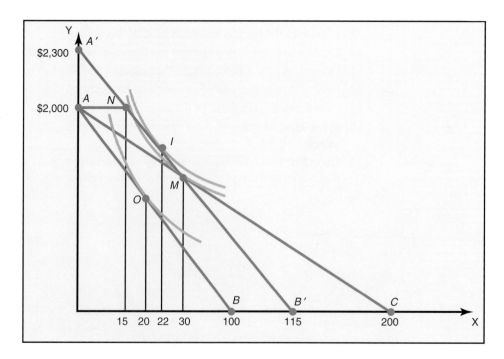

community's budget line $300 (so it hits the vertical axis at $2,300) while leaving its slope –$20; equivalently, it would shift the community's budget line to the right by 15 units of X ($300/$20 = 15), so the new budget line would be $A'B'$ and the community would choose point I ("income"). Clearly, the increase in X chosen by the community would be smaller with the $300 unconditional grant than with the $300 matching grant—to illustrate, the diagram shows an increase of just 2 units to 22. Suppose instead that the state gave the community a $300 grant that must be spent on X (a conditional block grant for X). The community would be able to buy 15 units of X without reducing its spending on other goods below $2,000. But thereafter, each additional unit of X would require it to spend $20 less on other goods. Thus, the community's budget "line" would be ANB'. As the diagram shows, the community should choose an X of 22, exactly as it would under the $300 unconditional grant when its budget line was $A'B'$. In effect, the community should use the state grant of $300 to buy 15 units of X, which frees up $300 of its own money to be spent however it wants.

Thus an open-ended matching grant, which causes a price reduction and makes the budget line flatter, results in a larger increase in X than an equal dollar unconditional block grant or conditional block grant for X—each of which has only an income effect that moves the budget line out parallel.

Chapter **Eleven**

Education

Getty Images

This chapter is divided into three parts: coverage of what schools do, elementary and secondary education (grades K–12), and higher education (college, vocational school, and graduate education).

WHAT SCHOOLS DO

In order to analyze what role government should or should not play in schooling, it is important to recognize that schools provide a set of distinct services. Some services primarily benefit students, but some services also benefit the rest of society, providing a positive externality that may justify a subsidy. Let's consider the distinct services that schools provide.

Skills, Knowledge, and Human Capital

Most obviously, schools teach specific skills and knowledge that will raise a student's future economic productivity. Elementary schools teach reading and math, secondary schools and colleges teach various subjects with direct job relevance, and college courses often impart particular knowledge that will make a graduate more productive on the job. Economists say that students at school are accumulating **human capital**—skills and knowledge that will raise their economic productivity (just as physical capital, like machinery, raises their economic productivity). Schooling is an investment: Time is spent today not on producing goods but in accumulating skills and knowledge that will enable a higher production of goods in the future.

Work Ethic

Schools teach students how to be responsible workers. School requires students to show up on time every day and complete assignments on time. It teaches students how to receive instructions for an assignment, work at the assigned task, and turn in a completed project or how to demonstrate learning by a certain date through performance on a test. This is similar to the process employers will require.

How to Learn

Schools teach students how to learn. Students learn how to study, memorize, think analytically, and formulate questions and criticisms. When a student is faced with a new subject on the job, the skill and experience of how to learn (acquired and practiced in school) raises productivity on the job.

How to Enjoy Learning

Throughout life, learning can provide satisfaction and pleasure. A course taught by an inspiring teacher can teach students how to enjoy learning for its own sake.

Screening and Sorting

Schools screen and sort students for employers. An important function of schools is to produce a track record on each student. Schools assign students academic tasks, grade their performance, and keep a record. Consequently, this provides employers with useful information on which to base hiring decisions. Suppose instead that employers had no information on job applicants. There would be an enormous waste of time throughout the economy in hiring, trial periods on the job, initial training, and firing of workers. Schools enable students to signal their qualifications to employers through their performance and therefore provide benefits that accrue to individual students. Screening and sorting by schools greatly improve the efficient allocation of labor to employers in the economy.

Citizenship

Schools teach how our democratic system works and the role that citizens are expected to play to make it function well. It may be hoped, for example, that learning history and political science will make citizens alert to attempts of a potential dictator to seize power. The alertness of each citizen benefits other citizens.

Reducing the Number of Criminals

Schools provide skills, work ethic, and track records that enable individuals to obtain and maintain productive jobs. Schools therefore reduce the number of individuals who resort to crime. This reduction in crime benefits other citizens.

ELEMENTARY AND SECONDARY EDUCATION

Most children in the United States receive their elementary and secondary (K–12) education at local public schools that are financed by local property taxes and by grants from the state government, which raises its revenue mainly from sales and/or income taxes. However, it is useful to begin our analysis by asking the question: What would happen if the government played no role in schooling?

Private Schools without Government

We begin with the extreme case of absolutely no government role in education: no operation of any school, no financial aid for any children, no regulation of schools or the admissions process, and no requirement that parents send their children to school.

Because many parents would be willing to pay for schooling, private schools would spring up. Each school would charge a price—a "tuition"—that covers its cost. Competition among schools would keep price close to cost. Some schools would be high quality, charging high tuition to cover their high cost, while others would be low quality, charging low tuition to cover their low cost. Private schools would compete for parents by trying to provide a given quality for the lowest possible cost and tuition (equivalently, trying to maximize quality for a given cost and tuition). Each school would feel pressure to perform well or face an exit by paying consumers.

There would be substantial variation in school quality among children. Poor families would have difficulty affording even a low-tuition, low-quality school, while most affluent families would send their children to a high-tuition, high-quality school. There would also be quality variation due to variation in parental priorities about education; at any income level, some parents would buy more quality for their children than others. Some parents would buy no schooling at all for their children, preferring to spend their money on other things; their uneducated children may grow up to burden others in society by committing crimes or going on welfare.

An educational **separation process** would emerge. In selecting a school, many (but not all) parents would be interested in the socioeconomic characteristics of other children in the school. Many high-income parents would want their children to go to school mainly with other high-income children for both educational and social reasons. In response to this preference, schools trying to attract high-income children would have an incentive to try to limit admissions of low-income children. The main instruments for achieving this would be to charge high tuition, locate in high-income communities, and use an admissions process to screen applicants. If many high-income families succeeded in sending their children to mainly high-income schools, then most middle-income families would have to settle for mainly middle-income schools, leaving most low-income children to attend mainly low-income schools. The separation process would be governed by more than income. In selecting a school, some parents would also consider the race, ethnicity, and religion of other children in the school.

The school admissions process would be similar to the one currently used by colleges and private elementary and secondary schools. Children would be subject to entrance exams and rejections. There would be no guarantee that neighborhood friends would be able to attend the same school. Children with special educational needs or problems would be charged high tuition to cover their high cost, or schools would avoid admitting them. Many schools would discriminate in admissions on the basis of family income, and in response to the preference of some parents, some schools would discriminate on the basis of race, ethnicity, or religion.

Private Schools with Vouchers from Government

Now let's consider what would happen if government does not operate any public schools but does intervene in education through regulation and student financial aid.

To protect children from negligent parents and to protect others in society from the crime and welfare burden that would eventually result from uneducated children, government could require all parents to buy schooling for their children. This immediately raises the question: What about poor families who can't afford even a low-tuition school? Government could provide financial aid to poor families to enable them to afford a low-tuition school. One way to do this would be to have poor families apply for aid by submitting information on family income and assets just as colleges do currently.

Alternatively, the government could avoid requesting income and asset information by adopting a **uniform voucher plan** that gives every family with children the same dollar voucher per child—money that must be used for private school tuition. The voucher would be just large enough to enable even poor families to afford a low-tuition school. Any family would be free to add its own money to the voucher to buy higher quality from a school charging higher tuition. The voucher plan would require much more tax revenue than a financial aid program restricted to poor families.

The government would try to prohibit private schools from discriminating in admissions on the basis of race, just as it tries to prohibit private firms from discriminating by race under the Civil Rights Act of 1964. There would be the usual problems of detecting discrimination and of whether and how to apply affirmative action, but experience with the Civil Rights Act indicates that such regulation should be able to reduce racial discrimination.

With the uniform voucher plan just described, there would still be substantial variation in school quality across children according to family income. The government could reduce this variation by adopting a **variable voucher plan**. Low-income families would get a large voucher, middle-income families a middle-sized voucher, and high-income families a small voucher. To vary the voucher with family income, it could be implemented as a refundable tax credit on the annual personal income tax return.

Even with a variable voucher plan, the problems of the admissions process would remain. Children would still be subject to entrance exams and rejections; there would still be no guarantee that neighborhood friends would be able to attend the same school; and children with special educational needs or problems would be charged high tuition to cover their high cost, or schools would avoid admitting them. It would be possible for the government to try to counter these problems with regulation, but this might prove difficult in practice.

Although the theory behind vouchers has been debated by policy analysts, there have been only a few attempts to actually implement voucher plans in the United States. The voucher experiment that has probably received the most attention and generated the most controversy is the program that has been operating in Milwaukee since 1990. Low-income children are given vouchers that can be used to help pay private school tuition. The experiment has been passionately supported by voucher advocates and passionately resisted by voucher opponents. Analysts are divided on whether actual voucher experiments have been successful.[1]

Public Schools

An alternative approach for elementary and secondary education is in fact utilized in the United States and many other countries. School boards—elected by voters or

[1] Caroline Hoxby, "Does Competition among Public Schools Benefit Students and Taxpayers?" *American Economic Review* 90, December 2000, pp. 1209–38; Jesse Rothstein, "Does Competition among Public Schools Benefit Students and Taxpayers? A Comment on Hoxby (2000)," *American Economic Review* 97, no. 5 (December 2007), pp. 2026–37; Caroline Hoxby, "Competition among Public Schools: A Reply to Rothstein," *American Economic Review* 97, no. 5 (December 2007), pp. 2038–55.

appointed by elected local government office holders—operate public schools for local residents. Tuition is zero and all local residents are guaranteed admission; children are not subject to entrance exams and rejections. Most elementary schools are neighborhood schools open to all neighborhood residents, so neighborhood friends are guaranteed the opportunity to attend the same school. Financing is from taxes—partly local school district taxes and partly state taxes that are distributed by formula to local school districts. Local school districts raise most of their revenue from the property tax (which we examined in Chapter 10). States raise most of their revenue from sales and/ or income taxes. Parents can choose to send their children to a private school but must then pay the private school's tuition instead of receiving free public school education.

This system is acceptable to many high-income parents because of a residential separation process. Many high-income people seek to live in high-income suburban towns with other high-income people. These towns enact zoning laws that limit low- and middle-income housing for owners and renters and thereby limit the number of nonaffluent people who can reside in the town. Thus, the school "admission process" is governed indirectly by residential zoning laws rather than directly by schools. Once a family is able to obtain residency in a town, it has passed the admissions "test" and is guaranteed admission to local public schools. Any high-income family that moves into the high-income town knows that most other children in the public schools will come from high-income families. Middle-income families then have to settle for mainly middle-income towns, leaving low-income families in low-income cities.

Public schools in affluent towns feel substantial competitive pressure from public schools in other affluent towns and from private schools. If an affluent town's public schools do a mediocre job, some affluent residents would move to other high-income towns and many others would send their children to private schools. Teachers and administrators in affluent public schools feel pressure to do a good job to avoid the layoffs that would result if parents send their children to private schools.

By contrast, inner-city public schools that enroll low-income children feel little competitive pressure. Most low-income families are trapped in inner-city neighborhoods and are unable to afford housing in surrounding suburban towns. Moreover, low-income families cannot afford to send their children to private schools. So even if public schools do a poor job, few low-income children can exit. Teachers and administrators do not face the possibility of layoffs caused by the exit of children.

Public Schools plus a Refundable Tax Credit for Private School Tuition

Under the current public school system, it would be possible to give low-income children the same ability to escape their local public school as high-income children. This could be achieved through a refundable tax credit that partially reimburses a low- or moderate-income family for tuition expense. The credit would be highest for low-income families (for example, 90% of tuition up to $6,000 of tuition) and phased down as income rises. If the tax credit is *refundable*, its full value would be available to low-income families that owe no income tax; they would file an income tax return and after processing, receive a check for the full value of the tax credit.

With this refundable tax credit, low-income families as well as high-income families would have the option of private school. Public schools would still be favored because it would still cost a low-income family more to attend a private school than the public school (the tax credit would be less than 100%). However, the credit would make a private school affordable. Public schools in low-income neighborhoods would feel competitive pressure from private schools just as public schools do in high-income neighborhoods. To prevent a significant exodus of children to private schools, public schools would have to offer satisfactory quality.

Would the exit of some low-income children to private schools help or hurt the low-income children who remain at their public school? On the one hand, families that are motivated and informed enough to exit are more likely to have children who would have been positive role models for other students; the exit of these students may have a negative impact on the students who remain. On the other hand, the threat of exit exerts pressure on public school teachers and administrators to work harder to provide satisfactory quality to students; this pressure should have a positive impact on the students who remain.

Tuition versus Taxes

Why don't public schools charge any tuition? The answer is obvious in low-income, inner-city neighborhoods: Any significant tuition would pose a serious financial barrier for many poor families. It is less obvious why no tuition is charged in affluent suburbs. Public schools in affluent towns could raise revenue at least partly from tuition, so that less revenue would have to be raised from taxes. Of course, even affluent suburbs usually have some low-income families, so scholarships would have to be provided to enable these families to afford a significant tuition, requiring these families to submit information on income and assets. One explanation for setting zero tuition is that it avoids the need for a scholarship application process.

A more important explanation for zero tuition in affluent towns is the voting power of the parents of public school children. When schools are operated by an elected local school board or a board appointed by elected local officials, voters influence the financing. Parents with public school children would prefer zero tuition and full reliance on taxes, while voters without public school children would prefer significant public school tuition that enables lower taxes. If public school parents outnumber other voters, then the school board may well set tuition at zero.

Of course, the greater the reliance on taxes rather than tuition, the greater the political resistance of voters without public school children to raising public school quality. Imagine instead that public schools were financed completely by tuition and not at all by local taxes. Then voters without public school children would offer no resistance to raising public school quality by raising public school tuition. So public school parents face a trade-off. They benefit directly from zero tuition, but they then face greater political resistance from other voters to higher public school quality.

The Public-Private School Tuition Gap

Zero tuition drastically tilts the playing field between public and private schools. Consider a parent choosing between a zero-tuition public school and a high-tuition private school. Even if the quality of the public school is lower than the private school, the parent may choose the public school because of the huge gap in tuition.[2] The gap is made possible by the tax financing of public schools.

Economists generally oppose subsidizing one good but not others because the subsidy gives an artificial advantage to the subsidized good and distorts the choice of consumers, steering them toward the subsidized good through an artificially low price. Economists agree that a level playing field undistorted by subsidies is usually best.

Nevertheless, an argument can be made that it is socially optimal to encourage parents to send their children to the neighborhood public school rather than a private

---

[2] This point is illustrated in the appendix to this chapter, using an indifference-curve/budget-line diagram.

school. Consider the benefits for you and your child if your neighbors send their children to the neighborhood public school. Your child will be able to go to school with neighborhood friends. It will be easier to arrange after-school and weekend socializing for your child with school friends because they live nearby. You will be more likely to meet neighbors when you take your child to after-school and weekend recreation programs; the neighborhood school will promote friendships among neighbors and strengthen community bonds. You won't have to apply to a private school and submit your child to an admissions process that may end in your child's rejection from the same school that accepted his best friend. By contrast, if most of your neighbors send their children out of the neighborhood to private schools, then your child may be unhappy attending the neighborhood public school, and you may feel pressure to seek a private school.

Thus, according to this argument there is a *positive externality*. When some parents choose to send their children to the neighborhood public school, they confer a benefit on other neighborhood parents and children. Whenever one person's choice of X rather than Y benefits another person, economists say there is a positive externality and a subsidy to encourage the choice of X over Y may be warranted.

What is the socially optimal tuition gap between public and private schools? It is possible that the optimal gap is the current one: public school tuition of zero and private school tuition equal to the full cost of private schooling. It is also possible that the optimal gap is, for example, half the current gap. There are two ways for the government to halve the current tuition gap. One way would be to set public school tuition equal to half of private school tuition. The other way would be to keep public school tuition zero but have the government reimburse half the tuition at a private school through a tuition tax credit or a voucher.

The Optimal Quality of a Public School

Consider a town deciding on the quality of its public school. Higher quality requires a higher cost per child (higher salaries to attract higher-quality teachers, a higher teacher/pupil ratio, better computers and lab equipment, etc.). Whatever quality is chosen for the school will apply to all pupils. We can therefore use a diagram from Chapter 3 on public goods to examine this further.

In Figure 11.1, the marginal cost (MC) curve indicates the marginal cost of each additional unit of quality. Each unit of quality costs $600, so the MC line is horizontal at a height of $600.

Assume that there are only two families Y (young) and O (old) in the town. Each has a marginal benefit (MB) curve that indicates the maximum amount the family is willing to pay for another unit of quality. Suppose the height of the MB_Y curve is twice the height of the MB_O curve, so at any level of quality the ratio MB_Y:MB_O is 2:1; this means that for each unit of quality, family Y would be willing pay twice as much as family O. For example, at a quality of 10 units, MB_Y = $400 and MB_O = $200. The ΣMB curve indicates the *vertical sum* of the MBs of the two families. For example, at a quality of 10 units, ΣMB = $600 ($400 + $200).

The socially optimal quality, where the ΣMB curve intersects the MC curve, is 10 units. Why? Suppose quality is less than 10 units—for example, 8 units. Then it would be possible to make both families better off by raising quality. Starting from 8 units, suppose quality is raised by 1 unit and the cost is divided, so that Y pays $400 and O pays $200. From the diagram, each family's MB would be greater than its *cost-share* (its share of the cost), so both families would be better off if quality were increased from 8 to 9 units; the same would be true from 9 to 10 units.

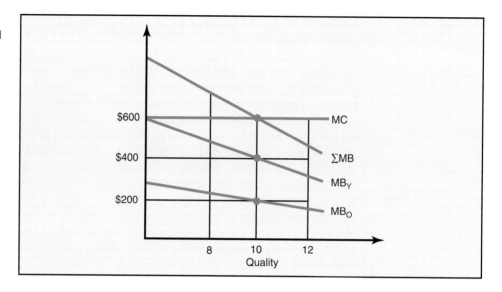

Symmetrically, suppose quality is greater than 10 units—for example 12 units. Then it would be possible to make both families better off by choosing a lower quality. How? Starting from 12 units, suppose they save the $600 cost by making quality 1 unit less and then divide the savings, so that Y saves $400 and O saves $200. From the diagram, the MB that each family gives up would be less than its cost saving, so it would be better off if quality were reduced from 12 units to 11 units; the same would be true from 11 units to 10 units.

If quality is 10 units, it would *not* be possible to make both families better off by raising or lowering quality. When it is not possible to make everyone better off by making a change from a particular situation, economists call the situation *efficient*. So 10 units is the socially optimal (i.e., efficient) quality of the public school for this town of two families.

Each family's preferred quality depends on its cost-share, or *tax price*. Suppose the local government divides the tax burden among the families in the ratio of 2:1, the same ratio as their MBs. Because the cost per unit of quality is $600, Y will be taxed $400 per unit and O will be taxed $200 per unit. With these tax prices, each family looks at its own MB curve, compares the height of its MB at each level of quality to its share of the marginal cost, and decides how much quality it would want. Note that each family's MB curve is its demand curve, because at each price that the family faces (its cost-share), the curve tells how many units of quality the family would want to "buy" (i.e., demand). With these tax prices, both families would want 10 units of quality. Up until 10 units, each family's MB exceeds its tax price, but beyond 10 units, each family's MB is less than its tax price.

Suppose that the local government divided the tax burden equally among the two families, so that each family is taxed $300 per unit of quality. Then from Figure 11.1 clearly Y would have wanted (i.e., demanded) more than 10 units, while O would have wanted less. There would have been no unanimity.

The local government cannot know with certainty the height of the MB curve of each family. Suppose that each family's tax is set at *t* percent of the property value of the family's home (so *t* is the property tax rate). Suppose that the height of every family's MB curve just happens to be proportional to its property, so if one family has twice the property of another family, its MB is twice as high. Then a property tax would induce the families to unanimously support the socially optimal quality.

However, if each family's MB is not proportional to its property, then a property tax would not induce a unanimous vote in favor of the socially optimal quality. Consider a town where a family's property usually varies directly with age, so an old family (O) usually has more property than a young family (Y). A young family has school-age children, while an old family does not, so the young family's MB is higher than the old family's (as shown in Figure 11.1, family Y's MB is twice as high as family O's MB). A property tax would impose a higher tax price on the old family (the family with the lower MB) than on the young family (the family with the higher MB). Consequently, the young family would prefer more than 10 units of quality, while the old family would prefer less than 10 units. With a property tax financing the public school, most young families would vote for high quality, while most old families would vote for low quality.

State Funding of Public Schools

The residential separation process results in high-income towns, middle-income towns, and a large low-income "town" (the inner city). If public schools were financed solely from local taxes, then high-income towns would have higher-quality public schools. For example, suppose schools are financed entirely by a local property tax, and the ratio of the total property value in the town (the **property tax base**) to the number of pupils in high-income town H is twice as great as in low-income town L. Then if both towns levy the same property tax rate, property tax revenue raised per pupil will be twice as great in H as in L. With spending per pupil twice as great in H as in L, school quality will be higher. Thus, school districts differ in their **fiscal capacity**—their property tax base per pupil. Hence, two districts that set the same tax rate will raise different amounts of revenue per pupil.

Some citizens believe that all children should have equal educational opportunity regardless of the income or property wealth in their school district. This goal has been called **income neutrality**, or **wealth neutrality**. Several court decisions have held that a state must act to reduce the disparity in spending per pupil among its school districts because a significant disparity violates either the equal protection clause of the Fourteenth Amendment to the U.S. Constitution or a similar provision of a state's constitution (e.g., the *Serrano v. Priest* decision in California in the 1970s).

If citizens want to reduce the disparity in school quality between towns H and L, they can use the state government as a vehicle to redistribute funds from high-income towns to low-income inner cities. The state can levy taxes on households and/or business firms throughout the state, thereby extracting revenue from affluent suburban (and urban) households and from corporations and other business firms. The state tax revenue can then be distributed to local public school districts by a formula that favors low-income districts.

We consider three approaches: a foundation plan, a district power equalizing plan, and a variable matching grant plan.

A Foundation Plan

A foundation plan gives each district a grant per pupil that provides a basic minimum foundation upon which the district can add its own spending. The purpose is to make sure that every district can achieve a basic minimum expenditure per pupil. The grant per pupil is usually phased down as the wealth of the district increases. A shortcoming of the foundation plan is that it doesn't provide a financial incentive for a district to increase its own effort or spending.

A District Power Equalizing Plan

Some states implement a **district power equalizing plan**, also called a **guaranteed tax base plan**. Under this plan, the state designates a target property per pupil (a target tax base) and gives a grant to any district with property per pupil less than the target. Specifically, it gives each district the difference between the tax revenue that the district actually raises and the revenue it would have raised if it had the target amount of property per pupil (the target tax base). It is as though the state brings the district's tax base up to the target (the "guaranteed" level). Note that the greater the property tax rate that the district sets, the larger its state grant, so this plan should encourage local tax effort and spending.

A Variable Matching Grant Plan

Although a variable matching grant plan has seldom been implemented, it deserves serious consideration. Under a **variable matching grant plan**, the matching rate would be highest for low-income districts and would phase down sharply as income per pupil rises. For example, the state might give $20 for every $10 a low-income district raises itself (a matching rate m of 2), $10 for every $10 a middle-income district raises ($m = 1$), and $1 for every $10 a high-income district raises ($m = 0.1$). Each school district would know its matching rate when it chooses its local school tax rate. By giving a low-income district a much higher matching rate than a high-income district, the variable matching grant program should narrow the quality gap between high- and low-income school districts.

A matching grant reduces the "price" of education to the local school district. With the grant, the low-income district can obtain $30 of education for $10, so its price is 33% ($10/$30); the middle-income district can obtain $20 of education for $10, so its price is 50% ($10/$20); and the high-income district can obtain $11 of education for $10, so its price is 91% ($10/$11). Hence, the grant program cuts the price 67% for the low-income district, 50% for the middle-income district, and 9% for the high-income district.

$$\text{District's price} = 1/(1 + m)$$

$$\text{District's price cut} = m/(1 + m)$$

For example, the low-income district's price equals $1/(1 + 2) = 33\%$, and its price cut equals $2/(1 + 2) = 67\%$. Table 11.1 shows the price and price cut for the three districts.

If the state matching rate m for the low-income district is set very high so that the price for the low-income district is set near 0%, then the low-income district is likely to choose to increase its spending a lot. Conversely, if the m for the high-income district is set very low (near zero) so that the price for the high-income district is set near 100%, then the high-income district is likely to choose to increase its spending only a little. Thus, the gap between districts in total expenditure (local plus state) per pupil—and therefore in school quality per pupil—should narrow.

TABLE 11.1
Price Cut for Three Districts

District's Income	State Matching Rate m	District's Price	District's Price Cut
Low	2.0	33%	67%
Middle	1.0	50	50
High	0.1	91	9

The variable matching grant plan has two advantages over the district power equalizing plan. First, each school district would be told its matching rate *m,* so it can easily see that it would receive *m* state dollars for each dollar that it raises itself for education. Second, the state would explicitly choose *how much* it wants to vary the matching rate as property per pupil varies across school districts; if the current degree of variation in matching rates does not reduce inequality as much as the state desires, the state could adjust its formula to explicitly increase the degree of variation of matching rates.

State versus Local Funding of Public Schools

States *on average* provide about 50% of the revenue spent by local public schools, but the state share varies widely. Local governments on average provide a bit more than 40%, and the federal government on average provides a bit less than 10%. What should make a citizen favor a high or low state percentage?

State government can redistribute funds from high- to low-income districts. A citizen who supports such redistribution should favor a high state percentage, whereas a citizen who opposes such redistribution should favor a low state percentage.

The larger the state percentage, the more likely the state will impose regulations. Local districts will probably retain greater control over the curriculum in their schools if the state percentage is low.

A state matching grant reduces the price of education to the local school district below its cost; the larger the state's matching rate, the lower the price the local school district faces. If a district's matching rate is 2, it must raise only $10 to obtain $30 of education because the state will match its $10 with $20. If there were no positive externality, this would induce the local school district to spend too much on education. If there is a positive externality—if others outside the school district benefit from the district's education spending—then a state subsidy via a matching grant is exactly what is needed to induce the district to spend optimally. Suppose many affluent suburbanites want low-income children to receive higher education spending per pupil than the low-income district could afford on its own. Then there is a positive externality, so a subsidy equal to the external benefit induces a socially optimal expansion.

Improving Public Schools

Many approaches have been taken to try to improve the performance of public schools. Here we consider two of them: paying teachers for performance and holding schools accountable for results.

Paying Teachers for Performance

Throughout most of the U.S. economy, efficiency is promoted by paying workers according to job performance and discharging workers who perform poorly. Workers are motivated to work hard and perform well when they are paid more, and they fear discharge if they slack off. Yet in some sectors of the economy, workers are paid by seniority and are protected against being discharged. Studies and common sense suggest that efficiency suffers when pay doesn't depend on performance and when workers can't be discharged for bad performance. Some workers and unions, however, understandably prefer pay by seniority and protection against discharge. Private sector employers who face intense pressure from competition and who fear that customers will switch to more efficient rivals usually insist on retaining the ability to vary pay with performance and discharge slacking workers. When employers are subject to less competitive pressure, however, they sometimes give up this ability.

One sector where this has often occurred is public schools. New teachers are given a relatively short trial period when they are subject to discharge for poor performance. After this period, they receive tenure and can no longer be discharged for mediocre or poor teaching; thereafter, their pay is usually determined by seniority. Some teachers defend tenure as a protection of "academic freedom" that enables them to hold and express views that are unpopular with the elected officials on their school board or their administrators. Some teachers defend pay by seniority rather than performance as a further protection of their academic freedom.

Some teachers say they object to pay by performance, not in theory but in practice. They point out the difficulty of measuring performance and fear that if a defective measure is used, it will distort teaching and actually harm students. For example, if students' scores on a particular standardized test are used to judge teacher performance, then teachers may spend excessive time preparing their students for this test. Teachers also worry that their performance will be judged simplistically and unfairly. They argue that what they do is much harder to judge than the production of most goods and services.

There are many other sectors of the economy where it is also hard to measure a worker's performance. Despite the difficulty, employers and supervisors make decisions about whom to promote and how much more to pay worker A than worker B. These decisions are often guided by intangible subjective judgments rather than by objective numerical measures. Obviously some judgments are incorrect and unfair, but most economists believe that throughout the economy pay for performance generally works better than pay strictly by seniority.

It follows that one priority for improving public schools might be to give less weight to seniority and more to performance and to restore the ability of administrators to discharge slacking or poor-quality teachers. Teachers judged as excellent would be paid high salaries regardless of their seniority. Wide pay differentials between outstanding and mediocre teachers would attract talented individuals to become teachers.

Local citizens who favor pay for performance would need to vote for school board members who promise to implement it. Of course local school boards might meet resistance from some teachers and teachers' unions or associations. The resistance will be harder to overcome if local teachers can correctly claim that other districts are staying with seniority. Thus there is an argument for a state to provide matching grants to school districts as a reward for tightening the link between teacher pay and performance.

Holding Schools Accountable for Results

With the signing into law of the No Child Left Behind (NCLB) Act by President George W. Bush in 2002, the federal government joined state governments in attempting to hold local public schools accountable for results by using standardized tests. NCLB requires states to devise and annually administer standardized tests to all students from grades three to eight. The state must keep track of each school's standardized test scores. Schools with students who fail to make adequate progress must permit those students to transfer to other public schools, pay for tutoring for low-income students, and replace some teachers and/or change curriculum; schools with extreme failure may even be shut down. According to one study, testing and school penalties implemented by states in the 1990s appear to have improved student achievement.[3] NCLB has

---

[3] Eric Hanushek and Margaret Raymond, "Does School Accountability Lead to Improved Student Performance?" *Journal of Policy Analysis and Management* 24, no. 2, pp. 297–327.

certainly caused many schools to make efforts to improve student performance on the annual standardized tests.

However, critics contend that the focus on standardized test scores has negative effects. They argue that too much time is spent "teaching to the tests" at the expense of learning, creative problem solving, and imaginative thinking which are harder to measure but more important to a child's long-run academic development. Defenders of NCLB reply that without standardized tests, accountability, and penalties for the school and the school board, too many students will continue to fail to learn the most important basic skills.

HIGHER EDUCATION

Most people agree that all children should attend school through high school. Once high school has been completed, many graduates are physically, mentally, and emotionally ready to take a full-time job. A hundred years ago, most graduates did start working full time at this stage. Yet today most graduates enroll in higher education instead of going to work. Is this a good thing?

The Costs and Benefits of Higher Education

Attending college is costly. There are two large costs. The first is **forgone earnings**—the wage income that the student could have earned if he were not attending college. A college student does not work at all or only works part time, so he contributes less output to the economy and earns correspondingly less income. If a high school graduate could earn $20,000 a year for the next four years but instead goes to college, his forgone earnings are $80,000. The second cost is *tuition*. Colleges incur costs (e.g., teachers' salaries and facilities, etc.) to provide education to students, and the costs are covered partly or fully by charging tuition. If tuition is $15,000 a year for four years, the total tuition cost is $60,000. The student in this example faces a cost of $35,000 per year ($20,000 forgone earnings + $15,000 tuition) or $140,000 to attend college over four years—$80,000 in forgone earnings and $60,000 in tuition. These costs are shown in Figure 11.2.

FIGURE 11.2
The Benefits and Costs of Higher Education
The financial benefit is the rise in rest-of-life earnings; the costs are tuition and forgone earnings.

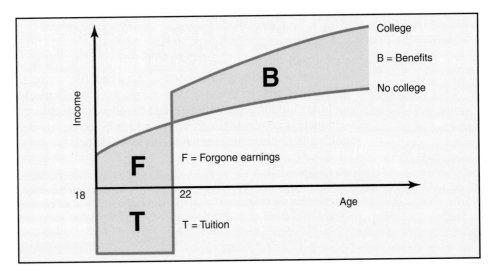

College, of course, has benefits. The first is the increase in rest-of-life earnings. A college degree will usually enable an individual to obtain a higher-paying job. The increase in earnings is shown in Figure 11.2 as the difference between the rest-of-life earnings curve with college and the earnings curve without college.

To properly compare future benefits to present costs, recall from Chapter 4 that it is necessary to take the present value (PV) of the future benefits. For example, if 10 years after graduating, you will earn $10,000 more than you otherwise would have earned because you attended college, then the present value of $10,000 ten years in the future equals $10,000/(1 + r)^{10}$ where r is the interest rate; if the interest rate is 3%, then the PV of $10,000 ten years in the future equals $7,441. Next you should sum the PV of future earnings benefits in every year you will be working. If the PV of your future earnings benefits exceeds the cost (forgone earnings plus tuition) of your four years of college, then you gain financially by attending college.[4] It's too late for this calculation to help you decide whether to go to college, but it's not too late to make this calculation to help you decide whether to go to graduate school.

The second benefit is increased rest-of-life job satisfaction—college opens the door to jobs that wouldn't be available with just a high school degree, and it should therefore raise job satisfaction. The third benefit is simply that being at a college campus for four years may be more satisfying and enjoyable than working. Do your best to put a dollar estimate on the second and third benefit. Then sum the three benefits. If the sum of all three benefits exceeds the cost of college, then you achieved a net benefit by going to college. Note that economists are well aware that college benefits go beyond higher future earnings—the first benefit—and we urge you to consider both financial and nonfinancial benefits when you decide whether to pursue higher education.

Private Colleges without Government

Suppose government played no role in higher education. Private colleges would charge tuition to cover cost, and individuals attending college would pay full tuition. Would the outcome be socially optimal?

College raises the productivity of an individual and therefore the output of the economy. However, this doesn't mean that government should help pay private college tuition or operate a college that charges tuition that is lower than cost. It is economically efficient for an individual to attend college as long as the increase in rest-of-life productivity (plus nonmonetary benefits) exceeds the cost of college. Therefore, an individual will attend college without government help as long as the increase in rest-of-life earnings (plus nonmonetary benefits) exceeds the cost of college. As long as the increase in earnings equals the increase in productivity, individuals pursuing self-interest will do what is economically efficient; they will attend college when the increase in productivity (plus nonmonetary benefits) exceeds the cost of college and won't attend when it doesn't. In an economy with competitive labor markets where employers bid for labor, earnings tend to follow productivity. At first glance, it might seem there is no reason for government to help pay private college tuition or operate a public college charging a tuition that is less than cost.

[4] We simplify by treating the four years of college as though it were a single year. Also, note that by computing the present value of your future benefits, you are taking into account the interest cost you incur if you borrow to help pay for college, so you shouldn't add your interest cost to your cost of college. Even if your family has enough funds to avoid borrowing, your family could have earned interest (forgone interest) on those funds. So there is an interest cost to attending college even if you don't borrow. Whether you borrow or not, your interest cost is taken into account when you compute the present value of your future benefits.

There would, however, be a major problem. The cost of education occurs during college, but the benefit occurs after graduation. To make the economically efficient decision, the individual must either have family funds for college or be able to borrow. Low- and even middle-income families don't have sufficient funds and must borrow. But why should this be a problem? As long as the increase in earnings really exceeds the cost (including interest) of college, the borrower will be able to repay the loan. The problem is that a lender cannot be sure that the individual's earnings will be sufficient to repay the loan. Lending to an individual who buys a college education is riskier than lending to an individual who buys a home. With a home, the lender usually requires that the home be used as *collateral* for the loan, so if the individual fails to make the agreed repayments on schedule, the lender has the right to take the home. With college, collateral may not be available. Without collateral, the lender may insist on a much higher interest rate or refuse to make the loan. Thus, low- and moderate-income individuals may be unable to get loans even though it would be economically efficient for them to attend college.

The outcome would be inequitable as well as inefficient. The collateral problem would drastically limit college attendance by low-income high school graduates, but hardly at all by high-income high school graduates. Affluent families usually have funds on hand to finance college, so they don't need to borrow. Thus, access to college would depend on family income.

Public Colleges with Tuition below Cost

One approach to the collateral problem is public colleges. In the United States, every state government operates at least one public college that charges tuition well below cost to residents, with the difference made up by state tax revenue. Tuition is generally much higher for out-of-state residents though still usually below full cost. Low tuition enables low-income high school graduates to attend college with little or no borrowing. Moreover, local governments operate two-year ("community") colleges and vocational training schools that charge tuition below cost with the difference made up by local tax revenue.

There are several shortcomings with this approach. First, it requires state taxes. Most of the tax burden falls on families that don't send their children to the state college. Moderate-income taxpayers without children at a state college help pay for the education of young people who will go on to earn a relatively high income.

Second, this approach distorts the choice of college for in-state high school seniors. Consider a family choosing between its low-tuition state college and a full-tuition private college or a public college in another state that charges high out-of-state tuition. The family may choose the state college because of the huge tuition gap even if it prefers another college.[5]

Third, it causes some economic inefficiency by inducing some high school graduates to attend college because tuition is well below full cost, even if the benefits (monetary and nonmonetary) of college are less than the full cost of college.

Student Loans and Financial Aid

Another approach to the collateral problem is government assistance in providing loans and financial aid to students.

---

[5] If a state college were content to enroll only its own residents, it would feel less pressure to operate efficiently, given its artificial advantage; however, most state colleges seek to attract out-of-state students at high tuition, and to do so, they must operate efficiently.

Case Study   College Grants on a Postcard

Susan Dynarski and Judith Scott-Clayton of Harvard's Kennedy School of Government have analyzed the complexity of the current system of college grants for students in a 2006 journal article and have proposed a simple remedy in a 2007 paper.*

They show that the current federal aid application, "Free Application for Federal Student Aid" (FAFSA), has several severe flaws. First, the application form asks a lengthy set of financial questions that is a surely a substantial hurdle for many low-income parents, and Dynarski and Scott-Clayton include the daunting pages of questions in their 2006 article. Second, awards of financial aid are not made until the spring of the student's senior year in high school, too late to help the student decide where to apply and what tuition can be afforded. Third, the complexity of the basis for awards makes it impossible for the student's parents to estimate, at the time that the student is deciding where to apply, how much aid is likely to be received.

They propose a simple remedy. The postcard below would be mailed to each high school junior and high school guidance counselor. The grant would be obtained by claiming the amount as a refundable tax credit on the household's annual income tax return. Today, many low-income households already file a tax return to claim another refundable tax credit, the Earned Income Tax Credit (EITC), which is discussed in Chapter 12. For those parents not yet filing, high school guidance counselors might provide a list of local tax preparers that would assist parents with filing a tax return and claiming the credit.

* Dynarski and Scott-Clayton, "The Cost of Complexity in Federal Student Aid: Lessons from Optimal Tax Theory and Behavioral Economics," *National Tax Journal,* 59, no. 2 (June 2006), pp. 319–56; and "College Grants on a Postcard: A Proposal for Simple and Predictable Federal Student Aid," The Hamilton Project of the Brookings Institution, Discussion Paper 2007-01, February 2007.

If Your Parents' Adjusted Gross Income Is . . .	Then Your Annual Grant Is . . .
$ 0–$14,999	$4,050
15,000– 19,999	3,700
20,000– 24,999	3,300
25,000– 29,999	3,000
30,000– 34,999	2,400
35,000– 39,999	1,600
40,000– 44,999	800
45,000– 49,999	600
50,000– 74,999	450
75,000– 99,999	300

Plus $250 for each dependent child other than the student, up to an additional $1,000.

- Grants will be adjusted for attendance status (if you attend half-time, your grant would be half the amount listed).

- If you are legally independent from your parents, your aid will be based on your (and your spouse's) income.

- You can obtain your grant by filing a federal income tax return, claiming the college tax credit, and documenting your enrollment.

Student Loans

Currently the federal government provides student loan assistance in two ways: direct loans and guaranteed loans. With direct loans, the government itself provides low-interest loans to students and often defers repayment until after graduation. With guaranteed loans, private banks make low-interest loans with the government guaranteeing repayment if the student defaults. To qualify, students must come from families with limited income and financial assets—the limits must be documented when applying for the loans.

Even low interest rates may not be enough to encourage economically efficient borrowing for higher education. Consider a student from a nonaffluent family deciding whether to incur a large debt in order to attend vocational training, college, or a graduate program. Incurring large debt is risky. Under a standard loan, the student will be obligated to make fixed monthly payments regardless of future earnings. If the investment in education pays off well and the student's income rises more than the loan repayments, the loan will have been financially beneficial. But if the investment pays off poorly and the student's income rises less than the loan repayments, borrowing for education will turn out to have been a serious financial mistake. Risk-averse individuals might hesitate to pursue more education even if the payoff, on average, would cover the loan repayments. Yet it is economically efficient for individuals to borrow to pursue more education when payoffs, on average, exceed the costs of loans.

One way to overcome this hesitation would be to offer loans with *income-related repayments;* the required repayment would vary with the income that the borrower actually earns after graduation. With this kind of loan, risk would be shifted from the student borrower to the lender. Government would be able to adjust required repayments by using income tax returns.

Financial Aid

For several decades, the federal government has given grants to students from low-income families (Pell grants or work-study grants that require some on-campus work by students); applicants must document family income and assets. For the past decade, assistance has been given to middle-class families through income tax credits (HOPE and lifetime learning tax credits) and income tax deductions for interest payments on student loans and expenses for higher education. The tax credits and deductions, however, do not help low-income families that owe little or no federal income tax.

Assistance could be extended to low-income families by using a *refundable* tax credit. In fact, it might be desirable to channel all federal financial aid through a single refundable tax credit. Like other families, low-income families would annually file a federal income tax return and claim the refundable tax credit to reimburse a portion of college tuition. For example, a low-income family that owes no income tax would receive a check from the U.S. Treasury to partially reimburse tuition expenses. The credit would be highest for low-income families and phased down as income rises. For a further discussion, see the box "College Grants on a Postcard."

Summary

Schools provide a set of distinct services. Schools impart skills, knowledge, and human capital; teach students a work ethic, how to learn, and how to enjoy learning; screen and sort students for employers; teach citizenship; and reduce the number of criminals. Benefits to others imply a positive externality which may justify a subsidy.

Most children in the United States obtain elementary and secondary education in public schools. If government played no role, private schools would compete for students; high-income students would attend high-quality, high-tuition schools, and low-income students would attend low-quality, low-tuition schools. This inequality could be reduced if government provided tuition vouchers that were higher for low-income than for high-income children. A system of private schools with variable vouchers would still have certain problems that arise from selective admissions. Public schools remove these selective admissions problems within the school district by guaranteeing admission to all residents, but high-income towns can afford higher-quality public schools than low-income inner cities. While high-income parents apply some pressure to public school teachers and administrators by their ability to send their children to private schools, low-income parents cannot exert this pressure; a refundable tax credit for private school tuition would enable parents to exert this pressure and give them a means to escape an unsatisfactory public school.

By setting zero tuition, public schools must be financed entirely by taxes. This financing benefits the parents of public school children but not other taxpayers. It also creates a large tuition gap between public and private schools that creates certain problems. The optimal quality of a public school occurs where the marginal benefit from additional quality equals the marginal cost of providing additional quality. Whether the optimal quality is chosen depends partly on the tax used to finance schools. State government is a vehicle to redistribute funds from high- to low-income school districts. There are pros and cons to raising the percentage of school financing that comes from state rather than local government. One method of improving public school quality would be to link each teacher's salary more to performance and less to seniority.

Obtaining higher education has costs and benefits. The costs are forgone earnings and tuition. The benefits are monetary and nonmonetary. Except for the affluent, obtaining higher education usually requires borrowing. In a system of private colleges charging full tuition with no government involvement, there would be a serious problem: Many individuals for whom the benefits of college exceed the costs would be unable to get a loan to attend because they cannot offer lenders collateral in case of default. Public colleges that charge tuition well below cost alleviate this problem. However, these colleges require taxes that often burden families that do not have children attending the public colleges. Government low-interest loans and financial aid also alleviate the collateral problem, but it might be possible to improve their design. Loan repayments might be adjusted according to the graduate's income, and federal financial aid might be delivered by a refundable tax credit on the federal income tax return that gives the largest help to low-income students and phases down gradually as family income rises; parents of high school juniors could be notified of the amount of the credit through a simple postcard.

Key Terms

human capital, *276*
separation process, *277*
uniform voucher plan, *278*
variable voucher plan, *278*
property tax base, *283*
fiscal capacity, *283*

income neutrality, *283*
wealth neutrality, *283*
district power
  equalizing plan, *284*
guaranteed tax
  base plan, *284*

variable matching
  grant plan, *284*
forgone earnings, *287*

Questions

1. List seven things that schools do, and give an example of each.
2. What would happen if there were private schools but no government intervention?
3. What would happen if there were private schools with vouchers from the government?
4. Discuss the residential separation process and public schools.
5. What happens with public schools plus a refundable tax credit for private school tuition?
6. Is the private-public school tuition gap socially optimal? Explain why or why not.
7. Draw a diagram that shows the socially optimal quality of a public school and explain it.
8. Describe three state plans to reduce the disparity in quality between high-income suburban and low-income inner-city schools.
9. Discuss two approaches to improving public schools. Do you think they would work?
10. Use a diagram to show the costs and financial benefits of going to college.
11. What would happen if there were private colleges but no government intervention?
12. What are the pros and cons of having public colleges that charge tuition below cost?
13. Describe the proposal for "College Grants on a Postcard." Do you think that this is a good plan?
14. Go online to find differing opinions about the No Child Left Behind Act. Express them.
15. Go online to find opinions pro and con about the Milwaukee school voucher program. Express them.

Appendix

Education

In this chapter, the following statement was made: "Zero tuition drastically tilts the playing field between public and private schools." Consider a parent choosing between a zero-tuition public school and a high-tuition private school. Even if the quality of the public school is lower than the private school, the parent may choose the public school because of the huge gap in tuition. Figure 11A.1 explains this statement using an indifference-curve/budget-line diagram (review the appendix to Chapter 1, which introduces the indifference-curve/budget-line diagram).

Suppose the parents' income is $50,000 and each unit of education quality has a price of $1,000. The parents' budget line is AC. Without public schools, the parents would select a private school with quality V—10 units of education quality—and therefore spend $10,000 on their child's tuition and $40,000 on other goods.

Now suppose the parents have the option of a public school with zero tuition that offers 9 units of education quality, so that the parents have the option of choosing point B—9 units of education quality from the free public school and $50,000 of other goods. The parents still have the option of choosing a private school with tuition—the parents can still choose point V on AC. As the diagram shows, it is quite possible that point B is on a higher indifference curve than point V. If so, then providing a public school with zero tuition will cause the parents to reduce the quality of education they choose for their child from 10 to 9 units. In effect, the parents reason: "The public school has somewhat lower quality than the private school with $10,000 tuition that we would otherwise have chosen, but zero tuition saves us so much money that we'll settle for the somewhat lower quality of the public school."

FIGURE 11A.1
The Tuition Gap
The gap may reduce the quality of education.

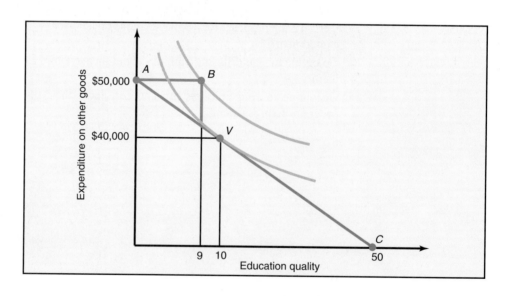

Chapter **Twelve**

Low-Income Assistance

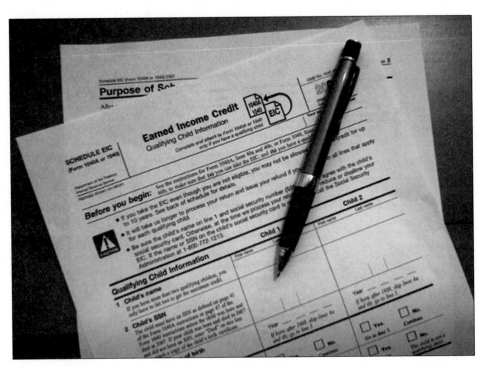

Meredith Desmond

Citizens differ in their philosophy on providing assistance to low-income people. Some prefer that assistance be provided through voluntary contributions to charities that administer the help, while others prefer having government provide assistance through direct spending or refundable tax credits; others support both methods. Some citizens support giving assistance to poor people regardless of why they are poor, but for many citizens, it matters why they are poor. Some citizens support giving cash assistance with no restrictions on how the money will be spent, but many citizens prefer assistance aimed at specific purposes.

Voluntary giving to charities is encouraged by the federal tax deduction for charitable contributions, the exemption from tax of nonprofit charitable institutions, and the estate tax. Under the charitable deduction, every hundred dollars given to charity is a hundred dollars not subject to personal income tax (provided the household takes itemized deductions rather than the standard deduction). Under the nonprofit exemption, nonprofit charitable institutions are not subject to a corporate income tax. Under the estate tax, every hundred dollars given to charity at or before death is a hundred dollars not subject to the estate tax (the estate tax applies to only the top 1%, but these wealthy individuals have a large sum that they divide between charities and heirs—the portion given to charities is not taxed, whereas the portion given to heirs is taxed).

The rest of this chapter focuses on assistance to low-income people that is provided by direct government expenditures or refundable tax credits.

FEDERAL SPENDING TO ASSIST LOW-INCOME PEOPLE

Table 12.1 shows federal spending on selected social insurance and income support programs ranked according to dollars spent. The "big three" are Social Security, Medicare, and Medicaid. Of course Social Security and Medicare provide assistance to people of all income levels, as well as to low-income people.

Programs that are targeted to assist only low-income people are called **means-tested** programs because a person's eligibility for a benefit depends on whether the person's income and/or wealth—the person's "means"—is sufficiently low. The program requires that applicants provide information about their means: either their income or assets (wealth) or both. It should be noted that the income tax is also means-tested: How much tax a person owes depends on her income; the required information is provided on a tax return. If a means-tested program is run separately from the federal income tax, the applicant must supply income and possibly asset information to the program. Alternatively, as explained later in this chapter, a means-tested program can be run through the annual income tax process for which households already supply information about their income; the program can use refundable income tax credits to deliver benefits that can vary with household income as reported on the tax return.

Table 12.1 suggests that most citizens care about why a family is poor and how money is spent to help them. Citizens are willing to spend a very large sum to provide medical care to poor people (Medicaid). They support targeting money for food (food stamps and child nutrition). They support aid to the blind and disabled, to low-income families in which someone is actually working and earning income, and to workers who have been laid off (unemployment insurance). Their support for welfare—cash benefits to low-income single mothers with children—is much less than their support for medical care and food for these same families.

Unrestricted versus Restricted Assistance

Should low-income assistance take the form of unrestricted cash, or should the assistance be restricted in some way (e.g., Medicaid, food stamps, and rental housing supplements)? Restricted assistance can be cash (e.g., a refundable tax credit to

TABLE 12.1

Federal Spending on Selected Programs in Fiscal Year 2007

Source: Congressional Budget Office, *The Budget and Economic Outlook: Fiscal Years 2008 to 2018* (January 2008), Table 3-3, pp. 56–57.

Program	Spending ($ Billions)
Social Security	$581
Medicare	436
Medicaid	191
Earned income and child tax credits	54
Aged, blind, disabled	36
Food stamps	35
Unemployment insurance	33
Welfare family support	24
Child nutrition	14
Foster care	7
State children's health insurance	6

reimburse the purchase of health insurance) or **in kind** (e.g., free medical care under Medicaid).

If each recipient is regarded as the best judge of how to maximize her family's utility or well-being, and if taxpayers care only about the recipient's utility—not how it is achieved—then it would be best to give unrestricted cash rather than restricted assistance. Recipients have different preferences and needs, and each will reach a higher utility if free to allocate her funds accordingly.

Many taxpayers, however, question whether the recipient will be the best judge of how to maximize her family's utility. There is concern that some recipients will use unrestricted cash in ways that will not maximize the utility of their children or even of themselves. Restricted assistance can be viewed as a method of educating recipients about the best way to maximize their family's well-being.

Moreover, many taxpayers care about the means that a recipient uses to pursue utility. Even if a recipient feels happier using taxpayer money in a particular way, taxpayers may have different preferences about how their money should be used. Taxpayers may be glad that their tax money helps recipients buy medical care and food for their children but not expensive entertainment or fancy clothes. In other words, there may be a **consumption externality**. When a recipient uses taxpayer money to buy medical care or food for her children, taxpayers may experience an increase in their own utility, whereas if a recipient uses taxpayer money to buy expensive entertainment or fancy clothes, taxpayers may experience a decrease in their own utility.

In the United States and many other countries, restricted assistance for low-income families is much larger than unrestricted cash assistance. This may be socially optimal if recipients are not good judges of how to maximize their family's utility, or if there are significant consumption externalities so that the utility of taxpayers is significantly affected by how their money is used by recipients.

Medicaid

By far the largest program that assists only low-income people is Medicaid, as is evident in Table 12.1. **Medicaid** provides health insurance for people with low income and low assets. Medicaid helps two groups: poor families with children and the elderly who have used up their assets paying for nursing home care. Medicaid is an *in-kind* benefit rather than a cash benefit: Instead of giving cash to people, Medicaid pays their medical bills so they get medical care for free. Note a striking fact from the table:

> *Federal spending on Medicaid ($191 billion) is eight times greater than federal spending on cash welfare for low-income single mothers with children ($24 billion).*

It should be pointed out that an important share of Medicaid recipients are elderly residents of nursing homes who were not poor while they worked but who have become poor by paying for nursing home care. Still, Medicaid goes only to people who currently have low income and low assets.

Medicaid is a joint federal-state program—the federal government pays a larger share for low-income states than for high-income states. On average Medicaid absorbs about 20% of state budgets. In each state Medicaid sets a fee schedule for paying doctors and hospitals. Medicaid pays most or all of each patient's medical bill; there is little or no patient cost sharing. To qualify for Medicaid, a family must sign up at a Medicaid office by documenting its low income and low assets (bank balance, etc.).

Medicaid is an all or none program: Either a family qualifies or it doesn't. If the family qualifies, it gets medical care for free.[1] However, if its income and assets rise above certain thresholds, the family loses its Medicaid coverage. Taking a job often means losing Medicaid eligibility, so unless the job provides health insurance or enough income to buy health insurance, Medicaid recipients may be reluctant to take the job. The solution to this problem is to make sure that people who take jobs are able to obtain and afford health insurance.

The Earned Income Tax Credit

The Earned Income Tax Credit provides about $40 billion in assistance to about 20 million low-income families that earn income by working. The **Earned Income Tax Credit (EITC)** is a *work bonus*. Unless a household actually earns labor income, it does not receive an EITC. An EITC has to be "earned" by working. Initially, the more wage income earned, the greater the EITC until a maximum is reached; then as further income is earned, the EITC is gradually phased out. The dollar amount of the EITC at each level of income depends on the number of children. For a married couple with two or more children, the EITC reaches its maximum, roughly $4,800, when income reaches about $12,000, and phases out completely when income reaches about $40,000. A household is ineligible for the EITC if its investment income exceeds about $3,000 (because this implies that it probably has about $100,000 in wealth, assuming a 3% return). All dollar amounts in the EITC are indexed to increase automatically each year with wage income in the economy.

A household receives its EITC annually by filing a federal income tax return reporting its labor earnings, investment income, and number of children. After its tax return is processed, the household receives a check from the U.S. Treasury. For example, suppose the family's EITC is $2,400; if it would otherwise owe no federal income tax, it receives a $2,400 check; if the family would otherwise owe $400 in federal income tax, it receives a $2,000 check. The EITC is called a *refundable* tax credit, because it triggers a check from the U.S. Treasury as though the household were obtaining a tax refund.

Figure 12.1 shows the fundamental difference between the EITC and welfare. Figure 12.1(*a*) shows an EITC schedule: When earnings are zero, the benefit is zero;

[1] Sometimes a very small payment by the patient is required.

FIGURE 12.1
The EITC and Welfare
If there is no work, there is no EITC but welfare is at its maximum.

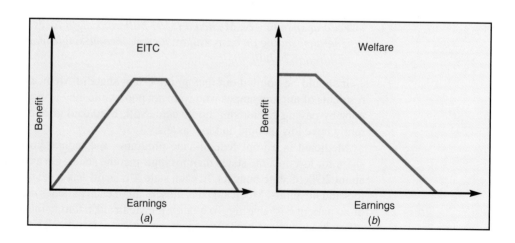

FIGURE 12.2
The EITC
For a family with
two children, the
phase-in rate is 40%,
the maximum EITC
is $4,800, and the
phase-out rate is 20%.

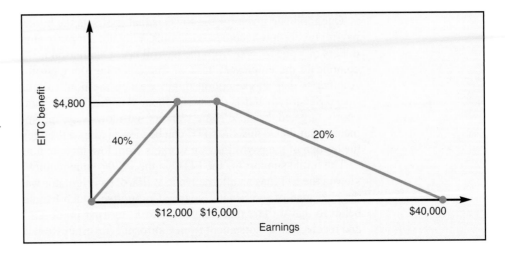

as earnings increase, the benefit increases until a maximum benefit is reached. After a brief flat range, as earnings increase, the benefit is phased out. Figure 12.1(*b*) shows a welfare schedule: When earnings are zero, the benefit is at its maximum; after a brief flat range, as earnings increase, the benefit is phased out. The EITC encourages and rewards working rather than not working; when a person who was not working goes to work, the EITC raises the reward from working. By contrast, welfare does not encourage or reward work: The benefit is at its maximum amount when a person doesn't work, and working reduces the benefit.

Figure 12.2 shows the EITC schedule (using rough, round numbers) for a married couple with two or more children. The family receives an EITC of $40 for each $100 of wage income it earns (the phase-in rate is 40%) until its wage income reaches $12,000 and its EITC benefit reaches $4,800. As its income increases from $12,000 to $16,000, its EITC stays $4,800. Further family income beyond $16,000 causes a phaseout of the credit; the credit is reduced $20 for every additional $100 of income the family obtains (the phase-out rate is 20%), so that the credit falls to zero when the family's income reaches $40,000. Note that the credit phases in over an income range of $12,000 at a phase-in rate of 40% and phases out over an income range of $24,000 (from $16,000 to $40,000) at a phaseout rate of 20%.

If the family has one child, the phase-in rate is 34% (instead of 40%), the maximum credit is about $2,900 (instead of about $4,800), and the phase-out rate is 16% (instead of 20%). If a household has no children, there is a small EITC for persons between the ages of 24 and 65 (thereby excluding most college students and retirees); the phase-in rate is only 7.65% (chosen to offset the employee payroll tax which is 6.2% for Social Security and 1.45% for Medicare), the maximum credit is a bit over $400, and the phase-out rate is also 7.65%.

History of the EITC

The Earned Income Tax Credit was enacted in 1975. Under the original version, a household with at least one child received a supplement of 10% of its wage earnings until earnings reached $4,000 and the credit reached $400; then for each $100 of income above $4,000, the credit was reduced $10, so that the credit completely phased out when household income reached $8,000. By comparison, today for a household with two children, the phase-in rate is 40%, not 10%, and the maximum credit is $4,800, not $400.

One rationale given for the EITC is that it offsets the burden of the Social Security payroll tax for low-income households. Why not simply exempt the first few thousand dollars of wage income from the payroll tax? One reason is that this exemption would complicate the employer's task of implementing the payroll tax for Social Security. Another is that an exemption might weaken the political claim of these workers to Social Security benefits upon retirement. Another is that such an exemption would be poorly targeted, because some workers with low-wage income are members of high-income families. Thus, the EITC can be viewed as a well-targeted vehicle for offsetting the burden of the payroll tax on workers from low-income households.

The initial support for the EITC in the 1970s came mainly from conservatives who viewed the EITC as an alternative to welfare. Its originator was Senator Russell Long, the chairman of the Senate Finance Committee which handles all tax legislation; he believed that welfare discourages work. Long first proposed his work bonus in 1972 and received an endorsement from California Governor Ronald Reagan. It wasn't until the recession of 1975 that Long got the EITC enacted as a provision of the Tax Reduction Act of 1975, which gave a tax rebate to all households to stimulate consumption spending to counter the recession. To include low-income working households who hadn't paid income tax, Long attached to the bill a new refundable 10% tax credit for poor families—the Earned Income Tax Credit. Thus, the Earned Income Tax Credit became law, not as part of a debate on low-income assistance, but as part of an effort to respond to a recession. With most other Americans receiving a new income tax rebate, it seemed only fair to give some cash assistance to the working poor, all of whom were subject to the payroll tax but many of whom did not pay any income tax. Hence, the new tax credit was made refundable in order to reach the working poor.

Over the next decade and a half, the EITC remained a small program with only a modest increase in the phase-in rate and a modest increase in the maximum credit. The EITC's conservative origins delayed its acceptance by liberals, but eventually they came to appreciate the EITC as an effective instrument for helping an important share of low-income people—those who worked. Liberals realized they could make more political headway with the EITC that conservatives supported than with welfare or the minimum wage, which conservatives opposed. By 1990, liberals had become supporters of the EITC, despite its conservative origins.

With bipartisan support, two major EITC expansions were enacted in 1990 and 1993. The 1990 expansion raised the phase-in rate to nearly 20% for a family with two or more children. The expansion raised the maximum credit from under $1,000 in 1990 to over $1,500 in 1993, and total credits doubled from $7.5 billion in 1990 to over $15 billion in 1993. The 1993 expansion doubled the phase-in rate to 40%, more than doubled the maximum credit from $1,500 in 1993 to $3,500 in 1996, and doubled total credits from $15 billion in 1993 to nearly $30 billion 1996. Thus, the two expansions nearly quadrupled total credits from $7.5 billion 1990 to nearly $30 billion in 1996.

Two opposite concerns have been expressed about the EITC. One is that some low-income people who are entitled to the EITC are not getting it. For example, some eligible people have never heard of the EITC and don't file a tax return because they owe no income tax. Outreach and publicity campaigns have tried to reduce the "under-participation" rate. The opposite concern is that some people obtain the EITC who are not supposed to or get more than they should. For example, some intentionally commit fraud by falsely claiming labor earnings or children in residence; some are confused about EITC rules concerning the definition of a qualifying child, the required filing status, and the determination of which family member (parent or grandparent with whom the child is living) should file for the EITC. Efforts have been made to reduce the "overparticipation" rate. A helpful measure has been the requirement that each child must be identified by a Social Security number. The Taxpayer Relief Act of 1997 included provisions that deny the EITC for a decade to taxpayers who fraudulently claim the EITC and impose "due diligence" requirements on paid preparers of tax returns involving the EITC.

The Marginal Tax Rate Generated by the Phasedown of the EITC

Whenever any government benefit phases down as a person earns additional income, the phasedown reduces the person's net gain from earning additional income. For example, suppose that when a person earns an additional $100, the government benefit is reduced $20. Then the person's net gain from earning the additional $100 is $80. It is *as though* the person were being taxed 20% on the additional earnings. Economists therefore describe this situation by saying the person faces a *marginal tax rate* of 20%.

Of course, the person is not actually being taxed. The person is not making a payment to the government; the government is making a payment to the person; and the person is better off because of the program. The marginal tax rate, however, does tell how much a person gains by earning another $100. If the phase-down rate (the marginal tax rate) is 20%, then the person gains $80 by earning another $100. Thus, a high marginal tax rate may discourage individuals from making the effort to earn more. Even if they do earn more, they may be discouraged because their net gain is less than their additional earnings.

The EITC versus the Negative Income Tax

It is important to clarify the relationship between the EITC and the **negative income tax (NIT)**. The NIT was proposed several decades ago and is often mentioned in textbooks, but it has never been enacted. Like the EITC, the NIT would deliver cash benefits to low-income households through the personal income tax filing and refund process. For this reason, some have called the EITC a version of the NIT.

However, the NIT, as it was originally proposed, is fundamentally different from the EITC, because the NIT has the same benefit schedule and diagram as welfare except for the flat range [look again at Figure 12.1(*b*)]: When income is zero, the NIT is at its maximum; as soon as income increases, the NIT benefit is phased down. Hence, the EITC is a work bonus, but the NIT, like welfare, is *not* because it gives its maximum benefit to a household that doesn't work and has no income. The NIT lacks a phase-in range that encourages and rewards work.[2]

The NIT can be described in two equivalent ways. First, the NIT gives a household a benefit equal to a percentage of the gap between the household's income and a target income. For example, the NIT might give a household a benefit equal to 75% of the gap between its income and $8,000. If a household's income is $0, its benefit is $6,000, but if its income increases to $4,000, its benefit is only $3,000. Note that earning $4,000 raises the amount it can spend only $1,000 (from $6,000 to $7,000), so this NIT imposes a marginal tax rate of 75%.

Second, the NIT gives the household the maximum benefit if its income is zero but reduces the benefit as the household earns income. For example, the NIT might give the household a benefit of $6,000 if its income is zero but would reduce the benefit

---

[2] The impact of the EITC and the NIT on labor supply is shown in the appendix to this chapter, using an indifference-curve/budget-line diagram.

$75 for each $100 the household earns. If its income is $4,000, the benefit is reduced by $3,000 to $3,000. So this NIT imposes a marginal tax rate of 75%.[3]

The EITC versus a Wage Subsidy

Under a wage subsidy, the government would pay a worker an hourly benefit that depends on the hourly wage. The hourly benefit would equal a percentage of the gap between the wage and a target wage. For example, the wage subsidy might give an hourly benefit equal to 75% of the gap between the wage and $10; if the wage were $6, the hourly benefit would be $3.

An advantage of the wage subsidy over the EITC is that benefits would only be paid to low-wage workers. Under the EITC, it is possible for someone who earns a high wage to receive a benefit because she works few hours and therefore has low wage income; the EITC is based on wage income, not the hourly wage.

But the EITC has two advantages over the wage subsidy. First, the EITC pays benefits only to low-income households. Under the wage subsidy, low-wage workers from high-income households would receive benefits. Second, under the wage subsidy, it may be easy for some workers to understate their hourly wage in order to obtain larger benefits. Currently employers are required by the government to report the wage income but not the hourly wage paid to each employee. Thus a government auditor can easily cross-check the wage income that a worker reports against the wage income paid by her employer when she claims the EITC; no communication with the employer would be necessary. Currently an auditor cannot easily cross-check the hourly wage a worker reports to claim the wage subsidy; presumably the employer has a record of each employee's hours worked and wage per hour, but the auditor would need a communication with the employer to obtain that information.

The EITC versus the Minimum Wage

When the government enacts a minimum wage law, any worker previously paid less than the minimum wage who retains her job enjoys an increase in wage income. However, it is likely that some employers will lay off some workers rather than raise a low wage up to the minimum wage; obviously any worker who does not retain her job suffers a decrease in wage income. In the future, some jobs that would have been offered at a wage below the minimum wage won't be offered.

An advantage of the minimum wage over the EITC is that there is no budgetary cost to the government. An advantage of the EITC over the minimum wage is that it raises the income of low-income households while increasing, rather than decreasing, employment.

Reform of the EITC

The EITC has some problems that might be reduced by making a few changes. Consider three possible changes in the EITC:

1. Reduce the phase-out rate to further encourage work.
2. Further raise the EITC of a married couple relative to single parents to reduce the marriage penalty that the EITC sometimes (but not always) imposes.
3. Give a higher EITC for a third child to further reduce poverty.

Let's consider each change in turn.

---

[3] According to the first way of describing the NIT, the benefit is $B = t(Y^* - Y)$, where Y^* equals target income and Y is the household's income. Multiplying yields $B = tY^* - tY$, which is the second way of describing the NIT: The household with zero income ($Y = 0$) receives a benefit of tY^*, but each dollar of Y reduces the benefit tY.

The EITC encourages a person to work rather than not work. However, once a person works enough to reach the phase-out range, the phase-out rate (i.e., the marginal tax rate) provides some discouragement to additional work. Reducing the phase-out rate—for example, from 20% to 16% for a married couple with two or more children—would enable the couple to gain $84 instead of $80 for each additional $100 earned in the phase-out range.

The EITC causes a marriage bonus in some cases but imposes a marriage penalty in other cases. Consider a single man who works for $12,000 and a single mother of two children who doesn't work. The single man gets a small EITC and the nonworking mother gets none. But if they marry, they will get the maximum EITC of about $4,800. In this case, the EITC gives a marriage bonus. But consider a single mother of two children who works for $12,000 and gets an EITC of $4,800. If she marries a single man who works for $28,000 and she continues to work for $12,000, she will lose the EITC because the couple's income will reach $40,000. In this case, the EITC imposes a marriage penalty. Due to a recent change in the law, the EITC already gives some advantage to marriage by delaying the income at which the phasedown begins according to marital status. Further raising the EITC of a married couple relative to single parents (e.g., by extending the married couple's phase-in range above $12,000 and hence raising its maximum EITC) would reduce the marriage penalty in cases like this one.

The EITC phase-in rate is 34% for one child and 40% for two children, but it remains at 40% for three children. Yet a family with three children needs more income to escape poverty than a family with two children. Giving a higher EITC for a third child—for example, raising the phase-in rate to 42% for three children—would reduce poverty for working families with three or more children.

Of course each of these three changes would raise the cost of the EITC to taxpayers, so the additional cost of each change must be weighed against the additional benefit.

Welfare

A welfare program gives a cash benefit to a family according to its need; it therefore gives its maximum benefit to a family with no income. The welfare benefit is at a maximum when the recipient doesn't work, and the benefit is reduced as the person works and earns income. Thus, welfare does not encourage or reward work. Welfare is motivated by the liberal sentiment to help families to the degree that they need help.

There is broad support and not much controversy over the federal welfare program that spent $36 billion in 2007 to provide assistance to the aged, blind, and disabled—supplementary security income (SSI)—because recipients are often unable to work and need help. Also not very controversial is the federal food stamps program that spent $35 billion in 2007 to make food cheaper for poor people. More controversial is the welfare program called Temporary Assistance for Needy Families that provided $24 billion of cash benefits in 2007 to poor single mothers and their children. This welfare program for single mothers is controversial because the mothers are generally able to work, and citizens disagree about whether these women should work, whether some mothers are to blame for their predicament, and whether the absent fathers rather than taxpayers can and should be made to support their children.

The Welfare Reform Act of 1996 moved the U.S. welfare program for single mothers and their children in a conservative direction. The act imposed time limits, work requirements, and certain conditions on young unwed mothers; converted the federal contribution from a matching grant to a fixed block grant in order to limit federal funding; and changed the name of the program from Aid to Families with Dependent Children (AFDC) to Temporary Assistance for Needy Families (TANF) in order to emphasize that aid to any family would be temporary. In the late 1990s, the Welfare Reform Act, a strong economy, and the expansion of the EITC together cut the number of people on welfare in half and induced many recipients to go to work.

Temporary Assistance for Needy Families

Temporary Assistance for Needy Families (TANF) is a joint federal-state program that provides cash benefits to low-income families with children in which one parent is absent; most TANF recipients are mothers. A family with no income receives the maximum TANF benefit. As family income increases, the benefit is phased down as shown in Figure 12.1(*b*). The maximum benefit and the phase-down rate vary substantially across states. The benefit in the highest-benefit states is several times greater than the benefit in the lowest-benefit states. The phase-down rate in most states is high, so most recipients face a substantial marginal tax rate and discouragement to work.

Under TANF, the federal government imposes time limits and other restrictions on recipients. There are two federal time limits. Under the first, recipients must go to work after receiving benefits for 24 consecutive months (a state can require work sooner). Under the second, over a lifetime, a recipient cannot receive more than 60 months of benefits. The federal government requires that half of a state's TANF recipients be working. Teenage mothers cannot qualify for benefits unless they live with their parents and stay in school; the benefit is cut for mothers who won't identify the father; and a state is permitted to impose a family cap—a limit on how many children it will support per family.

TANF also limited the federal government's expenditure obligation for welfare. Previously, the federal government had an open-ended commitment to match state spending for every recipient who qualified for welfare. Under TANF, the federal government gives a fixed block grant to each state for welfare, so federal welfare spending no longer varies automatically with state welfare spending or with the number of recipients who qualify for welfare. This limit on the federal obligation gives each state government a stronger incentive to try to limit its own spending and to limit the number who qualify for welfare, because the state will not automatically receive any additional help from the federal government.

TANF Replaced AFDC

Aid to Families with Dependent Children was enacted as part of the Social Security Act of 1935. It was a joint federal-state program in which the federal government matched each state's share. Its purpose was to assist widows with children; at the time there were few divorces and few mothers who had never married. As the decades passed, both divorced and never-married mothers increased, and AFDC coverage was extended to these mothers and their children. As more women in society began working for pay instead of staying at home full time, many citizens came to the view that paid work should also be expected of poor mothers. When moderate Democrat Bill Clinton ran for president in 1992, he promised to reform welfare in this direction. When Republicans won the House and Senate in the 1994 election, they drafted welfare reform legislation that replaced AFDC with TANF. After negotiation with Congress, and despite opposition from some liberal Democrats, President Clinton signed the Welfare Reform Act. By the end of the 1990s, the number on welfare had been cut in half and has remained low since, even through the 2001 recession.

THE IMPACT OF ASSISTANCE ON POVERTY

What is the combined impact of all these programs on poverty—on the well-being of low-income people in the United States? Specifically, what is the impact on the **poverty rate**—the percentage of the population living below the *poverty line*?

When the official U.S. government poverty line was first propounded in the 1960s, it was estimated that low-income families spent roughly a third of their income on food. Thus, the poverty line was set at three times the amount of money a family would need to purchase a nutritionally adequate diet for all its members; it was assumed that the family would need twice what it spent on food for other necessities. Hence, the official poverty line amount varies with family size and is automatically raised each year according to price inflation in the economy. The poverty line should differ across geographic areas because of the variation in prices (the cost of living), but it doesn't.

So what is the impact of government programs on poverty? To answer this question, clearly all important programs need to be counted and included. Medicaid is the single largest program targeted for low-income people. Medicare spends a very large sum on elderly, low-income people while also spending a large amount on the rest of the elderly population. The Earned Income Tax Credit delivers cash to low-income working families. Yet none of these programs affects the *official* government measure of poverty in the United States. How can this be?

The official government measure of poverty is based on a family's pretax cash income. Cash transfers like TANF are counted, but huge *in-kind* benefits like Medicaid and Medicare are not counted. Nor are other in-kind benefits programs that pay for food, housing, or education and training. Nor is the EITC counted because it is treated as an effect of the tax system that doesn't affect "pretax" cash income. Table 12.2 shows the striking difference between the official poverty rate before in-kind government programs and the EITC, and the poverty rate after all government programs.

The table presents data for the five years 1980, 1985, 1990, 1995, and 2000, and for two additional years when the U.S. economy felt the effects of a recession, 1992 and 2002. Three points are evident from the table. First, in-kind government programs plus the EITC significantly reduce the percentage of the population living below the poverty line; over the period shown in the table, the reduction was roughly one-third (for example, in 2002 from 12% to 8%). Second, the relationship between the two columns has been fairly stable since 1980—the numbers in the right column are roughly two-thirds of the left column over the period. Third, each recent recession temporarily raised the poverty rate about one percentage point.

TABLE 12.2
Poverty Rates

Source: Committee on Ways and Means, U.S. House of Representatives, *2004 Green Book,* table H-11

	Poverty Rate (Official) Before In-Kind Government Programs & EITC	Poverty Rate After All Government Programs
1980	13.0%	8.6%
1985	14.0	10.1
1990	13.5	9.5
1992	*14.8*	*10.5*
1995	13.8	9.0
2000	11.3	7.6
2002	*12.1*	*8.2*

Why aren't medical benefits included in assessing poverty? Defenders of the exclusion claim that it is not obvious how to calculate a family's benefit from Medicaid. They note, correctly, that Medicaid is insurance, so it has value even to families that don't use medical care in a given year. But Medicaid's insurance value can be measured as Medicaid's total expenditure divided by the total number of families covered—that is, Medicaid's per capita expenditure can be included in each covered family's income.

To assess the case for inclusion of the benefits from all government programs in measuring poverty, imagine a society that initially has no government programs for low-income families. Now imagine that all the government programs are enacted: Medicare, Medicaid, food stamps, the EITC, and so on. According to the official definition, these programs have no effect on poverty. Now suppose that instead of enacting all these programs, the government gives families an amount of cash welfare equal to the amount spent on these government programs. The official measure of the number of families in poverty would drop significantly. The enactment of the set of government programs would have no effect on the official measure of poverty, but the enactment of an equal amount of cash welfare would have a large effect.

REFUNDABLE TAX CREDITS

The EITC is a refundable tax credit that delivers cash assistance to low-income households through the annual federal income tax process. By contrast, tax deductions, tax exclusions, or ordinary tax credits cannot help low-income households who owe little or no income tax. Currently there are very few refundable tax credits, but it would be possible to assist low-income households by converting current tax deductions, tax exclusions, or ordinary tax credits to refundable tax credits.

The advantage of a set of refundable tax credits for particular categories rather than a single refundable tax credit that can be used for any purpose (unrestricted cash assistance) is that taxpayers may get utility when recipients use their money for certain purposes (medical care or education) rather than others (expensive entertainment or fancy clothes).

Let's consider several categorical refundable tax credits that have been proposed but have not yet been enacted.

Home ownership: The current mortgage interest deduction could be converted to a refundable tax credit for a home purchase. For example, any household could claim a refundable credit equal to X% of the home purchase expense up to a $50,000 expenditure where X would decline as income rises.

Retirement saving: The current individual retirement account deduction and the current ordinary tax credit for retirement saving could be converted to a refundable tax credit for retirement saving. For example, any household could claim a refundable credit equal to X% of its saving in a retirement account up to $2,000 of saving where X would decline as income rises.

Higher education: The current ordinary tax credit for higher education tuition could be converted to a refundable tax credit. For example, any household could claim a refundable credit equal to X% of its tuition expense up to a $5,000 expenditure where X would decline as income rises.

Health insurance: The current exclusion of an employer's expenditure on health insurance for an employee (from the employee's total income on her 1040 income tax return) could be converted to a refundable tax credit for health insurance.

For example, any household could claim a refundable credit equal to X% of the premium up to a $10,000 expenditure where X would decline as income rises.

A refundable tax credit has two advantages over a direct government program. First, it can vary the amount of assistance with family income because income is reported on the tax return. A direct government program cannot vary assistance with family income unless it asks families to report their income, duplicating the income tax return process. Second, the family uses the same process (the 1040 income tax return) and bureaucracy (the IRS) each year, regardless of how its income fluctuates: One year its income is low, so it a files its return and receives a large refundable tax credit; the next year its income is high, so it files its return and receives a small refundable tax credit. One disadvantage is that the IRS provides less monitoring and supervision than most direct government programs.

UNEMPLOYMENT INSURANCE

An employed individual who is paid an adequate wage generally does not need assistance. However, things can go wrong. The individual can lose her job, suffer an injury on the job, or become disabled. The typical individual would be willing to pay for insurance against these adverse events—a guarantee of some financial assistance should the event occur. Insurance has developed for each of these contingencies: unemployment insurance, workers' compensation, and disability insurance. These insurance programs are similar to old age insurance (i.e., Social Security), which we examined in Chapter 5, and health insurance, which we examined in Chapter 6—they provide benefits contingent on an adverse event.

As in the case of old age insurance or health insurance, it is not immediately obvious whether these insurance programs should be provided by government or by private insurance companies, whether they should be voluntary or required, and whether the appropriate level of government is federal or state. In the United States, unemployment insurance and disability insurance are provided by the government. States require private firms to buy **workers' compensation**—job injury insurance—from private insurance companies (just as many firms voluntarily buy health insurance for their employees). **Unemployment insurance** is mandated by the federal government but administered by the states; it was originally enacted as part of the Social Security Act of 1935 to give cash benefits to workers laid off from their jobs. **Disability insurance** is a federal program introduced in 1957 to assist people with career-ending disabilities; it is part of the Old Age, Survivors, and Disability Insurance (OASDI) program along with Social Security. The remainder of this section focuses on unemployment insurance.

When a person is laid off from her job, she usually qualifies for unemployment compensation from the government and will be paid periodic cash benefits for up to 26 weeks (and an additional 13 weeks if the economy is in recession); in a normal economy, most workers collect for less than 10 weeks before finding a new job. Because each state administers its own unemployment insurance program under federal regulations originally established in the Social Security Act of 1935, provisions vary across states. An unemployed worker's benefit depends on her recent wage income; on average the benefit is roughly 40% of recent wage income—this "replacement rate" is generally higher than 40% for low-income workers and lower than 40% for high-income workers. Unemployment benefits are included in the adjusted gross income when the household computes its federal income tax. The unemployment insurance program is financed by an employer payroll tax. The tax varies somewhat according to the employer's past experience with laying off workers—hence, it is partially experience-rated (only "partially" because if one firm has twice the layoffs of another firm, it pays less than twice the tax). Under this experience rating, employers who frequently lay off workers have to pay more tax, so that they have an incentive to try to avoid layoffs.

Not all unemployed workers qualify for unemployment compensation. The worker must apply at her local unemployment insurance office and demonstrate several things in order to receive benefits. First, unemployment compensation is usually restricted to workers who are laid off due to economic conditions facing their firm; a worker who voluntarily quits her job or is fired for misconduct usually does not qualify. Second, a worker's earnings in the preceding year must exceed a specified minimum amount; a person must therefore earn eligibility through recent employment and wage income. Third, the unemployed person must agree to look actively for work and accept any job with a wage near her previous wage. Even workers who qualify do not always claim benefits. To receive benefits, an unemployed person must first be interviewed at the unemployment insurance office. As a consequence of these restrictions and lack of full participation by eligible workers, only about half the unemployed actually receive unemployment benefits.

Setting the replacement rate (currently about 40% in most states for workers with average wage income) involves a trade-off. If the replacement rate is set too low, it won't provide enough help to unemployed people. If it is set too high, unemployed people might delay obtaining another job; it has been estimated that an increase of 10 percentage points in the replacement rate (for example, from 40% to 50%) raises the duration of unemployment between 1 and 2 weeks. Similarly, setting the time limit for benefits (currently 26 weeks) involves a trade-off. If the time limit is too low, it will expire before many of the unemployed have a chance to find work. If it is set too high, unemployed people might delay obtaining another job; one study found a spike in job finding wherever a state sets its time limit for benefits. In most economically advanced Western European countries, the replacement rate is higher and the duration of benefits is longer than in the United States.

Summary

The largest federal program that assists only low-income people is Medicaid (Social Security and Medicare help people at all income levels, including poor people). Federal spending for Medicaid is nearly eight times federal spending for cash welfare.

Citizens generally prefer to give low-income assistance that is restricted to a particular purpose, like medical care or food, rather than to give unrestricted cash that can be used for any purpose. This may be socially optimal if recipients are not good judges of how to maximize their family's utility or if there are significant consumption externalities so that the utility of taxpayers is significantly affected by how their money is used by recipients.

Medicaid pays poor people's medical bills. It helps two groups: families with children and the elderly who have used up their assets paying for nursing home care. It's an all or none program: A family either qualifies or it doesn't; obtaining a new job can cause a family to lose Medicaid.

The Earned Income Tax Credit (EITC) is a work bonus. The EITC provides assistance only to families that earn income from work. Initially, the more wage income that is earned, the greater is the EITC until a maximum is reached; then as further income is earned, the EITC is gradually phased out. The dollar amount of the EITC at each level of income depends on the number of children. A household receives its EITC annually by filing a federal income tax return. Spending on the Earned Income Tax Credit is nearly twice the spending on welfare.

The U.S. welfare program for single mothers with children is called Temporary Assistance for Needy Families (TANF) in order to emphasize that aid to any family is temporary. The Welfare Reform Act of 1996 imposed time limits, work requirements, and certain conditions on young unwed mothers; and it converted the federal contribution from a matching grant to a fixed block grant. The Welfare Reform Act, a strong economy, and the expansion of the EITC together cut in half the number on welfare in the late 1990s.

The official measure of poverty is based on a family's pretax cash income and omits the impact of in-kind benefits, like Medicaid and Medicare, and of the Earned Income Tax Credit. If they were counted, in-kind government programs plus the EITC would significantly reduce the percentage of the population living below the poverty line (from 12% to 8%).

A refundable tax credit is a policy instrument for providing low-income assistance. The EITC reaches low-income people because it is refundable. By contrast, tax deductions, tax exclusions, and ordinary tax credits do not help low-income people who pay little or no federal income tax. Refundable tax credits have been proposed for saving, education, health insurance, and home ownership.

When a person is laid off from a job due to economic conditions facing her firm, she usually qualifies for unemployment insurance from the government and will be paid periodic cash benefits for up to 26 weeks; the benefit for the average worker is roughly 40% of her recent wage income (more than 40% for low-income workers, less than 40% for high-income workers).

Key Terms

means-tested, *296*
in kind, *297*
consumption externality, *297*
Medicaid, *297*
Earned Income Tax
  Credit (EITC), *298*

negative income tax
  (NIT), *301*
wage subsidy, *302*
Temporary Assistance
  for Needy Families
  (TANF), *304*

poverty rate, *305*
workers'
  compensation, *307*
unemployment
  insurance, *307*
disability insurance, *307*

Questions

1. What is one argument for unrestricted cash assistance? What is one argument for restricted assistance?

2. What is the largest category of federal spending targeted on low-income people? How much larger is its spending than welfare?

3. Draw two diagrams to illustrate the difference between EITC and welfare. Explain.

4. Draw the EITC diagram, and put in round numbers for a family of four. Explain your diagram.

5. Give a brief history of the EITC. How was it enacted, and how has it changed?

6. Compare the EITC with the negative income tax (NIT).

7. Compare the EITC with the minimum wage.

8. List three possible reforms of the EITC. What are the arguments for these reforms?

9. What does the "T" stand for in TANF? Give two provisions of the Welfare Reform Act of 1996 that implement the "T."

10. Name two important programs that are ignored in measuring the official poverty rate. Explain why these programs are ignored.

11. List three kinds of "tax breaks" that do not help low-income people. List one that does. Explain.

12. Convert the current homeowner tax break so that it benefits low-income homeowners. Explain how your changes enable those benefits.

13. Explain the trade-off in setting the replacement rate for unemployment compensation.

14. Go online to read about proposals to reform the EITC. Choose one proposal and explain it in detail.

15. Go online to read about the debate over the Welfare Reform Act of 1996 and analyses of the effects of the act over the past decade.

Appendix

Low-Income Assistance

THE EITC AND LABOR SUPPLY

We now use an indifference-curve/budget-line diagram to analyze the effect of the EITC and the NIT (or welfare) on labor supply (review the appendix to Chapter 1 which introduces the indifference-curve/budget-line diagram). We assume that a person gets "utility" (i.e., subjective well-being) from two goods: leisure and income. For each hour that a person works, she earns income but sacrifices an hour of leisure. We assume the person is offered a job with a specific wage but is given a choice about how many hours to work per year—that is, how many hours of labor to supply per year. The person can vary her annual hours of labor supply by varying her hours per day, her days of work per week, and/or her vacations. Of course, employers usually do not give an employee completely free choice over the number of hours—but many employers do give some choice.

Figure 12A.1 shows the indifference-curve/budget-line diagram for the EITC. Leisure hours are plotted horizontally, and income is plotted vertically. With 365 days in a year and 24 hours in a day, there are 8,760 hours in a year. We *define* any hour that the person is not working in the marketplace to be an hour of *leisure* (so leisure includes time sleeping, caring for children, doing home chores or repairs, etc.). As shown in the diagram, the maximum possible hours of leisure per year is 8,760 hours, so point *M* is a point on the person's budget line (a point she could choose). Suppose the wage she is offered is $10 an hour. Starting from point *M* with 8,760 hours of leisure and no income, for every hour of leisure she gives up to work she moves up $10 if there is no EITC. The slope of her budget line *MN* without the EITC is –$10, and she chooses point *O* with 8,260 hours of leisure per year, so she works 500 hours per year and earns $5,000 of income (note that a person working 40 hours per week for 50 weeks works 2,000 hours per year).

FIGURE 12A.1
The EITC and Work
The EITC usually induces a person in its phase-in range to work more.

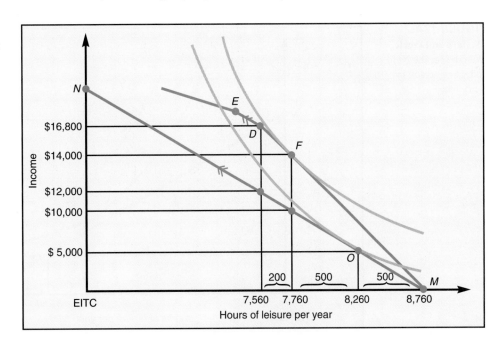

Suppose, as shown in Figure 12.2 in the text, that the EITC has a phase-in rate of 40% until earnings reach $12,000 and the EITC reaches $4,800. Then for each hour of leisure she gives up for work, she gets a wage of $10 plus an EITC of $4 for a total of $14 per hour. The slope of her budget line *MF* is –$14, and she chooses point *F* with 7,760 hours of leisure per year, so she works 1,000 hours per year and earns $10,000 of income plus $4,000 of EITC. Note that if she had worked 200 hours more for a total of 1,200 hours, she would have reached point *D,* earned $12,000 plus an EITC of $4,800 for a total of $16,800; point *D* is the end of the EITC phase-in range; from point *D* to point *E* the EITC is constant (see Figure 12.2), and the EITC budget line is therefore parallel to *MN*. To the left of *E*, the EITC phaseout causes the EITC budget line to be flatter than *MN*.

To summarize: The EITC causes this individual to choose to move from point *O* to point *F,* thereby increasing her hours of work per year from 500 to 1,000, her earnings from $5,000 to $10,000, and her earnings plus EITC from $5,000 to $14,000. For this person, point *F* is to the left of point *O*—in response to the EITC, she chooses less leisure and more work.

It should be noted that for another individual with other indifference curves, it is possible that the point *F* she chooses would be much closer to point *M* on the EITC budget line and actually to the right, not left, of point *O;* such a person would choose more leisure and less work in response to the EITC. It must be admitted that while the EITC is likely to increase hours of work for a person in its phase-in range, the reverse is possible. Also note that this diagram examines the response of a person who begins and ends up in the EITC phase-in range. The results would be different for a person who begins in the EITC flat or phase-down range.

THE NIT (OR WELFARE) AND LABOR SUPPLY

Suppose the same person is faced with a negative income tax (or a welfare program) instead of the EITC. This is shown in Figure 12A.2. With the NIT(or welfare), the person gets a maximum amount if her earnings are zero (e.g., $5,000, as shown in

FIGURE 12A.2
Welfare and Work
Welfare (or the NIT) induces a person to work less.

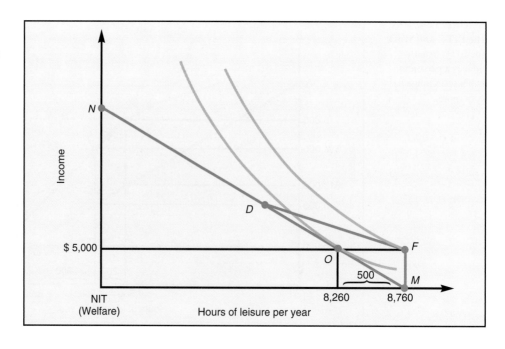

Figure 12A.2); as soon as she earns income, the NIT is phased down (the NIT is similar to welfare except that welfare usually has a flat range before the phasedown begins; neither the NIT nor welfare have a phase-in range, in contrast to the EITC). With the NIT the person's budget line is *FD,* which is flatter than *MN* due to the NIT phasedown. In response to the NIT, this person chooses point *F*—zero hours of work and an income equal to the NIT $5,000.

The flatter the NIT budget line (the higher the phase-out rate—the marginal tax rate), the more likely she will choose point *F* directly above *M* and work zero hours. The steeper the NIT budget line (the lower the phase-out rate—the marginal tax rate), the more likely she will choose a point *F'* (not shown) to the left of point *M* on a higher indifference curve than point *F* and therefore she will choose some hours of work; the point *F'* that she chooses would still lie to the right of point *O,* so that she would work less under the NIT than without it.

If a welfare program has a flat range before the phasedown begins, her budget line would extend northwest from point *F* parallel to *MN* (not shown) until the phasedown begins; then it gets flatter, taking the same slope as *FD* (not shown). She would choose a point *F''* (not shown) that lies to the right of point *O,* so she would choose to work less under the welfare program than without it.

Chapter **Thirteen**

Government Borrowing

Hisham F. Ibrahim/Getty Images

Throughout most of this book, we have implicitly assumed that government spending would be financed by taxation. This chapter investigates another option: borrowing.

GOVERNMENT DEBT

Deficit versus Debt

We begin by clarifying the distinction between two terms: *deficit* and *debt*. Suppose in year 0 the government spends $150 billion, collects $100 billion in taxes, and borrows $50 billion by selling $50 billion in government bonds to the public. Then the government *deficit* in year 0 is $50 billion. The **deficit** is defined as spending minus taxes in a given year.

Suppose the government does the same thing in year 1, so its deficit in year 1 is also $50 billion. At the end of year 1, the government *debt* is $100 billion, because the public holds $100 billion in government bonds ($50 billion bought in year 0 and $50 billion bought in year 1). Thus, the **debt** at the end of year 1 is the *cumulative* result of the deficits in years 0 and 1. Hence:

> *The debt is a stock that is measured at a point in time, and the deficit is a flow that occurs during a period of time—one year.*

Suppose in year 2 the government spends $100 billion and collects $150 billion in taxes, so the government *surplus* is $50 billion. With the surplus, it buys back $50 billion in bonds from the public, "retiring," or paying off, $50 billion of its debt. At the end of year 2, government debt is down to $50 billion.

Thus, running a deficit causes government debt to increase, and running a surplus causes government debt to decrease.

Commonsense Concern about Excessive Borrowing

Let's begin with a commonsense concern about excessive borrowing for an individual or a business firm and then consider whether it applies to a government.

A person who borrows money to spend more than he earns is relying on creditors (i.e., lenders) who will exact a price—interest payments—for their service. It takes self-discipline to limit spending to earnings—borrowing is tempting. However, excessive borrowing today means heavy payments (principal plus interest) to creditors tomorrow. Ultimately it may lead to a day of reckoning: If a time comes when you are unable to make the heavy payments, you will face personal bankruptcy, and your creditors will have the legal right to take your property. Moreover, you will be spurned by creditors in the future, unable to borrow even in an emergency.

This warning about *excessive* borrowing does not mean that all borrowing should be avoided. Borrowing in a genuine emergency is appropriate. Borrowing to finance a long-lived durable such as a house or tuition for education that will raise productivity and earnings is warranted, provided that the interest plus repayments are not large relative to your future earnings. If your income is low today but is sure to be high tomorrow, it makes sense to borrow so that your consumption is "smoother"—that is, stays more even than your income between today and tomorrow. You must keep your debt from becoming large relative to your earnings, so that your interest payments do not absorb too large a percentage of your earnings.

This commonsense view applies to a business firm as well. Borrowing to finance a long-lived productive asset, such as a machine, is warranted provided that the additional earnings generated by the machine will be enough to cover interest plus repayments. But excessive business borrowing can lead the business into bankruptcy and the taking of its property by creditors.

The same concern applies to a government. Like a business firm, a government is justified in borrowing to finance a long-lived productive asset—such as a highway or a school building. However, a government that borrows in order to spend more than it collects in revenue must rely on creditors who will exact a price—interest payments—for their service. Heavy borrowing today means heavy repayments to creditors tomorrow. There might come a day of reckoning: If the government is unable to make repayments when they come due, it will default and creditors will go unpaid. After a default, the government may find it difficult to borrow because creditors will be wary. The government will then be forced to spend only what it collects in tax revenue, and this may require a sudden painful cut in its spending or an increase in taxes. It may lose the ability to borrow in an emergency. Although the federal government has the power to print money, such a solution would be inflationary and therefore harmful to the economy. Thus, it is important for the federal government to avoid excessive borrowing.

The Burden of the Debt

Does borrowing burden future generations? Let's explore this question with regard to a family, and then we will turn to government. Do parents burden their children by borrowing? Does the government burden future generations by borrowing?

The Burden of Family Borrowing

Suppose parents borrow to finance their own consumption—every year they travel to a vacation resort and leave their children with a sitter. Then they die in debt. What happens? If children were legally responsible for their parents' debt, then their children would be required to repay their parents' debt, and the borrowing by the parents would impose a burden on their children. However, under the law children are not legally responsible for their parents' debt. Hence, borrowing by the parents does not directly burden the children.

Does this mean that children are unaffected by their parents' borrowing? Not necessarily. Even if the parents die in debt, their children may be affected because creditors may say: "I'm not going to lend to these children because their parents never repaid their loan, and these children may turn out to be just like their parents." Thus, the children may judge that they have to pay off their parents' debt in order to preserve their own ability to borrow in the future. If so, then the parents' borrowing imposes a burden on their children.

The Burden of Government Borrowing

Now consider a government. To pay for this year's spending, suppose the government borrows instead of collecting taxes. What's the consequence of borrowing instead of taxing? If the government collects taxes, today's taxpayers bear the burden of this year's spending, whereas if the government borrows, today's taxpayers bear no burden this year. To borrow, the government sells bonds. When the bonds come due, the government can pay the old bondholders by selling new bonds to new bondholders. But in all future years, the government must pay interest to bondholders. To pay the interest, future taxpayers must pay additional taxes. Thus, the future interest payments will impose a burden on future taxpayers.

Of course, future taxpayers could refuse to pay the interest. Like the children whose parents left them with unpaid debt, future taxpayers could claim that they didn't incur the debt and therefore have no obligation to pay. But like the children, they may judge that they have to pay off their parents' debt in order to preserve their own ability to borrow in the future. If so, then future taxpayers will have to bear the burden.

Future bondholders receive the interest payments. Suppose the bondholders are foreigners—people, firms, and/or governments. Then future U.S. taxpayers pay interest to foreigners. In this case, it seems clear that government borrowing today burdens U.S. taxpayers tomorrow. Currently nearly half of U.S. government bonds are held by foreigners, so there is no doubt that nearly half of current U.S. government debt will impose an interest burden on future U.S. taxpayers.

But what about interest paid to domestic bondholders? In this case interest paid by U.S. taxpayers will be received by U.S. bondholders, and it is sometimes said that "we owe this debt to ourselves" so there is no burden. But there *is* a burden to *future U.S. taxpayers*. Taxpayers at the time that the government borrows are better off, while future taxpayers are worse off. The good deal given to today's taxpayers is offset by the bad deal given to tomorrow's taxpayers.

Government borrowing shifts the burden of today's government spending from today's taxpayers to tomorrow's taxpayers.

INVESTMENT

Capital Expenditures

Is it fair to shift the burden of today's government spending? It depends. If today's government spending benefits today's but not tomorrow's taxpayers, most would agree that the shift is unfair. But if today's government spending primarily benefits tomorrow's taxpayers, then most would agree that the shift is fair.

Consider two examples. Suppose today's government spending is a one-time cash transfer to today's elderly (a one-time supplement to today's Social Security benefits). Borrowing to finance the transfers would shift the burden to tomorrow's taxpayers who receive no direct benefit from the transfers. By contrast, suppose today's government spending is to repel an invasion by an aggressor nation or to build a highway that will last many years. Borrowing to finance these expenditures would shift the burden to tomorrow's taxpayers who benefit from both expenditures; taxing rather than borrowing would unfairly place the entire burden on today's taxpayers. Thus, borrowing is inappropriate when government spending doesn't benefit tomorrow's taxpayers, but appropriate when it does benefit them. This is sometimes expressed as the distinction between "current" expenditures and "capital expenditures." Current (or operating) expenditures should be financed by taxation, but capital expenditures should be financed by borrowing.

There is, however, a serious practical problem with this guideline. Politicians will try to classify any expenditure that they favor as a "capital" expenditure—an investment—that can be financed by borrowing rather than taxation. For many government expenditures, a good case can be made that the expenditure is an investment that will benefit future taxpayers, so that borrowing is appropriate. If the military buys a submarine, isn't this an investment that will provide protection for many years? If government provides grants to college students, isn't this an investment in human capital that will generate higher productivity for many years from these students after they graduate? If the government pays for medical care for poor children, isn't this an investment in health capital that will raise the productivity of these children in school and later in the workforce? In fact, it is hard to think of any government expenditures that can't be claimed to be an investment that yields returns in the future. However, if politicians are told they can borrow instead of tax, then politicians who advocate particular expenditures won't face the discipline of having to raise taxes to pay for them. It seems likely that more expenditures will be enacted if they can be financed by borrowing rather than taxation.

If it is feared that reclassification of government spending programs as "investments" will become widespread and that discipline on politicians will therefore be undermined, it may be better simply to prescribe that government expenditures (with perhaps a few exceptions) must be financed by taxation rather than borrowing, so that, ignoring exceptions, the budget must be balanced: Spending must not exceed tax revenue.

FIGURE 13.1
Government Borrowing
When the government borrows, the demand for loanable funds shifts to the right, raising the interest rate.

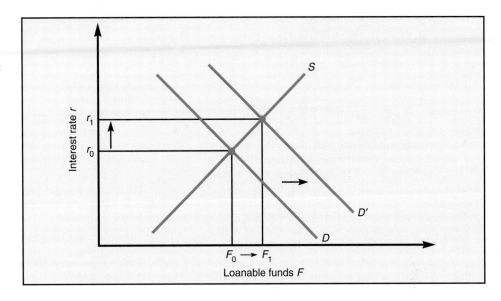

Government Borrowing, Interest Rates, and the Crowding Out of Investment

Suppose the government either cuts taxes on households or raises cash transfers to households and increases its borrowing—its demand for loanable funds—to finance its deficit. As shown in Figure 13.1, the demand curve for loanable funds shifts to the right. If households mainly consume, not save, their tax cut or transfers increase, then the supply curve of loanable funds (which comes from savings) hardly shifts right (Figure 13.1 shows no shift), and at the initial interest r_0, the demand for funds will exceed supply, causing the interest rate to be bid up to r_1. This rise in the interest rate causes business firms to reduce their borrowing and investment. Thus, government borrowing "crowds out" private investment, thereby reducing tomorrow's private capital stock and output per worker (i.e., productivity) in the private sector.

For a further discussion of Figure 13.1, see the box "The Deficit and Interest Rates: An Estimate from U.S. Data."

BALANCED BUDGET

Disciplining Politicians with a Balanced Budget Rule

Suppose government is required to adhere to a balanced budget rule: Spending must be financed entirely by tax revenue. Such a rule would impose desirable discipline on politicians. Why?

The public naturally likes the benefits they receive from government spending programs. If the public believes that such benefits can be obtained "for free," they will naturally demand an excessive amount of such spending, and politicians will naturally vote to provide it. Whenever the price of a private or public good appears to be zero, consumers will demand too much of it. By contrast, the optimal rather than an excessive amount of a private or public good results when consumers see that they must pay the cost of any benefit. For a private good, this is done by charging the consumer a price equal to its cost. For a public good, it is done by charging the citizen a tax equal to its cost. If citizens see that they must pay taxes to finance government spending programs, they will weigh cost against benefit and vote for politicians who do the same.

Case Study   The Deficit and Interest Rates: An Estimate from U.S. Data

In two papers in 2003 and 2004, Brookings Institution economists William Gale and Peter Orszag (now the director of the Congressional Budget Office) examined empirical evidence concerning the hypothesis that an increase in government borrowing following a tax cut raises interest rates (illustrated in Figure 13.1).* In these papers, they reviewed past empirical studies and provided a new empirical analysis of U.S. data.

In Figure 13.1 it is implicitly assumed that households spend rather than save their tax cut; if they saved the entire tax cut and deposited it in banks, then the supply curve of loanable funds would shift right as much as the demand curve for loanable funds and the interest rate wouldn't be bid up.† So a key question becomes: Do consumers mainly consume or save a tax cut? Gale and Orszag examined U.S. data to see how consumption responds to a tax cut. They found that a tax cut is mainly consumed, not saved, so that the supply curve of loanable funds hardly shifts right, implying that the interest rate would rise in Figure 13.1.

How much does the interest rate rise if, instead of running a balanced budget, every year the government runs a deficit of 1% of GDP? Gale and Orszag examined year-to-year variations in interest rates and the deficit (and "ran a regression" with the interest rate as the dependent variable and the deficit as one of the independent variables).

They estimated that a permanent increase in the deficit of one percentage point of GDP (for example, from 0% to 1% of GDP) raises the (long-term) interest rate roughly half of a percentage point (for example, from 4.0% to 4.5%).

It should be emphasized that estimating the relationship between the interest rate and the deficit is tricky. To see this, suppose consumer and business pessimism—for example, triggered by a plunge in the stock market—causes aggregate demand to fall and the economy to drop into a recession, reducing income and tax revenue and, hence, raising the deficit. The pessimism also reduces the demand for loanable funds by households and business firms, thereby reducing the interest rate. There would be a simultaneous increase in the deficit and a decrease in the interest rate.

All of this happened in 2001 in the United States. Thus, some U.S. data are generated by a recession causing an increase in the deficit and a decrease in the interest rate. But Gale and Orszag are interested in what happens to interest rates if the government enacts a tax cut that generates a deficit, not what happens to the deficit and interest rates if there is a recession due to pessimism. Actual U.S. data are generated by both occurrences. There are techniques to try to separate the two occurrences, but they don't work perfectly. Thus, any estimate should be treated with caution.

* William Gale and Peter Orszag, "Economic effects of Sustained Budget Deficits," *National Tax Journal* 56, no. 3 (September 2003), pp. 463–85; and "Budget Deficits, National Saving, and Interest Rates," *Brookings Papers on Economic Activity* 2004 (2), pp. 101–87.

† Economist Robert Barro contends that families will save their tax cut because they think they will have to pay higher taxes in the future and has called such thinking "Ricardian." No direct evidence has ever been provided that ordinary people think this way when they get a tax cut.

The simplest balanced budget rule would be a prohibition on borrowing (or printing money), so that government spending can never exceed tax revenue. No excuses would be permitted. This might be called an "always" balanced budget rule or a "no excuses" balanced budget rule. Such a rule would certainly make citizens, and politicians, weigh the tax cost of any program against its benefit.

Unfortunately, such a rule would be risky: It could force the government to take action in the middle of a recession that would make the recession worse.

The Problem with an Always Balanced Budget Rule

Suppose the economy is normal (not in recession or boom) and government spending equals tax revenue, so the budget is balanced. Then the economy falls into recession.

Automatically tax revenue falls because a recession reduces the output produced and income earned and, therefore, the tax revenue collected. With tax revenue down, the government borrows to keep spending from falling, and the budget goes into deficit. What would happen if the government were forced to adhere to an always balanced budget rule?

The government would promptly have to either cut spending or raise taxes. Consider the impact of each fiscal action on the economy. If the government cuts its purchases, firms supplying goods to the government—planes for the military, computers for public schools—would cut output and employment, making the recession worse. If the government cuts its cash transfer spending—Social Security or welfare benefits—the recipients would reduce their consumption, making the recession worse. If the government raises taxes, taxpayers would reduce their consumption, making the recession worse. No matter how the government balances its budget, its action would make the recession worse. Economists are virtually unanimous in agreeing that a rule that requires prompt budget balancing in the middle of a recession is dangerous, because it would make a recession worse.

Does this mean that any balanced budget rule would be dangerous? No. For more than half a century, most economists have advocated a particular kind of balanced budget rule that would not make a recession worse. It has been called the *full employment balanced budget rule (FEBAR)*. One practical problem with FEBAR is that there is disagreement about what constitutes full employment. Another is that actual employment often turns out to be less than full employment. To avoid these two problems, we replace "full employment" with "normal unemployment" and call the rule *normal unemployment balanced budget rule (NUBAR)*. Normal unemployment is defined as the average unemployment rate during the past decade. There is little disagreement about the average unemployment rate over the past decade, and the actual unemployment rate on average equals the average unemployment rate.

A Normal Unemployment Balanced Budget Rule

Under a **normal unemployment balanced budget rule (NUBAR)**, each year Congress must enact a *planned* budget for the coming fiscal year that *technicians estimate* would be balanced *if* next year the unemployment rate is normal (the average of the preceding decade). The technicians should probably be the staff of the Congressional Budget Office (CBO) which already performs similar tasks for Congress. Given the tax rates Congress has set, the technicians estimate how much revenue would be collected next year if the unemployment rate is normal. Given the features of the spending programs that Congress has enacted, the technicians estimate how much would be spent next year if the unemployment rate is normal. If the estimate of spending roughly equals the estimate of revenue, then the technicians would pronounce Congress' planned budget to be in compliance with NUBAR. If the estimate of spending exceeds the estimate of revenue, the technicians would pronounce Congress' planned budget to be in violation of NUBAR, and Congress would be required to amend its planned budget until the technicians pronounce it to be in compliance.

NUBAR would avoid making a recession worse because it applies to this year's *planned* budget for next year, not this year's actual spending and revenue. Suppose the economy drops into recession and NUBAR is in effect. Congress is *not* required to immediately cut spending or raise taxes in the recession, because NUBAR applies to the planned budget, not current spending and revenue.

At the same time, NUBAR would exert desirable discipline on politicians at the time they enact the planned budget for the coming year. Under NUBAR, they can only raise planned spending if they are willing to raise planned taxes, and they can only cut planned taxes if they are willing to cut planned spending.

Note that NUBAR would permit Congress to enact an automatic fiscal stimulus that would be triggered by recession and removed by recovery. For example, suppose Congress enacts a stimulus package of tax cuts and spending increases that would be triggered automatically whenever the unemployment rate exceeds the normal unemployment rate by a full percentage point and be terminated when the unemployment rate falls below this threshold. For example, if the normal unemployment rate (the average of the preceding decade) were 5.2%, then the stimulus package would be triggered as soon as the Department of Labor announces that the monthly unemployment has risen above 6.2% and would be terminated when the unemployment rate falls below 6.2%. In judging whether the planned budget complies with NUBAR, the technicians would ignore the stimulus package because it would not be in effect next year if the unemployment rate is normal. Thus, NUBAR does not prevent Congress from using fiscal policy to combat a recession, provided the fiscal stimulus would be removed if the unemployment rate declines to normal.

Several questions can be raised about NUBAR. First, how would it be implemented? Congress would need to adopt a planned budget in its entirety and get approval from the CBO technicians instead of just voting on individual components of spending and taxes. Second, how would it be enforced? Suppose Congress fails to adopt a planned budget that is in compliance with NUBAR. Would the penalty simply be bad publicity for Congress, or would Congress have to accept an across-the-board X% cut in the planned spending of each program; if so, would there be exceptions for any programs? Third, would there be a provision to suspend NUBAR in case of a severe recession or a war?

FUTURE CONSIDERATIONS

Fiscal Imbalance

The debt of a family, business, or government is an explicit obligation that must be managed in the future. But it would be misleading to look only at debt to assess the fiscal prospect of the family, business, or government.

Consider two families. The first has only one child, and it has decided that the child will attend the state university where the family lives and therefore pay a low tuition for college. The second has five children, and it has decided that all the children will attend private universities and therefore pay high tuition for college. Clearly, the second family faces a much more challenging future fiscal burden than the first. Its decision to send all five children to high-tuition private universities means that it has incurred a large implicit obligation. Suppose the explicit debt incurred by the two families is the same. It would clearly be wrong to conclude that they face the same future fiscal burdens.

The same logic applies to a government. Consider Social Security and Medicare. The federal government has scheduled cash benefits determined by a formula when workers retire, and the payment of retirees' medical bills. These scheduled benefits and bill payments are much larger than the tax revenue that it is estimated will be raised by current payroll tax rates (given projected ceilings on taxable payroll). The federal government has therefore undertaken an implicit obligation that is much larger than the taxes it has assigned to the task of meeting the obligation.

This gap between scheduled benefits and assigned taxes is called *the fiscal imbalance* of each of these two programs. More precisely, the **fiscal imbalance** is defined as the *present value* of future scheduled benefits minus the *present value* of future assigned taxes. An example will explain the meaning of present value (also called present discounted value) and why it is used to define fiscal imbalance.

Suppose taxes in year 0 (the "present") are $100,000, and scheduled benefits in year 1 are $110,000. Are the $100,000 of taxes collected in year 0 enough to finance the $110,000 of scheduled benefits in year 1? The answer depends on the interest rate. Suppose the interest rate $r = 10\%$. If $100,000 of taxes are collected in year 0 and saved for one year earning interest of $10,000, then in year 1 there will be $110,000 available to finance the $110,000 of scheduled spending. Equivalently, we can ask: To pay benefits of $110,000 in year 1, how much would we need to collect in taxes in year 0? We define the present value (PV) of $110,000 as $110,000/(1 + r) = $110,000/(1.10) = $100,000$. As long as taxes collected in year 0 equal the PV of benefits scheduled in year 1, then the taxes in year 0 will be just enough to pay benefits scheduled in year 1.

More generally, as long as the present value of assigned taxes equals the present value of scheduled benefits, taxes will be just enough to pay scheduled benefits. This is why fiscal imbalance is defined as the present value of future scheduled benefits minus the present value of future assigned taxes.

Note that the interest rate chosen to compute present value affects the dollar amount of the present value. According to one study, the fiscal imbalance of Social Security and Medicare together is $72 trillion—$62 trillion for Medicare and $10 trillion for Social Security. By contrast, the explicit federal debt held as bonds by the public (domestic and foreign) is about $5 trillion. Thus, the federal government has explicitly scheduled to raise $5 trillion to pay bondholders, but implicitly scheduled to raise $10 trillion to pay beneficiaries of Social Security and $62 trillion to pay beneficiaries of Medicare. Thus, rising Medicare spending is the main source of the federal government's long-term fiscal imbalance.[1]

Generational Accounting

Each generation pays taxes and receives benefits from government spending. But some generations may pay more in taxes than they receive in benefits, while others pay less in taxes than they receive in benefits. Generational accounting focuses on how particular generations fare with respect to government taxes and spending.

Consider the introduction of Social Security in 1935 and Medicare in 1965. As "pay-as-you-go" programs, payroll taxes were levied on workers, and benefits were paid to retirees. The people who were retired when each program was introduced received benefits even though they had not paid payroll taxes when they were working. Clearly, they gained from the introduction of each program, because the introduction raised the benefits they received without raising the taxes they paid. People who retired a decade after each program was introduced gained almost as much; they paid taxes to the program for only a decade but received benefits for their entire retirement. As time passes, eventually each new generation pays taxes its entire working life before receiving benefits.

Conversely, consider the introduction of the first public schools. Adults were taxed to pay for them even though they had not benefited when they were children. Adults who had no children therefore lost from their introduction because it raised their taxes

[1] Jagadeesh Gokhale and Kent Smetters, *Fiscal and Generational Imbalances* (The AEI Press, 2003); and "Fiscal and Generational Imbalances: An Update," in *Tax Policy and the Economy 20*, James Poterba, ed. (MIT Press, 2006), pp. 192–223.

without giving them benefits. As time passes, eventually each new adult generation that pays taxes had benefited from the public schools when they were young.

A natural measure of how a particular generation fares with respect to government is the present value of the benefits it receives minus the present value of the taxes it pays. Note that the interest rate chosen to compute present value affects the dollar amount of the present value. By this measure, the people who were retirees when Social Security and Medicare were introduced gained an amount equal to the present value of the benefits they received minus the present value of the taxes they paid (zero). The people who retired a decade after these programs were introduced received a smaller gain because they paid taxes for a decade before receiving benefits.

Suppose that, starting from an initially balanced budget, the government cuts taxes and keeps government spending constant by borrowing. Today's taxpayers use the tax cut to raise their consumption. In the future, the government must pay interest to bond-holders and finance the interest payments by raising taxes on future taxpayers. Today's tax cut therefore benefits today's taxpayers and harms future taxpayers. Today's generation gains, and tomorrow's generation loses.

Generational accounting makes the important point that some generations (or age cohorts) get a better or worse deal from government spending and taxes than do other generations. Moreover, generational accounting tries to quantify how much better or worse is the deal. Finally, it alerts citizens and policy makers to assess the impact on different generations (or age cohorts) of particular fiscal actions (spending, taxing, and borrowing) by the government.[2]

DEFICITS, DEBT, AND INTEREST

U.S. Deficits, Debt, and Interest during the Past Half Century

The U.S. federal government's gross debt can be divided into two components: debt held by the public (domestic and foreign) and debt held by federal government agencies such as the Social Security Trust Fund. The box "Deficits and Debt with Two Components of Government" gives a simple example of deficits and debt when the government is divided into two components.

U.S. Treasury Debt Held by the Public and by U.S. Government Agencies

As shown in Table 13.1, in 2007 U.S. Treasury debt held by the public was about $5 trillion ($5,000 billion) and U.S. Treasury debt held by U.S. government agencies (including Social Security) was about $4 trillion, so total U.S. Treasury debt was about $9 trillion. The total $9 trillion is called *gross* debt, and the $5 trillion held by the public is sometimes called *net* debt. For comparison, U.S. GDP in 2007 was about $14 trillion, so net debt was about 37% of GDP and gross debt was about 63% of GDP.[3]

U.S. Treasury debt held by the public (roughly $5 trillion) arises from past deficits in the federal budget. To finance a deficit (spending in excess of taxes), remember that the U.S. Treasury sells securities (i.e., "bonds") to various members of the public—households, businesses, and governments, both domestic and foreign. Central

---

[2] Alan Auerbach, Jagadeesh Gokhale, and Laurence Kotlikoff, "Generational Accounting: A Meaningful Alternative to Deficit Accounting," in *Tax Policy and the Economy* 5, James Poterba, ed. (MIT Press 1991), pp. 55–110; Laurence Kotlikoff, *Generational Accounting* (The Free Press, 1992); and Laurence Kotlikoff and Scott Burns, *The Coming Generational Storm* (The MIT Press, 2004).

[3] Using the rounded numbers $5 and $14, $5/$14 = 36%; more exact numbers yield 37%, so 37% is reported both in the text and in Table 13.1.

Deficits and Debt with Two Components of Government

Suppose we divide the government into two components: Social Security (a "government agency") and the Rest-of-Government. In the year shown, Social Security spends $50 billion and collects $75 billion in tax, while the Rest-of-Government spends $100 billion and collects $25 billion in tax.

Social Security runs a $25 billion surplus, and the Rest-of-Government runs a $75 billion deficit, so the government runs a $50 billion deficit. The Rest-of-Government borrows $75 billion—$25 billion from Social Security (which then increases its holding of government bonds by $25 billion) and $50 billion

from the public (which then increases its holding of government bonds by $50 billion). Debt held by the public rises by $50 billion, equal to the government deficit of $50 billion. Gross debt of the Rest-of-Government (debt held by the public plus Social Security) rises by $75 billion, equal to the deficit of the Rest-of-Government.

Thus, government debt held by the public arises from past deficits of the government. Gross debt of the Rest-of-Government held by the public and Social Security arises from past deficits of the Rest-of-Government.

	Social Security	Rest-of-Government	Government
Spending	$50 billion	$100 billion	$150 billion
Taxes	75 billion	25 billion	100 billion
Surplus or deficit	$25 billion surplus	$ 75 billion deficit	$ 50 billion deficit

banks including the U.S. Federal Reserve are counted as part of the public. About 90% of the debt consists of marketable securities—bills, notes, bonds, and inflation-indexed issues called TIPS; the remaining 10% are nonmarketable. The Treasury sells marketable securities in regularly scheduled auctions.

Perhaps the most striking fact shown in Table 13.1 is this: Foreign investors (private and governmental) currently hold *almost half*—about 45%—of U.S. Treasury debt held by the public. The largest foreign investors are China, Japan, and the U.K. (Britain), which together hold over half of foreign-held U.S. Treasury debt and about 25% of the total U.S. Treasury debt held by the public of $5 trillion.

U.S. Treasury debt held by U.S. government agencies (roughly $4 trillion) are nonmarketable securities. The securities represent credits to the various government agencies that hold them and are redeemed when needed to cover benefit payments or other expenses. More than half of this debt is held by the Social Security Trust Fund. Since the mid-1980s, Social Security has collected more revenue from payroll taxes and

TABLE 13.1

A Breakdown of U.S. Treasury Debt ($ Trillions)

U.S. Treasury Debt	
Held by the public (U.S. net debt)	$ 5.0
Domestic	2.8
Foreign	2.2
China, Japan, and UK	1.2
All other countries	1.0
Held by U.S. government agencies including Social Security	4
Total (U.S. gross debt)	9
U.S. GDP	14
U.S. Treasury debt held by the public as % of GDP	5/14 = 37%
Total U.S. gross debt as % of GDP	9/14 = 63%

interest every year than it has paid in benefits; its surplus has been invested in nonmarketable Treasury securities that pay interest and are now worth over $2 trillion.

When the Treasury issues debt to Social Security in exchange for Social Security's cash surplus, the Treasury uses the cash for other government spending. This does not mean the Treasury has "raided" the Social Security Trust Fund, but only that it has *borrowed* from the Trust Fund (borrowers always take cash and spend it while promising to repay the debt in the future). Once demographics cause Social Security's scheduled benefits to exceed its revenues, Social Security will ask the Treasury to redeem its securities for cash to pay scheduled benefits. The Treasury is obligated to provide this cash to Social Security in the same way it is obligated to provide cash to public bondholders when its bonds mature. Thus, in the future, Congress and the president must make sure that the Treasury is able to raise the cash to pay debt held by government agencies like Social Security as well as debt held by the public. It is therefore important to keep track of the government's gross debt ($9 trillion) as well as its net debt to the public ($5 trillion).

The Treasury's authority to issue gross debt to the public and government agencies is subject to a statutory limit, but whenever the gross debt approaches the limit, Congress votes to raise the limit (after representatives and senators have made speeches vowing to avoid more borrowing in the future).

The Interest Burden of the U.S. Treasury

Large deficits and borrowing during World War II in the first half of the 1940s raised U.S. Treasury debt held by the public (i.e., net debt) to over 100% of GDP by the war's end in 1945. In the next three decades, GDP grew a lot and government debt only a little (the budget oscillated between small surpluses and small deficits that were generally less than 1% of GDP), so net debt as a percentage of GDP declined to 26% in 1980.

Over the next two decades a dramatic fiscal story unfolded: The rise and fall of U.S. Treasury debt as a percentage of GDP. To follow the story, look back at Figures 1.11 and 1.12 in Chapter 1 and also look at the top row of Table 13.2.

From 1981 to 1992, the federal deficit (the excess of federal spending over federal tax revenue) ranged from 2% to 6% of GDP, averaging roughly 4% of GDP.

With federal spending roughly 20% of GDP and federal borrowing 4% of GDP, between 1981 and 1992 for every $100 the federal government spent, $20 were borrowed and only $80 came from tax revenue.

Net debt as a percentage of GDP rose from 26% in 1980 to 49% in 1993. In the rest of the 1990s, rapid GDP growth and the transformation of budget deficits to surpluses of 1% of GDP reduced debt as a percentage of GDP to 33%. Since then, deficits returned and raised debt as a percentage of GDP to 37% in 2007.

Table 13.2 shows the consequences for the interest burden of the U.S. Treasury and U.S. taxpayers. Net interest as a percentage of GDP is the product of two things: net

TABLE 13.2

Interest Burden of the U.S. Treasury and U.S. Taxpayers

Source: CBO, The Budget and Economic Outlook: Fiscal Years 2008 to 2018, tables F-2 and F-6.

	1980	1993	2001	2007
U.S. net debt as a percent of GDP	26%	49%	33%	37%
Interest rate on U.S. Treasury bonds	7.3	6.1	6.0	4.6
Net interest as a percent of GDP	1.9	3.0	2.0	1.7
Revenue as a percent of GDP	19.0	17.5	19.8	18.8
Net interest as a percent of revenue	10.0	17.0	10.0	9.0
Percent of revenue available to finance programs	90.0	83.0	90.0	91.0

debt as a percentage of GDP and the bond interest rate. Let's follow the story of the interest burden by moving from the left column to the right column in the table.

In 1980 net debt as a percentage of GDP was 26% of GDP, and the bond interest rate was 7.3%, so net interest was 1.9% of GDP (26% × 7.3% = 1.9%). With federal revenue 19.0% of GDP, 10% of federal revenue was needed to pay interest to the holders of Treasury debt (1.9%/19.0% = 10%), leaving 90% available to finance other federal programs.

By contrast, in 1993 net debt as a percentage of GDP peaked at 49%, and the bond interest rate was 6.1%, so net interest was 3.0% of GDP (49% × 6.1% = 3.0%). With federal revenue 17.5% of GDP, 17% of federal revenue was needed to pay interest to the holders of Treasury debt (3.0%/17.5% = 17%), leaving 83% available to finance federal programs.

Quite an improvement had been achieved by 2001. In that year, net debt as a percentage of GDP was 33% of GDP, and the bond interest rate was 6.0%, so net interest was 2.0% of GDP (33% × 6.0% = 2.0%). With federal revenue 19.8% of GDP, 10% of federal revenue was needed to pay interest to the holders of Treasury debt (2.0%/19.8% = 10%), leaving 90% available to finance other federal programs.

To bring things up to date, in 2007 net debt as a percentage of GDP was a few points higher, 37%, than in 2001 (33%), but the bond interest was much lower, 4.6% (instead of 6.0%), so net interest was 1.7% of GDP (37% × 4.6% = 1.7%). With federal revenue 18.8% of GDP, 9% of federal revenue was needed to pay interest to the holders of Treasury debt (1.7%/18.8% = 9%), leaving 91% available to finance federal programs.

The Deficit, Debt, and Interest as a Percentage of GDP

Suppose the government runs a deficit equal to 5% of GDP every year (e.g., suppose that every year federal spending including interest payments to bondholders is 25% of GDP and federal tax revenue is 20% of GDP). What would happen to debt as a percentage of GDP (b) in the long run? It turns out that the answer is given by the simple formula[4]

$$b* = f/g$$

where $b*$ = debt as a percentage of GDP in the long run
f = the deficit as a percentage of GDP
g = the growth rate of nominal GDP.

For example, if $f = 5\%$ and $g = 5\%$, then in the long run, debt as a percentage of GDP $b*$ would eventually become 100%.

Consider an example shown in Table 13.3, for which all money amounts are in the billions. Suppose that in year 0 debt is $5,000 and nominal GDP is $10,000, so debt as a percentage of GDP (b) is 50.0%. Assume that every year the deficit as a percentage of GDP (f) is 5% and the growth rate of nominal GDP (g) is 5%. Then in year 0 the deficit is $500.00, so in year 1 debt is $5,500; in year 1 nominal GDP is $10,500, so debt as a percentage of GDP (b) is 52.4%; and so on. Each year debt as a percentage of GDP (b) would rise until it eventually gets very close to but never exceeds 100%—we say that in the long run b "becomes" 100%.

Now let's look at what happens to interest paid to bondholders. Assume that every year the interest rate on government bonds (r) is 5%. Then in year 0 interest is $250

---

[4] The derivation of the formula is given in the appendix to this chapter.

TABLE 13.3
Debt and
Nominal GDP
($ Billions)

Year	Debt	g = 5% GDP	b	f = 5% Deficit	r = 5% Interest	i
0	$5,000	$10,000	50.0%	$500.00	$250.00	2.50%
1	5,500	10,500	52.4	525.00	275.00	2.62
2	6,025	11,025	54.6	551.25	301.25	2.73
•		•			•	
•		•			•	
•		•			•	
Long run			100.0%			5.00%

*Money in billions.

(5% of $5,000), so interest as a percentage of GDP (i) is 2.50%; in year 1 interest is $275 (5% of $5,500), so interest as a percentage of GDP (i) is 2.62%; and so on.

Note that in every year $i = rb$ (in year 0, $i = 5\% \times 50\% = 2.50\%$; in year 1, $i = 5\% \times 52.4\% = 2.62\%$). In the long run, interest as a percentage of GDP (i) is given by the simple formula

$$i^* = rb^* = r(f/g)$$

where r is the interest rate on government bonds. In this example with $r = 5\%$, $f = 5\%$, and $g = 5\%$, interest as a percentage of GDP (i) would eventually be 5% of GDP.

If tax revenue were 20% of GDP, then 25% of tax revenue (5% out of 20%) would have to be devoted to paying interest to bondholders, leaving only 75% of tax revenue available to finance government programs.

By contrast, if the deficit as a percentage of GDP (f) were only 2% of GDP, then from the formula $b^* = f/g$, eventually b^* would be 40% and $i^* = rb^*$ would be 2% of GDP. If tax revenue were 20% of GDP, then only 10% of tax revenue (2% out of 20%) would have to be devoted to paying interest to bondholders, leaving 90% of tax revenue available to finance government programs.

Inflation, Debt, and Deficits

Suppose a debtor—household, business, or government—owes a creditor $100. If inflation—a rise in the prices of goods and services in the economy—occurs, then when the debtor pays the creditor $100, the debtor is giving up less real goods and services than if there had been no inflation during the period of the loan. Thus, a debtor who owes a fixed dollar amount to a creditor enjoys a real gain when inflation occurs, and the creditor suffers a real loss. Inflation reduces the *real* (inflation-adjusted) value of a given nominal dollar debt.[5]

Suppose at the beginning of this year, government debt held by the public is $100 billion—the government is obligated to pay bondholders $100 billion in cash when the bonds reach maturity. Assume that there is 10% inflation during the year. At the end of the year, the $100 billion that the government owes bondholders can buy the same real goods and services that could have been bought with $91 billion at the beginning of the year ($100/1.1 = $91). The 10% inflation has reduced the real (inflation-adjusted) value of the debt from $100 billion to $91 billion.

[5] At the time the loan was made, both debtor and creditor may have anticipated inflation and agreed on a higher interest rate to compensate for it. It remains true that inflation reduces the real value of the dollar debt.

Suppose during the year that government spending equals taxes, so the nominal debt remains $100 billion. However, the real debt falls $9 billion (from $100 billion to $91 billion). Throughout this chapter, we have always said that if debt falls $9 billion this year, then there must have been a budget surplus of $9 billion this year; we've said that a surplus of $X causes debt to fall $X and a deficit of $X causes debt to rise $X. To preserve this relationship between the change in debt and the budget surplus or deficit, we define the **real surplus** and **real deficit** as follows:

real surplus = taxes − spending + reduction in real value of debt due to inflation

= nominal surplus + reduction in real value of debt due to inflation

real deficit = spending − taxes − reduction in real value of debt due to inflation

= nominal deficit − reduction in real value of debt due to inflation

This year the nominal surplus is zero, but the real surplus is $9 billion; the real debt falls $9 billion (from $100 billion to $91 billion). Thus, the real surplus equals the nominal surplus (taxes minus spending) plus the reduction in the real value of the debt due to inflation.

Suppose instead that spending exceeds taxes by $9 billion this year—the nominal deficit is $9 billion. The real deficit would be zero, because the nominal deficit of $9 billion would be offset by a $9 billion reduction in the real value of debt due to inflation.

Think of this from the perspective of the government treasurer. Your financial position is strengthened by a nominal surplus, weakened by a nominal deficit, but strengthened by a reduction in the real value of the debt you owe bondholders due to inflation. To the government treasurer or any other debtor, inflation is good news because it reduces the real value of the debt that must be paid to bondholders.

Generating Inflation

Although debtors have reason to like inflation, most debtors have no power to generate inflation. The federal government, however, does have the power. If the federal government spends more than it taxes not by borrowing but by printing money, then it injects a combined fiscal-monetary stimulus into the economy which raises aggregate demand for goods and services above supply and hence causes prices to rise—inflation. Thus, there is always a danger that if the federal government has gone deeply in debt, it may try to solve its debt problem by generating inflation which would "inflate away" the real value of its debt. Thus, excessive debt gives the federal government a motive to generate inflation—something it has the power to do. This is one reason why some analysts predict that a significant rise in federal debt as a percentage of GDP may eventually lead to inflation.

Fortunately, a *separation of powers* has been instituted within the federal government to reduce the likelihood that it will generate inflation in order to solve its debt problem. Congress and the president have the power to set spending, taxes, and borrowing by authorizing the Treasury to sell bonds. But Congress and the president do *not* have the power to print money to pay for spending that exceeds taxes. The control over injecting money into the economy has by law been given to the Federal Reserve (the Fed), which is the central bank. Fed decisions about injecting money are made by its Federal Open Market Committee (FOMC) consisting of the Fed chairman, the other six members of the board of governors, and the presidents of the 12 regional Federal Reserve banks. To inject money into the economy, the Fed buys government securities from members of the public (domestic and foreign) in the open market and pays with a check; the seller of the securities deposits the Fed's check in its bank account and then has money to spend by writing checks (or the Fed will supply printed money to banks that request it if the depositor wants printed money to spend).

Thus, due to this separation of powers, Congress and the president can only borrow from the public, not inject money into the economy. If Congress and the president can persuade the Federal Reserve to buy as many bonds from the public as the Treasury is selling to the public, then the federal government as a whole would really be injecting money to finance the excess of its spending over its taxes. But it must persuade the Fed.

The seven members of the board of governors are appointed by the president with the approval of Congress for 14-year terms. The chairman serves for a four-year term and then must be reappointed to continue as chairman. It is therefore possible that the Fed may succumb to pressure from Congress and the president. The fact remains that because of the separation of powers, it is the Fed that controls money. Congress and the president cannot, without the Fed's cooperation, inflate away the debt by printing money and injecting it into the economy.

Deficits and Inflation

Thus far we have focused on how excessive debt gives the federal government a motive to generate inflation through a combined fiscal-monetary stimulus. Now we turn to a different question: Do deficits directly cause inflation? Suppose the economy is at full employment and the budget is balanced. Then spending is raised and/or taxes are cut, thereby raising aggregate demand for goods and services above supply, causing prices to rise. It is the excess demand that causes inflation, but the excess demand in this case has been generated by shifting the budget from balance to deficit, so it might be said that the deficit generated inflation.

Clearly deficits do not have to generate inflation. Suppose again that the economy is at full employment and the budget is balanced. Then suppose a plunge in the stock market causes consumers and businesses to become anxious and cut their spending. This causes a fall in aggregate demand, output, employment, and income, and the economy goes into recession. The fall in income automatically reduces income tax revenue, so the budget goes into deficit, and the government must borrow to finance its spending in excess of taxes. In this case, aggregate demand decreases and prices rise more slowly—inflation decreases. Here the shift of the budget from balance to deficit is accompanied by less, not more, inflation. In the recessions of 1982, 1991, and 2001, budget deficits rose but inflation decreased.

Therefore, it is more accurate to say that excess demand raises inflation and deficient demand reduces inflation. Shifting the budget from balance to deficit can cause excess demand and inflation, but deficient demand can cause a recession which reduces inflation and shifts the budget from balance to deficit. Thus, in one circumstance the deficit increases and inflation increases, while in another the deficit increases but inflation decreases.

THE LONG-TERM BUDGET OUTLOOK FOR THE U.S

Over the past few years the U.S. federal budget deficit has been about 2% of GDP—the average over the past half century. Look back at Figure 1.11 in Chapter 1 to see that over the past few decades federal spending has ranged between 18% and 23% of

In a provocative 2007 article, Brookings Institution economist Henry Aaron contends that there has been a flawed diagnosis in the political arena of the source of the huge long-term fiscal imbalance facing the U.S. government and, as a consequence, a flawed prescription concerning what to do about it.* He says that if one examines carefully the numbers and projections, it is clear that the main source of the long-term federal budget problem is medical care costs—both Medicare and Medicaid (we noted in the text that Medicare's fiscal imbalance is *much* larger than Social Security's fiscal imbalance).

He says that over the past four decades, U.S. health care spending has had an annual growth rate that is 2.7 percentage points higher than the U.S. income growth rate and comments that "progress of medical technology, population aging, and the continuing indiscipline of U.S. health care financing give no reason to think that this gap will spontaneously narrow." Using Congressional Budget Office projections, he estimates that if a 2.5 percentage point gap persists in the coming decades and applies to Medicare and Medicaid as well as private health care spending, then federal budget spending (excluding interest) would grow from its current 18% of GDP to nearly 29% in 2050, generating huge deficits unless there is a huge increase in taxes as a percentage of GDP (currently 18%).

Aaron asserts that the costs of Medicare and Medicaid—costs for treating the elderly and the poor—cannot be controlled without also controlling medical costs for the nonelderly and the nonpoor. His assertion seems plausible once we note that the same hospitals, doctors, and nurses that treat the elderly and the poor also treat the nonelderly and the nonpoor, and these providers of medical care would regard it as unethical and impractical to practice medicine differently for the two groups. In particular, the elderly would expect to receive the same quality of medical care that they received before they became old. If costly technology and procedures are used for the nonelderly and nonpoor, then they will also be used for the elderly and the poor. Hence, neither the providers of medical care nor the majority of the public will support making Medicare and Medicaid costs grow more slowly than health care costs for the rest of the population.

Thus, Aaron argues, solving the long-term federal budget problem requires solving the medical cost problem for the entire population. He concludes that "rising health care spending is the only source of long-term budget shortfalls" and that "controlling spending under public-sector health care programs cannot proceed independently of control of private-sector health care spending." If Aaron is right, then the long-term fiscal imbalance problem must be solved in Chapter 6 on health insurance.

* Henry Aaron, "Budget Crisis, Entitlement Crisis, Health Care Financing Problem—Which Is It?" *Health Affairs,* November–December 2007, pp. 1622–33.

GDP (so spending has been roughly 20% of GDP) and tax revenue, between 16% and 20% of GDP.

Thus, on average federal spending has been about 20% of GDP, federal revenue about 18% of GDP, and the federal deficit about 2% of GDP.

An important component of federal spending is national defense, which constitutes about 4% of GDP and 20% (4% out of 20%) of federal spending. However, in this section we do not emphasize defense spending in our long-term budget outlook because most analysts do not expect defense spending to rise significantly above 4% of GDP.

Look back at Table 1.2 of Chapter 1. Based on projections of population demographics and medical costs (see the box above), the Congressional Budget Office (CBO) projects that spending on Medicare, Medicaid, and Social Security—the "big three" domestic (nondefense) programs—will rise from 10% of GDP in 2010 to 16% in 2040. If the rest of the budget components remain the same as a percentage of GDP, then federal spending will rise from 22% of GDP in 2010 to 28% in 2040. If tax revenue is 20% of GDP (it has never exceeded 20% and has averaged 18% in recent decades), the budget deficit will rise to 8% of GDP in 2040 (compared to its average of 2% of GDP over the past half century).

The CBO's long-term budget outlook presents a challenge for the public. The analysis in this chapter suggests that simply accepting a rise in the deficit to 8% of GDP would pose serious risks and burdens on future taxpayers. But to avoid it, either projected spending growth on Medicare, Medicaid, and Social Security must be significantly reduced or tax revenue as a percentage of GDP must be significantly increased. Hard choices lie ahead.

Summary

The commonsense concern about excessive borrowing for an individual or a business firm also applies to government. Any borrower, including a government, must rely on creditors who will exact a price—interest payments—for their service. Borrowing today means repayments to creditors tomorrow. If the government is unable to make repayments when they come due, it will default, and creditors will go unpaid; thereafter the government may find it difficult to borrow even in an emergency. Government borrowing shifts the burden of today's government spending from today's taxpayers to tomorrow's taxpayers. If the government borrows by selling bonds, the government must pay interest to bondholders. To pay the interest, future taxpayers must pay additional taxes. Taxpayers at the time the government borrows are better off, but future taxpayers are worse off.

Because today's capital expenditures (e.g., highways, schools) primarily benefit tomorrow's taxpayers, it is appropriate to shift some of the burden to future taxpayers by borrowing. However, politicians may try to classify any expenditure they favor as a "capital" expenditure—an investment—that can be financed by borrowing rather than taxation. To avoid undermining the discipline of politicians, it may be better to simply prescribe that government expenditure (with perhaps a few exceptions) must be financed by taxation rather than borrowing. If the government borrows, the interest rate is bid up, causing business firms to reduce their borrowing and investment; thus, government borrowing "crowds out" investment, thereby reducing tomorrow's private capital stock and output per worker (i.e., productivity).

A balanced budget rule would impose desirable discipline on politicians because, if they must levy taxes to finance government spending programs, they will weigh cost against benefit. But an always balanced budget rule would be risky: It could force the government to take action in the middle of a recession—either cutting spending or raising taxes—that would make the recession worse. Instead, many economists advocate a particular kind of balanced budget rule that would not make a recession worse—the full employment balanced budget rule (FEBAR). A normal unemployment balanced budget rule (NUBAR) is a slight modification of FEBAR. Under NUBAR, each year Congress must enact a planned budget for the coming fiscal year that technicians estimate would be balanced if next year the unemployment rate is normal (the average of the preceding decade).

A government's fiscal imbalance is a better measure of its financial future than its explicit debt. Under Social Security and Medicare, the federal government has scheduled cash benefits for retired workers, determined by a formula, as well as payment of their medical bills. These scheduled benefits are much larger than the tax revenue that it is estimated will be raised by current payroll tax rates (given projected ceilings on taxable payroll). This gap between scheduled benefits and assigned taxes is called the fiscal imbalance of each program.

Generational accounting illuminates how different generations (or age cohorts) are treated by government. Some generations may pay more in taxes than they receive in benefits, while others pay less in taxes than they receive in benefits. Generational accounting focuses on how particular generations fare with respect to government taxes and spending.

U.S. Treasury debt held by the public—domestic and foreign—was 37% of GDP in 2007. Foreign investors (private and governmental) currently hold *almost half*—about 45%—of U.S. Treasury debt held by the public. The largest foreign investors are China, Japan, and the U.K. (Britain), who together hold over half of foreign-held U.S. Treasury debt and about 25% of the total U.S. Treasury debt held by the public. Debt as a percentage of GDP rose from 26% in 1980 to 49% in 1993, then fell to 33% in 2001, and rose to 37% in 2007.

Excessive debt gives the federal government a motive to generate inflation in order to "inflate away" (or reduce) the real (inflation-adjusted) value of its debt. In contrast to other debtors who would also welcome inflation, the federal government has the power to generate inflation by injecting a combined fiscal-monetary stimulus into the economy that generates excess demand. Fortunately there is a separation of powers that reduces the likelihood of this happening.

The Congressional Budget Office projects that spending on Medicare, Medicaid, and Social Security (the "big three" federal domestic programs) will rise from 10% of GDP in 2010 to 16% in 2040 due to demographics and medical cost trends unless a way is found to curtail their growth. If the rest of the budget components remain the same as a percentage of GDP, then federal spending will rise from 22% of GDP in 2010 to 28% in 2040. However, federal tax revenue has never exceeded 20% of GDP. Difficult choices loom on the horizon.

Key Terms

deficit, *316*

debt, *316*

normal unemployment balanced
   budget rule (NUBAR), *321*

fiscal imbalance, *322*

generational accounting, *323*

real surplus, *329*

real deficit, *329*

Questions

1. Use a numerical example to show the difference between the deficit and the debt.

2. Why should the government avoid excessive borrowing?

3. Does government borrowing burden future taxpayers? Explain why or why not.

4. Give an argument for financing capital expenditures by borrowing.

5. Give a practical argument against letting government borrow to finance any capital expenditure.

6. Draw a diagram to show how government borrowing crowds out private investment. Explain your diagram.

7. What is the problem with an always balanced budget rule?

8. Give a balanced budget rule that avoids this problem. Explain.

9. What is the "fiscal imbalance" of a government program?

10. What does "generational accounting" focus on?

11. If the deficit is always 3% of GDP, and nominal GDP grows 5% per year, eventually debt will be __% of GDP.

    Which formula did you use? Explain each letter (i.e., variable) in the formula.

12. Why is a government that is deeply in debt tempted to generate inflation? Can a government generate inflation? Can Congress and the president? Explain your answers.

13. Why does the CBO's long-term budget outlook imply that hard choices lie ahead?

14. Go online to read about the debate in the mid-1990s over a constitutional amendment to require a balanced budget. Summarize the two sides of the argument.

15. Go online to read about fiscal imbalance and generational accounting. Explain the current discussions surrounding these issues.

Appendix

Government Borrowing
The Derivation of the Formula b* = f/g

Let b equal debt as a percentage of nominal GDP. By definition,

$$b \equiv B/Y$$

where B is debt and Y is nominal GDP. If the numerator B and the denominator Y grow at the same rate, b stays constant; if B grows faster than Y, b increases; and if B grows more slowly than Y, b decreases. What happens to b is determined by the "race" between the numerator B and the denominator Y. We therefore examine the growth rate of the denominator Y and the growth rate of the numerator B.

Let g be the growth rate of the denominator Y.

We assume that g is constant.

Let G be the growth rate of the numerator B. Then

$$G = F/B$$

where F is the deficit and B is the debt. For example, if debt B is $5,000 billion at the beginning of this year and the deficit F equals $500 billion this year, then debt B will be $5,500 billion at the beginning of next year, a 10% increase. Therefore, $G = F/B =$ $500/$5,000 = 10\%$; then G, the growth rate of debt B, is 10%.

$$G = F/B = (F/Y)/(B/Y)$$

But $F/Y \equiv f$, the deficit as a percentage of GDP; and $B/Y \equiv b$, the debt as a percentage of GDP, so

$$G = f/b$$

We assume that f is kept constant by the government.

FIGURE 13A.1

Debt as a Percentage of GDP

Debt as a percentage of GDP (b) moves to $b*$ where the growth rate of debt (G) equals the growth rate of nominal GDP (g).

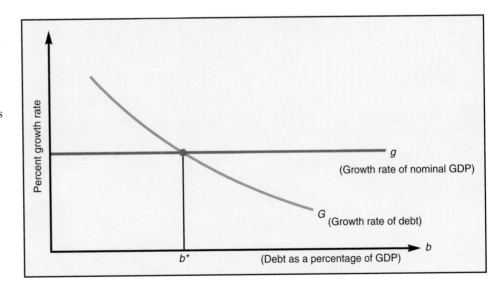

Because $G = f/b$, with f kept constant, as b gets larger, G gets smaller, as shown in Figure 13A.1. The figure plots b, debt as a percentage of GDP, on the horizontal axis, and G, the growth rate of B, and g, the growth rate of Y, on the vertical axis. Then G is a curve that declines as b increases, and g is a horizontal line that stays constant as b increases.

Call $b*$ the value of b where the G curve intersects the g line. If b is less than $b*$ (so b is to the left of $b*$ in the diagram), then G is greater than g. Therefore, B grows faster than Y, and $b \equiv B/Y$ increases until b equals $b*$. If b is greater than $b*$ (so b is to the right of $b*$ in the diagram), G is less than g. Therefore, B grows more slowly than Y, and b decreases until b equals $b*$. Thus, if f and g stay constant, the economy will converge to $b*$ where

$$G = g$$

$$f/b = g$$

Then $b*$ is the value of b that satisfies this equation; solving for b yields

$$b* = f/g$$

Glossary

A

ability to pay   The capacity of taxpayers to pay a tax.

actuarially fair premium   A health insurance premium that just covers the expected cost of enrollees.

adjusted gross income (AGI)   A household's total income minus adjustments.

adverse selection   When people have accurate "inside information" about their health prospects, it results in a bias (towards higher medical cost) in the mix of people who decide to buy insurance.

agglomeration economies   The gains in efficiency that come from having many firms and workers close to one another.

allocative efficiency   When producers allocate the optimal quantity of resources to the production of good X versus good Y.

alternative minimum tax (AMT)   A tax that replaces the regular income tax for a subset of high-income households. The intent is to make every high-income household pay at least a minimum amount of tax even if that household would owe little or no regular income tax.

altruistic   Willing to contribute to help others.

annuity   A payment made monthly for as long as the retiree lives.

assessed value   The value assigned by local government to each residential and business property.

assessment ratio   The ratio of assessed property value to market value.

assets   Items of value owned.

average indexed monthly earnings (AIME)   A concept used by the Social Security Administration to calculate a person's monthly benefit. It is the average of a person's adjusted annual wage incomes divided by twelve to put it on a monthly basis.

average tax rate (ATR)   The ratio of total taxes paid to total income earned.

B

bequest   A person's estate (wealth) that is given to heirs upon the person's death.

bureaucrats   Government officials who administer bureaus (government departments in charge of particular programs).

C

cap and trade   A permit method to allocate pollution where a *cap* is set on the total quantity of permits for a pollutant, and firms that initially obtain permits are allowed to *trade* them so there is an active secondary market in permits.

capital gain   An increase in the value of an asset.

capitalization   The effect on home prices of the desirability of the service-tax mix provided by the local government.

capitalized   Built into the price of the home.

catastrophic insurance   A type of health insurance where the insurance company will pay the entire medical bill above a high threshold.

categorical matching grant   A grant that gives the lower level of government funds only as a match for its own funds spent on a specified activity.

circuit breakers   A refund to partially reimburse the taxpayer for a local property tax that is high relative to the taxpayer's income.

closed-ended categorical matching grant   A grant with a ceiling (limit). Once the ceiling is reached, there is no further matching by the grantor.

coinsurance rate   The percentage of a medical bill that the patient is required to pay. Also called the cost-sharing rate.

command and control   A method of allocating pollution by *commanding* each polluter to emit a certain amount of pollutant or by *controlling* the production technology that firms can use.

compensating differential   The difference between the pay of two jobs due to the difference in the risk of on-the-job injury or death.

comprehensive income   A household's consumption plus its increase in wealth (saving). Equivalently, the maximum the household could consume in a given year while holding its wealth constant.

conditional block grant   A grant that gives the recipient a fixed dollar amount to spend on a specified activity.

consumption externality   When an individual's consumption affects the well-being of others but no compensation for this occurs.

consumption tax   A tax that imposes a burden on a household according to its consumption spending.

contingent valuation   Asking individuals hypothetical questions about how much they would be willing to pay to obtain the benefits of a project.

corrective subsidy   A subsidy provided by the government to eliminate the inefficiency that occurs when there is a positive externality and the market produces too little of a particular good.

corrective tax   A tax levied by the government to eliminate the inefficiency that occurs when there is a negative externality and the market produces too much of a particular good. Also called a Pigouvian tax.

corruption   Illegal and unethical behavior that sacrifices the public interest for personal gain.

cost-benefit analysis   Measuring the costs and benefits of a project to help decide whether to undertake the project and what scale the project should be.

cost-effectiveness   Achieving a given objective at minimum cost.

cost-share   The price that a family must pay per unit of a public good.

cost-sharing rate   The percentage of a medical bill that the patient is required to pay. Also called the coinsurance rate.

credit-invoice method   The method of computing value-added tax as equal to the tentative tax minus the tax credit.

D

deadweight loss   The reduction in society's welfare caused by the unfavorable change in the mix of goods when allocative efficiency does not hold. Also called efficiency loss, welfare loss, welfare cost, or excess burden.

debt   The amount owed to others. Also called liabilities.

deductible   Under health insurance, the first dollars of a person's annual medical bill which the patient is responsible for paying.

defer   To postpone payment.

deficit   Spending minus taxes in a given year.

defined-benefit plan   A retirement plan where a worker's retirement benefit is linked by a formula to that worker's pre-retirement wage history.

defined-contribution plan   A retirement plan where a worker's retirement benefits are paid from the sum that has accumulated in the worker's account from designated contributions made by the worker and employer plus investment income (interest, dividends, and capital gains).

depreciation   The annual cost of the wearing out of machinery.

disability insurance   A federal program to assist people with career-ending disabilities. Part of Old Age, Survivors, and Disability Insurance (OASDI).

district power equalizing plan   A school funding plan where the state designates a target property per pupil (a target tax base) and gives a grant to any district with property per pupil less than the target. Also called a guaranteed tax base plan.

E

earliest eligibility age (EEA)   The earliest age at which a person can begin collecting monthly Social Security benefits.

Earned Income Tax Credit (EITC)   A refundable tax credit to provide assistance to low-income families that earn income by working.

effective tax rate   The tax burden that a household bears as a percent of its income.

efficiency   When both productive efficiency and allocative efficiency hold. Productive efficiency holds when producers minimize the cost of producing a product of a given quality. Allocative efficiency holds when producers allocate the optimal quantity of resources to the production of good X versus good Y.

efficiency loss   The reduction in society's welfare caused by the unfavorable change in the mix of goods in response to a tax or subsidy when there is no externality. Also called inefficiency, deadweight loss, welfare loss, or welfare cost.

efficient   A situation where it would be impossible to make a change that makes everyone better off.

elastic   A demand or supply curve is elastic when a price change causes a large response in quantity (this happens when the curve is flat rather than steep).

elasticity   A measure of the percentage change in one variable resulting from a one percent change in another variable.

elasticity of demand   The ratio of the percentage *increase* in quantity demanded over the percentage *decrease* in the price.

elasticity of labor supply   The ratio of the percentage *increase* in hours supplied over the percentage *increase* in the wage.

equimarginal principle   The total cost incurred to achieve a pollution target has been minimized only if each polluter reduces pollution until its marginal abatement cost is the same as every other polluter.

excess burden   The reduction in society's welfare caused by the unfavorable change in the mix of goods in response to a tax. Also called the deadweight loss, welfare loss, or welfare cost of a tax.

excise taxes   Taxes on particular commodities such as gasoline, alcohol, and tobacco.

exclusion   A source of income that is not subject to the income tax.

expected value   The average or mean value.

externality   When a producer or consumer does *not* have to pay for a cost he generates (negative externality), or does *not* receive a payment for a benefit he generates (positive externality).

F

federal debt   The amount of money that the federal government owes to lenders (bond holders).

federal deficit   The difference between federal spending and tax revenue in a given year.

Federal Insurance Contribution Act (FICA)   The act that authorizes the financing of Social Security and Medicare through a payroll tax where half the tax is levied on the worker and half on the employer.

federalism   The assignment of some government spending programs and taxes to the federal government, others to state governments, and others to local governments.

fee for service (FFS)   A type of health insurance where health care providers receive a fee for each service.

fiscal capacity   The ability of a community to finance public services.

fiscal imbalance   The present value of future scheduled benefits minus the present value of future assigned taxes.

flat tax   A tax composed of a value-added tax on firms except that wage income is deductible and a wage income tax on households above an exemption at the same (single) rate used for the value-added tax.

flypaper effect   The tendency of a conditional block grant to increase spending on the specified activity more than an unconditional block grant even in cases where theoretically these two grants should have the same effect on the activity. The money "sticks where it hits."

foreign tax credit   A corporate income tax credit for taxes paid to foreign governments.

forgone earnings   The wage income a person could have earned if she were not attending school.

free market   The voluntary interaction of producers and consumers of goods and services.

free riders   People who choose to let others pay for a public good and then enjoy the benefits that they did not pay for.

free-rider problem   If there are too many free riders, reliance on voluntary contributions will result in an underprovision of a public good.

full benefits age (FBA)   The age at which a person can begin collecting full monthly Social Security benefits.

G

generational accounting   How particular generations or age cohorts fare with respect to government taxes and spending.

global public good　A good that benefits every nation whether or not each individual nation pays for it.

government reinsurance　A government commitment to reimburse private insurers for a fixed percentage of the amount by which a patient's medical bill exceeds a high threshold.

guaranteed tax base plan　A school funding plan where the state designates a target property per pupil (a target tax base) and gives a grant to any district with property per pupil less than the target. Also called a district power equalizing plan.

H

health maintenance organizations (HMOs)　Medical provider organizations that charge capitation (a fixed sum per patient per year regardless of how much service is provided).

human capital　Skills and knowledge that will raise a person's economic productivity.

I

in kind　Payment in the form of goods or services rather than cash.

income neutrality　The goal that all children should have equal educational opportunity regardless of the income in their school district.

incremental matching grant　A categorical matching grant where the match begins only *after* the recipient has first spent a fixed dollar amount (the threshold) on the specified activity.

indexing　Automatically raising the exemption, standard deduction and tax brackets, or the Social Security benefit, to keep up with either price inflation or wage growth in the economy.

inefficiency　The reduction in society's welfare caused by the unfavorable change in the mix of goods in response to a tax or subsidy when there is no externality. Also called efficiency loss, deadweight loss, welfare loss, or welfare cost.

inefficient　A situation in which it would be possible to reallocate resources and make everyone better off.

inelastic　A demand or supply curve is inelastic when a price change causes a small response in quantity (this happens when the curve is steep rather than flat).

inheritance　A gift or bequest received.

internalize the externality　When an appropriate adjustment (e.g., a corrective tax or corrective subsidy) is made so that producers and consumers face a price that reflects all external costs and benefits.

itemized deductions　Income tax deductions for certain kinds of expenses, subtracted from adjusted gross income.

L

liabilities　Items of value owed to others. Also called debt.

limited liability　Owners (shareholders) and executives are not personally responsible for the debts of the corporation.

lobbying　Communication from citizens or groups to legislators about their reasons for supporting or opposing a proposed bill.

logrolling　Trading of legislators' votes to ensure passage of each legislator's highest priority legislation.

lump-sum tax　A tax where the amount owed doesn't vary with the taxpayer's behavior.

M

marginal benefit (MB)　The maximum dollar amount that consumers would be willing to pay for another unit of a good.

marginal cost (MC)　The cost of producing another unit of a good.

marginal damage (MD)　The damage to the environment of producing another unit of a polluting good.

marginal private cost (MPC)　The cost producers will actually have to pay to produce another unit of a good.

marginal product of capital (mpk)　The output produced by another unit of capital.

marginal revenue product of labor (MRPL)　The revenue produced by another hour of work.

marginal social benefit (MSB)　The entire marginal benefit to society of consuming another unit of a good.

marginal social cost (MSC) The entire marginal cost to society of producing another unit of a good.

marginal tax rate (MTR) The ratio of the additional tax to additional income.

market failure An allocation of resources by the market that is *not* socially optimal.

marriage bonus When marriage lowers the income tax paid by two individuals.

marriage penalty When marriage raises the income tax paid by two individuals.

means-tested Programs that are targeted to assist only low-income people.

median voter The voter in the middle when voters are ranked in order of their preference.

Medicaid Government health insurance for low-income people.

Medicare Government health insurance for the elderly.

moral hazard The use of more medical care by insured people because they know that their insurer will pay part or all of the bill.

N

negative externality When a producer or consumer does *not* have to pay for a cost he generates.

negative income tax (NIT) A program that would deliver cash benefits to low-income households. The benefit would be maximum when income is zero and would be phased down as income increases.

nominal interest rate The interest rate actually paid.

nonexcludability When it is not possible to exclude any person from benefiting from a good or service even if the person won't pay for it.

nonrivalry When consumption of a good or service by one person does not prevent consumption of the good by other people.

normal unemployment balanced budget rule (NUBAR) A rule saying that Congress must enact a *planned* budget for the coming fiscal year that *technicians estimate* would be balanced *if* next year the unemployment rate is normal (the average of the preceding decade).

normative economics Makes value judgments about whether something in economics is good or bad.

O

Old-Age, Survivors, and Disability Insurance (OASDI) The official name for the Social Security program.

open-ended categorical matching grant A categorical matching grant without a ceiling (limit).

opportunity cost A project's opportunity cost is the benefit that could have been enjoyed by using the resources to instead produce other goods and services.

optimal federalism The particular assignment of programs and taxes to particular levels of government that best promotes the well being of the citizenry.

P

pay-as-you-go (PAYGO) Using current payroll taxes to pay current retirees' benefits (as Social Security does).

payroll tax ceiling The maximum amount of wages to which the Social Security payroll tax rate may be applied.

personal exemptions A fixed amount per household member that is subtracted from adjusted gross income.

Pigouvian tax A tax levied by the government to eliminate the inefficiency that occurs when there is a negative externality and the market produces too much of a particular good. Also called a corrective tax.

play-or-pay Health insurance plan where employers must either "play"—provide health insurance—or "pay" a tax that would help finance government efforts to cover the uninsured.

political economy The analysis of how government should and actually does make decisions concerning goods and services.

positive economics Explains what happens in economics without saying whether it is good or bad.

positive externality   When a producer or consumer does *not* receive a payment for a benefit he generates.

poverty rate   The percent of the population living below the poverty line.

premium   The price of insurance paid by the insured to the insurance company.

present value (PV)   The amount of money you would need to put in the bank today to have a certain future amount by a certain future date.

present value of the benefits   The amount obtained by discounting each future benefit and then summing.

price elasticity   The ratio of the percentage increase in the quantity demanded to the percentage reduction in the price.

price indexing   Automatically raising a dollar amount in the tax or Social Security schedule at the same rate as prices rise in the economy.

primary insurance amount (PIA)   A concept used by the Social Security Administration. It is a retiree's monthly Social Security benefit computed from the person's AIME which reflects his record of wage income.

private good   A good that has excludability and rivalry.

productive efficiency   When producers minimize the cost of producing a product of a given quality.

progressive benefit formula   The formula used to calculate a worker's monthly Social Security benefit based on his average indexed monthly earnings; the formula favors low earners more than high earners.

progressive income tax   An income tax where the ratio of tax to income rises as income rises.

progressive indexing   A compromise between wage indexing and price indexing of Social Security retirement benefits.

progressive tax   A tax that applies a higher tax rate to high-income households.

property rights   The rights of an owner to use or exchange property.

property tax base   The total property value in a town.

proportional income tax   An income tax where the ratio of tax to income stays constant as income rises.

proportional tax   A tax that applies the same tax rate to all households regardless of income.

public good   A good that is nonexclusive and nonrival.

R

rate of return   A percentage that compares a person's benefit in retirement to the sacrifice that person made as a worker.

rationing   Limiting the use of medical care other than by raising the price to patients.

real   Inflation-adjusted (measured in terms of purchasing power).

real deficit   The nominal deficit (spending minus taxes) minus the reduction in the real value of debt due to inflation.

real interest rate   The nominal interest rate minus the inflation rate.

real surplus   The nominal surplus (taxes minus spending) plus the reduction in the real value of debt due to inflation.

realize   Sell an asset for cash.

realized capital gains   The capital gain of an asset that has actually been sold.

redistributive   Reduces inequality between low- and high-income households.

refundable tax credit   A tax credit that benefits even people who owe no income tax.

regressive income tax   An income tax where the ratio of tax to income falls as income rises.

regressive tax   A tax that applies a higher tax rate to low-income households.

replacement rate   The ratio of the monthly retirement benefit to the pre-retirement monthly wage.

residence-based taxation   Taxation of workers and investors who reside in a city.

retail sales tax (RST)   A percentage tax on the sale of consumer goods by retailers.

revealed preference   Observing actual market behavior by individuals and inferring how much they would be willing to pay to obtain the benefits of a project.

revenue-rate curve   A curve showing the relationship between tax revenue and the tax rate.

S

saving An increase in wealth. Equivalently, income minus consumption.

separation process The process where the affluent move away from the nonaffluent, the nonaffluent try to follow, but the affluent use zoning laws to maintain their separation.

single-payer plan A health insurance plan with a single payer of all medical bills—the government.

social discount rate The rate that should be used to compute the present value of a government project's future benefits.

social insurance Old-age insurance, health insurance, unemployment insurance, disability insurance, and workplace-injury insurance.

Social Security A government program in which workers and employers pay payroll taxes each year to finance benefits to current retirees based on their wage histories.

Social Security Trust Fund The fund into which Social Security payroll taxes are deposited and from which benefits are paid.

social security wealth The wealth accumulated as workers work and pay Social Security taxes, thereby increasing the Social Security benefits to which they will be entitled when they retire.

socially optimal quantity The quantity of a good that maximizes society's welfare.

source-based taxation Taxation of labor and financial capital employed in the city and goods purchased in the city regardless of where the workers, investors, and consumers reside.

standard deduction An income tax deduction of a fixed amount. Subtracted from adjusted gross income.

subtraction method The method of computing value-added tax as equal to the tax rate multiplied by the difference of sales revenue and purchases.

T

tax A compulsory payment levied by the government.

tax bracket A range of taxable income subject to a given marginal tax rate.

tax competition Competition among local governments to cut business taxes to attract firms and jobs.

tax effort The ratio of tax collections to tax capacity.

tax exporting Levying taxes that burden outsiders.

tax-exclusive rate A tax rate where tax is not included as part of the tax base; it is larger than the tax-inclusive rate (example: if price is $80, tax is $20, and the consumer pays $100, the tax-exclusive rate is $20/$80 = 25%).

tax-inclusive rate A tax rate where tax is included as part of the tax base; it is smaller than the tax-exclusive rate (example: if price is $80, tax is $20, and the consumer pays $100, the tax-inclusive rate is $20/$100 = 20%).

Temporary Assistance for Needy Families (TANF) A joint federal/state program that provides cash benefits to low-income families with children in which one parent is absent.

Tiebout process Just as firms compete to attract and retain consumers, local governments compete to attract and retain residents by offering them a desirable mix of public goods and taxes.

total income A household's wage income plus investment income.

tradable Able to be bought and sold at the market price.

transactions costs The costs involved in organizing a class action suit and contacting the numerous parties to the suit.

turnover tax A tax on the sales of all firms (not just retailers) with no deduction or credit for the firm's purchases.

U

unconditional block grant A grant that gives the recipient a fixed dollar amount to use however the recipient wants.

unemployment compensation Cash benefits from the government to people who are laid off from their jobs.

unemployment insurance A social insurance program that provides cash benefits to workers who are laid off from their jobs. Mandated by the federal government but administered by the states.

unified transfer tax   A tax that coordinates the taxation of a person's estate at death with gifts given to heirs prior to death.

uniform voucher plan   An educational plan that gives every family with children the same dollar voucher per child for private school tuition.

unrealized capital gain   The capital gain of an asset that has not yet been sold.

V

value of a statistical life (VSL)   A rough dollar estimate for the value of the life of someone not known personally.

value-added tax (VAT)   A percentage tax on the value that is added at each stage of production.

variable matching grant plan   An educational grant plan where the matching rate would be highest for low-income districts and would phase down as income per pupil rises.

variable voucher plan   An educational plan where low-income families would get a large voucher, middle income families a middle-sized voucher, and high-income families a small voucher for private school tuition.

W

wage indexing   Automatically raising a new retiree's initial monthly benefit at the same rate as wages rise in the economy.

wage subsidy   Low-income assistance program where the government would pay a worker an hourly benefit that depends on the hourly wage.

wealth   Assets minus liabilities.

wealth neutrality   The goal that all children should have equal educational opportunity regardless of the wealth in their school district.

withholding   Taxes that an employer subtracts from each employee's paycheck and periodically sends to the government.

workers' compensation   Workplace-injury insurance.

X

X tax   A tax equivalent to the flat tax except that households' wage income above the exemption is taxed at graduated bracket rates rather than a single rate.

Z

zoning laws   Laws that limit the type of residential construction or land use within a locality.

Index

Page numbers followed by n indicate material found in notes.